BUSINESS AND SOCIETY IN JAPAN

BUSINESS AND SOCIETY IN JAPAN

Fundamentals for Businessmen

Edited by
Bradley M. Richardson
Taizo Ueda

East Asian Studies Program,
Ohio State University

PRAEGER

New York
Westport, Connecticut
London

Library of Congress Cataloging in Publication Data

Business and society in Japan.

Reports of a study of Japanese business by the East
Asian Studies Program of Ohio State University.
Includes index.
1. Japan—Economic conditions—1945–   . 2. Japan—
Social conditions. 3. Japan—Commerce. I. Richardson,
Bradley M. II. Ueda, Taizo. III. Ohio State University.
East Asian Studies Program.
HC462.9.B86   330.952′048   81-2710
ISBN 0-275-91701-0 (alk. paper)   AACR2

Library of Congress Catalog Card Number: 81-2710

ISBN: 0-275-91701-0

First published in 1981

Praeger Publishers, One Madison Avenue, New York, NY 10010
A division of Greenwood Press, Inc.

Printed in the United States of America

The paper used in this book complies with the
Permanent Paper Standard issued by the National
Information Standards Organization (Z39.48-1984).

10 9 8 7 6 5

FOREWORD

The United States has its own American cultural sphere just as Japan is its own Japanese cultural entity. As is true throughout the world, each cultural sphere has its own characteristics and historical background. I believe that cross-cultural communications are possible only if one clearly recognizes what is common to and what is different among the various cultural traditions.

The Japanese are born with and raised in the Japanese culture, and their culture is an integral part of their lives; and this is true of Americans with respect to the American culture. Neither the Japanese nor the American can possibly abandon his or her own culture. The first step to understanding another culture, while maintaining one's own cultural background, is to compare, analyze, and grasp the characteristic qualities of the other culture, such as customs, sense of values, expressions, manners of action, and exterior appearance.

There are many aspects of the Japanese people's actions of which they themselves are not conscious. For example, they follow Shintoist ceremonies for such festive occasions as weddings, celebrations for children reaching the ages of 3, 5, and 7, and the dedication of a new building. The same people follow Buddhist rites on such sad occasions as funerals and memorial services. At the same time, the parent-child relationship, manners between superiors and subordinates, and relations among neighbors are governed by Confucian traditions. The coexistence of these three different religions and belief systems has become so much a way of life in Japan that the Japanese feel nothing strange in following these different traditions and seldom are conscious of the existence of Shintoism, Buddhism, and Confucianism.

Shintoism is a polytheistic religion, and its philosophies and dogmas are very vague. It is perhaps this vagueness of Shintoism that has enabled Buddhism and Confucianism, both imported from China in the sixth century, to coexist in Japan without causing any serious religious conflicts in the people's minds. Herein lies the fundamental difference from Christianity or Judaism, both of which teach rigid relations between God and man.

Foreigners visiting Tokyo are often surprised to find the coexistence of Western and Japanese traditions in Japanese food, shelter, and clothing. Traditional Japanese *kimonos* and business suits just like those of Americans, high-rise skyscrapers and Japanese-style houses, foods of all origins, music and paintings of Japanese and Western cultures all maintain their identities and influence each other but never conflict against one another. Strange though this may appear to visitors from the West, it is this co-existence that characterizes the Japanese culture.

Nobody would deny that the automobile, which is a product of modern civilization, symbolizes one culture. Japanese automobiles, which are products of Japan's historical and social traditions, are meant to meet the needs of the Japanese consumers and society, and that is why they are fuel-efficient. The fact that the Japanese industry has achieved a high level of quality control has not just stemmed from the Japanese acquiring the American quality control techniques of W. E. Deming, but rather, his ideas have formed a perfect match with the group orientedness and the sense of participation of the Japanese social traditions. This is how the quality of Japanese industrial products has come to be recognized throughout the world.

In short, the Japanese are prepared to accept anything from the outside, and have transformed whatever has been imported and made it part of the Japanese culture.

Today the whole world is faced with such extremely difficult tasks as reorganization of the international economic orders, solution of the energy problem, and rectifying stagnation in technological innovations. And the circumstances surrounding these problems are rapidly changing. A solution to these problems cannot be expected of one nation or one enterprise alone, and it requires cooperation and effort on the part of many international organizations. Corporate activities overseas must also be aimed at contributing positively to the furtherance of the international division of labor.

Yet, internationalization of a corporation and elevating the international sense of businessmen are easier said than done. Investing overseas requires difficult decision making on the part of a corporation, and has a variety of impacts on the economy and industry of the host nation and its local community. Unless the investment is welcomed by the recipient nation or community, the resulting production activities are not expected to succeed.

International interchanges begin with efforts to recognize the differences in culture, custom, and sense of value of each other and to fill those gaps. Frictions are inevitable whenever different cultures meet. But a majority of such frictions can be resolved through mutual understanding of different cultures. International communications in the truest sense of the term can be achieved when peoples of different cultures collaborate to work together and create together, as it is often said that working together makes friends.

It is for the promotion of better international communications that we have sought to analyze and enhance understanding of the origins of Japan's unique cultural heritage, the characteristics of the Japanese culture, and how it is common to and differs from the American culture by tackling questions in a wide variety of fields such as politics, economy, management, and labor. It is our great pleasure that through the cooperation of the East Asian Studies Program of Ohio State University, we are able to present this book incorporating the results of studies conducted by scholars who are experts in the cultures of Japan and the United States.

It is my sincere hope that this book will be of some interest and value to those who are interested in Japan, those who have some relations with Japan, and especially those who have business relations with Japan.

MICHIHIRO NISHIDA

Formerly Executive Vice-President and currently advisor of Honda Motor Co., Ltd., Michihiro Nishada is also Director of the Honda Foundation and Vice-President of the International Association of Traffic and Safety Sciences.

EDITOR'S PREFACE

Japan is the number three economic power in the world, and is rapidly overtaking the Soviet Union to become the number two power. In the non-Socialist world, Japan's gross national product is already much larger than that of any country other than the United States. In terms of per capita income, Japan ranks among the top industrialized countries of the world with a per-person GNP in 1979 that was almost identical to that of the United States. All in all, Japanese economic growth in the post-World War II era was a true miracle both in view of Japan's situation of virtual total natural resource poverty and in comparison with the growth records of other major world economies.

Yet in many ways Japan is not very well known in the West. Popular attitudes toward Japan's culture and experience have often been superficial and have typically been either extremely positive or extremely negative. Japanese art was a fad in nineteenth-century Europe, just as Japanese products are sometimes praised without restraint in the West today. Also, Japanese culture is uncritically viewed as an optimum of humanity and collective bliss by some observers. In contrast, Japanese were seen in World War II as primitive persons, too degraded to be considered civilized or human by Western standards. Obviously, both extremes are unwarranted; but the broader dimensions of Japanese culture are still too often treated in the West today in terms of such superficial stereotypes despite the enormous improvements in intercultural communications that have occurred in recent decades.

Western attitudes toward Japanese business successes are similarly divergent and shallow. Some observers see Japan as a business culture to be emulated in the West, arguing that human values are ignored in American business organizations to the detriment of successful labor relations and maintenance of satisfactory productivity and quality control. Others see Japanese economic and trade successes as the result of an unholy alliance between Japan's government and its business sector, both of which are believed to engage in actions designed to thwart the honest foreign entrepreneur. Neither interpretation is adequately buttressed by in-depth factual evidence.

Obviously there is a middle ground in foreign reactions to Japanese culture and business, and some writings on Japan are remarkably thoughtful. Yet perhaps more than foreign commentaries on other societies, foreign discussions of Japan are often unbalanced in the direction of positive or negative evaluations. This book is directed toward rectifying the imbalance in evaluations of specifically Japanese business practices and their sociocultural, political, economic, and historical background. On the one hand, Japan has had an economic miracle and this should be explained. Also, some unfortunate myths about Japanese economic and government practices need to be challenged in order that Japan's economic successes be understood in terms of their real origins and causes. On the other hand, Japan's economic success has not been solely beneficial for Japanese society; there have been negative payoffs like severe pollution and over-crowded cities. Moreover, housing and social capital investments in Japan have generally lagged far behind economic growth for a variety of reasons. Japan has also had the usual social security problems that accompany urbanization and industrialization with the exception of the comparatively small scale of unemployment during the high growth years.

Our discussion of Japanese business and its overall environment is designed for foreign businessmen who want to know more about Japan and who want to have a more balanced understanding of the Japanese business scene. This book is organized in major sections that deal serially with business and labor, the Japanese economy, and the overall social and political environment both past and present. Also included as a fourth major part of the book are some practical considerations regarding entrance into the Japanese market and other aspects of social and business relationships with Japanese business colleagues. A series of common stereotypes, misperceptions, and areas of ignorance concerning Japan have been taken as a starting point. The stereotypes or areas of inadequate knowledge addressed here have been identified through a study of letters to the editor from foreign residents in Japanese English-language newspapers and from articles in the news media or special journals on aspects of Japanese business by foreign businessmen and journalists. We have taken the editorial liberty to convert these perceptions of Japan into questions that highlight areas of misunderstanding or incomplete information.

This book was written by American academic specialists on Japan, but it was not written for fellow scholars. Rather, it is designed for Western business persons who are interested in Japan or involved in some way in trade relationships with that country. We also hope that the information in this book will be useful to students in colleges and universities studying Japanese business and its environment. In preparing this work, we have tried to avoid academic pretentiousness while still adhering to scholarly standards of accuracy in order to make the book simultaneously valuable and interesting.

The multidisciplinary team of contributors includes economists, a lawyer, specialists on education, business, and the media, a sociologist, political scientists, and a historian. Each academic field has its own perspective on Japanese experience, and there are inevitable differences in emphasis and interpretation in the different subchapters in this book as a result. Some specialists see Japanese cultural traits of cooperation and harmony as the main point of emphasis in such areas as business organization and history, while others tend to see more institutional or cultural diversity and conflict, such as the subchapters on law, labor, and politics report. Whatever the variations in emphasis within this book, the contributors are in agreement that Japan is a different culture and simultaneously a complex and diversified nation in which tradition and modernity are intimately interwoven in ways that at times defy disentanglement. Japanese business practices and the overall economic record reflect this complexity.

This book is the product of a joint project between the Honda Motor Company of Japan and the East Asian Studies Program of Ohio State University. Former Executive Vice-President Michihiro Nishida of Honda Motor Company felt that a book of this kind was needed and provided encouragement at many points. The topics, questions and layout of the book were decided upon jointly in consultations between Taizo Ueda, Chief Economist of Honda Motor Company, and Bradley Richardson of Ohio State with help from the individual contributors; the Honda Motor Company also supported the production of the book with a generous gift to Ohio State University. While the analysis and judgments expressed in this book are those of the individual scholars, we are greatly indebted to the Honda Motor Company for its support of this effort to provide more information about Japanese business to Western business persons. We are also personally indebted to the members of the scholarly team contributing to the book for their written efforts and participation in the various team meetings that led to refinement in the book's format and substance.

CONTENTS

	Page
Foreword	v
Editor's Preface	viii
PART I. BUSINESS AND LABOR IN JAPAN	1

Chapter
1 JAPANESE BUSINESS ORGANIZATION	3
The Japanese Corporation	5
The Sōgōshōsha	14
Patterns in Economic Organization	21
2 LABOR IN JAPAN	29
Permanent Employment	31
Enterprise Unions	36
Labor Conflict	42
Labor Regulations	52
PART II. THE JAPANESE ECONOMY	63
3 JAPAN'S ECONOMIC GROWTH	65
Japan's Economic Modernization	67
Japan's Growth Record	75
The Postwar Economic Miracle	82
Resource Dependency and Energy Problems	89
4 JAPAN'S TRADE COMPETITIVENESS	99
Research and Development	101
Cheap Labor	108
The Contemporary Myth of Japanese Protectionism	115

Chapter		Page
5	INCOME DISTRIBUTION, PURCHASING POWER, AND THE CONSUMER MARKET	124
	Income Distribution in Contemporary Japan	125
	Consumer Spending in Japan	134
PART III. THE JAPANESE BUSINESS ENVIRONMENT		139
6	LAW IN JAPAN	141
	The Japanese Legal System	143
	Litigation in Japan	149
	Crime in Japan	155
	The Japanese Constitution	162
7	THE POLITICAL ENVIRONMENT	169
	Political Interests and Political Parties	172
	Movements and Political Stability	179
	Pollution Problems and Response	185
	Business and the Bureaucracy	194
	Japanese Foreign Policy	200
	Japan's Social Welfare System	207
8	SOCIOHISTORIC TRENDS	215
	Militarism in Japan's Tradition	217
	Religion in Japan	224
9	SOCIETY AND CULTURE	233
	Japan's Educational System	236
	Cultural Values in Japan	244
	Leisure and Entertainment	251
	The Media in Japan	258
	The Status of Women	268

Chapter			Page
PART IV. TRADING WITH JAPAN			279
10	ENTERING THE JAPANESE MARKET		281
	Realities of the Japanese Consumer Imports Market		283
	Exports to Japan by Small Firms		290
	Export Assistance for Foreign Firms		299
11	SOCIAL RELATIONS AND JAPANESE BUSINESS PRACTICES		304
	Negotiations with Japanese Firms		305
	Dos and Don'ts of Japanese Etiquette		312
	Friendships with Japanese Counterparts		317
PART V. JAPAN'S MODERN EXPERIENCE			323
12	THE IMPACT OF MODERNIZATION ON JAPAN		325
	Modernization Versus Westernization in Japan		326
ABOUT THE CONTRIBUTORS			333

PART I

BUSINESS AND LABOR IN JAPAN

1

JAPANESE BUSINESS ORGANIZATION

Many observers of Japan's recent economic growth attribute a heavy portion of this success to the nature of Japanese business organization. The differences between the model Japanese firm and the model American firm are indeed striking, as are some other distinctive features of Japanese business organization, and these could be important to economic success. However, there are some similarities in Japanese business behavior to that in other countries which should not be overlooked. Also, it must be emphasized that Japanese corporations are not uniquely successful at all times in all of their activities: Japanese firms do make mistakes and fail, and life in Japanese firms is not always smooth. It is important to see how corporate organizational patterns are different in Japan, and how these could have effects on firm behavior. But we should avoid the current tendency to overromanticize Japanese life while looking at the Japanese phenomena with a balanced eye.

As Yoshi Tsurumi points out, Japanese business organizations are different from those in America. While corporations in both countries have functional divisions and hierarchies of authority, decision making in at least the ideal Japanese firm tends to flow upward from middle-level management rather than downward from top echelons as typifies the American case. This apparent major difference in national management styles is related to a parallel difference in company cultures, wherein personnel matters receive much more emphasis in Japanese firms in efforts to create strong employee loyalty.

Underlying the emphases on loyalty and decentralized participation among employees is a Japanese orientation toward long-term perspectives;

this long-term outlook affects business strategy as well as company organizational matters. On the personnel side, Japanese corporate leadership currently looks for *permanent* commitments among its core employees and provides them with rewards and incentives designed to induce this kind of commitment. Elsewhere, in making decisions about products and facilities, business leaders define firms' goals in terms of long-term market shares more than short-term profits and sales. It is this long-term orientation in all areas of business activity that is probably most basic about Japanese firms, and permits the evaluation of capital investments in terms of future rather than immediate payoffs; such an outlook is probably a major factor in economic growth where decisions are based on accurate predictions of future market behavior and where the general economic environment permits growth.

Given Japan's prowess as an economic giant, it is perhaps surprising to many foreign observers that individual firms in Japan are often much smaller than large American multinational corporations like General Motors and Exxon. Yet as Albert Keidel II illustrates, Japanese firms in an important number of cases operate in tandem with other firms in large business groups. These groups emerge around relationships with major banks which parallel, albeit in a looser sense, the ties which bound together Japan's prewar *zaibatsu* and their parent holding companies. The major groups like Mitsubishi, Mitsui, and Sumitomo actually have annual business volumes that are considerably greater than the economic output of most countries or for that matter the major multinational corporations. (Comparisons of this kind actually give a good appreciation of the strength of Japanese business even though there are some inevitable distortions in comparing groups with individual corporations given the "looser" operating styles and integration of the groups in some cases.)

The tendency to affiliate with groups is probably closely related to another Japanese business tendency to engage in monopsonistic economic practices through a variety of cartel or cooperative relationships with other firms in particular product areas. Japanese firms thus tend to look toward cooperative relationships with other firms in "output" decisions as well as in regard to "input" decisions about capital accumulation and material supply.

At the center of the major economic groups are the trading companies, which are themselves sometimes very large, as in the case of Mitsubishi or Mitsui. Today the trading companies generally perform two functions for their groups and other customers: specialization in raw materials trade and initiation of overseas investment projects (which themselves are often in the area of raw materials procurement). In the process of dealing with worldwide sources of supply, which are critical to Japan's well-being, the trading companies have developed elaborate and far-flung organizations that to some degree resemble the foreign services of nations in their common esprit de corps and worldwide global communications facilities.

The large Japanese corporation has its own management styles and culture, and concerns itself with long-term aspects of personnel management and market behavior. Large Japanese corporations are also typically affiliated with major economic groups and participate in some form of collective market activity. The large firms operating through groups and cartels are clearly the core organizational unit in the Japanese economy. Yet Japan is a *dual* economy in terms of the continued existence of an important small-firm sector, and the frequently close ties that exist between large corporations and suppliers in the small-firm sector. While the large corporations have spearheaded growth, smaller firms have provided a cushion during economic slumps for the "permanent" operations of the giants. At the same time, large firms have provided financial resources for small firms that are often otherwise unavailable to small businesses.

The Japanese Corporation

What is the nature of company organization in Japan? What are the major positions in a typical Japanese company, and how are powers distributed among these positions? What variations also exist between companies on these matters? Also, what are the most typical patterns of decision making among Japanese companies today?

In order to compare corporate organizations in the United States and Japan, we should first identify some of the major contrasts between the types of organizations found in these two countries. In general, we can make the following observations about American and Japanese firms.

Key Characteristics	Japanese Firms	American Firms
1. Business orientation	Global; toward long-term growth	Domestic; toward short-term growth
2. Business target	Market share at home and abroad	Quarterly profit
3. Management attitude toward job security of rank-and-file employees	Seen as efficient means to ensure employees' long-term commitment to growth and technological innovation	Considered inefficient and an obstacle to growth
4. Staffing of executive positions	Promotion from within	Hiring from outside
5. Internal control of organization	Through implicit rules and shared goals among managers and employees	Through explicit rules and management by objective

Purely theoretical models of Japanese and American corporations are best illustrated in Figure 1.1. The triangular figure in the middle denotes the ordinary hierarchy from top echelon down to the rank-and-file employees.

The very highest echelon of management in both Japanese and American firms is expected to maintain the broadest commitment to the firm's long-range goals. In most American firms, the lower the individual's position is in the hierarchy of the firm, the more markedly his commitment to the goals of the firm tapers off. In most Japanese firms, even employees at the lowest level, the rank-and-file regular employees, are encouraged to maintain a long-term interest in their firm's future.

TWO MODELS OF CORPORATION

What can be observed here are two distinct types of corporations—Model J and Model A. The former is found predominantly but not exclusively among Japanese firms in Japan, while the latter is predominantly but not exclusively found among American firms in the United States. But in Japan, there are firms that act more like the Model A type. And in the United States, there are such firms as Xerox, Kodak, IBM, and Texas Instruments that have developed their internal working systems more like the Model J type of organization. In reality, we should be prepared to observe different mixtures and weights of Model J and Model A types of behavior in the same firm. And this mixture may well change depending on the firm's stage at its growth cycle, too. A priori, we have no way of determinimg which of these types is more efficient in carrying out a given corporate task. The only significant difference lies in their approach to achieving their corporate goals.

Model A

Strategic decision-making tasks such as formulating the firm's growth goals, deciding on new investment, and implementing long-range planning prerogatives, are the executive functions of upper-echelon executives.

Epitomized by the phrase "hired hands," the Model A firm, based on its requirements, maintains that few idiosyncratic skills are unique to the firm itself. Any unique skills required to accomplish a given task within the firm may be added easily to the general skills each employee has already acquired elsewhere through his or her general or vocational education or prior job experience outside the firm. This type of procurement of necessary skills from outside markets influences promotion and selection of personnel at even the highest rung on the corporate ladder.

FIGURE 1.1

Japanese and American Corporate Structure

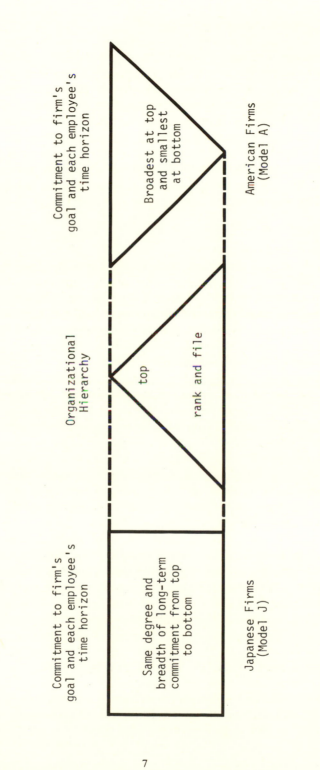

Source: Reprinted with permission from *The Japanese Are Coming,* Copyright 1976, Ballinger Publishing Company.

Once the firm's long-range goals are determined by executives at the uppermost level, the implementation required to achieve these goals is then "subcontracted" out to the next level down, namely, to operational units such as production divisions or to functional units such as marketing, manufacturing, research and development (R&D), and to general administration, including accounting and finance departments. These subunits are in turn given explicit performance goals (objectives) described in terms of "quantifiable variables" such as target profits, costs, production units, financial costs, and an assortment of indexes designed to "measure" the subunit's performance.

Model J

Strategic decision making is considered to be the collective responsibility of all in the middle-management echelon and above. Furthermore, even rank-and-file employees and newly recruited college graduates are encouraged to take an active interest in the long-term goals of their firm.

The Model J firm holds that both managers and employees must acquire idiosyncratic skills unique to the firm in order to accomplish their assigned tasks. Consequently, this type of firm hires human beings *in toto*, not merely their skills and personal traits. Through on-the-job training, which often emphasizes job rotation among various divisions within the firm, not only requisite idiosyncratic skills but also specific corporate "ideology" and "culture" are inculcated in the workers of the firm.

Even when top-level managers formulate certain strategic projects, they do not finalize their plans until middle- to lower-echelon managers have had an opportunity to refine and often revise these strategies to fit the means that middle- to lower-echelon managers have for implementing such plans. As extensive consultations take place among the individuals involved in implementing these plans who are scattered throughout the various subunits of the firm, a chosen course of action, once put into effect, is well understood by the corporate members. This implicit understanding among corporate members concerning each individual's task and the relationship of each task to all of the other jobs involved in carrying out a plan replaces the explicit performance goals the Model A corporation applies to the subunits involved in implementing its strategy.

CORPORATE CULTURE OF MODEL J FIRMS

As may be deduced from the preceding accounts of the two models of corporate organization, the most marked distinction between Model A and J corporations lies in the corporate cultures (atmospheres) that permeate their respective company hierarchies from middle echelon on down through the rank and file. In contrast to their counterparts in Model A firms, even the rank-and-file employees of a Model J firm are very much aware of their company's long-range goals. They are encouraged to participate actively in the performance of their firm and, most notably, are urged to contribute to the growth and potential of their company through their work. In order to nurture a long-term orientation on the part of corporate members, which will in turn foster a strong personal identification with their own company, a Model J firm spares no effort or expense in keeping even its rank-and-file employees informed about the firm's growth goals, its new achievements in R&D, and its marketing and manufacturing activities.

By implication, the job security of employees in a Model J firm becomes both the cornerstone of a long-term orientation on the part of the firm's workers and an incentive that spurs cooperative rather than adversary relationships among the various subunits of the firm and among management and rank-and-file employees.

The job security of Model J employees often eliminates the necessity for such cumbersome measures as the arbitration of job-related grievances and the policing of individual members' behavior to ensure that their actions are not damaging to the firm. Mutual trust between management and employees, as well as among individual employees, is thus not only a cost-saving means but also a source of organizational productivity.

The ideological commitment of management to job security for their rank-and-file employees orients them toward remaining alert to dynamic changes taking place in the company's business environment. Since misjudgment of market conditions and the company's competitors on the part of management can result in declining sales and profits (which cannot easily be cushioned by expedient layoffs of rank-and-file employees), managers must constantly be concerned with possessing the organizational flexibility needed to cope with rapid shifts in the firm's business environment.

DECISION-MAKING PROCESSES OF JAPANESE FIRMS

The commitment of individual employees to the widely accepted goals of their firm has produced an often mentioned decision-making system in Japanese firms that is called *ringi seido*. Observers of this decision-making process will note that new proposals—marketing or investment decisions, for example—are often initiated at the lower or middle echelons of the firm. These proposals are passed along through the hierarchy, collecting seals of approval or undergoing minor revisions, on their way up to the president. The initiators or collaborating parties of such proposals are busily engaged on an informal basis in pinpointing key personalities whose support is needed. Some proposals fade away or die on their journey to the top echelon. But those proposals that do survive cannot be attributed solely to their initiator(s). By the time a proposal is accepted by top management, there will be a corporate consensus concerning its feasibility.

This process of building a consensus among the individuals who will be affected by a decision takes the decision out of the hands of any specific initiator or implementor. The decision-making process in Japan is inextricably intertwined with the later process of implementation. This explains why American managers often complain of the length of time it takes Japanese managers to reach decisions. It is inconceivable to Japanese managers that any decision could be made without consulting those individuals who are directly responsible for the internal workings of the organization. The specifics of such a procedure would be rather time consuming to list here. But when a decision is made and communicated to a third party such as a customer, that may be deemed tantamount to the commencement of its implementation.

Consensus-building practices in the decision-making process of Japanese firms have created two characteristics that are distinctly Japanese: first, a substantive involvement of middle management (section chiefs up to department heads) in strategic decision making; and second, the expectation that presidential leadership will confine itself to coping mainly with crisis situations or with abrupt, clear-cut changes in the direction of the firm. Once the firm's general direction is communicated to middle management, both operations decisions and incremental changes tend to be entrusted to the initiative of lower to middle management echelons.

In actual practice, the conceptual demarcation of the roles of upper and middle echelons in a Japanese firm is often blurred. In general, one may view the upper and middle echelon as a group that concerns itself with not only the day-to-day fine tuning of the company's accepted strategies but also with the search for new strategic moves. In this context, members of the middle-management level of a Japanese corporation act as planning aides and advisors to upper-echelon management as well as day-to-day supervisors in the implementation of agreed-upon strategies. In turn, the upper echelon is expected to take an active interest in the details of middle management's activities, while remaining one step removed from any actual involvement.

WHO HOLDS POWER IN JAPANESE CORPORATIONS?

As it is with their American counterparts, the influence of Japanese executives generally stems from their position in the company hierarchy. The only marked difference between Japanese and American corporate power stucture lies in the influence of a Japanese executive vice-president in charge of personnel affairs and his office. In American corporations, personnel managers are often treated as glorified file clerks who screen routine application forms and other personnel matters. In view of the Japanese firm's emphasis on human resources development, the personnel department works closely with the company's president and manages all aspects of human resources management. The position of personnel manager is often considered to be one of the most important positions in the company. This management skill is deemed one of the managerial skills vital to anyone desiring to reach the upper echelon of the corporation.

The other difference between Japanese and American corporations is the inability of managers to fire their subordinates. It is the collective entity known as the firm that hires all employees and decides on their fate. Individual managers assume responsibility for training their staffs, evaluating their personal performance, and acting as their personal counselors. They do not have any right, however, to fire their subordinates. They can only influence their promotion.

MIDDLE MANAGEMENT: CENTER OF MEANINGFUL INFLUENCE

A deep-rooted feeling exists among Japanese employees and managers that the Japanese corporation belongs to *all* of its members. This accounts for the substantive influence and authority that is delegated, de facto, to middle management. At minimum, middle management is expected to initiate questioning when it is not convinced of the wisdom of a specific decision reached by the upper echelon.

In the case of American subsidiaries I have studied in Japan, this conception of the roles of middle management in relation to upper-echelon authority has caused considerable conflict between Japanese employees and American managers. These employees, working for the long-term goals of their firm, tended to challenge actions on the part of their superiors that they might have deemed detrimental to the good of the firm. The Japanese employees expected explanations from their superiors with regard to how certain actions would benefit the firm over a longer period of time than that which American managers would care to consider. Most American managers took such requests to be personal affronts to their management prerogatives. American managers, bred in American corporate culture, expected the Japanese middle management to follow their decisions. Little did they expect their subordinates to confront them with questions concerning their decisions.

In my studies of Japanese subsidiaries in the United States, American plant and sales managers have often been bewildered when they discovered that they were expected to resolve problems among themselves without bothering Japanese top executives. American managers would report on problems to the Japanese president of the firm, and would offer suggested solutions. The Japanese president would politely suggest in turn that if American managers were able to identify the problem and knew the solution, they should have quietly gone ahead and solved it. Once American managers learned that de facto delegation of managerial authority was materially prevalent in the Japanese corporate environment and that this culture was tolerant of managerial mistakes far more readily than the American culture, American managers began to enjoy a position of managerial authority that in their former American companies had belonged only to a higher level of management.

MANUFACTURING PRODUCTIVITY AND THE INFLUENCE OF WORKERS

"Permanent employment" in Japan is not a legal or contractual system. It is a psychological and moral contract between the firm (as represented by its president) and its employees. It means that managers will not use layoffs to shift the blame for their mistakes onto workers. When disaster strikes the firm, its burdens will be shared first from the top down. The first to suffer is usually the company's dividends. Then, the firm's president and executives would take cuts in salary. After that, all management personnel would be asked to take cuts in salary before some voluntary layoffs are called for among the rank and file in order to lighten the economic burden on the firm.

As we discussed in our appraisal of the two models of corporation— Model J and Model A—the job security of rank-and-file workers in Model J types of firms has evolved as those workers' unique skills and manufacturing experience became important to their firm. As a result, even today in Japan, unskilled construction workers and temporary subcontractors whose skills can easily be procured from open markets do not enjoy job security to any particular extent. However, as Japan began to experience a labor shortage starting in the mid-1960s, the general ranks of temporary workers hired on a daily-wage basis rapidly began to dwindle in size.

The Japanese system of job security for rank-and-file workers has allowed Japan to excel in mass-production process technologies in which worker-machine interactions determine productivity. The participation of workers in innovations in their production processes has been encouraged and honored by management. Management expects workers to tell them what should be done about mass-production processes. Plant engineers mingle freely with production workers and help them to solve technical problems that crop up in their work.

After about a quarter of a century of holding ordinary production workers responsible for their own product quality and cost-cutting measures, Japan's manufacturing industries today have come to possess unique production systems that permit both mass production and zero-defect quality for varying products. Mass production and product quality in Japan are not considered trade-offs. Workers have been trained to utilize a variety of analytical tools for statistical quality control and operational research methods to improve their production methods. Some plants have even encouraged their production workers to stop their assembly lines rather than send defective products on to the next stage.

Inside Japanese factories, quality control is built into the production processes. And this obviates costly and cumbersome quality checks at the end of production lines. This is perhaps responsible for the difference in manufacturing productivity between comparable Japanese and American factories. For example, when a leading American automobile firm experienced difficulty maintaining an assembly-line productivity of 75 cars per minute at its ultramodern facility, a comparable factory of a Japanese automobile firm in Japan was easily topping 100 cars per minute. Also, the American firm was beseiged with quality-control problems at Lordstown, while the Japanese factory was turning out its subcompacts with impeccable workmanship as a result of its dedication to zero defects.

After World War II, Japan learned the analytical tools of statistical quality-control methods and other operational research techniques from the United States. Japan even bought industrial equipment from the United States. While the American management was not introducing these manufacturing tools onto their production floors, their Japanese competitors had invested time and money in modernizing their production facilities and in training and retraining their workers, engineers, and managers to use them. What accounted for this difference? Perhaps it is because of the difference in corporate culture between the Model J type of Japanese firm and the Model A type of American firm.

Japanese managers willingly shared their power with their rank-and-file workers. Indeed, as far as improvements in production processes are concerned, the Japanese system practices the use of authority from the bottom up, which allows workers to tell their superiors what they think should be done with the production processes.

Yoshi Tsurumi

BIBLIOGRAPHY

Rohlen, Thomas. *For Harmony and Strength*. Berkeley: University of California Press, 1974.

The Sōgōshōsha

All Western businessmen dealing with Japan know about the famous trading companies, but sometimes details of their size and operations are hard to find. How do the trading companies stack up with regard to share of import and export markets and volume of operations? Also, what is the nature of their relationship with banking groups, and direct investments in productive capacity? Are there exceptions to the "rule" that the best way to trade with Japan is through trading companies? If so, what are they?

TRADING COMPANIES IN JAPAN

In terms of the breadth of products and services in which they deal, Japanese trading companies may be divided into two groups: large, general trading companies (*sōgōshōsha*), of which there are nine; and specialty trading companies (*semmonshōsha*), which number more than five thousand. The latter handle a limited range of products and services. Many of the latter group are not much different from import and export specialty firms found in the United States. And many specialty trading firms in Japan function as wholesalers and distributors.

The most visible and best known of the Japanese trading companies are the nine largest trading concerns called sōgōshōsha. Not only have these firms grown into multinational conglomerates, but they have also come to handle a diversity of products and services ranging from ground nuts to missiles for Japan and other countries. Among them they still handle approximately 30 percent of Japan's imports and exports.

Table 1.1 provides an economic profile of the nine sōgōshōsha. One may observe the wide variation in size even among the nine sōgōshōsha from such Class A firms as Mitsubishi and Mitsui to Class C firms as Kanematsu-Gosho, Tomen, and Nichimen.

One should note from Table 1.1 that there are two distinct characteristics of sōgōshōsha. First, sōgōshōsha thrive on the economies of scale provided by the size of their organizations. The larger the total number of employees is, the larger their annual business volume and profit becomes. Second, sōgōshōsha clearly pursue volume in their business, thriving on the total cash flow associated with the massive movements of goods and services rather than on net profit, which the histories of the sōgōshōsha have shown that, with the exception of Mitsubishi and Mitsui, each of the other seven sōgōshōsha have transformed themselves from specialty trading firms into large general trading companies during the last quarter of a century since World War II.

Furthermore, two additional characteristics of influential sōgōshōsha should be recognized. These firms are involved in both domestic and international trade in goods, services, finances, and information. In fact, it is not unusual for sōgōshōsha to derive better than one-half of their business from wholesale and other distribution business in Japan. Trading companies in general, and sōgōshōsha in particular, derive their main business from linking the marketing activities of their interconnecting suppliers and users of specific products and services with the financing needs of their clients. Sōgōshōsha often act as intermediaries between banks and a multitude of manufacturing and retailing concerns. The sōgōshōsha absorb the financial risks associated with banks' eventual loans that are channeled through the sōgōshōsha to their client firms. In return, the sōgōshōsha establish captive business relations with their manufacturing and retail clients who either purchase goods and services from the sōgōshōsha or who supply the sōgōshōsha with necessary products for the sōgōshōsha's domestic and overseas offices.

The sōgōshōsha and semmonshōsha in Japan are noted for their export-import assistance to both Japanese and foreign firms. Japanese trading companies have helped other small- and medium-sized Japanese manufacturing firms to export their products and to import necessary raw materials, technology, and products. They have also assisted even large Japanese manufacturing firms in exporting their products to many small pockets in the world markets. By utilizing worldwide networks for market information and other financial services, Japanese sōgōshōsha are able to pool the exportable products of many Japanese manufacturers. Likewise, by pooling the import needs of several Japanese firms, Japanese trading firms are able to carry out a worldwide search for necessary raw materials, products, and technologies, and bring them to Japan in quantity and at prices that are advantageous to their Japanese clients.

TABLE 1.1

The Nine Sōgōshōsha, 1978

Company by Size	Annual Turnover	No. of Japanese Employees	Annual Turn- over per Employee	Annual After- tax Profit
Class A				
Mitsubishi	$38 billion	9,645	$4.0 million	$67 million
Mitsui	36	10,382	3.5	42
Class B				
C. Itoh	28	8,120	3.4	8
Marubeni	27	7,961	3.4	16
Sumitomo	25	6,062	4.0	31
Nissho-Iwai	18	6,627	2.8	15
Class C				
Kanematsu- Gosho	9	3,079	3.1	3
Tomen	9	3,330	2.8	4
Nichimen	8	3,664	2.1	6

Note: The original figures in Japanese yen have been converted into U.S. dollars at the rate of ¥240 to $1.00.

Source: Compiled by the author from the Annual Reports of Respective Firms, 1978.

THE GROWTH OF JAPANESE TRADING COMPANIES

Contrary to popular belief, trading companies are not unique to Japan. The United States and the nations of Europe gave birth to their own trading firms during their early stages of industrial development. What is unique about the Japanese trading firms is that they have survived well into the postindustrial era in Japan. The European and American counterparts of an earlier era have either faded out of existence or have survived by choosing to specialize in the narrower functions of international trade in agricultural commodities or in retailing or wholesale business in a limited range of products.

The growth of Japanese trading firms is very much a product of the approach Japan has taken to achieve rapid industrial growth. In the 1870s, when Japan was embarking upon its concerted effort to catch up economically with the West, divisions of labor had evolved among trading firms, banks, and manufacturing firms with each group specializing in what it did best. Thus, manufacturing firms came to entrust domestic and international marketing activities to the trading firms and corporate finance to the banks. The growth of Japanese trading firms was facilitated by their functioning as the central marketing arms of their respective industrial groupings.

THE MYTH OF OMNIPOTENT SŌGŌSHŌSHA

Contrary to popular belief, sōgōshōsha are by no means omnipotent. They have become adept at handling bulk commodities. They are now good at exporting and importing industrial machinery and plants. However, they singularly lack the experience and skill of marketing at home and abroad such consumer products as automobiles, electronic appliances, fashion apparel, cosmetics and other products that require extensive consumer marketing activities. Even in the fields of industrial equipment, sōgōshōsha do not possess extensive technical capabilities of providing requisite sales engineering services.

As Japanese exports and imports grew to consist more and more of consumer and industrial products requiring extensive and sophisticated customer services, sōgōshōsha have often come to be bypassed by the manufacturers that are handling for themselves both overseas and domestic marketing activities.

INVESTMENTS OF TRADING COMPANIES
IN MANUFACTURING FIRMS

Both inside and outside Japan, Japanese sōgōshōsha have gone about obtaining their own captive manufacturing suppliers and clients through partial or whole ownership of promising manufacturing firms. Even in 1980, nearly one quarter of the Japanese manufacturing subsidiaries established overseas have one or more Japanese trading companies as their founding business partners.

In the case of large-scale projects in natural resource and agricultural development, the participation of Japanese trading firms is often deemed necessary. Trading firms are relied upon to provide their share of investment funding and to market the products of such ventures throughout the world.

Of late, many foreign fast foods and soft drinks have been introduced into Japan as the sōgōshōsha diversified their operations into direct "downstream" business. In this case, the capability of sōgōshōsha to procure necessary food ingredients and their ability to provide financial and managerial resources have been matched with foreign investors' proprietary business know-how. The most notable success stories in Japan are those of Kentucky Fried Chicken and McDonald's.

SŌGŌSHŌSHA'S INVESTMENT IN NATURAL RESOURCES DEVELOPMENT

As the world supply of such vital natural resources as oil, copper ore, iron ore, bauxite, timber and agriproducts turned to shortage from glut, sōgōshōsha that had built their influence over processors of these raw materials through their ability to procure these vital raw materials sought to invest in the development projects of natural resources abroad. This new worldwide strategy of sōgōshōsha became apparent toward the end of the 1960s and was intensified after the first oil crisis of 1973.

Most notable examples are C. Itoh's project of the copper ore development in Zaire, Mitsubishi's copper ore and natural gas development in Brunei, and Mitsui's participations in the international consortium of iron ore development in Australia. In addition, sōgōshōsha are deeply involved in the lumbering operations in the Philippines, Indonesia, Malaysia, Canada, and in the United States. Petrochemical projects in the Middle East were organized by Mitsui and Mitsubishi.

Sōgōshōsha's attempt to develop captive supply sources of natural resources abroad produced another bold strategy of acquiring a substantial interest of the existing foreign firms that had already developed their own positions in such natural resource based industry as aluminum and oil. Mitsui's acquisition of 50 percent of the voting shares of the aluminum subsidiary of AMAX in 1973 was the harbinger of the similar moves by other sōgōshōsha. Mitsubishi's acquisition of a sizable minority ownership position of the existing oil refinery and retail firm on the west coast of the United States is another example of such moves.

ORGANIZATIONAL STRENGTH OF GENERAL TRADING COMPANIES OF JAPAN

Sōgōshōsha's organizational flexibility and strength stems from a corporate structure and culture typical of the Model J type of firm discussed earlier. The firm consists of sōgōshōsha professionals (male) most of whom have attended a handful of leading universities in Japan and gone through the same kind of socialization processes during and after their college days.

This is why sōgōshōsha professionals can swap trades, information, and commodities among themselves. The internal workings of sōgōshōsha resemble very much the efficient market trading place to which various biddings for information and commodities and services are tossed by literally thousands of sōgōshōsha professionals. In order to link many trading posts scattered all over the world, sōgōshōsha use telex, telephone, and other modern communications networks that are operated by the computers. Mutual trust and interwoven obligations permit sōgōshōsha professionals to conclude their urgent deals in a short period of time. Their codes of conduct are implicitly understood by sōgōshōsha professionals. Long years of acculturation and apprenticeships within sōgōshōsha help every sōgōshōsha professional to understand clearly the implicit but binding rules of conduct.

True to the Model J type of corporation, sōgōshōsha have implicitly incorporated their strategy formulation in their process of day-to-day operations. Sōgōshōsha professionals are encouraged to think of the future in the global context of their businesses. This is because sōgōshōsha cannot stand still. They thrive on flows of goods and services. Even junior members of sōgōshōsha professionals are often encouraged to develop trade and investment development plans that may take years to implement. These plans are refined by initiators' peers and bosses as they go through check-and balance scrutinies up the hierarchical echelon of sōgōshōsha.

HIGH-RISK OPERATION OF SŌGŌSHŌSHA

Since sōgōshōsha are operating on a thin profit/sales margin (on the average, 1.5 percent), and since sōgōshōsha are highly leveraged with debts, they are exposed to high financial risks. Besides, over two-thirds of sōgōshōsha's costs and expenses are related to human costs of salaried sōgōshōsha professionals. This is inevitable because sōgōshōsha professionals are the real assets of the large general trading firms. However, financially speaking, the job security of salaried professionals increases the fixed operating expenses of sōgōshōsha, and thus increases the financial risk of downturn in sōgōshōsha's businesses.

Of recent, multinational investments of Japanese sōgōshōsha have increased their operational and financial risks so much so that any sudden failure of sōgōshōsha's overseas ventures might destroy them. This is actually what happened to the now defunct sōgōshōsha Ataka. Ataka was one of the ten leading sōgōshōsha. However, its investment in an oil refinery in Canada was properly checked by its headquarters. When the refinery went bankrupt, so did Ataka.

In order to mitigate high-risk characteristics of sōgōshōsha, they now need to develop cadres of capable managers who can manage not only trading activities but more importantly diverse investment projects at home and abroad. Furthermore, in order to manage diverse projects abroad and in order to penetrate overseas markets more deeply than before, sōgōshōsha will have to bring non-Japanese professionals into the intimate communications networks that we discussed in the preceding section.

Accordingly, we cannot rest assured that by 1989 all the leading nine sōgōshōsha of Japan will survive in their present form. We may well see further concentration of the top nine sōgōshōsha as their ranks thin out.

Such operating risks as mentioned above come from within Japan itself. A number of manufacturing firms, small and large, that have utilized sōgōshōsha in the past have developed their own experience of international trade and investment. And they try to handle for themselves their own international trade. Besides, there are many Japanese government policymakers who do not understand the functions of sōgōshōsha and their benefits to Japan as a whole. Accordingly, there have been increasingly many attempts by the Fair Trade Commission (the antitrust arm of the Japanese governmentt) and by other branches of the government to curb sōgōshōsha's abilities to borrow from Japanese banks and to invest in many ventures. These officials do not understand that sōgōshōsha have provided a vast amount of "venture' capital to fledgling small- to medium-sized firms and in turn have benefited from expanding trade volumes related to the growth of such venture businesses.

Unfortunately, the public image of Japanese sōgōshōsha is not favorable. And some sōgōshōsha have exhibited a few embarrassing acts of getting caught in commodity speculation. As a result, politically, sōgōshōsha are difficult to defend publicly even though their ultimate demise and disappearance are likely to damage the Japanese economy beyond repair.

Yoshi Tsurumi

BIBLIOGRAPHY

Tsurumi, Yoshi. *Sogoshosha: Engines of Export-based Growth*. Montreal: Institute for Research on Public Policy, 1980.

Patterns in Economic Organization

> The Japanese economy is said to be dominated by large firms, cartels, and other producing or marketing arrangements. Just what is the state of economic organization in Japan, and how does it compare with the situation in the United States?

Although superficial statistics indicate that industrial organization in Japan and America is formally quite similar, a closer look at the nature of Japanese business organizations, and in particular the encouraging posture of the Japanese government, reveals profound differences not only in industrial organization but also in national philosophy. In spite of an American attempt at the dissolution of occupied Japan's giant prewar industrial holding companies and the establishment of the Antimonopoly Law and many features of American antitrust legislation, Japanese government strategists favor rather than discourage industrial collusion and co-operation.

The principal reason is that the Japanese distrust the ability of a purely laissez-faire economic environment to create in Japan the efficiency and innovation her economic survival requires. Coordinated guidance has been perhaps one of the single most important ingredients in Japan's overall economic success. Nevertheless, within those same colluding industries, Japan has been able to foster creative and productive competition. From cheaper ships and more efficient steel production to smaller cameras, economical electronics, and fuel-efficient, pollution-free cars, the Japanese industrial milieu produces goods with quality and ingenuity matching and often surpassing that of the United States. This combination of open oligopolistic collusion and creative competition in turn perhaps points to more basic differences in American and Japanese industrial and managerial philosophy, differences for which patterns in industrial organization are more a symptom than a cause.

SIMILAR PATTERNS: U.S.-JAPANESE INDUSTRIAL CONCENTRATION

In formal terms, industrial concentration is the percentage share one or a few firms controls out of a whole market or out of total productive capacity. For example, the top four firms in an industry could control 80 percent of their market, while the top four in another less-concentrated industry might control only 25 percent of sales. That percentage is called an industry's four-firm concentration ratio. Comparing concentration ratio data from the 1960s for Japan and the United States, we find that for all manufacturing industries, the concentration ratios are about the same, and that if anything, there is somewhat less concentration in Japan than in the United States. The top four firms in an "average" industry controlled between 35 and 40 percent of its 1960s market, whether the firm was American or Japanese. This dispels the popular belief that there is some gross degree of measurable monopoly or oligopoly concentration in Japanese manufacturing when compared to that of the United States.

In addition, the same individual industries that are highly concentrated in Japan are by and large also the same industries that are concentrated in the United States (for example, paper, steel products, motor vehicles, synthetic fibers, photographic film, and beer). These and other results lead some scholars to conclude that both the pattern and level of market concentration is roughly the same in both countries. However, scholars disagree about whether these concentration ratios represent relevant measures of industry control over prices, profits, and competition in general.

This point is made more clearly by noticing that comparisons of American and Japanese industrial structure in the 1930s also reveal statistical similarities. And yet, by the time of the Pacific War, roughly 25 percent of all Japanese industries was controlled by just four giant holding company groups: Mitsui, Mitsubishi, Sumitomo, and Yasuda. Clearly, concentration ratios, as important as they may be for analyzing competitive levels in American industry, cannot give an accurate picture of the interrelations and degree of cooperation among Japanese industrial firms.

In fact, the most important form of Japanese business combination is not centered around control of a single market, but rather around oligopolistic influence in an entire range of related industries and markets. Hence, to understand the economic power of business groupings in Japan, one must be familiar with a tangle of intercorporate ownership, market, and credit relationships.

HORIZONTAL INDUSTRIAL CONGLOMERATES: NOT THE WHOLE STORY

In general, the major corporate combinations in Japan are chiefly in the capital-intensive industries, and the associations follow a pattern in which the core corporations include a bank or banks and several insurance firms, a dozen or so mining and industrial firms (steel, chemicals, shipbuilding, for example), and a collection of commercial and other firms (a trading company, real estate, food processing, shipping). Clustered around these in turn are tiers of subsidiary firms, linked by ownership, interlocking directorates, and controls on credit.

The clearest examples of such "associations" are the ones descendant from the "big three" prewar *zaibatsu* holding companies: Mitsui, Mitsubishi, and Sumitomo. In addition, a group related to the Fuji Bank is a descendant of Yasuda, the fourth major prewar conglomerate. Other combinations are related to the Daiichi Bank and the Sanwa Bank, while still others are more closely connected along product lines, such as Matsushita.

There is, however, no formal holding company as there was before 1945. The various ownership, credit, and other control mechanisms are so much weaker than before World War II that it is difficult to know whether these groupings do in fact operate in some centrally disciplined way for the benefit of some higher good, or whether they operate only as individual corporations in close contact for purposes of mutual cooperation, information, and assistance.

There is, nevertheless, close contact. For the largest combinations, this contact has traditionally taken place in monthly clubs. For example, presidents of the core Mitsui banks and industries meet in a Monday Club, and presidents of a more select subgroup of those same firms meet in a Second Thursday Club. Mitsubishi core presidents meet at a Friday Club, while for the Sumitomo group's presidents it is the White Waters Club, and so on.

It is important to realize, however, that the Japanese economy is not made up entirely of large firms in loose cooperative combination with one another. Far from it. One of the most interesting features of the Japanese economy is the very great number of extremely small firms in the industrial structure. Japanese manufacturing employment levels in firms with fewer than 10 workers are five times as great as in the United States. Although some Japanese officials and Ministries consider the large number of small firms a problem, many of those same firms have histories going back to the Meiji Restoration and before. They are an integral part of the Japanese economy, and their juxtaposition with the industrial giants leads many to analyze Japan's industry as one with a dual structure, part modern and highly efficient, part traditional, with much lower labor productivity and wages.

The gulf between the two kinds of business firms is not as great, however, as it might seem. There is often a close monopsonistic relationship between these small firms and the much larger industries they very often serve. In some extreme cases the only product of such small firms is a specific service performed inside a large factory or the provision of a single specialized part to some giant manufacturer. Thus, although formally independent, a significant portion of Japan's small industrial businesses are often closely linked to parent firms through tight subcontract relationships.

PRICING ARRANGEMENTS:
A TOLERATED TRADITION

Given the traditional public tolerance for industrial cooperation in Japan's economic past as well as the relatively weak Japanese government interest in prosecuting discriminatory arrangements and practices, it is not surprising to find widespread collusive and cooperative pricing arrangements. In many oligopolistic concentrations there are patterns of price leadership and price following similar to those in the United States. For other retail markets there are often trade associations that provide pricing information to member suppliers, and many wholesale businesses (30 to 40 percent of those employing more than 50 workers) are controlled by the manufacturers who supply them. In short, even though single firms or small groups of firms cannot dominate a market, the Japanese have exploited a host of mechanisms for regulating price competition, and hence for supporting profit levels.

Hard evidence of the degree to which cartels actually control markets is difficult to find. Only in the case of legal cartels, sanctioned by the government's Fair Trade Commission, are there data on the extent of cartelization. Table 1.2 shows legalized cartels and the degree to which they dominate their respective markets as measured by their share of total shipments in the market.

These figures do not include illegal cartels, for which there are of course no data, but they do show that sanctioned business collusion in price fixing is widespread and actually increased in the 1960s, though the record is very mixed. The most significant aspect of the above data, however, is not the extent of cartelization, but rather the fact that the cartels have legal status. Such legitimization is just one of many ways the Japanese government has come to cooperate with and even urge business collusion.

GOVERNMENT INVESTMENT COORDINATION

In fact, one of the most important cartels of all is what some refer to as a de facto cartel in investment funds. In 1966, The Ministry of International Trade and Industry (MITI), the principal government champion of industry, reached an agreement with the Japanese Fair Trade Commission that exempted most investment adjustments from the Antimonopoly Law. Government investment guidance is in the form of coordination panels for each industry, which consult with firms about their investment plans. The purpose is to avoid overcapacity, and yet some researchers claim that the administrative quotas implied by such a system actually increased compe-

TABLE 1.2

**Importance of Legal Cartels
(in percent of shipments)**

Industry	1960	1970
Food Products	34.2	17.9
Textiles	78.1	69.1
Clothing	64.8	67.0
Lumber and wood	9.8	74.2
Furniture, fixtures	5.7	—
Pulp and paper	27.4	8.5
Publishing-Printing	47.0	—
Chemicals	22.6	22.7
Rubber products	13.2	42.7
Leather	7.4	13.4
Stone, clay, glass	41.2	17.6
Iron and Steel	34.5	58.8
Nonferrous metals	50.8	29.9
Metal products	7.0	19.9
Nonelectric Mach.	15.5	27.5
Electrical Mach.	8.3	26.3
Transport Equip.	1.9	31.9
Precision Instr.	25.8	55.6
Other mfgd. goods	6.7	6.5
Total	28.0	30.7

Source: Ken'ichi Imai, *Gendai Sangyo Soshiki* [The organization of contemporary industry] (Tokyo: Iwanami, 1976), chap. 1, translated in *Japanese Economic Studies*, Spring-Summer 1978, p. 40.

tition among manufacturers to modernize their plant and equipment so as to qualify for higher MITI quota shares.

This government involvement in cartels and investment discipline is perhaps itself the single most important feature of industrial organization in Japan. The Japanese are under no delusions about perfect competition, and they clearly do not believe that laissez-faire economic policy is the best way to promote rapid growth. In fact, the government strategy for molding Japanese industrial combinations does more than promote technical efficiency, it addresses Japan's whole international strategy of maximizing value-added exports while minimizing necessary imports for domestic consumption.

As mentioned above, MITI is instrumental in overseeing the expansion in capacity for evolving growth industries. An additional and particularly effective effort to make firms more efficient and reduce unnecessary competition has been the government encouragement of strategic mergers. These attracted the most attention during the 1960s, when the recombination of splintered shipping giants and the reunification of major steel combines, broken up less than 20 years earlier, caused popular speculation in Japan that the prewar zaibatsu giants themselves would also be re-created. That has not happened and shows no sign of happening in the future, but government efforts to assist the concentration of industry continue, especially in heavy industries and industries important for exports.

PLANNED INEFFICIENCY:
DOMESTIC CONSUMPTION INDUSTRIES

The close cooperation between MITI and industry to promote exports and industrial rationalization is familiar and widely studied. But there is much less attention paid to the government role in maintaining *poor* efficiency in domestic commercial and service industries. The purpose of this latter strategy is to increase as much as possible both the share of consumer income spent on domestic value added and the availability of domestic employment opportunities not related to exports. High expenditures for domestic value added reduce demand for consumer imports, while employment growth relieves employment pressures on the export industry sectors, where labor-saving investments are emphasized.

The clearest examples of this domestic value-added strategy are in agriculture and housing, where government trade and investment policies support exorbitantly high prices. But from the viewpoint of cartels and commercial combinations, the government role is perhaps most visible in the area of retail distribution. In addition to the legalized cartels and producer-controlled arrangements mentioned above, there are what amount to statutory restrictions on the establishment of supermarkets and other large cost-effective retail outlets.

According to laws revised as recently as 1973, opening a new department store or supermarket requires the permission of MITI, which in turn consults with the equivalent of the proposed location's chamber of commerce or other local retail representatives. The effect is to give local merchants who stand to lose business a degree of veto power over new stores, with the result that the spread of efficient labor-saving retail innovations are considerably retarded. An interesting exception is apparently made for luxury supermarkets, though it is probably going too far to say this is done to earn foreign exchange from Western residents who frequent them.

In any event, it is significant that the Japanese government influence over industrial behavior has this dual nature and at the same time is consistent with an overall international strategy for husbanding potentially scarce imported resources. By encouraging efficiency in export industries, the Japanese strengthen their foreign-exchange earnings; by discouraging efficiency in domestic market firms, they conserve foreign exchange by blunting the import impact of increased consumer purchasing power.

The above greatly oversimplified presentation of the Japanese government's part in supporting industry cartels and encouraging industry market discipline is not meant to imply that there is some all-powerful central command or soviet-style national plan. Nor are individual firms and combinations the meek followers of ministerial orders. Planning in Japan is indicative planning, the setting of suggested industry targets, with limited enforcement powers. Even the various government agencies themselves disagree on major policy questions, and even within a single ministry different departments have different goals that often conflict.

Government enforcement is limited to exhortation, which can nevertheless be very effective, and in major policy programs, to the use of tax incentives and threats, or the extension or withdrawal of credit. Individual firms chafe under unpopular directives, and often find ways to circumvent MITI's overall wishes, but in general there is not the opposition between government and industry so often seen in the United States. If anything, Japanese business sees itself as the instrument of national policy, its own best interests not very different from those of the economy as a whole.

It is clear, then, that simple concentration ratios hardly allow a fair comparison of American and Japanese industrial organization. A considerable portion of the spirit of zaibatsu Japan lives on, though the conglomerates themselves have very weak abilities to discipline and control subsidiaries when compared to prewar conditions. This loss, however, seems to be compensated to a significant degree by the active role played by the Japanese government, a role at present unthinkable in the United States, not only because of differences in economic ideology but also because Americans might feel that such a concentration of economic control may not be far removed from some similar potential for concentrated political power.

Albert Keidel

BIBLIOGRAPHY

Caves, Richard E. "Industrial Organization." In *Asia's New Giant: How the Japanese Economy Works,* edited by Hugh Patrick and Henry Rosovsky. Washington, D.C.: Brookings, 1976.

Hadley, Eleanor M. *Antitrust in Japan.* Princeton: Princeton University Press, 1970.

Roberts, John G. *Mitsui: Three Centuries of Japanese Business.* New York: Weatherhill, 1973.

2

LABOR IN JAPAN

The nature of labor relations is of course critical to the operation of businesses and to overall economic performance. Other things being equal, an institutionalized labor movement can be an important factor in increasing production costs over time. Labor strife also obviously bears its own costs in the production process. While it is often believed abroad that Japanese labor is compliant, and therefore not a disturbing factor in the business process on the scale found elsewhere, this is far from true. While Japan has some fairly idiosyncratic patterns in labor market organization and unionization, Japan's labor relations are far from the cooperative state sometimes attributed to them.

One of the more important features of Japan's labor market is the existence of permanent employment schemes in some industrial sectors. Under the permanent employment system regular workers and employees are hired by firms upon graduation from school or college and continue in the enterprise work force until their retirement, usually at the age of 55. Roughly one-third of Japan's work force is actually employed under the permanent employment system, which affects mainly males working in large firms. As Robert Cole demonstrates, the permanent employment system has been treated as a highly distinctive feature of Japan's labor scene, whereas in reality for men above 35 years of age there is more comparability between Japan and other countries than has been assumed. Still, the permanent employment system exists, and there is considerably less worker mobility between firms in Japan among younger male workers than in the United States.

The permanent employment system has been viewed as an expression of Japan's traditional cultural values that emphasized paternalistic relations between superiors and their subordinates. Though culture may have provided the model for the permanent employment system, the system was actually established self-consciously after World War I by employers who sought a stable work force for their firms.

In addition to the fact that the system is the result of conscious managerial policy, recent experience shows that permanent employment is also dependent on economic conditions more than was generally thought to be the case earlier. The permanent employment system was not challenged during the period of high economic growth in the 1960s; however, in the prolonged recession of the 1970s some industries have been forced to substantially pare down their permanent work force through interfirm transfers, delayed hiring, early retirement, and other practices.

The existence of a permanent employment system in Japan's larger firms has implications for the nature of Japanese unionism: it might be expected that employment security and seniority-based wage systems might take away some of the incentives for union organization. Nevertheless, a substantial union movement has developed in Japan since World War II, and unionization levels in Japan are slightly higher than those in the United States even though they are considerably lower than the case for northern Europe.

Still, the Japanese union movement is quite different from that of the United States and Europe. Unions tend to organize principally around specific enterprises in Japan rather than on an industry basis, and both white- and blue-collar workers are union members. Cole shows that there are several plausible political and economic reasons for the enterprise union phenomenon. Whatever the causes, enterprise unionism means that bargaining between union and management tends to focus on the individual firm (even though pattern bargaining across firms and unions also exists). Enterprise unionism, according to Cole, also enhances workers' parochialism on some national political issues and increases their dependence on their firm, even though at the same time it increases intrafirm egalitarianism and union knowledge of firm operations through inclusion of white-collar employees.

Enterprise unionism in Japan and cultural stereotypes about the docility of Japanese vis-à-vis their superiors have encouraged the view abroad that labor conflict is less intense in Japan than in other industrialized countries. This view is supported by statistics that show that fewer man-hours are lost through labor strife in Japan than in several other countries. However, these figures are misleading because they assume that labor strife, which assumes different forms, can be measured in terms of the *time* dimension alone. As Solomon B. Levine conclusively shows, worker participation in strikes is quite extensive in Japan even though Japanese strikes are typically of very short duration. (Also, labor strife has been on the increase in Japan since the emergence of the union movement after World War II.)

So it is clearly incorrect to view the Japanese worker as compliant, and important to realize that Japanese labor conflict takes different forms from that prevailing in other countries. The short duration and broad worker participation in labor conflict in Japan relates to a practice begun in the 1950s of spring labor drives that are conducted on an economywide basis. (The Spring Wage Offensive, known as *shuntō*, is a pattern-bargaining effort by Japan's major industrial and public employee unions; the shuntō accounts annually for between one-half and two-thirds of the man-days lost by labor conflict in Japan.)

Unions were severely suppressed in pre-World War II Japan, and the union movement only gained momentum in the favorable environment created by the postwar constitution and labor laws. However, as a result of the postwar legislation and subsequent rulings, aspects of labor-management relations such as labor organization, bargaining processes, labor standards, minimum wage levels, and job security are now institutionalized roughly as in other advanced industrialized countries. The relevant legislation and institutions are discussed here by Levine.

Permanent Employment

The Japanese permanent employment system is famous, but little is actually known about it. What does permanent employment really mean and has it always existed since Japan modernized its economy? And what are current trends in managerial recruitment and general employment practices?

THE JAPANESE PERMANENT EMPLOYMENT SYSTEM

Westerners have come to see the practice of permanent employment as a striking symbol of a unique industrial relations system in Japan. The term refers to the practice whereby an employee enters a company after school graduation, receives in-company training, and remains an employee of the same company until the retirement age of 55. Until recently, Westerners viewed permanent employment as an extension into the modern era of feudal principles that dominated preindustrial Japan. This view has been shown to be false as it is now recognized that employer changing was quite high in the early period of Japan's industrialization. It was not until after World War I that the system had its beginning primarily among white-collar employees. At this time, management sought to reduce the loss of skilled workers who were in short supply. The system received a boost during the wartime period at which time employer changing was discouraged. It spread to blue-collar workers in large firms after World War II as workers and unions tried to improve employment security during the chaotic early postwar period. Although the permanent employment practice may be seen as having traditional elements, in terms of drawing upon selected preindustrial values and practices, its evolution has been characterized by the pragmatic application of this tradition by the various parties to the labor market.

Despite extensive historical and contemporary scholarship on the subject, the serious analyst immediately discovers that we do not know how many employees currently are covered by this "guarantee." Government statistics do not help us delimit the number of workers covered by the practice of permanent employment because they use the rather nebulous category of regular workers. Similarly, labor contracts between unions and employers in Japan tend to be general and abstract, without specifying the rights and obligations of either party. With the exception of special categories such as temporary workers, Japanese labor contracts generally bind the contracting parties together for an indefinite period of time. Legally, the courts provide no bar to discharges or layoffs that are seen as a legitimate response of firms experiencing economic difficulty during a recession. There is also no bar to employees voluntarily changing employers. In short, the difficulty of determining who has permanent employment derives from the practice not being a formally guaranteed right. It should be seen rather as a social custom and a societal norm. Permanent employment has been established as a company practice and employee-behavioral pattern that is reinforced by the distribution of rewards according to age and length of service (*nenkō* system) and strengthened by social and judicial pressures. The practice is strongest among male employees in the large private-sector firms and in the government bureaucracy. Generally, it is estimated that from 20 to 35 percent of all wage earners are covered by the permanent-employment practice. The rapid economic growth in postwar Japan further clouds the issue of whether employees have permanent employment or whether employers are simply in a better position to guarantee continuous employment. Throughout much of the postwar period, at least until the oil shock of 1973, rapid economic growth made it easy for employers to dispense with layoffs and discharges. In the context of Japanese values, de facto continuous employment among regular male employees lends itself to being interpreted by management and workers alike as evidence of permanent employment. In the final section of this subchapter, however, we will have the opportunity to discuss the impact on employment patterns since 1973 of the lowered economic growth rate. Finally, it should be noted that workers and management do not always make the same evaluations with respect to the presence or absence of permanent employment much less its desirability. Workers in large firms are likely to emphasize their loyalty to their firm and management's obligation to keep them employed until retirement age. The smaller the firm, the more likely it is that employees will assert their willingness to quit should an attractive offer come along. Similarly, the smaller the firm, the more likely it is that management finds itself needing to adjust their labor force to the ups and downs of the business cycle.

To put the matter differently, employment security is weakest and permanent employment least relevant in the following areas and for the following categories of workers: first, it is least applicable to the small-scale private sector, where working conditions are poor, product demand unstable, and capital often in short supply. It does not apply to female workers to any great extent and of course it does not apply to the variety of temporary worker categories. It is less likely to be available to blue-collar than to white-collar employees. Finally, the early retirement age of 55 means that the guarantee is far shorter than the actual labor market participation of individuals. This introduces considerable flexibility into the system.

SOME COMPARATIVE OBSERVATIONS
ON PERMANENT EMPLOYMENT

If we take as our meaning of permanent employment the percent of employees never changing employers, we can compare the labor-force experiences of employees in Detroit and Yokohama to give us a sense of the national differences. Holding age constant, Cole (1979) found that 35 percent of his Yokohama sample had never changed employers compared to 14 percent of his Detroit sample. However, the differences between the employed in the two samples were quite small for those with the longest labor-force experiences. Moreover, in both cities, an examination of job changers reveals that with increasing age, education, and size of employing firm, the amount of employer changing tends to decline. Thus, there are some striking similarities in pattern of labor market behavior in the two cities even if the volume of employer changing is lower in Yokohama.

In any comparison of labor market behavior in Japan with that of the United States, it is tempting to see any differences as reflecting the unique traditions of the Japanese. It has been common for Americans to look at differences from this perspective. An alternative tack is not to ask why employer changing is so low in Japan but to ask why it is so high in the United States. Although cross-national comparisons are notoriously difficult, turnover in North America is said to be notably higher than in Western Europe. A survey of job separation rates in the early 1970s by the Japanese Ministry of Labor reported that they are highest in the United States and France, with West German and English rates running about 80 percent of the American rates. The Japanese recorded about 60 percent of the American rates. In a survey carried out by Gallup International, 2,000 young people between the ages of 18 and 24 were interviewed in 11 nations. It was found that 60 percent of the Japanese sample never changed employers as compared to 23 percent of the American respondents. However, the comparable percentages in Western European nations are: West Germany 52, France 51, Switzerland 48, and England 37 percent. In short, although Japan still scores higher in this respect than the Western Europeans, it is the Americans who appear more out of line than the Japanese.

In a mid-1960s survey of American workers, it was reported that 26 percent of those interviewed had started their job less than one year before. This is a remarkably high percent and raises the possibility that perhaps we have in the United States not a marked case of modernity but rather excessive labor mobility. To say that individuals as resources must be separable from their work organizations in order for the economy to make maximum use of them does not mean that the more the job changing the better. Purposeless reshuffling leads to the imposition of extra costs, which are borne by employers, workers, and the society at large. This is not to deny that there are important advantages in the American practice of encouraging movement between firms, both from employee and employer perspectives. Nevertheless, our discussion should establish that the use of the American labor market as a yardstick for measuring Japan's modernity distorts our interpretations.

CONTEMPORARY CHANGES IN JAPAN'S EMPLOYMENT SCENE

My final observations concern changes in the permanent-employment practice currently occurring and the prospects for the future. In the period since 1973, the permanent-employment practice has been exposed to its greatest challenge in the postwar pepriod. The dramatic decline of the economic growth rate from the two-digit figures of the later 1960s and early 1970s to 4 and 5 percent of the mid-1970s has led to some major readjustments. In some industries such as steel and shipbuilding the worldwide slump accentuated the employment adjustments that needed to be made. Demographic changes are also important here. Coinciding with the decline in economic growth rates was a dramatic aging of the Japanese work force. Japan is moving quickly from an industrial nation with a relatively youthful work force to one that is aging rapidly. The wage sytstem that rewarded age and length of service thus is becoming a significantt burden on Japanese employers. Employers are increasingly questioning the benefits of permanent employment.

The Japanese manufacturing sector, in the course of the four years from the end of 1973 to the beginning of 1978, shed some 1 million employees or almost 10 percent of all manufacturing employees. In the early period, part-time employees, women, and older workers provided for the bulk of reductions. Most of the employees in these categories would not fall into those thought of as having a permanent employment guarantee. To keep the discharges from becoming a major social problem, the government took the new step of providing subsidies to employers to encourage them to hold on to excess labor. That is to say, the government was in effect subsidizing the permanent employment system during this critical period of adjustment. They sought to buy time for attrition and new growth to take place. Japanese employers also sought to cut labor costs through a variety of means as an alternative to employee discharges. Thus, many companies have moved away from the steeply inclined seniority-wage system so that wages will now tend to level out for those over age 40. There was also a good deal of sharing of labor within interdependent company groupings. Notable here was the loaning of steel and shipbuilding workers to the still expanding automobile industry. In short, a variety of mechanisms developed all of which served to preserve the core of permanent employees. There was some whittling down of this core in severely hit industries, but for the most part large-scale employers did manage to save the jobs of regular male employees. Now that most of the surplus has been taken out of manufacturing employment, however, there is relatively little flexibility that would permit the permanent employment system to survive some new world crisis. In the process of making these adjustment to the post-1973 world, the permanent employment system has continued to develop in new directions. Whatever the traditional elements in the permanent employment practice, it has never been static, but rather a constantly evolving response to the needs of various social actors.

Robert E. Cole

BIBLIOGRAPHY

Cole, Robert E. *Work Mobility and Participation: A Comparative Study of American and Japanese Industry*. Berkeley: University of California Press, 1979.

Crawcour, Sidney. "The Japanese Employment System." *Journal of Japanese Studies* 4 (Summer 1978):225–46.

Rohlen, Thomas. "Permanent Employment Faces Recession, Slow Growth and an Aging Work Force." *Journal of Japanese Studies* 5 (Summer 1979):235–72.

Enterprise Unions

Japan is said to have a history of enterprise unionism. Just what does this mean, and how does it apply today? Also, where enterprises are organized rather than trades or industries, are white-collar workers members of the same unions as blue-collar workers? And, overall, what are the characteristics of levels of union membership in Japan?

JAPANESE UNIONISM

As of 1978 there were some 12.4 million union members in Japan. After the initial spurt of the early postwar period when the number rose almost overnight from barely any members in 1945 to close to 5 million in 1946, the number of union members has grown gradually but quite steadily.* The 1978 organization rate (the number of union members divided by the number of those eligible) was 32.6. The rate has been relatively stable since the late 1950s. It represents a decline from the high of 55.8 reached in 1949, which is to say that since 1949 the labor force has been growing at a faster rate than union membership. The overall organization rate of 32.6 is well above that of the United States. In the United States, 34 percent of the nonagricultural labor force was organized in unions in 1953 as compared to 26 percent in 1974. More generally, the rate of organization in Japan is higher than much of southern Europe as well, but far below the high levels of unionization achieved in northern Europe.

As in the United States, the larger the firm in the private sector, the higher the rate of unionization. For example, in Japanese firms of 1,000 or more employees, some 57 percent of all employees are organized; this

---

*This paper draws on the thorough analysis of Japanese-style unionism recently provided by Taishiro Shirai. See "A Theory of Enterprise Unionism," in *Contemporary Industrial Relations in Japan,* edited by Koshiro Kazutoshi and Shimada Haruo. Japan Institute of Labor, Tokyo (forthcoming).

compares to a rate of unionization of only 9.3 percent in those firms with 500 to 900 employees. A notable difference in the structure of unionization in Japan and the United States is the higher rate of unionization among white-collar employees in Japan, the reasons for which will be discussed below. Related to this difference are divergent unionization rates by industry. Notable here are the high rates of unionization achieved by the Japanese in the following sectors: finance, insurance and real estate (60.5 percent), transportation and communication (65.3 percent), and electricity, gas, water, and heat (83.5 percent).

Many of Japan's 34,163 unions affiliate to one of four national centers. Of the four, Sōhyō (strongest in the public sector) accounted for 4,525,000 workers in 1978; Dōmei (strongest in the private sector) covered 2,182,000; and the Federation of Independent Unions and the National Federation of Industrial Organizations enrolled 1,321,000 and 61,000 respectively. A large number of unions representing some 4,600,000 workers or 37 percent of all unionized workers, do not affiliate to a national center. (Although there have been numerous attempts to merge Sōhyō and Dōmei, divergent political philosophies have contributed to keeping them apart.) Sōhyō is the major organizational support for the left-wing Japan Socialist Party and Dōmei plays a similar role for the middle-of-the-road Democratic Socialist Party. (Generally at the level of the national federations the union is a political organization committed to national programs involving workers as citizens rather than as employees or union members.) The national unions offer few direct benefits to the local unions and their members. The annual Spring Wage Offensive (shuntō) begun in 1955 under the leadership of Sōhyō was a relatively successful attempt to involve the national centers more deeply in wage matters. In recent years, however, shuntō has played a diminished role in the face of the growing differences among firms and industries in their "ability to pay."

ENTERPRISE UNIONS IN JAPAN

Apart from the national centers, there are union federations for industries like iron and steel, shipbuilding and heavy machinery, automobiles and textiles. Despite an increased role for such organizations in recent years, they do not play a major role in negotiating contracts and in the day-to-day activities of the union on the shop or office floor. Rather, the basis of the trade-union movement is the autonomous *enterprise union*. The enterprise union covers all employees below the management level employed in a particular enterprise or it may be a federation of unions representing the plants that make up the enterprise. In the case of the automobile industry, it would be as if employees at General Motors had their own autonomous union composed of locals at given plants plus the locals organized at subcontractors. Each GM local would then conclude its own contract based on local collective bargaining only within the frame-work of a master agreement negotiated by the companywide GM union. The industrial union would provide only weak guidance in these efforts. Such an industry framework is absent in Japan.

Japanese enterprise unions, even if members of industrial federations or one of the national centers, have complete autonomy to make decisions. They collect dues, formulate and revise their constitutions, call strikes and elect their own officers. An examination of the form of union organizations conducted by the Ministry of Labor in 1975 reports that 93.6 percent of Japanese unions may be classified as enterprise unions, 1.6 percent as craft unions, and 3.1 percent as industrial unions. The remaining 1.7 percent are general unions that are composed primarily of workers in small firms who are organized regardless of the trade, industry, or enterprise to which they belong.

Enterprise unions are notable for the following organizational charac-teristics:

1. Blue-collar and white-collar employees are organized in the same union.
2. Membership is limited to regular employees of the same enterprise. Those employed on a part-time or temporary basis are not eligible for membership.
3. Union officers are elected from among the regular employees of the enterprise; as union officers they retain their employee status but are paid by the union. Union offices and other administrative facilities are commonly provided by the company.
4. Regular employees automatically join the union and their union dues are commonly collected through automatic checkoffs.

ORIGINS OF ENTERPRISE UNIONS

This form of unionism has no obvious counterpart in the dominant union organizations of western Europe and the United States. Conse-quently there is a good deal of interest in its origins and a number of factors have been cited. Among the most popular explanations discussed by scholars are the following.

First, the American occupation encouraged rapid formation of unions pursuant to implementing the Potsdam Declaration. The Japanese re-sponded in the quickest and easiest fashion by organizing workers at the plant or firm.

Second, enterprise unions developed as a response to the pressure of the Communists, who played a major role in the radical labor movement in the immediate postwar period. Following the policies advocated by the left-wing World Federation of Trade Unions, the Communists allegedly supported the policy of a single union in each plant.

A third explanation stresses that enterprise unionism was an outgrowth of the wartime patriotic labor organizations organized at each plant and company. The Sangyō Hōkokukai (Sanpō) was organized by the government to ensure industrial peace and high productivity during the wartime crisis. When the American Occupation authorities stressed the formation of unions, it is argued that they simply replaced the wartime government role and enterprise unions became a logical successor to Sanpō.

A final explanation given for the development of enterprise unions is that they are the only form of union organization that employers would tolerate. In fact, Japanese employers have continually opposed the intrusion of "outsiders" into their bargaining relationship with unions. They have strongly endorsed unions composed of only their regular employees and led by their regular employees. Often they have refused to allow nonemployees, freely elected by the membership, from participating in the collective bargaining process. Moreover, it is not uncommon for employers and government officials to explicitly recognize the advantages of enterprise unions from their point of view. They stress the stability enterprise unions provide to Japanese industrial relations practices.

Despite a clear element of truth in all these explanations, there are some problems. First, it is hard to imagine a system of unionism emerging that seems to have served simultaneously the interests of so many different parties to the labor market. Is it possible that the practices served equally management, left-wing unions, and the American occupation? Second, while these various factors may help explain the origins of enterprise unionism, they don't explain its persistence. What are the institutional factors that sustain enterprise unionism? Finally, recent research provides evidence that forms of enterprise unionism emerged in the pre-World War II period, thereby invalidating some of the proposed explanations such as the importance of Sanpō and the American Occupation.

With these considerations in mind, Taishiro Shirai has recently proposed an explanation that is quite consistent with an emerging consensus among scholars on the importance of "internal labor markets" in Japan. The internal labor market refers to those jobs in the firm (and the linkages between them) that are shielded from the direct influence of competitive forces in the external market and are filled by the promotion and transfer of workers who have already gained entry. Such a set of characteristics seems to have been particularly important in the historical development of large Japanese firms. Notable here are the combination of the lifetime employment system, skill development through extensive enterprise training programs, a seniority-based wage system, and extensive employee welfare programs. These practices generate a strong loyalty on the part of employees to the firm. They tend to see themselves as part of a "community of fate." Put differently, these practices create a strong sense of dependency on the part of the employee to the firm. However one evaluates the situation, it is clear that enterprise unionism becomes a quite logical form of unionization under the conditions described above. The employees' feelings of solidarity and identification with the firm are given ample room for expression under enterprise unionism. Employees will support enterprise unionism because they perceive they can achieve their major interests under this form of unionization. In this sense, enterprise unionism may be seen as a "countervailing force" to the dominance of employers in constructing strong labor markets that developed in large firms during the course of Japanese industrialization. One of course can also address the reasons for employers developing strong internal labor markets in Japan but this would take us too far afield from the major subject under consideration.

CONSEQUENCES OF ENTERPRISE UNIONISM

Finally, we may consider the basic strengths and weaknesses of enterprise unionism. Some U.S. observers equate enterprise unionism with company unionism, thereby emphasizing the domination of the union by employers. Such an explanation appears far too simplistic. Nevertheless, enterprise unions are particularly vulnerable to employer domination. In the 1950s, despite various laws designed to protect workers from such intervention, employers intervened to support workers sympathetic to management interests. This intervention led to the removal of many of the most militant unions in the private sector. Under enterprise unionism, union members tend to become overdependent on the fortunes of their company. This strong identification with the interests of the company makes the union susceptible to company manipulation. The rapid scaling down of union wage demands after the oil shock of 1973 shows the weakness of the unions in the face of *employer claims* that their demands would hurt the enterprise. Employers have not been reluctant to make such claims throughout the postwar period. Second, the enterprise union commonly lacks interest in problems outside the enterprise based on national needs and social responsibilities; they are rather indifferent to the organization of unorganized workers outside the company. Indeed, they have opposed the organization of the temporary employees in the firm. Third, because enterprise union leaders commonly maintain their status as company employees and their term of office is quite short, Japanese union leaders are not highly professionalized. As a consequence, union leaders often see their union activities as an opportunity to provide service to the company and a means of enhancing their promotion opportunities. Just how realistic an expectation this is may be seen in the results of a recent survey of 134 major firms. Forty-six of the firms had directors who had previously served as officials in the firm's enterprise union. Such expectations on the part of union officers can only be expected to weaken union defense of worker interests.

On the other side, a number of strengths are associated with enterprise unionism. First, a major achievement of the postwar enterprise unions was to dramatically level the differences between blue-collar and white-collar employees with respect to their treatment by the company. The strong egalitarian character of Japanese firms must be attributed to a large extent to the activities of enterprise unions and the joint participation of blue-collar and white-collar workers. A symbolic manifestation of this leveling is seen in the contrasting layout for employee parking at American and Japanese firms. In American firms, salaried employees are commonly provided separate parking privileges that are located closer to their work. This is a constant source of irritation for hourly employees. Second, although it is difficult to separate out the effects of union demands on wage increases, it can hardly be said that the rate of increase of Japanese wages has been inferior to those achieved in Western nations in the postwar period. Indeed, they have risen more rapidly than in almost any other advanced industrial nation. It may also be argued that union-company relations tend to develop according to the realities of the enterprise under enterprise unions. The participation of salaried employees in particular, increases union knowledge about the actual financial situation of the firm. The probability is thereby increased that the union will make reasonable demands in accordance with the firm's ability to grant them. In addition, the raison d'être of the enterprise union lies in maintaining its members as employees in the company. It is thus possible to mobilize strong resistance on the part of the regular employee to work-force reductions. This strongly contributes to the employment security among union members and can be contrasted with the United States, where surveys report that lack of employment security is one of the great concerns of blue-collar workers. Finally, because union leaders commonly come from within the firm, it is possible to develop strong bonds between union leaders and the rank and file. This conttributes to the maintenance of union democracy. Enterprise unionism is based on the enterprise consciousness of employees and not only loyalty to the employer or management alone.

In conclusion, *it may be seen* that enterprise unionism is firmly embedded in the institutional fabric of Japanese life. Without doubt, it makes a significant contribution to the character of Japanese industrial relations.

Robert E. Cole

BIBLIOGRAPHY

Cole, Robert E. *Japanese Blue-Collar*. Berkeley: University of California Press, 1971.

Levine, Solomon B. *Industrial Relations in Postwar Japan*. Urbana: University of Ilinois Press, 1958.

Okochi, K; B. Karsh; and S. B. Levine. *Workers and Employers in Japan*. Tokyo: University of Tokyo Press, 1973.

Shirai, Taishiro. "A Theory of Enterprise Unionism." In *Contemporary Industrial Relations in Japan*, edited by Kazutoshi and Shimada Haruo. Tokyo: Japan Institute of Labor, forthcoming.

Labor Conflict

Some countries like Britain and the United States have many labor disputes while others such as Germany have relatively few. Does Japan have a high or low rate of industrial conflict, and why is this the case?

LABOR-MANAGEMENT CONFLICT IN VARIOUS NATIONS

According to the few measures of labor-management conflict that are available on an aggregate national basis for the past three decades, the United States and the United Kingdom as well as Australia, Canada, Italy, and Finland rank relatively high, while West Germany, Austria, the Netherlands, Norway, Sweden, and Switzerland score relatively low. Japan's record on the average has been close to the midpoint of the extremes—about comparable over the years to France, Belgium, Denmark, and New Zealand. It shows that Japanese labor relations are not devoid of open conflict as the commonly held belief alleges.

A major problem in assessing the amount of industrial conflict in a nation is that we do not know precisely how to measure it. Even if we did, obtaining the data is difficult. The problem is compounded by country-to-country differences in the definitions and data collection methods utilized, so that cross-national comparisons must be made with great caution. In Japan statistics are published only for work stoppages (strikes and walk-outs) that last four hours or more (even though it is well known that numerous strikes of shorter duration occur). Other nations use still different counting methods. Moreover, conflicts between labor and employers may take many different forms, not all of which find expression in work stoppages and man-days lost from work. In Japan, for example, the number of strikes lasting more than four hours in any given period usually is less than half the number of labor disputes monitored and recorded by the government authorities.

LONG-TERM TRENDS

What do the available statistics indicate for postwar Japan? First, they show that since 1945 Japan has averaged a much higher annual level of work stoppages—in number of strikes, workers involved, and man-days lost—than in the years between World War I and World War II. One study estimates that the strike level rose at least 400 percent between the two eras, probably the highest such increase for any advanced industrialized country in the world. Of course, during the interwar period, especially in the 1930s as well as during the war, government and employers forcibly repressed trade union activity and organization. The labor reforms under the Allied Occupation were sweeping, if not revolutionary, guaranteeing to almost all workers through the new postwar Constitution and laws the right to organize, engage in collective bargaining, and conduct concerted activities, including strikes. By and large the reforms have remained intact to the present. Japanese labor has utilized these rights quite extensively, with almost one-third of all wage and salary earners now organized in unions.

Second, if one looks at the long-term trends for Japan in the postwar period alone, there has been a steady increase in the number of labor disputes, with and without work stoppages, from a level of about 1,500 a year in the late 1940s to well over 8,000 in the mid-1970s. The number of work stoppages, too, displays the same trend, rising from about 800 a year to around 4,000. Yearly variations, of course, take place but with new peaks every few years. On an annual basis, man-days lost to work stoppages have varied from as low as about 1.5 million (1967, 1977, 1978) to as high as 10 to 15 million (1952, 1974), with most years about midway between these figures. Since 1975 a notable downward swing in the number of disputes with and without stoppages and man-days lost has set in, but it is not yet known whether this recent development signals a permanent decline and/or leveling off, or just another trough in the steady upward movement over the long term.

Most work stoppages and other visible manifestations of industrial conflict take place where workers are organized. Japan is no exception. The rise in the number of labor disputes and work stoppages in the postwar eras has in fact outpaced the increases in both wage and salary employment and in union membership during most of the period, indicating that organized workers have resorted more and more to overt conflict with their employers with the passage of time. The recent downturn in disputes and strikes has accompanied a virtual leveling off of paid employment and a slight decline in the number of unionists.

Ups and downs in strike activity occur in most advanced industrialized countries. In Japan, as elsewhere, the variations appear to be related to changes in the state of the labor market. Since 1960, for example, changes in the amount of man-days lost from stoppages have varied in the opposite direction from the rate of job quits with a lag of about three or four years. That is, when the percent of voluntary separations from employment goes up, in the next few years the level of man-days lost goes down; when that percentage drops, the level increases within about the same time. Voluntary separation rates on an annual basis have fallen and leveled off since about 1973, so that, if the relationship continues to hold, the level of man-days lost will soon rise again. As in other countries, this may be explained, at least in part, by an accumulation of grievances and dissatisfactions among workers the longer they remain in the employ of one enterprise and their inability to move to more satisfying jobs (mainly because of the rise in unemployment and, hence, competition in the labor market). A recent survey, published in the *International Labour Review*, indicates that among several advanced industrial nations Japan appears to have the lowest percentage of workers "satisfied" with their employment. As one analyst puts it, workers eventually resort to "voice" rather than "exit" under these conditions. However, the correlation is at best only a rough one, indicating that a large number of complex factors may explain variability in the extent of strikes in addition to labor market conditions.

SHORT STRIKES VERSUS BROAD PARTICIPATION IN JAPAN

Compared to other countries, Japan averages a relatively low duration of strikes, but a relatively large number of workers involved per work stoppage. These seemingly contradictory figures make strikes in Japan appear to foreign observers as mild affairs, but to many Japanese themselves they are seen as most serious. Short work stoppages show up in figures for man-days lost per worker involved. In 1974, for example, one of the years of high strike activity in Japan's history, days lost per worker involved averaged only 2.7, far below the 17.6 in the United States and 9.1 in the United Kingdom for the same year. (However, it was above the French average of 2.2 days and not much below the West German average of 4.2.) Yet, at the same time, Japan's number of workers involved per stoppage averaged 695, considerably exceeding those for the United States (456), United Kingdom (554), France (461), and West Germany (282). The comparatively high participation of workers in strikes in Japan is seen also in the figures for 1974 when 10 percent of all wage and salary workers went on strike at one time or other; while the American ratio was 3.3 percent, Great Britain's 7.4 percent, France's 7.0 percent, and West Germany's 1.1 percent. Comparisons such as these make it difficult to judge whether Japanese industrial relations are more or less harmonious than other countries. It depends, of course, on which dimensions of dispute activity one chooses to emphasize.

SPRING LABOR OFFENSIVES

The comparatively large involvement of Japanese workers in stoppages and the short duration of Japanese strikes reflect a bargaining strategy that organized labor in Japan has developed since the mid-1950s to seek gains in wages and other benefits on an economywide basis. The main part of this strategy is the so-called *shuntō,* or Spring Wage Offensive, which has been staged every year from 1955 on (with recognizable predecessors going back to 1946). Shuntō usually accounts for one-half to two-thirds of all man-days lost in stoppages annually and has grown to involve almost 10 million workers in strikes, pickets, or demonstrations (including wearing of headbands and pasting up wall posters). Approaching the scope of a general strike, shuntō is a means for mobilizing the accumulating worker dissatisfaction within companies on a mass basis. Because of its importance, the process and function of shuntō needs to be fully understood.

Shuntō, as its name implies, takes place from March to May and involves negotiations of general wage and benefit increases throughout most of Japanese industry. In a sense, it is pattern bargaining on a national scale, in which, once certain settlements are made in key industries and major enterprises, a benchmark is set for most of the remaining economic sectors, organized and unorganized, private and public, to follow with variations by industry and enterprise that depend upon such factors as profitability, cost of living, and degree of unemployment. The timing of the offensive coincides with the beginning of the fiscal year (April 1) when the government and private businesses formulate annual budgets, grant automatic length-of-service salary raises, and make promotions and other personnel changes, and with the end of the school year, when enterprises and organizations recruit the new school graduates.

Union and management planning for shuntō begins as soon as the preceding offensive ends. A joint "struggle" council, representing the participating union organizations, actually proclaims the specific wage demands well in advance of shuntō itself, as early as December or January, and draws up and announces a schedule of waves of short walkouts, industry by industry, for the Spring offensive season. Simultaneously, spokesmen for employers, principally Nikkeiren (Japan Federation of Employers' Association), issue counterdemands. The positions are rarely close together. Negotiations then begin formally and informally at the enterprise and, in a few cases, industrywide level; but usually there is considerable behind-the-scenes maneuvering and meetings among leading government, industry, and labor figures as well as mediation efforts by neutrals. Compromises are struck in this process, and by about mid-April key settlements emerge throughout the private sector in industries such as steel, electric machinery, shipbuilding, and private railways. With these as pacesetters other settlements are reached in the ensuing few weeks. The public sector usually awaits the outcome in the private sector. For the latter, where the right to strike is legally forbidden, the Public Corporation and National Enterprise Labor Relations Commission attempts first to mediate the wage dispute, following in large measure the pattern already set in the private sector. Almost inevitably, as provided by law, the commission issues a final and binding arbitration award close to its mediation proposal. Illegal stoppages usually occur among these public-sector workers.

Emergence of the shuntō strategy in the 1950s resulted primarily from two interrelated factors. One was the basic organizational characteristics of Japanese labor unions, decentralized as they are into enterprise-level organizations. By themselves, each enterprise union individually had weak bargaining power vis-a-vis the employer. Thus, shuntō became a means to coordinate, unify, and support separate union bargaining efforts.

The other factor stemmed from the fact that, after a remarkable spread of unionism following Japan's surrender and a show of considerable union radicalism and militancy up to about 1950, organized labor was placed on the defensive by a series of restrictive amendments to the postwar labor reforms, the Occupation's purge of left-wing union leadership, bitter rivalries and ideological differences within the labor movement itself, reorganization of the national labor centers, and restoration of power and prestige to employers once redevelopment of the Japanese economy began. Some of Japan's severest strikes, notably in the coal mining, electric power, steel, and automobile industries, occurred during that transitional period.

Leaders of Sōhyō took the initiative in devising shuntō, at first developed around a few major industrial union federations in the private sector. Year by year, shuntō gained adherents, eventually including, in addition to Sōhyō, other national labor organizations, although Dōmei, Sōhyō's chief rival, has not formally entered the joint struggle committee (but Dōmei's constituents engage in a parallel set of shuntō negotiations with similar demands). Also, the focus of the key bargaining over the years shifted to the growth industries whose union federations comprise the Japan Council of Metal Workers' Unions (IMF-JC). Until the mid-1970s, shuntō appeared to be a resounding success. Not only were settlements on the rise each year, largely reflecting Japan's rapid economic expansion, but also the patterns set became increasingly uniform. With the slowdown since 1975, however, the annual increases have fallen and disparities in wage increases have grown.

Shuntō-type strategy also is followed in other "seasonal" bargaining, particularly negotiations for the semiannual wage bonuses at midyear and year-end. These "bonuses," which amount to as much as six months' additional earnings and are paid almost universally throughout Japan, are subject to negotiations with the unions. Because they often depend upon the amount of the shuntō settlements, the extent and duration of these offensives tend to be less than shuntō itself. By concentrating the bulk of dispute action in the pattern-setting shuntō, stoppages have been less necessary at other times of the year.

Since the early 1970s, the unions have labeled shuntō the People's Spring Offensive. Up to that time, the main preoccupation of shuntō had been with general wage increases, although almost from the beginning it was coupled with political campaigns to place pressure upon budget deliberations in the Cabinet and Diet, support candidates for public office, and whip up opposition to government policies in both foreign and domestic affairs. Shuntō, however, had come under increasing criticism for loss of vitality and routinization. As collective bargaining itself expanded to include additional subjects (e.g., retirement payments and pensions, retirement age, overtime payments and other allowance, hours of work and days off, starting wages, injury compensation, loans for worker property purchases, and so forth) and the government itself gave increasing attention to social welfare matters (e.g., social security benefits, income redistribution, taxation rates, environment improvement, and so forth), the joint struggle committee has broadened its demands by appealing for support from the whole community on a large number of issues. These demands are aimed as much at the government as at employers.

Negotiations, of course, occur at times of the year besides shuntō or other seasonal campaigns and are usually confined to industrial enterprises and local plants. Employment adjustment practices, renewal of basic comprehensive labor agreements, and other nonwage issues often come up in the Fall, in between the seasonal offensives. Disputes in these instances are relatively few but often intense.

CONSTRAINTS ON LENGTHY STRIKES

Prolonged strikes are not frequent in Japanese labor-management negotiations because of constraints faced by both sides. Shuntō and the bonus drives are displays of strong worker solidarity and determination that employers defy at their risk. Labor demands are backed up by the enterprise unions, which, as discussed elsewhere, typically are highly democratic and unified organizations. The resort to demonstrations and work stoppages usually comes at the outset of bargaining rather than at the point negotiations reach an impasse. Likewise, the enterprise unions themselves as well as employers are particularly mindful of permanent damage that a lengthy strike may inflict upon market position, production, and employment in their respective enterprises. Thus, both sides are careful in calculating their respective strengths, although as in strikes everywhere emotional, and ideological, elements emerge. This mutually recognized "balance of power" probably not only averts long work stoppages but also supports the widespread and regular use of labor-management consultative committees, usually established by the comprehensive basic agreements, to share information, discuss, and dispose of a wide range of issues that otherwise would proceed to collective bargaining. In addition, with such well-established institutions like length-of-service wages, benefits, and promotion within the enterprise, uncertainty over terms and conditions of employment is greatly reduced for most regular workers in the large-scale enterprises. These practices obviate the need to negotiate many issues that become collective bargaining problems in the United States. In this stable context, Japanese labor relations has had little conflict over seniority rights, order of layoffs, work assignments, job rates, and technological and organizational change—unless they involve dismissals of regularly employed personnel.

Fundamentally, ever since the labor and other reforms under the Occupation, unions and employees in Japan have accepted one another's right to continued existence. No doubt, the widesweeping reforms firmly implanted labor rights with little employer resistance. Most major Japanese unions today were established years ago and have expanded through union shop provisions as enterprise work forces themselves have grown. Japan experiences very few disputes over the right to organize and bargain, issues which continue to be important sources of conflict in the United States with its exacting legal requirements (absent in Japan) for designating appropriate bargaining units and holding recognition elections for exclusive bargaining rights. That Japanese workers chose for the most part an organizational pattern on a enterprise basis facilitated this employer acceptance and also avoided jurisdictional disputes among unions. It should be noted, too, there have been few new large-scale drives for unionization since most of the enterprise unions are preoccupied with conditions within their respective enterprises and, with strong "internal" labor markets, fear little competition from unorganized workers.

Acceptance of unionism carried with it implicit guarantees of the organized workers' job and income security. A major accomplishment of the enterprise union has been fortification of such protection of its members against arbitrary discharge and layoffs. This protection, coupled with the regular annual wage increases through both length-of-service and shuntō gains and with intensive company investment in sizable departments of personnel administration, probably dispels grievances and issues which in the United States could break out into disputes and stoppages. Yet, in Japan the severest strikes have occurred in cases where management moved to terminate workers who believed they were entitled to long-term or permanent employment within their enterprises. Such was the case, for example, in the almost yearlong strike at the Mitsui Miike coal mines in the early 1960s, when Japan rapidly converted from domestic coal to foreign petroleum as its chief industrial fuel. While it may be said that the union lost that strike, the Miike experience is well-remembered on all sides as a caution to plan carefully any mass displacement of permanent workers. Still other cases where employment security has been a dramatic issue, involving lengthy strikes, are maritime shipping and the national railroads. Several such strikes have involved foreign-owned companies. On the whole, however, discharge and dismissal have not been frequent occurrences as long as Japan's economy expanded rapidly and operated at full employment.

INCIDENCE OF WORK STOPPAGE

Contrary to common belief, the large private firms in Japan appear to suffer the highest incidence of work stoppages, even though they are reputed to provide the greatest employment security (permanent employment) and the best wages, benefits, and working conditions. Enterprises with 500 employees or more are the most fully unionized, with almost two-thirds of their workers organized, a ratio more than two times the average for the whole private sector. It is in these large-scale firms where the great bulk (two-thirds) of workers is involved in stoppages and mandays lost annually, even though they employ only about one-fourth of the total number of wage and salary earners. Man-days lost to strikes per thousand employees often are double or triple the average in the small-scale companies. The number of workers involved in stoppages as a ratio of all workers in those organizations reaches as high as 25 percent (three times higher than in small firms), probably reflecting the high rate of participation in shuntō and bonus-dispute walkouts. Duration of strikes, however, tends to be shorter than the average.

A widespread impression is that the public sector exhibits the severest overt industrial conflict in Japan. This is true only in certain respects. Since strikes of workers in the public sector are illegal, they usually are largely visible in receiving considerable attention in the news media. The government, central and local, is a major employer. From 1945 to 1947, public employees were accorded the same right to strike as private-sector workers under the labor reforms; but, following a threat of a general strike scheduled for February 1, 1947 (but outlawed and not carried out), the Occupation and government authorities amended the new laws to prohibit striking in the public sector. Organized labor's demand for restoration of this right has remained a highly controversial political issue ever since and often is used to justify the illegal stoppages. However, forbidden by law from striking, the public-sector workers, even though three-quarters organized, actually account for less than one-fourth of all workers involved in work stoppages, and about one-fifth of the man-days lost in strikes. Days lost per thousand workers, workers involved as a percent of all workers, and days lost per worker involved in the public sector are less than those in the large-size private firms with 500 or more employees.

ROLE OF GOVERNMENT

One observation on the extent and severity of work stoppages in industry is that they often vary inversely with the amount of labor relations conflict that takes place in the political realm. This is difficult to measure, but it is believed that the more the issues are handled through the government, the less they will generate strikes in industry itself. That the Japanese government, beginning with the labor reforms of the Occupation, suddenly took far more direct responsibility for legislating and enforcing a wide range of new labor standards may well have removed many issues from collective bargaining and shifted conflict away from industry to politics. The standards cover a whole host of items, from minimum wages to industrial health and safety and social security, for example. Battles fought over such questions have often taken place in and around the Diet and government ministries and agencies rather than in union-management bargaining. With the leading national labor centers and industrial union federations closely tied to competing opposition parties, particularly the Marxist-oriented Socialists and the moderate Democratic Socialists, organized labor in Japan, like their counterparts in Western Europe, has placed considerable emphasis on political and ideological movement directed toward government policy. This emphasis, however, may be undergoing change as organized labor has become more and more oriented toward collective bargaining and, with increasing affluence, collective bargaining itself embraces additional issues especially in the fringe-benefit area.

Finally, also as part of the postwar labor reforms, Japan developed a comprehensive network of permanent machinery at the national level and in each prefecture for conciliation, mediation, and arbitration of industrial disputes and for employer unfair labor practices. This machinery is composed of one set of tripartite labor relations commissions for the private and local public sectors, another set for the maritime industry, and a third for central government-owned corporations and enterprises. The courts, too, are available for processing disputes in the unfair labor practice area. These bodies and their staffs tend to be highly active in monitoring disputes and assisting the parties to reach agreements through conciliation and mediation. While they are often slow in handling cases, they cater to the proclivities of many Japanese to attempt to avoid direct confrontation in negotiations. Rarely is there resort to arbitration, as so often is found in American grievance procedure.

In summary, the degree of industrial conflict, overt and latent, in Japan, has been neither remarkably high nor low during the postwar period compared to other advanced industrialized democracies. As best as they can be measured, long-run trends show an increasing resort to disputes, but with a high degree of volatility in the short term. A complex set of factors—economic, technological, political, legal, social, and cultural—requires analysis for explaining these trends and differences from other countries.

Solomon B. Levine

BIBLIOGRAPHY

Fujita, Wakao. "Labor Disputes." In *Workers and Employers in Japan: The Japanese Employment Relations System*, edited by Kazuo Okochi, Bernard Karsh, and Solomon B. Levine, pp. 308–59. Princeton and Tokyo: Princeton University Press and University of Tokyo Press, 1973.

Hanami, Tadashi. *Labor Relations in Japan Today*. Tokyo: Kodansha International, 1979.

Japan Institute of Labour. *Labor Unions and Labor-Management Relations.* Japanese Industrial Relations Series, Series 2. Tokyo, 1979.

Levine, Solomon B., and Koji Taira. "Interpreting Industrial Conflict: The Case of Japan." In *Labor Relations in Advanced Industrial Societies: Issues and Problems,* edited by Benjamin Martin and Everett M. Kassalow, pp. 61–88. Washington, D.C.: Carnegie Endowment for International Peace, 1980.

Sugimoto, Yoshio. "Quantitative Characteristics of Popular Disturbances in Post-Occupation Japan (1952–1960)." *Journal of Asian Studies* 37, no. 2 (February 1978):273–91.

———. "Comparative Analysis of Industrial Conflict in Australia and Japan." In *Sharpening the Focus,* edited by R. D. Walton, pp. 198–219. Brisbane: School of Modern Asian Studies, Griffith University, 1977.

Labor Regulations

What kinds of labor regulations must firms in Japan adhere to? In other words, what are some of the main labor laws and their requirements to which companies must comply?

BACKGROUND

As in the United States and other countries, employers in Japan must observe a large number of labor laws and regulations. Legal obligations are abundant in the major areas of labor and employment relations, labor standards and protections, and social security and welfare. They are as complex and detailed as found in any advanced industrialized nation, although their substance differs in some respects. Only the most important relating to private employers are covered in this chapter.

By and large, the legal requirements in force today had their beginnings during the Occupation period, when the Japanese government adopted wholesale reforms in the labor field as part of Japan's democratization. Since then they have undergone numerous amendments, additions, and elaboration over the years as the Japanese industrial economy has grown in size and changed in structure. Labor law is a dynamic area requiring employers (and labor organizations), both public and private, to monitor its development and conform to changes in regulations.

THE JAPANESE CONSTITUTION

To describe Japanese labor law, one must begin with the postwar Constitution of Japan, adopted in 1946, which provides the basis for all legislation in this field. The Japanese Constitution is rather exceptional among democratic countries in including explicit provisions for guaranteeing fundamental worker rights as inviolable and unalterable. Specifically as part of a "bill of rights" lengthier than found in the American Constitution, Article 25 states that "all people shall have the right to maintain the minimum standards of wholesome and cultural living . . . the State shall use its endeavors for the promotion of social welfare and security . . ."; Article 27 sets forth that "all people shall have the right and the obligation to work . . . standards for wages, hours, rest and other working conditions shall be fixed by law . . . children shall not be exploited"; and Article 28 provides that "the right of workers to organize and to bargain and act collectively is guaranteed." A basic assumption in the Constitution is that even in a democratic society workers inherently are in a disadvantaged position in relation to employers and therefore are in need of State protection.

LABOR RELATIONS

Turning first to the area of labor and employee-relations law, the employer must make a distinction between the individual worker and workers as a collectivity (or union). The protections for the individual are found mainly in the Labor Standards Law (LSL), first adopted in 1947 and subsequently amended on various occasions, and in related legislation, since they provide for basic and minimum conditions under which wage and salary workers of all categories are employed. They specify the nature of individual employment contracts, rights and duties of employers and employees during the employment relationship, working time, methods of pay, worker incapacity, job security, equal treatment, employee grievances and disputes, and similar matters. Collective agreements that provide (and most do) higher standards than the LSL and related laws supersede the latter because of the constitutional inviolability of the workers' rights to organize, bargain, and act collectively. In other words, an individual employment contract may not be used to undercut a collective agreement. If it does, it is null and void. Of course, there may be conflicts between collective agreements and the Constitution, in which case the Constitution is overriding. For example, because of the constitutional guarantees, the employer cannot require an employee to promise not to form a union (the so-called yellow-dog contract).

There is no parallel stipulation in Japanese law granting employers the right to organize, bargain collectively, and carry out concerted activities such as lockouts (as is sometimes the case in Western European countries). While employers have the freedom to join industrial or regional associations, and most of any size actually do so, only in very few cases (e.g., maritime shipping, private railways, textiles) do the associations bargain on behalf of their members. Rather, bargaining in almost all cases is the responsibility of the individual employers. Associations, however, may play a vital role in issuing guidelines for bargaining, providing research and information, representing employees before government and other bodies, and conducting education services for management.

Under the Trade Union Law (TUL) of 1949 (which had a predecessor adopted in 1946), the employer may be subjected to charges of unfair labor practices almost identical to provisions in U.S. law. An employer is forbidden to interfere in any way with the right of workers to organize unions of their own choosing. He must recognize a union of his employees for purposes of collective bargaining as long as the union promotes the interests of the workers against the employer and is independent of both employer and government. (Such a bona fide union can gain certification as a democratic and independent organization by submitting to a qualifications examination by an appropriate government-established labor relations commission.) The law does stipulate, however, that the union must not include managerial personnel (usually above first-line supervisors) or employees with access to confidential information; but no distinction is made among employees as to their status of blue or white collar, or craft or occupation. Employers cannot, as under U.S. law, even raise the question of appropriate bargaining units and demand that a union seeking employer recognition undergo a representation election to obtain certification; those matters are left to the workers themselves.

Other charges of unfair labor practices against the employer as in U.S. law include discharge of or discrimination against employees for union activities, although the employer may agree to require union membership as a condition of employment when the union represents a majority of the workers in the work place or plant. (Most collective agreements have such "union-shop" provisions.) Also, the employer must not refuse to bargain in good faith with his employees collectively "without fair and appropriate reasons," provide financial support for the union except office space and similar facilities, or penalize a worker for filing complaints, requesting review, or giving testimony in unfair labor practice cases. There is no parallel set of unfair labor practices against unions, although they must meet bona fide union requirements to avail themselves of remedies against employer unfair labor practices and to gain recognition as a juridical person.

Similar to the functions of the American National Labor Relations

Board, the tripartite labor relations commissions in Japan, provided for in the TUL and Labor Relations Adjustment Law (LRAL), process complaints of employer unfair labor practices. Only the public members of the commissions sit on these cases, and usually they first attempt through informal procedures to get the parties to settle voluntarily. The law has established several sets of commissions at both national and prefectural levels for the private sector, the maritime industry, and the national enterprises and public corporations of the central government. For private employers, the Central Labor Relations Commission, situated in Tokyo, is the most important. When informal methods fail to resolve an unfair labor practice case, a commission proceeds to formal investigation, hearing, and decision. If the commission finds against the employer, it may order the employer to comply with the law and turn to the courts for enforcement. Remedies may include reinstating employees with back pay, posting notice of compliance, and the like. Charges of unfair labor practices may also be pressed directly through the courts as an alternative procedure to the labor relations commission.

Usually between 500 and 1,000 unfair labor practices cases are filed formally each year with the labor relations commissions. The majority are eventually compromised or withdrawn, but about 150 a year end with formal decisions and orders from the commissions. These numbers for the labor relations commissions are far less as a percent of total cases than in the United States; but twice as many than received by the commission cases are processed through the courts, where formal litigation is more frequent. The resort to the courts is due primarily to the relatively long time it takes to reach settlements through the commissions. Most cases deal with discharge or discrimination for union activity.

COLLECTIVE BARGAINING AND AGREEMENTS

Within the typical large-scale, multiplant enterprise (in which usually all the nonmanagerial employees have a single union), management may expect to bargain collectively at least at three levels: first, with the enterprisewide union as a whole about general working conditions and other matters in common; second, with the plant branches of the union about issues pertaining only to that plant; and third, with subdivisions within the plant branch union in the application of the wider agreements. It is unusual for representatives of national industrial union federations to which an enterprise-level union is affiliated to conduct negotiations with the employer, although the union is free to designate its own collective bargaining agent. In some cases, however, industrial union federation representatives may be present at negotiations.

Since a collective bargaining agreement is legally binding as a contract under law, it must be put into writing and signed by the qualified representatives of the parties. (Of the organized workers eligible to bargain collectively, 90 percent are covered by written agreements.) The parties usually agree upon procedures to follow in bargaining in order to establish that they have negotiated in good faith. Unlike the American National Labor Relations Board, the Japanese commissions have not specified what are mandatory and nonmandatory subjects of collective bargaining. In theory, bargaining in the private sector is wide open in that almost every management practice may affect conditions of work.

However, most collective bargaining agreements in Japan provide for joint union-management consultative committees so that various matters such as personnel assignment, production planning, and technological and organizational change are discussed in those committees, and, as a result because of mutual understandings reached in joint consultation, do not get to the bargaining table. The right to joint consultation, it appears, must be respected as part of the legally enforceable collective agreement.

The TUL sets a limit of three years as the maximum duration for an agreement. Most agreements actually are for one year, mainly as the result of the annual shuntō, and often allow for reopeners in addition to joint consultation. In theory, an agreement implies that neither side will resort to an act of dispute as to items in the agreement while it is in effect. In practice, because of the vagueness of many clauses and omission of certain items, legal strikes may take place at any time. In the event of a legal strike that causes "damage" to an employer, the latter has no right to sue either unions or workers for losses; and, indeed, if there is damage to customers or third parties, the employer runs the risk of liability himself.

There are also provisions under the TUL for extensions of collective agreements to other plants of a company and to a whole industry in a given locality. When an agreement expires and a new agreement has yet to be reached, the previous agreement usually remains in force if so originally stipulated by the parties.

WORKING CONDITIONS

Even where there is no union of the employees, a management that employs at least ten persons regularly is required under the Labor Standards Law (LSL) to inform, consult with, and seek the opinion of worker representatives about work rules and make sure that the rules meet at least the legal minimums. As for most other facets of the law, the Ministry of Labor, especially the Labor Standards Office, is charged with enforcing this provision and maintains a host of labor inspectors through bureaus and officers at the national and prefectural level. Work rules must cover most working conditions: hours of work, rest time, holidays, vacations, and shifts; methods of deciding and computing wages; dates of wage payment, minimum wages, bonuses, promotion procedures, retirement age, and pay allowances; discipline and dismissal; charges to employees for food, equipment, and the like; regulations for safety and sanitation; vocational training and apprenticeships; accident compensation, relief for injury and illness, and any other requirements set forth by the LSL and related ordinances. An employer must post all of these conditions and rules. LSL often is a substitute for a collective agreement, especially when there is no union of the majority of employees.

Among other items, the LSL stipulates a maximum of 8 hours per day and 48 hours per week (for adult workers) with certain exceptions for employees in agricultural, supervisory, irregular, and emergency work. It also provides for rest time at work and rest days per week. In practice, at least 12 national holidays with pay are observed; and the 5-day, 40-hour week has become increasingly prevalent. (In fact, average working hours per week in manufacturing firms with 30 employees or more are now only slightly above the American level.) Overtime must be paid at least at time and one-quarter and except for certain hazardous work may be unlimited for adult males. Graveyard-shift work also must be paid at the overtime rate. In addition, a worker must receive at least six days of annual paid vacation after a year of continuous employment with an 80 percent attendance record or more. Each year a day of paid vacation must be added up to a maximum of 20 days. Vacation pay must equal the worker's average or normal pay. The worker is permitted to take his vacation at any time, either all at once or spread over the year unless the normal schedule of the plant operations is thereby interrupted. In practice, relatively few workers in fact take entitled vacation all at once, and often vacation days go unused and are worked into overtime. (Many Japanese workers appear to prefer income to leisure.)

A large number of legal regulations protect women and minors in employment. Their overtime hours are usually limited. Maternity leave for six weeks prior to and after delivery is guaranteed. So are nursing time and leave for menstruation. Equal pay for equal work must be paid regardless of sex. The law also prohibits discrimination for other working conditions on the grounds of nationality, creed, or social status, but omits any mention of sex. Actually, however, because of the constitutional provisions, the employer runs considerable risk in discriminating against women in other working conditions. Recent court decisions, for example, have prohibited earlier mandatory retirement ages for women than men and retirement of women and not men because of marriage.

As for minors, there are a large number of restrictions for minors under

18 years of age. Indeed, even up to the age of 20 a minor cannot have a contract of employment (or anything else) without parental guidance or consent. Children between the ages of 12 and 15 may be hired for work not harmful to their health or welfare, but not at all in manufacturing, mining, construction, and transportation, and then only outside school hours and with permission of the Labor Standards Office. Only theaters and the film industry may employ children under age 12, with the same permission. Restriction of hours and of types of work, similar to those for women, also apply to minors under age 18.

Employers must pay all wages in cash and directly to the workers themselves, not less than once a month on a fixed date except for bonuses and other unusual payments as approved by the Labor Ministry. Payment-in-kind is allowed under special conditions and limitations, while wage deductions are permitted only as provided by law or written agreement with the union or representatives of a majority of the employees if there is no union. Deductions usually include income taxes, social security con-tributions, union dues and fees if a checkoff is present (this, like the union shop, is widespread), and other agreed-upon payments for benefits and goods that the employer provides. Delays in paying wages are punishable by a fine. In case of bankruptcy, wage claims for three months have priority over other claims (and since 1976 the government by law pays the balance of unpaid wages).

MINIMUM WAGES AND TERMS OF EMPLOYMENT

Japan has also developed a legal minimum-wage system, although unlike the United States and other countries there is no universal minimum. The Minimum Wage Law of 1959 stipulates procedures for setting daily minimums by industry, occupation, or region. Most workers are now covered by minimum wage orders.

The employer is obliged to pay wages in various circumstances beyond the worker's control. When a worker is laid off or required to take "rest" days because of the company's financial difficulties, lack of materials due to a strike elsewhere, or the like, he must be paid at least 60 percent of his average wage. He is paid at the same rate when incapacitated by a work injury or disease, although this is actually covered by Work-men's Compensation insurance. Employers also must allow workers to take time off to vote and perform other duties as citizens (usually with pay although not legally required). Short leaves, or days off, for illness, family matters, or even union activities are usually granted without docking wages (one reason for not taking all of one's vacation time).

Employers in Japan do not take dismissals or discharges lightly on legal grounds alone. In law, there is the presumption that an employee whom a company hired without an individual labor contract specifying a definite duration of employment will remain continuously on the payroll. Usually, fixed-term contracts are made only with temporary employees, who are placed on legal notice from the time of hire of the date they will be terminated. Even then, the law prohibits individual employment contracts with definite terms of more than one year with certain limited exceptions. Otherwise, to terminate an employee legally requires at least 30-days' notice (or the equivalent wages).

As Article 27 of the Constitution has been interpreted by the courts, job security for the individual appears to be well safeguarded under the guaranteed right to work. This means that an employer has to show "just cause" or "inevitable reason" in dismissing a worker, even when rendering the required 30-day notice. Financial or economic conditions or even natural disaster, it should be noted, do not necessarily constitute sufficent grounds.

Thus, from the legal standpoint alone, an employer must be extremely cautious in terminating workers who are not temporarily employed under an explicit fixed-term contract of employment. This obligation is in distinct contrast to the United States (but not most other countries), where dismissal and layoff of individual workers are accepted practices except as constrained by seniority-type rules under collective bargaining agreements or by laws preventing discrimination against union members, women, and minorities. The constitutional and legal principles in Japan fit well with the idea of continuous employment of a regular worker with a single company. They also make less necessary resort by unions in Japan to bargain for seniority or other types of job-security systems for layoffs or reductions in the work force. In other words, an employer can dismiss an individual worker only for the strongest reasons.

However, when due to adverse business conditions a company finds it must either cut down its regular work force or perhaps go bankrupt, there is the serious legal question as to which employees should be dismissed—the older or younger, the higher or lesser paid, the married or single workers, or men or women. If this question goes to court, there are no set standards in law or practice. Each case is examined and decided for its particular circumstances. Mandatory retirement at a stipulated age, of course, is an accepted grounds for nondisciplinary discharge. Usually, retirement age is set at least at age 55, but in a growing number of cases it is rising to between 55 and 60.

Furthermore, in case of disciplinary action, an employer is expected to spell out in the collective bargaining agreement or approved work rules the exact penalties or sanctions to be imposed for infractions, ranging from warnings to discharge. According to court rulings, laziness, inefficiency, or minor rule infractions often are not grounds enough to order dismissal. Should an individual be terminated, the employer is required under the LSL to provide the worker with a certificate showing details of his employment as required by the worker. Black lists are absolutely forbidden.

SOCIAL SECURITY

As in the United States and elsewhere, social security laws in Japan place a number of obligations upon the employer. If he employs five or more workers regularly he must contribute to government-enacted schemes for employee health and pension insurance. If fewer are employed, the contributions may be voluntary. Regardless of the number of employees (with certain exceptions in agriculture, forestry, and fisheries), the employer must also contribute to the government's employment (really unemployment) insurance, workmen's accident compensation insurance, and children's allowance fund.

Contributions to these schemes are roughly about the same for employer, employees, and government, except for workmen's compensation and children allowances to which the employer and government alone contribute. It is estimated that, in recent years, public social security programs amount to at least 6 percent of total labor costs. In addition, especially in the large enterprises, collective bargaining agreements provide for additional benefits beyond those required under the obligatory social security programs. Usually, they about double these fringe-benefit costs. Since the Japanese population and labor force is aging and Japan is placing increasing emphasis upon social welfare programs, rates and levels of contributions to the various government-sponsored insurance schemes are likely to rise in the years ahead. Similarly, it may be expected that collective bargaining will see growing demands for welfare-type fringe benefits.

Solomon B. Levine

BIBLIOGRAPHY

Ariizumi, Toru. "The Legal Framework: Past and Present." In *Workers and Employers in Japan: The Japanese Employment Relations System,* edited by Kazuo Okochi, Bernard Karsh, and Solomon B. Levine, pp. 89–132. Princeton and Tokyo: Princeton University Press and University of Tokyo Press, 1973.

Hanami, T. A. *Labor Law and Industrial Relations in Japan.* Kluwer-Deventer, The Netherlands, 1979.

Japan Institute of Labour. Japanese Industrial Relations Series: *Labor Unions and Labor-Management Relations,* Series 2. Tokyo, 1979; *Wages and Hours of Work,* Series 3. Tokyo, 1979; and *Social Security,* Series 5. Tokyo, 1980.

Takahashi, Takeshi. "Social Security for Workers." In *Workers and Employers in Japan: The Japanese Employment Relations System,* edited by Kazuo Okochi, Barnard Karsh, and Solomon B. Levine, pp. 441–84. Princeton and Tokyo: Princeton University Press and University of Tokyo Press, 1973.

PART II

THE JAPANESE ECONOMY

3

JAPAN'S ECONOMIC GROWTH

Economic growth in Japan has attracted world attention: Japan is the most highly industrialized nation outside of Western Europe and North America, and the only major non-Caucasian economic power. Japan has grown dramatically since World War II to a position second only to the United States among free-world economies and occupies third rank among all industrialized nations including the USSR. While Japan's rapid economic growth has not come without some domestic costs, as we discuss elsewhere, Japan is clearly the world's growth economy par excellence, a fact made more dramatic by her heavy dependency on imported raw materials.

A model of the factors affecting economic growth has emerged from the study of the experience of Western nations that began their industrialization as far back as two centuries ago. Internally, nations must have adequate pools of potential entrepreneurs to lead industrial development and skilled persons to staff factories and laboratories; a sufficient supply of potential workers who have some education and an ability to adjust to modern production processes must also be present. Nations must in addition have an adequate supply of capital from either internal or external sources, and markets must be available for the products that are produced. Finally, as has become abundantly apparent in the third-world economies, the will to develop and industrialize must be present, either in the form of entrepreneurial motivation or in the commitments of government leaders.

Pre-World War II economic development in Japan followed closely the patterns of industrial development found in other nations, and resembled particularly the trend among late developing economies, where access to established technologies and international markets became additional variables in the assemblage of factors influencing development. Japan entered the modern world with a pool of persons having some education and its elites had managerial and bureaucratic skills. The will and self-discipline to develop also existed in the form of both centralized guidance and entrepreneurial initiative. Monetary stability was provided by fiscal reforms, and taxation of the agricultural sector plus foreign borrowing provided funds for investment. Moreover, World War I absorbed the energies of the combatant powers and gave Japan an opportunity to gain a vital economic foothold in nearby Asian markets and elsewhere. The result was an economic growth pattern from 1880 to 1960 which matched that of model growth economies such as the United States.

The same factors present in earlier periods contributed to the phenomenally high growth experienced by Japan in the 1960s, and, according to Albert Keidel II, Japan's "economic miracle" can be seen as an accelerated continuation of earlier growth patterns. Leadership from the government was present in centralized indicative planning, and "administrative guidance" from the Ministry of International Trade and Industry and other government offices. Corporate officials were also committed to long-term growth for their own companies, as we have seen in Chapter 1. The postwar land reform and emergence of an organized labor movement after occupation legislation laid the way for the development of a mass consumer market for the products of Japan's industries. As a result, although export led in some cases, Japan's postwar economic production depended far less on export markets in the aggregate than that of any other industrialized country with the exception of the United States. High growth was favored on the input side by Japan's high savings ratio, and the consequent availability of both private and corporate savings for investment, and on the output side by the absorption of roughly 86 percent of product in the expanding domestic market.

That Japan was able to achieve growth rates as high as 14 percent per year in the 1960s was by itself a miracle; that this was accomplished in a nation where almost all energy and raw materials were imported is even more remkarkable. However, as Keidel argues, raw material dependence and the ensuing awareness of vulnerability among Japan's economic leaders may actually have encouraged a commitment to increasing productivity and developing competitive export products that help pay for needed raw materials. As Keidel's carefully marshaled figures show, Japan has been able to substantially reduce the amounts of energy used in productive processes since the early 1970s, whereas the United States lags in this area. Likewise, efficient productive processes have been developed in industries particularly dependent on other kinds of imported supplies, such as the steel industry, and this has been a factor of overall importance in Japan's competitive cost position.

Forecasts of Japan's economic futures have ranged from Herman Kahn's prediction that Japan would be the dominant power of the world to Zbigniew Brezinski's estimate that Japan's economy was a "fragile blossom" that would wither because of inherent weaknesses in its internal dynamics and external dependency. Keidel, in contrast, predicts a moderate growth rate for Japan in the 1980s, which, while not as dramatic as earlier experience, may well be a dramatic event in the difficult years ahead for the industrial economies of the world. Because there is political consensus that favors growth in Japan, even though there are arguments about the most appropriate pace between fiscal conservatives and supporters of more rapid growth, the commitment to economic development will continue. In terms of emphasis, while Japan has actually reached the pinnacle of world technological development in several industries, it is also committed to further development of "knowledge-intensive" industries across the board. As Japan's economic maturation continues, Keidel feels that Japan will export more and more services like shipping and banking credits, and will expand technological and producer-good exports beyond their already substantial levels. Given Japanese world leadership in quality control and shared leadership in innovation, the main factors that will shape economic futures are political. Access to external markets must not be disrupted by the political actions of other states, while domestic monetary policies and governmental ability to help in the problems of declining industries will also be critical.

Japan's Economic Modernization

Japan entered the modern world a little later than some countries, although at about the same time as Germany and Italy. What were the reasons that Japan's economy was able to modernize and industrialize so rapidly?

Japan's economic modernization following the Meiji Restoration of 1868 represents the world's only noncaucasian incidence of successful industrial revolution. By the end of World War I, Japan had in essence completed the transition to modern economic growth. Although the already existing backlog of world scientific and engineering knowledge certainly made this record possible, that backlog has been available to all aspirant economies. Successful adaptation of that knowledge is clearly no automatic process, and to understand such a singular pattern of achievement, we must include in our study the origin of Japanese skills in management and commerce, skills that did not have to be borrowed from abroad.

OSCILLATIONS IN EARLY JAPANESE GROWTH

Japan's industrialization path from 1868 until the Pacific War is best introduced as a series of interlocking periods or "swings" of investment and output. For roughly the first 20 years following the Restoration there is no acceptable measure of economic growth; national efforts concentrated on the transition from feudal to more modern social institutions, while the country as a whole reeled in an attempt to absorb the ideas and technical possibilities that flowed in from the West. However, beginning in the mid-1880s and continuing to the turn of the century, Japan passed through its first period of modern economic growth, relying on rural taxation and government sponsorship of social overhead construction such as roads and ports, while commerce, banking, and nascent small-scale industry flourished under the stimulus of military victory in the Sino-Japanese War.

A second important period of growth lasted from the turn of the century until about 1912 or 1913. Government encouragement of shipping, railroads, metallurgy, and other large-scale industry added to the growth contribution of rapidly expanding private small-scale manufacturing, in particular textiles. Japan's increasing international stature and victory in the Russo-Japanese War were important elements in this period's success. In both of these early periods of growth, significant increases in agricultural productivity through better use of traditional methods was a crucial source of investment resources, captured through the use of very high rural taxation and rent levels.

The final two swings in Japanese growth before the Pacific War were those associated with World War I and with Japanese military preparedness efforts in the 1930s. A noncombatant in World War I, Japan increased production and export of textiles and heavy manufactures, while the iron, steel and machinery industries began the expansion they later resumed in the decade of the Great Depression. The 1920s were years of slow and sometimes negative growth in output and investment, but in the 1930s rapid growth began again, depending mainly on metals and machinery, and continued until Pearl Harbor.

GROWTH SPURTS FOR INDUSTRIAL LATECOMERS: A STATISTICAL COMPARISON

Japanese growth after World War II is treated in another chapter, and it suffices to say here that by 1953–54 Japan had recovered from the dislocations of war and began an unprecedented period of sustained high growth extending into the 1970s. Overall, we can study the pace of Japan's industrial revolution and modern economic growth by referring to Table 3.1, which compares Japan with the world's other major industrial powers for comparable periods in their early industrial expansion.

TABLE 3.1

Long-Period Growth of National Product, Selected Countries (percentage growth per decade)

Country	Growth Rate
Japan	
1879–81 to 1959–61	42.0
United Kingdom	
1700 to 1780	5.3
1780 to 1881	28.2
1885–95 to 1957–59	21.1
United States	
1839 to 1960–62	42.5
France	
1841–50 to 1960–62	20.8
Russia/USSR	
1860 to 1913	30.2
1913 to 1958	35.7
1928 to 1958	53.8
Italy	
1861–65 to 1898–1902	9.7
1898–1902 to 1960–62	26.8
Germany/West Germany	
1851–55 to 1871–75	17.6
1871–75 to 1960–62	31.1

Source: Simon Kuznets, *Modern Economic Growth* (New Haven: Yale University Press, 1966), pp. 64–65. Used with permission.

Table 3.1 shows that during the 80-year period presented, Japan grew at a rate of 42 percent a decade (an annual average of 3.6 percent), a rate considerably faster than the growth of the other industrial powers, with two exceptions: the United States, whose relatively high growth over more than 120 years had placed it in the position of world economic dominance it enjoyed in the 1960s, and the Soviet Union, whose five-year plans of command growth also propelled her to a place of world leadership. It must also be remembered that the United States was experiencing a very rapid growth of population from immigration, while that of Japan was considerably slower. If we take population into account by comparing growth rates in per capita product, and if we also extend the period of comparison to 1967 for the two countries, the respective growth rates are 32 percent for Japan and 18 percent for the United States.

This relatively later but more rapid industrial achievement conforms to an overall pattern observed internationally as the industrial revolution has spread from its origins in eighteenth-century Great Britain: countries beginning industrialization later tend to grow more rapidly and under more centralized guidance than did Great Britain or France, for example, two of the earliest industrializers. This is particularly true of the earliest years of each country's industrial revolution; the statistics above span two world wars that were particularly destructive in Europe and Japan, and hence they tend to underreport the rapidity with which "latecomers" began their industrial expansion.

MANAGEMENT AND LEADERSHIP:
JAPAN'S INDIGENOUS RESOURCE

In investigating the reasons for Japan's rapid industrialization, we must keep in mind both the advantages common to all economic latecomers as well as the special circumstances bequeathed to modern Japan by the earlier feudel Tokugawa order. These two factors summarize the major determinants of her early success. As a relative latecomer, Japan could draw on the wealth of technical and practical information already known to the Western world, not to mention their already established markets. On the other hand, the West did not automatically hand over to Japan a full complement of modern industrial establishments and institutions; Japan had to go out and acquire them.

Such acquisition is itself in many ways a process of innovation, ingenuity, and self-discipline, both at the personal and at the national level. Scholars agree with near unanimity that at the time of the 1868 Meiji Restoration the organizational, bureaucratic, and commercial skills of the Japanese were far in advance of their scientific abilities. Furthermore, the feudal Tokugawa order had succeeded in maintaining a strict sense of personal discipline and sacrifice at all social levels. In short, the Japanese who in 1868 found themselves with the task of "catching up" were in many ways ideally suited to the task.

Because of the suddenness with which Japan began commerce and intercourse with the West it is easy to overlook the long, slow development of commercial and management skills during the Tokugawa period. For over a hundred years before the arrival of Perry, the feudal governments and their retainers had found themselves in increasing financial difficulty. The economy was overwhelmingly an agrarian one with more than 80 percent of housueholds in subsistence farming. Long periods of peace and political stability had swelled the total population so that food production was barely adequate and population growth slow. Attempts by the ruling samurai to extract larger surpluses from the static productive base were largely unsuccessful, and it became increasingly necessary to resort to currency debasements and borrowing from the socially inferior but well-to-do merchant class.

The slow evolution of relations between urban merchants and poorer samurai formed a hybrid group composed of merchants who had purchased or otherwise obtained some minimal samurai rank and of poorer samurai who had adopted commercial and artisan livelihoods. These merchant and samurai elements were not only literate but well educated and by many standards sophisticated, living in some of the largest cities of the world at that time. In addition, they functioned well in an organizational and bureaucratic framework, and perhaps most importantly they saw Japan as a unified state requiring national leadership. If there was any single element in Japan's industrialization drive that set her apart from other economies whose growth efforts have failed, it was this network of educated managerial and leadership potential.

ECONOMIC TRANSITION FROM FEUDALISM

The principal economic tasks of the new Meiji government were institutional and financial reform and the acquisition of Western technology. With as much as 80 percent of the population in agricultural pursuits, the most important economic reform was the introduction of private-land ownership and the shift to a monetarized agricultural tax based on fixed rates and assessed values rather than on fluctuating harvest levels, as had been the case. But agrarian tax revenues proved insufficient for government fiscal needs, which included the costly quelling of a serious rebellion of former samurai and the capitalization of samurai pension obligations inherited from the Tokugawa. Paper money provided short-term financing in the late 1870s, but the resulting inflation and financial chaos threatened to destroy permanently the government's fiscal foundation. Without a strong and active government promoting economic expansion, successful growth would have been highly unlikely.

The solution to the crisis of the late 1870s was four years of deflation and financial contraction known at the Matsukata Deflation, named after the finance minister who carried it out during the years 1880–84. The Matsukata Deflation is considered by many to have been the single most important policy responsible for subsequent growth, and it ushered in the first of the upward "swings" in investment and output. The deflation was engineered through higher taxes, reduced expenditures, and the application of the resulting government surplus toward redemption of the national debt. The money supply decreased by 20 percent in four years, and prices fell substantially. As a result, the government-issued currency acquired respectability and traded at par with precious-metal specie. A single central bank, the Bank of Japan, was established in 1885, and Japan had at last acquired the minimal financial institutions it needed.

It is important to note, however, that the Matsukata Deflation also inflicted considerable costs on the economy, costs difficult to measure. Because nominal land taxes did not fall while the price of foodstuffs plummeted, many farmers found themselves forced to sell their only recently received land, leaving them poor tenant farmers in a rural economy of considerable income inequality, inequality which lasted until the land reform following World War II. It is difficult to gauge the damage inflicted on Japan by the imposition of this pattern of rural poverty. Even conservative orthodox economists have speculated that such an economic base may have influenced and seriously restricted the response of the Japanese to economic and other circumstances in the 1920s and 1930s. Speculation aside, we should remember that there is more to economic success than fast growth, which is itself deceptively easy to measure and hence easy to promote. The Matsukata Deflation clearly served its purpose, but we must ask ourselves, at what price?

GOVERNMENT AND FARM SUPPORT FOR EMERGING INDUSTRIAL POWER

Examining the actual pattern of growth, we find that the first two periods of industrial expansion, from the 1880s to the turn of the century and from then to just before World War I, exhibited a number of common attributes. In both the share of government investment in the total was greater than private investment, and the government investment was in turn financed by the taxation of steadily increasing farm output. Both periods were punctuated by victories in foreign wars and the acquisition of colonial territory (Taiwan and Korea). Small-scale light manufacturers, in particular textiles and food processing, dominated the expanding manufacturing sector, while metals (most importantly iron and steel) and machinery remained in a stage of early development.

Two points that deserve emphasis are the direct role of the Meiji government and the very great importance of agriculture for the financing of industrial growth. An important problem for almost any industrializing economy is how to provide cheap foodstuffs for its growing urban work force without spending precious foreign exchange on imports and without diverting significant sums of investment resources away from industry and into an ailing agricultural sector. For the periods prior to World War I Japan solved the problem by rejecting the U.S. model of mechanized agriculture in favor of a successful campaign to improve and diffuse existing indigenous seeds, planting techniques, fertilizers, and crop rotations. The most successful and experienced farmers were hired to travel the countryside and show others their secret techniques. The success thus achieved has been studied by generations of agricultural development economists around the world as the best-known example of indigenous techniques used to sustain rural-urban resource transfers in support of industrialization.

In spite of their many similarities, these two earliest growth swings also showed important differences. Perhaps the most striking was the shift in Japan's international position. She adopted the gold standard just before the turn of the century and renegotiated her unequal treaties, leaving her free from extraterritoriality and foreign controls on customs and tariffs. The victory over Russia was largely financed by Japan's first major foreign borrowing, and after 1905 growing Japanese international indebtedness was used to finance both increased imports and the continued fiscal deficits needed to support military and infrastructure programs. By the end of the period, these deficits and international loans had produced an inevitable inflation and the loss of large amounts of foreign reserves. Financial crisis was averted only by the onset of World War I and the large market it provided for Japanese manufacturers. It was this third period of war boom that completed Japan's industrial revolution.

WORLD WAR I AND EMERGING ECONOMIC MATURITY

Early industrial activity in almost any economy is dominated by light manufacturers such as food processing and textiles. With economic maturity, heavier industries, in particular machinery and metals, become more important. The prosperity accompanying Allied demand for Japanese munitions and other manufactures spurred the beginning of this transition in Japan. Food products as a share of manufacturing output fell from 42 percent in 1902–11 to 32 percent in 1912–21 (measured in constant prices). At the same time, production of metals increased from 2.6 to 6.8 percent of the total and machinery from 5.6 to 12.5 percent. In addition, for the first time, private sources of investment became more important than public ones, and the ability of the agricultural sector to sustain growth and resource transfers based on traditional methods came to an end. With this period Japan began to rely increasingly on food imports from her colonies, in particular Korea's high-quality rice.

A further indication of Japan's increasing economic maturity in this period was her growing integration into the world economy. The war opportunities allowed her to capture markets all over the world previously dominated by Great Britain and Western Europe. This was perhaps most true for cotton goods, and many of the gains and inroads made during the war were maintained after the signing of the armistice. By the 1920s, then, Japan had made the transition to an industrial nation. The disastrous Tokyo earthquake of 1923 and other economic difficulties of the 1920s resulted in slow growth, and the military expansion and forced heavy industrialization of the 1930s may be viewed by some as artificial stimuli outside the usual path of modernization, but that is beside the point. By the third decade of the twentieth century Japan had essentially completed an industrialization process that had taken other countries as long as a hundred years.

Successful and rapid industrialization by a non-European race has tremendous significance for the world economy as a whole. This quick review of the Japanese experience shows how a latecomer in the industrialization process can succeed in learning existing techniques and apply those techniques to meet foreign and domestic opportunities as they arise. The Japanese achievementns imply that a recipe for industrialization requires more than engineering and financial ingredients. The educational and in a sense managerial background of the preindustrial society must be given considerable credit for the success of millions of decisions, large and small, which are the real stuff of growth.

Albert Keidel

BIBLIOGRAPHY

Lockwood, William W. *The Economic Development of Japan: Growth and Structural Change, 1868–1938*. Princeton: Princeton University Press, 1954.

Ohkawa, Kazushi, and Henry Rosovsky. *Japanese Economic Growth: Trend Acceleration in the Twentieth Century*. Stanford: Stanford University Press, 1973.

Japan's Growth Record

Japan is said to have one of the fastest economic growth records in the world. If this is true, when did such growth occur, and what were its causes?

It must seem to the average American reviewing the last 30 years that Japanese products and economic achievements have exploded into our markets and lives. And indeed they have. Japanese production of goods and services, both for export and for home use, has expanded since the Korean War at a pace unmatched by any other economy in the world. Why didn't the United States grow that fast? Or Germany? Or some country like India? Experts haave analyzed Japan's performance and gained some understanding of the changes and patterns associated with her growth, but a search for the actual causes of Japanese success points beyond the borders of traditional economic analysis. The importance of supplemental leadership initiative and discipline from Japanese national agencies shows that a passive laissez-faire government role may not be sufficient if economic growth is a major goal.

The suddenness of Japan's ascent might also imply an oriental conspiracy, an economic Pearl Harbor of sorts, but that is not the case. To be sure, balanced plans to develop markets, apply new technology, and conserve foreign exchange have greatly improved Japan's efforts, but hard work, practical decisions, and disciplined cooperation deserve most of the credit. In fact, values usually associated with Western economic success— thrift, individual industry, and the work ethic—are also largely responsible for Japan's remarkable and sustained increases in productivity, industrial efficiency, and overall output.

Nor is the Japanese growth success the "result" of America's postwar occupation and the "democratization" of its conquered enemy. For over a hundred years Japan's economic performance has been extraordinary. Her emergence as a world economic power is not a recent event, and Japanese success since the 1950s can best be viewed as the accelerated continuation of a pattern of adaptation and achievement maintained for at least as long as Japan has been open to the West.

EXTRAORDINARY GROWTH:
A STATISTICAL WONDER

But let's look first at the record of Japan's recent economic growth, because it has indeed been unique. In the 25 years after 1953 Japan's economy grew faster than that of any other country in the world. An economy's growth rate in any one year is the percentage by which some measure of its output has increased over the previous year. In any single year, it is not unusual to find very high growth rates for individual countries, especially when the previous year was one of very low production because of harvest failure or national disaster. However, it is unusual to see high rates of growth continue year after year. A record of *sustained* high growth implies that the economy has found some out-of-the-ordinary motor of success. Japan's record is remarkable because the high annual rates of growth have not only been sustained, but sustained over a very long period.

Several sets of international comparisons are presented in Table 3.2. The first set is for different irregular periods of growth in different countries in the 1950s and 1960s. The second and third sets show comparisons for the 1960s and 1970s. The first column in the table shows the period of growth for each country in the earlier period. The remaining columns show the respective average annual growth rates for each period.

Table 3.2 shows that Japan's growth has been superior to that of any other Western industrial power for virtually all of the post-World War II period. For both Japan and the Western industrial powers, the periods of fastest growth were those of the Korean War years and of the 1960s. Slower periods have been in the late 1950s and in the 1970s following the 1973 Arab-Israeli War. In each of these subperiods, however, Japan's growth has been significantly more rapid than that of the other powers.

The data in column 1960–70 of Table 3.2 show that the 1960s were the years of Japan's most rapid growth; growth in some individual years was as high as 13 and 14 percent. It is important to emphasize just how extraordinarily rapid these rates of growth are. Because annual growth has a compounding effect, 10 percent growth will double national output in roughly seven years. That in fact was the much-debated and often ridiculed Japanese goal in 1960, to double the national product within the decade. That they succeeded rather easily in such an ambitious plan points to the more interesting aspect of the Japanese growth miracle: the degree to which government and industry policies were responsible for the growth record. What is the history of this record growth? And does such economic growth just happen, or are there understandable causal forces that can be influenced and exploited?

EARLY GROWTH SUCCESS AND WAR RECOVERY

The story of Japan's postwar economic growth cannot be cleanly separated from the more than a century of growth that began with the Meiji

TABLE 3.2

Comparison of International Growth Rates
(percent annual growth rates—corrected for inflation)

Country	Irregular Period	Growth Rate[a] (Irregular Period)	Growth Rates[b] (1960–70)	(1970–76)
Japan	1953–71	9.2	10.5	5.6
United States	1948–69	3.9	4.3	2.5
Canada	1950–67	5.2	5.6	4.8
Belgium	1950–62	3.2	4.7	4.0
France	1950–62	4.9	5.4	3.9
West Germany	1950–62	7.3	4.6	2.2
Italy	1950–62	6.0	5.3	2.9
United Kingdom	1950–62	2.3	2.9	2.3

[a]National income.
[b]Gross domestic product.
Sources: Irregular period data from Edward F. Denison and William K. Chung, *How Japan's Economy Grew So Fast* (Washington, D.C.: Brookings, 1976), p. 40; 1960–76 data from World Bank, *World Development Report* (New York: Oxford University Press, 1978), p. 77. Used with permission. Lawrence Krause and Sueo Sekiguchi, "Japan and the World Economy," in Hugh Patrick and Henry Rosovsky (eds.), *Asia's New Giant: How the Japanese Economy Works* (Washington, D.C.: Brookings Institution, 1976), p. 386. Copyright © 1976 by the Brookings Institution.

Restoration opening Japan to the West. Economic achievement before World War II in the Pacific also had its spurts of respectable growth: 6.7 percent in 1905–12, 7.0 percent in 1912–19, and 7.5 percent in 1931–38. If measures of output are plotted on a graph, there is of course a clear break corresponding to the years of war destruction, but overall one can see a long trend of growth stretching back to the late nineteenth century. To be sure, there are irregularities, and there has been acceleration since the 1950s, but Japan was already one of the leading world economic powers by the 1930s, and it was perhaps only natural that she eventually continue her progress, once she had recovered from defeat.

The Pacific War left Japan with tremendous destruction of economic plant and equipment, with the loss of a large colonial hinterland in Taiwan, Korea, and Manchuria, and with the repatriation of millions of formerly overseas Japanese. The several years immediately following the armistice were ones of economic chaos, inflation, and adjustment to the American occupation forces.

However, there were also important economic reforms. The land reform of 1946–50 successfully redistributed Japan's single most valuable asset category to individual cultivators, three-fourths of whom had been tenants paying at least half their annual crops in rents. Reforms in industrial labor laws, also begun in 1946, gave unions a protected legitimacy and the right to participate actively in the elective political process. Union membership grew rapidly and became less militant with the continuing passage of prolabor legislation. It is important to remember these early changes in the status of previously underprivileged groups. In subsequent decades, mass domestic consumer demand for services and consumer durables was important in buoying Japan's overall growth effort. It is difficult to imagine that this demand element would have been as significant had there been a national distribution of assets and income patterned on that of prereform Japan.

The years of the Korean War "boom" are rightfully considered the period of transition between recovery from war and resumption of modern economic growth. In a five-year period, the Japanese provided over 1.5 billion dollars of "special demand" goods and services. Weapons, coal, automotive products, and textiles, as well as services for construction, transport, and machine repair provided lucrative opportunities for both small individual entrepreneurs and large industrial concerns. The giant prewar zaibatsu conglomerates had been only half-heartedly dismantled by the occupying authority. During this same war period a number of economic indicators reached a normal prewar (1934–36) level: industrial output, real gross national product, real consumption, machinery investment, and per-worker productivity all in 1951; per capita gross national product and per capita consumption in 1953.

JAPAN'S MODERN MARKETS: BOTH DOMESTIC AND FOREIGN

By 1953, then, Japan was poised for the *Wirtschaftswunder* that would earn her the respect and admiration of economic policymakers everywhere. Her labor force was educated and skilled, and the large pool of workers in low-productivity agricultural and service activities represented a significant resource that could be freely tapped well into the 1960s, when the supply of labor first became tight. Machinery and other forms of physical capital to combine with that labor were needed, as were markets in which to sell output runs large enough to benefit from the economies of large-scale production. Both were forthcoming in the quarter-century that ensued.

A brief account of Japan's recent growth can only point to the markets Japan developed to absorb her output and the sources of productivity she continuously amassed. As interesting as these observations are, however, they do not really explain Japan's success. Economic plans and export drives have failed in so many other parts of the world that we can be fairly sure they are not *the* key to success.

International interest in Japan's economic miracle has often focused on her successful penetration of foreign markets, but it is perhaps equally important to note that without her own growing domestic demand for consumer durables and other goods and services, rapid growth could never have been sustained. It is true that Japan's postwar growth has been "export-led" in the sense that exports have grown faster than gross national product. It could not really be otherwise, given the almost total lack of natural resources and raw materials in Japan proper. Nevertheless, by the mid-1970s Japanese exports were still no more than 14 percent of gross national product, lower than any other Western industrial power, with the exception of the United States (which exported 8 percent of gross national product during the same period).

The strong domestic demand for industrial production is due to both the high rate of capital investment and the great surge in first-time purchases of refrigerators, washers, televisions, cameras, motorcycles, and automobiles, to name just the principal products which, although rare in the 1950s, had become commonplace by the mid-1970s (by 1975 over 95 percent of Japanese owned color televisions, 97 percent refrigerators, 56 percent stereos, 82 percent cameras and transistor radios, and 22 percent air conditioners). Hence, an understanding of Japan's growth success cannot be based on a simple export-dependence view. It is perhaps more accurate to say that Japan has taken advantage of existing international opportunities and coupled her success there with expansion of domestic demand to form a well-balanced development program.

COMPONENTS OF JAPANESE GROWTH:
NO OBVIOUS SOURCE OF SUCCESS

Questions of demand aside, how was Japan able to produce so much so fast and hence profit from these market opportunities? Considerably detailed work has been done to isolate the statistically significant components of Japanese growth. The approach to the question is straightforward. To produce output, it takes inputs of various kinds of labor, inputs of machinery, inputs of new techniques, as well as inputs of training, education, new structures, and a host of other factors, including even the effects of weather, labor relations, and increased efficiency from large-scale operations. If all of these recognized inputs increase, output should also increase, and it does. Measurement of the increases of these various growth components can reveal which of them are the most important.

In the Japanese case, however, as in studies of other industrializing nations, the influence of these inputs can explain only part of the overall growth. While fully two-thirds of the growth seems to be the result of increased inputs of labor and capital equipment combined with efficiencies of large-scale production, as much as one-quarter of overall Japanese output growth cannot be explained by growth of inputs. Analysis of U.S. growth shows a strikingly similar percentage breakdown of explained and unexplained growth, though in the Japanese case all the individual growth components are larger, including a considerably larger unexplained input contribution.

These research results leave two unresolved problems for efforts to understand Japanese growth. In the first place, why is it that *all* of the major productive inputs grew faster in Japan than in other countries? A study of the growth of major input components, such as investment in capital equipment, requires further individual study. In the second place, there is nothing in the research to indicate that these component contributions are the *causes* of growth rather than merely part of the growth process. It could easily be that some overall influence or plan is responsible for the orchestrated increases in inputs as well as for the resulting economic growth. A brief look at capital accumulation and economic planning in Japan, however, can bring us only a little closer to understanding the true sources of Japanese growth.

The accumulation of productive capital necessarily requires output in forms not suitable for consumption, and hence the economy as a whole must save a considerable portion of its income rather than seek to spend it on consumer items. The Japanese rate of savings and hence reinvestment has been extraordinarily high by international standards. Developing countries seeking to finance investment resources often have trouble saving 20 percent of gross national product. Japan, in contrast, saved an average 24 percent of gross national product in the years 1952–54, and by the early 1970s (1970–72) the savings rate had risen to over 39 percent of gross national product, though it fell again to the low thirties following the 1974 recession.

Corporate-retained earnings and government saving have made up the largest portion of Japanese gross savings, but private individual saving has also been traditionally high in Japan, accounting for a third of the total by the early 1970s. These figures represent a tremendous commitment to future growth at the expense of current consumption, especially when compared to the much lower rates of gross savings in the United States (roughly 18 percent of gross national product in the early 1970s). In attempting to explain the size of perhaps the single most important contributing *input* to growth, therefore, we must recognize a willingness in Japan greater than that in the United States to sacrifice consumption and comfort in the present in return for greater productivity and output in the future.

GROWTH-ORIENTED LEADERSHIP: JAPAN'S SOURCE OF SUCCESS

Is this kind of savings behavior, along with the other elements of growth, something that just happens? For Japan, clearly not. Since the very earliest years of Westernization in the Meiji period, the Japanese government has encouraged modernization, introduced new industries and techniques, coordinated expansion of capacity, and disciplined national saving through heavy taxation of rural incomes and the control of food prices. Direct government involvement in economic policy since the Pacific War has been much less direct than the heavy-handed policies of Japan's military era. Nevertheless, a significant degree of national coordination and planning within a competitive industrial framework is considered by many scholars to be perhaps the single most important causal force in Japan's growth experience.

And it is ironic that the Japanese are perhaps better trained intellectually than Americans to understand and undertake such a task. The economic theory that has long dominated Japanese universities, the same universities which train businessmen and bureaucrats alike, is the Marxist analysis of economic dynamics and growth in a free-market economy. In contrast, the passive orthodoxy of laissez-faire economics, which so commands American economic education, deemphasizes any possible role for government other than noninterference. It is curious and to a certain degree amusing that the Japanese might improve their management and coordination of free-enterprise industry through the study and application of Marx's analysis.

Here again, however, experience in other economies attempting to plan growth shows that a national plan or national planning agencies often do more harm than good, and that such powers in the hands of government can easily become the vehicles through which elites and special interest groups advance their own welfare at the expense of healthy growth. What then is the source of Japanese success? The answer is a vague but nevertheless meaningful one: In contrast to the leadership in many countries that feigns or affects progrowth policies, the Japanese groups with most influence, elected, corporate, bureaucratic, and even laboring, have actually made economic growth their *first* priority. Japanese leadership at all levels has simply been growth-oriented. While President Kennedy was challenging the United States with the task of flight to the moon, Prime Minister Ikeda was publicly spurring Japan to double national income in a decade.

In sum, then, the record shows that Japan's economy has grown significantly faster than that of any of the other Western economic powers, propelling her to a position in overall output second only to the United States. Behind this success lies the resourceful exploitation of foreign and domestic markets and the thrift and decision making needed to assure adequate capacity and levels of productivity. Perhaps most significant of all, however, has been the agreement within Japan's effective leadership of the primacy of the growth goal.

Albert Keidel

BIBLIOGRAPHY

Denison, Edward F., and William K. Chung. "Economic Growth and Its Sources." In *Asia's New Giant: How the Japanese Economy Works*, edited by Hugh Patrick and Henry Rosovsky. Washington, D.C.: Brookings, 1976.

Patrick, Hugh, and Henry Rosovsky. "Japan's Economic Performance: An Overview." In *Asia's New Giant: How the Japanese Economy Works*, edited by Hugh Patrick and Henry Rosovsky. Washington, D.C.: Brookings, 1976.

The Postwar Economic Miracle

Some Western scholars and journalists have called Japan a growth miracle and others term it a "fragile blossom." What are the best predictions for the future of Japan's economic development, especially as the industrialized world seems to have reached some degree of trade impasse in recent years? In addition, what are the current policy debates on these matters?

Predictions of "moderate" growth are boring. We should either say that Japan will fall on her face, or else say that Japan will rocket past us all to colonize the moon; anything in between is ho-hum. And yet there is nothing boring about the prospect of a maturing industrial Japan gradually crowding out simplistic world notions of caucasian economic superiority. Japan's permanent ascendancy to a position of shared economic leadership is one of the most exciting stories of modern economic history, and the 1980s and 1990s will see that position confirmed.

Just as we don't judge trees and bushes by their size alone, we can say that the vigor, adaptability, variety, and flexibility of the Japanese economic experience are welcome mutations in a world economic garden sorely in need of cross-pollination. Japanese growth will be moderate. But in an era of energy crisis and world macroeconomic confusion, moderate growth will be a considerable accomplishment. Japanese domestic pressures for more consumption rather than continued sacrifice will no doubt increase, yet very strong popular awareness of the continued need for international commercial success will prevail. Japanese technical brilliance and marketing imagination will keep her competitive internationally. A certain boldness in considering international projects will secure her world stature, and the developing two-thirds of the world's demand for capital goods and industrial know-how will ensure markets for a whole range of products previously supplied by Western Europe and the United States.

In the most general policy sense, Japan in the 1980s must face the consequences of her own industrial success. A strategy of continued rapid economic growth is in many ways in conflict with decisions to speed up consumption of the fruits of earlier growth. Investment in housing rather than plant and equipment, increased consumption of leisure and vacation time, labor demands for individual rather than corporate rewards: these trends have been expected by many observers for over a decade. They reflect the experience of earlier world industrial leaders, Great Britain and the United States. Such trends could indeed sap the strength of Japan's ongoing industrial modernization and rationalization programs. But so far they have not.

POLICY DEBATES: GROWTH VERSUS PRICE CONTROL

There is a strong sense in Japan of the nation's overall resource vulnerability and of the nation's need for continued application of the consistent and disciplined formula that has thus far ensured its economic survival. The several recent world crises in petroleum pricing and supply, rather than signaling disaster for Japan's economy, have instead renewed and strengthened indigenous awareness of economic isolation and of the need for limitations on economic indulgence. As a result, policy disagreements have been tactical and technical, rather than fundamental or divisive. It is likely that this is the way they will remain for some time to come.

As the 1980s began, economic policy debates centered on a rather traditional trade-off: more growth and more inflation on the one hand, or less inflation with less growth on the other. At least within the dominant Liberal Democratic Party, this was the principal issue. The origins of this debate actually go back at least to the early 1960s, at which time growth proponents prevailed over more conservative financial opinions. At the center of the debate is the principal issue of how best to carry out Japan's overall economic survival policy: the continued export of enough value added to pay for needed strategic imports. Ever-increasing oil prices in the 1970s and the prospect of further increases in the 1980s have added a degree of importance, and some would say even urgency, to the discussion.

Recession and financial contraction were required to contain the inflation that followed the first oil shock of 1973. The middle to latter 1970s were years of successful growth recovery and renewed balance of payments surpluses. However, in late 1978 Japanese wholesale prices again began to rise, and in mid-1979 the balance of payments moved into deficit, where it remained into 1980. These turns for the worse can be explained largely by rising oil prices; Japan imports 99.8 percent of all petroleum consumed. The policy debate of the early 1980s, then, has been how best to respond to this on-going challenge to Japan's basic international strategy.

The expansionists point out that growth, productivity increases, and successful competition abroad all go together and represent the soundest long-run strategy for both beating inflation and strengthening the balance of payments. The argument is based on certain fundamentals of economics. Technical change and hence increased productivity seem directly related to the investments that accompany economic expansion. Productivity increase, in turn, is the single most fundamental form of long-run inflation control. If an economy can produce the same output with reduced inputs, the rising costs of those inputs are not completely passed on. Growth proponents in the economic policy debate also maintain that an aggressive program is the best way to expand exports and hence strengthen the international value of the yen. Because oil is priced only in dollars, a continually strengthening yen would cushion the domestic impact of price rises.

The emphasis on growth is strongest among industry representatives and the government's Ministry of International Trade and Industry. More cautious forces, however, are represented by the Ministry of Finance, the Bank of Japan, and the Economic Planning Agency. They argue that priority should be given to stabilization policies involving tight credit restrictions and other monetary controls to dampen inflationary spirals set off by injections of increasingly higher-priced oil. In the late 1970s and early 1980s their arguments by and large prevailed. Budgets were cut, and the rediscount rate was set at a record-matching high of 9 percent.

With recession in the United States, the financial conservatives came under pressures to allow some expansion, but they maintained that the only way to reduce the 8 percent inflation rate was with continued tight credit and monetary controls. Such arguments are also founded in respected economic logic. Inflation itself can be seen as the root cause of most other difficulties: inflation weakens foreign competitiveness, also leads to a weaker international value for the yen, and discourages normal financial operations. Inflation can also be seen as the simple result of too much purchasing power, money and credit, in the economy. And since the only accepted cure for inflation in a free-market economy is reduction of that purchasing power, Japan's financial conservatives represent a strong and consistent policy for economic health.

And so the policy debates within the Liberal Democratic Party at the beginning of the 1980s reflected the two major policy choices offered by orthodox economic theory: more growth or more price control. There can be no final resolution of such a debate, and intermediate solutions will most likely be determined by world economic conditions rather than by factional political victories. World recession or depression will strengthen the position of growth advocates. Renewed growth in the United States and elsewhere will justify more cautious financial policies. Perhaps even more importantly, whatever the resulting policy shifts, they will involve well-thought-out compromises between both camps. Many recent developments point to Japan's ability to maintain both increased productivity and effective controls on excessive purchasing power. In a world of both rising prices and economic slump, Japan seems to be succeeding in maintenance of at least moderate growth as well as only moderate inflation.

For the fiscal year ending in 1980, the Japanese economy did indeed grow at an inflation-adjusted rate of 6.1 percent, largely because of greater-than-expected capital expenditures and export sales. For the following year, however, growth of 4 to 5 percent is expected. That is lower, largely because of monetary contraction both in Japan and in the United States, but it is still respectable in a year when U.S. growth will probably be negative. This same 4 to 5 percent rate is the best guess for Japan's average performance into the mid-1980s.

CHALLENGING WORLD TECHNICAL LEADERSHIP: MICROPROCESSOR SUPERIORITY

Crucial to Japan's continued moderate growth and future balance of payments health is the strength of her competitive position in the emerging major world markets of the 1980s. This implies that Japan must continue her climb to higher levels of technical sophistication, a climb she began with textiles in the Meiji era and then evolved through stages of machinery, iron and steel, chemicals, motorcycles, radios, cameras, televisions, automobiles, and most recently computer components and systems. There is evidence that Japan is no longer climbing but has rather reached the top of the world technological pyramid. This arrival at the frontier of world technology is probably the clearest sign of Japan's new place in world economic leadership.

The Japanese move to the forefront of advanced world technology is most vividly seen in basic semiconductor "chip" technology. By 1980 their work was actually superior to American, both in terms of quality and in some kinds of innovation. This poses a tremendous challenge to American producers of very large-scale integrated circuits, for no less than considerable portions of the most important new market of the 1980s are at stake.

For components such as semiconductor integrated circuits, reliability, that is, failure rates, is a very important consideration for potential buyers. By the 1980s, Japan had been provided with clear proof that her computer memory chips were more reliable than American ones. In a comparison that quickly gained attention within the industry, Hewlett-Packard, one of the largest American makers of hand-held calculators, small computers, and other scientific instruments, tested over 300,000 memory chips from three American and three Japanese suppliers. The failure rate of the worst Japanese supplier was six times better than the failure rate of the best American supplier. American producers themselves eventually conceded that Japanese mass-produced chips have lower failure rates than American ones and that they may also be better during their useful operating life.

PASSING THE AMERICANS:
A MORE ADVANCED PROCESSOR CHIP

But in addition to quality control, the Japanese have also come to challenge the American position as the leading innovator. In mid-1980 the Japanese announced that they had succeeded in producing the world's largest memory on one chip, 256K, ahead of American efforts to produce one of the same size. Up until then, it had always been the Americans who had come out with the new larger memory chips (meaning larger memory on the same sized chip). The Japanese were always trailing behind, at first by years, but then only by months. In 1980 it was the Americans who were trailing.

Such a combined reputation for both superior quality control and leading innovation could help Japanese producers capture a very large share of the world semiconductor market in the 1980s. Just as iron, steel, coal, and petroleum have been the building blocks of industrial growth in much of the twentieth century, it is very likely that semiconductor chips will become the basic building materials of economic expansion for the remainder of the century and beyond. Everything will be made of them.

The nation that becomes the best supplier of these "raw" components will gain a decided economic edge over those whose output is inferior.

During the middle 1970s the Japanese captured roughly 10 percent of the world market away from American producers, a market valued at as much as $6 billion in 1980. The Japanese share in 1978 was 26 percent, compared to 63 percent for the United States. The more recent advances in Japanese quality and innovation, however, could point to an acceleration of such erosion in American market leadership.

To understand better Japan's possible technological place in the future world economy, it is also useful to note the Japanese strategy for developing the above-mentioned integrated circuit. Just as the American government greatly stimulated semiconductor technology in its space program of the 1960s, so the Japanese government aided its own industry's development of integrated circuits. The Japanese Ministry for International Trade and Industry (MITI) established a Large-Scale Integrated Circuit Project to pool the knowledge of Japan's leading companies. It was information from this project that eventually led to the record-breaking memory circuit. Such cooperation among major Japanese researchers under government aegis is likely to reappear in the 1980s and in following decades, whenever conditions warrant. And from the point of view of American competition, it is difficult to criticize any such strategy that speeds up the world accumulation of useful knowledge.

The Japanese also promise to challenge American leadership in consumer-oriented applications of the microcomputer technology. Just as the Japanese were the first to introduce the hand-held calculator in 1970, in 1980 they were the first to introduce a complete hand-held computer, programmable in BASIC, perhaps the most widespread of computer languages. The miniature computer, selling for less than $125, is an excellent example of the continued aggressiveness of the Japanese in developing mass consumer products from the latest world technology. It is also a good example of the healthy influence of Japanese competition in an American-dominated industry. Some American producers of advanced hand-held calculators tend to slow the timing of new product releases to maximize revenues from earlier lines.

GROWING WORLD COMMERCIAL AND FINANCIAL LEADERSHIP

But technical prowess is only one reason why the Japanese economy will continue to perform well in the coming decade. The Japanese are already showing daring in planning for large-scale international construction projects, they are an increasingly more important provider of world commercial services, strengthening the yen as an international currency, and they are aggressively seeking and winning markets in the poorer countries of the world that will be buying the building blocks of their industrialization during the 1980s and 1990s.

Possible Japanese construction of a second Panama Canal is one dramatic example of how Japan can attempt to increase her share of the world market for shipping and other commercial services. Japan's exports have always included not only manufactured goods, but direct services and other "invisibles." In particular, shipping services and large construction contracts (in the Middle East, for example) have provided Japan with a significant element in her foreign exchange earnings. Sponsorship of or participation in a New Panama Canal project would place Japan in a position assumed by the United States in the beginning of the twentieth century: as an underwriter of improvements in world commercial capacity. The active planning already underway in Japan may be premature, but it symbolizes the aggressive aspirations that will certainly add to her international stature in the 1980s.

The most recent example of growing foreign activity by Japanese banks is the start of a correspondence relation between Japan's huge Agricultural Bank and the Bank of China. The Agricultural Bank is known for its large domestically raised funds, and is also Japan's largest private institutional investor. It is the size of these vailable assets that give the correspondence relationship significance; and although at first it perhaps will only facilitate bilateral trade in agricultural products, it is more likely the beginning of a major role for the bank in financing China's modernization. The bank has already begun making large agricultural loans to Brazil.

Japanese financing of development efforts will also facilitate Japanese sales of producers' goods. For example, India has agreed to a five-year project to produce 2 million watches annually, using a license for Japanese technology. With 1980 Indian production inadequate at roughly 6 million, the new capacity will represent a substantial increase. This is an excellent example of the future expansion of Japanese licensing and producer-goods exports. Japanese construction of an $85 million chemical plant in Singapore by 1988, and new motor vehicle parts factories in Indonesia are other recent examples of Japanese contract commitments or plans for sale of investment goods to developing countries. Hence, in addition to gaining a leading place in advanced world technology, Japan will continue to diversify her international payments position with exports to those areas of the world which themselves are likely to be going through stages of rapid if not "miracle" economic growth in the remainder of the twentieth century.

In sum, Japan is not a "fragile blossom." The motors of her exceptional growth in the past, electronics, motor vehicles, steel, and ships, will continue to support her world economic position. But more significantly, Japan's continued maturation in all areas of economic activity will give her leadership in areas heretofore reserved for Europe and North America. There is not likely to be serious domestic opposition to Japan's basic reexport survival strategy, and what debates do continue to occupy Japanese policymakers will represent an ongoing decision-making process rather than serious discord about strategic alternatives.

Albert Keidel

BIBLIOGRAPHY

Patrick, Hugh, and Henry Rosovsky. "Prospects for the Future and Some Other Implications." In *Asia's New Giant: How the Japanese Economy Works,* Washington, D.C.: Brookings, 1976.

Resource Dependency and Energy Problems

Japan is noted among industrialized countries for its nearly total lack of the raw material resources needed for modern industry. How has Japan dealt with this problem and been able to become such a strong economic power? In particular, how have energy costs and supplies affected the Japanese economy? Where will Japan go in the future with regard to energy development, and will energy problems ever slow down Japan's growth?

The Japanese claim they are a small nation, which of course they are not. What they mean is that their country is cramped and extremely poorly endowed. Although the first reports of Japan to reach Renaissance Europe were ones of fabulous mineral riches, especially gold, Japan is seriously deficient in almost all of the natural resources needed by an industrial society, including petroleum. Her successful strategy has been to reexport enough processed imports to pay for the other imports consumed at home. This strategy dominates Japanese economic policy. It is interesting to note that such international vulnerability greatly strengthens Japan's perceived need for domestic cohesion and sacrifice, and hence, ironically, Japan's paucity of raw materials may itself be one of the secrets to her industrial success.

Most recently, the world energy crises of the 1970s have reemphasized Japan's foreign dependence. Following the basic strategy, Japan has introduced conservation measures and sought alternative energy sources faster than the world's other industrial powers, allowing her to maintain and even strengthen her world competitive position. The real danger from such natural resource "shocks" for Japan, however, is in a sense political. The imposition by foreign governments of excessive quantity restrictions on either imports into or exports out of Japan is disastrous for her basic strategy, and hence Japan's efforts in the future will continue to center on the arrangement of long-run resource procurement agreements and the maintenance of an international atmosphere of free trade sufficient to ensure adequate export sales.

It must be said at this point, however, that Japan's general resource shortage, and her petroleum shortage in particular, are not necessarily all bad, and have probably strengthened Japan's economy in one crucial way. As discussed in other chapters, the most important single element in Japan's extraordinary economic success is perhaps the strong sense of discipline, personal sacrifice, and growth orientation that pervades her work force at all levels, both laboring and managerial. This "extra efficiency" born of an insular psychology the the continual propagation of a "small country" mentality could be the most important causal component of Japan's overall productivity achievement. The resource shortages in general, and the oil shock above all, have served to maintain this internal discipline just when rising incomes and general affluence might otherwise speed its erosion. Hence, the productivity gains from such internal "siege" cohesion represent the transformation of an early growth impediment into an important source of economic strength.

DESPERATE RESOURCE SHORTAGE

Japan's shortage of resources was of course not serious for a pre-modern economy, but as her industries developed during and after the Meiji era, their dependence on imported raw materials, both agricultural and mineral, also grew apace. Early in her industrialization drive, Japan actually exported some of the few raw materials available domestically: gold and silver at first, as well as coal, copper, and silk. This is the normal pattern for a developing economy: the export of unprocessed or semi-processed raw materials in return for imports of machinery and finished consumer goods.

For Japan, however, the number of exportable items was very small, their extraction expensive, and their supply limited. Only silk exports, the dominant single earner of Japanese foreign exchange into the 1920s, can truly be considered representative of such a primary export pattern. With the disappearance of the American silk market in the Great Depression, Japan completed her transition to virtual total dependence on foreign sources of all primary products for industrial inputs as well as dependence on their reexport in processed form for her sources of foreign exchange.

It is difficult to convey a sense of just how poor Japan's endowment of resources really is. For practical purposes, she has no iron ore or coking coal; there is essentially no lead, bauxite, or tin; no nickel, tungsten, platinum, cobalt, or vanadium. There is some copper, but it is expensive, and there is a little zinc and manganese. There is no oil to speak of, and very little natural gas. Japanese coal mined for fuel is heavily subsidized because of the mediocre quality, thin discontinuous seams, and a host of other geological difficulties. Japan is mountainous, but the river runoffs are so steep and short-lived that there is poor storage for reservoirs; what hydroelectric plants there are must be backed up with thermal units for seasonal use. And finally, Japan has so little cultivatable land that it is completely uneconomical to use it for cotton, sheep, or other textile fiber sources.

The seriousness of Japan's resource shortfall can be seen in Table 3.3, which gives raw material imports as a percentage of total domestic use.

TABLE 3.3

Imports of Selected Raw Materials, 1971

Product	Imports as a Percent of Total Consumption
Crude Petroleum	99.7
Coal	58.4
Iron Ore	99.3
Manganese Ore	84.4
Copper Ore	94.2
Zinc Ore	78.5
Lead Ore	100.0
Bauxite	100.0
Wool	100.0
Cotton	100.0
Rubber	27.4[a]

[a] Imports of natural rubber as a percent of consumption of natural plus synthetic rubber.

Source: Japanese Bureau of Statistics, presented in Lawrence Krause and Sueo Sekiguchi, "Japan and the World Economy." In *Asia's New Giant: How the Japanese Economy Works*, edited by Hugh Patrick and Henry Rosovsky. (Washington, D.C.: Brookings, 1976), p. 386.

Used with permission. Edward F. Denison and William K. Chung, *How Japan's Economy Grew So Fast: The Sources of Postwar Expansion* (Washington, D.C.: Brookings Institution, 1976), p. 40. Copyright © 1976 by the Brookings Institution.

SUBSTITUTE FOR NATURAL RESOURCES:
VALUE-ADDED EXPORTS

When all is said and done, Japan seems a very unlikely candidate for industrial leadership in the world. And yet, one of her few great natural gifts also points to the solution she has found for her situation: her geographical location is ideal for trade and commerce. Rather than being landlocked like the Soviet Union, she is a nation of islands on one of the most important great circle routes of the world. What is more, her harbors and habitable plains face the Pacific Ocean rather than the Sea of Japan, and the Inland Sea gives her a coastal lake for protected domestic shipping between many of the most densely populated regions. Trade and commerce are Japan's substitutes for natural resources, and the diligence of her labor force, strengthened by perceived national deprivation, is the wealth she sells in the world.

As mentioned at the outset, Japan's basic strategy is to import raw materials, add to their value by processing them as much as possible in Japan, and then reexport them to foreign markets. The reexported raw materials, of course, have paid for themselves. The value added, exported in the form of improvements and processing, is used to pay for imported raw materials that are not reexported. In this way, Japan's only pure export is the value added, the labor of Japanese workers.

It is fairly clear that the only way such a strategy can work is if other nations are willing to part with their raw materials and if they are in turn willing to buy Japan's exports. Ideally, this should always be the case, but in fact, world crises in raw materials supply, world recession, or both can compel nations to husband supplies, protect sources with political agreements, and exclude foreign products to appease domestic labor. These are the threats to continued Japanese economic progress, and because they are in essence political problems, Japan's international efforts to maintain her economic position require sensitivity to the political impact of even her own success.

Perhaps a helpful way to understand Japan's approach to her resource shortage and its inherent dangers is to consider the feudal analogy of commoner merchant classes. These townspeople depended on the sale of their value-added for a source of livelihood. Historically, landlord and nobility demand for urban products and services was great, and the merchant towns often ended up creditors, and hence threatened to gain eventual control of the land and other assets usually "reserved" by the feudal order for nobility. If the feudal nobility was powerful enough, it could resort to various forms of legal discrimination and physical abuse directed against the merchant groups. If the merchant groups were a racial minority, the legal and administrative controls and "corrections" were particularly easy to apply. The Chinese merchants in Southeast Asia and the Jews in Europe come immediately to mind. One might add that the situation of merchants in feudal Tokugawa Japan also fits the pattern described above. The merchant class had to proceed very carefully and make careful alliances with the nobles and samurai who legally held the power to find them guilty of some technical infraction and confiscate their wealth.

Just as merchants in feudal times had to pay careful attention to the political environment of their economic activities and the dangerous consequences of excessive success, so the Japanese have come to pay close attention to the world environment and the impact on it of their own economic ascendency. This posture is an integral part of the reexport strategy on which Japan has based her livelihood.

THE OIL CRISIS AND JAPAN'S NATURAL ENERGY SHORTAGE

This potentially precarious reexport strategy has been visible most recently in Japan's response to the world crises in crude oil supply following the 1973 Arab-Israeli War and the 1979 Iranian Revolution. Of all the industrial powers, Japan is by far the most dependent on imported forms of energy. The shortages of the 1970s signaled serious crises. In general, the Japanese have responded with impressive conservation efforts in both industry and in homes. But the dangers of world recession and discriminatory petroleum rationing in the event of hostilities in the Middle East both represent potentially serious threats to Japan's economic stability.

With the introduction of cheap supertanker transport, energy has become the world's single most important resource requirement for industrialization. By 1973 petroleum had come to dominate a world energy consumption pattern once shared more equally with coal. With her many ocean ports, few domestic energy interest groups to protect, and the opportunity for total reconstruction, Japan, even more than other economic powers, embraced petroleum as the energy basis for her industrialization. Hence, Japan was stunned by the oil shock more than other nations, and certainly much more than the United States. This is because not only is Japan more dependent on imported energy than Western economies, but petroleum is also a larger share of that energy consumption, and in terms of petroleum imports themselves, Japan depends more heavily than other countries on the unpredictable Middle East for her supplies. In all, Japan is the most vulnerable industrial petroleum consumer in the world. This vulnerability is seen most succinctly in Table 3.4.

TABLE 3.4

International Energy Dependence, 1977

Country	Imported Energy per Total Consumption	Oil per Total Energy Consumption	Imported Oil per Total Oil Consumption
Japan	88.2%	71.9%	99.8%
United States	22.1	46.3	47.4
Great Britain	25.3	44.2	64.2
Canada[a]	−3.9	43.9	32.1
France	75.1	64.3	99.1
Italy	80.8	68.3	99.0
West Germany	55.7	53.0	94.8

[a]Canada is a net energy exporter.

Source: International Energy Agency and Ministry of International Trade and Industry, as reported in Foreign Press Center, *Facts and Figures of Japan, 1980*, (Tokyo: Foreign Press Center, 1980), pp. 70–71.

The data in Table 3.4 show that Japan imports almost all (88.2 percent) of her energy, and certainly a much larger share than the United States (22.1 percent). Furthermore, oil is a larger part of total energy consumption than it is for any other economy shown (column 2); virtually all (99.85 percent) is imported. Comparatively and absolutely, then, Japan is a prisoner of the international oil situation.

Japan's precarious predicament is seen even more clearly when we notice the degree to which she depends on the Middle East for her oil imports. Unlike the United States and Western Europe, who get significant portions of their oil from Africa and Latin America, data for recent years show that Japan depnds on the Middle East for 78 percent of her oil, the rest obtained from Southeast Asia. In comparison, only 28 percent of U.S. oil imports come from the Middle East. Combining these data with those in Table 3.4, we find that a full 56 percent of all Japanese energy comes from the Middle East, while the same figure for the United States is a mere 6 percent.

Japan's relative weakness is also reflected in her international market position. International supply and demand of oil is managed with a combination of long-term contracts on the one hand and ad hoc purchases and sales on the "spot" market on the other hand. European access to

African and Latin American oil is in large part the result of historical relations formalized in long-term purchase agreements. Until the early 1970s, Japan, too, relied on long-term agreements, mostly with the principal international oil companies, known as the "majors." In 1972 they supplied Japan with 77.5 percent of her oil, but by 1980 the majors could provide only 44.4 percent, requiring her to resort to government-to-government purchases from the Middle East and to purchases on the spot market. Such spot purchases had become as much as 10 percent of Japanese purchases by 1979—a measure of growing instability in Japan's petroleum supplies.

We can now see clearly the current and future threats to the Japanese economy as a result of her lack of domestic petroleum resources. These are political interruptions of oil supplies on the one hand, and world recession on the other. World recession, of course, can itself be an indirect result of world oil crises, because oil price rises can trigger general inflation, the only known cure for which is deliberate economic contraction and unemployment. If such contractions are severe enough, the protectionist pressures within Japan's foreign markets might jeopardize the basic strategy of reliance on industrial reexports.

On the other hand, prolonged war in the Middle East could be disastrous for Japan, since without oil much of her industrial activity would have to stop. In anticipation of such an emergency, the Japanese have been stockpiling petroleum for the last decade, until by early 1980 there was enough stockpiled to supply Japan with just under 100 days of industrial and government activity, a little more than three months.

ENERGY CONSERVATION AND JAPAN'S IMPROVING COMPETITIVE EDGE

The increasingly higher price of oil, however, does not itself imply crisis for Japanese industry. As long as the impact of price increases is worldwide, Japanese reexports will still be competitive. The prices of oil-intensive products produced anywhere in the world must all go up in step. The only potential differences would result from unequal success in efforts to conserve energy in production methods. It is in just these efforts, however, that the Japanese have excelled.

More than the other industrial powers, Japan has been able to produce the same outputs with lower and lower input requirements of oil and other energy sources. A comparison of total primary energy consumption to total Gross National Product shows that in the five years from 1973 to 1978 Japan reduced its energy consumption per Gross National Product unit by 14 percent; the United States reduction was only 3 percent.

Conservation is impressive in absolute terms as well. By 1978 Japan used less energy per dollar of output than the other industrial powers, including West Germany. The same superiority can be seen in the energy efficiency of individual industries. Data for 1976 show that in iron and steel, for example, the Japanese use far less heat per ton (4.8 billion calories) than the other major producers (the United States uses 6.8 billion calories, Germany 5.7 billion). In other industrial areas, such as chemicals and cement, the results are similar.

The basic strategy of financing necessary domestic consumption with value-added exports has also spurred Japan to reduce those "necessary" levels of domestic raw materials consumption. And in fact, Japan has been much more successful than the other industrial powers in curtailing domestic petroleum consumption. In 1978 Japan used only 42 percent of her energy consumption for nonindustrial uses (transport, residential, commercial, and other uses); the United States, in contrast, used 68 percent outside of industry.

In transportation, while actually enforcing much higher emission pollution standards than the United States, Japan has succeeded in raising automobile fuel efficiency far above what it is in the United States. It is true that climatic and geographical differences greatly favor fuel conservation in Japan (for example, dense population patterns favor fuel-efficient public transportation), but these are not sufficient reasons for the great gaps in per capita energy and oil consumption that persist. Table 3.5 shows a quick comparison.

TABLE 3.5

Per Capita Energy and Oil Consumption
(in tons of oil equivalent per person)

Country	Energy	Oil
Japan	3.11	2.26
United States	8.44	4.04
West Germany	4.44	2.32
United Kingdom	3.79	1.68

Source: International Energy Agency, as reported in unpublished statistics of the Japanese Embassy, Washington, D.C., 1980.

The figures show that Japan has followed the European pattern of energy consumption rather than that of the United States. Whether in home and office heating, transportation, or any other consumption use, the Japanese have been able to enforce significant conservation and hence reduce the burden of necessary exports and required foreign exchange earnings. These conservation efforts, both in industry and in domestic consumption, represent the continued application of Japan's basic re-export strategy for coping with the fundamental problem of overall natural resource deficiency.

Finally, Japan has committed herself to the development of nuclear power as a long-run alternative source of energy, but major dependence on petroleum is planned at least until 1990. By 1980 Japan had 19 nuclear power plants with total capacity of 13,000 megawatts, and the first fast-breeder prototype reactor began tests in 1977. Sixteen additional reactors are either under construction or in the planning stage. These developments, however, do not promise relief from energy import pressures any time in the intermediate future, and so Japan's energy and general resource poverty will continue to dictate her policy response.

In sum, successful conservation both in production for reexport and in "necessary" home use have maintained and will continue to maintain Japan's world competitive lead. The oil and other energy crises do not threaten Japan's ability to compete and survive in the world market. In fact, the "underdog" psychology reinforced by such severe foreign dependence probably strengthens Japan's economy in vital ways. The real threats to economic security are the direct and indirect political ones outlined above: short and intermediate range cutoffs in oil supplies from the Middle East, and protectionist policies in world markets in an atmosphere of world recession.

Summarized differently, Japan is extremely poorly endowed in virtually all industrial raw materials, especially petroleum. Her successful strategy has been to market value-added exports in the form of reexported processed raw material imports. This strategy has proved surprisingly buoyant in the face of repeated oil crises and will most likely continue to be so. However, the threat of world economic contraction, war in the Middle East, or both leaves Japan in a particularly vulnerable position. It goes without saying that Japan will continue her successful conservation measures, but the more important part of her strategy must be to diversify the geographical sources of her energy and stabilize them in the form of long-term agreements. At the same time, she must continue efforts to tread carefully in her penetration of foreign markets to avoid permanent protectionist backlash.

Albert Keidel

BIBLIOGRAPHY

Ackerman, Edward A. *Japan's Natural Resources and their Relation to Japan's Economic Future*. Chicago: University of Chicago, 1953.

Caldwell, Martha. "Japan's Policy Response to the Oil Crisis: Consensus and Contradiction in Petroleum Policy Making." Ph.D. dissertation, University of Wisconsin–Madison, 1980.

Committee for Energy Policy Promotion. *Japan and the Oil Problem*. Tokyo, 1980.

4

JAPAN'S TRADE COMPETITIVENESS

Japanese exports have become increasingly successful in recent years in the markets of the industrialized countries of Europe and North America as well as in developing nations. Reflecting the demand for Japanese products, Japanese exports rose from 3 percent of world trade in 1960 to 8 percent in 1978. As a testimony to this trade success, one has only to observe the current proposals in the European Economic Community (EEC) countries and in the United States and Canada to limit popular Japanese imports, such as automobiles, because of their disruptive effects on internal markets.

It was long thought that the success of Japanese products, i.e., their competitiveness, reflected low domestic labor costs. Solomon B. Levine addresses this view, and demonstrates persuasively that wages in Japan are now much closer to those of other industrialized nations than is popularly believed. While Japanese labor was indeed comparatively cheap in the 1950s and 1960s, wages in Japan trebled in the 1970s to a level equal to that of France and exceeding the comparable British figure. Reflecting the increased wage levels, labor costs in Japan were roughly two-thirds of those in the United States as of 1978; probably the gap has closed even further since that time. (Also, fringe benefits are a similar percentage of labor costs in these two countries, and the rising relative costs of labor in Japan reflected a combination of declines in actual hours worked, rigidity of nonwage parts of labor costs—such as fringe benefits—and increases in wages.)

A second view of Japanese competitiveness in foreign markets argues in its simplest form that Japan can be likened to a corporation (Japan,

Incorporated) wherein government and business work in tandem like components of the same firm. According to this idea, Japan's Ministry of International Trade operates like a firm's management, determining its business policies and underwriting its weaknesses with supportive economic policies.

While Japan has never operated as monolithically or effectively as the Japan, Incorporated image would suggest, it is true that the Japanese government gave considerable assistance to industrial development in the 1950s and 1960s. The government sponsored a protectionist foreign trade and investment policy in this period, in part because of severe foreign exchange limitations and in part because of a protectionist outlook. As Bradley Richardson reports, there were very extensive quota restrictions on imports in the 1950s, as well as high tariffs and severe limitations on imports of foreign capital. These protectionist trade policies were supplemented by various corporate tax benefits for exporters. However, the supports for Japan's industries were gradually withdrawn during the 1960s as both government and business leaders became convinced of the need for trade liberalization. As a result, by the mid-1970s, Japan's foreign trade policies resembled those of other industrialized countries: import restrictions affected only a handful of items, mostly farm goods, and foreign investments were freed from most kinds of control. Japan's tariff structure also came to resemble that of other industrialized nations, and Japan could not be seriously accused of protectionism, even though the protectionist image lingered in the foreign media.

Still, cultural and institutional differences between Japan and the other industrialized nations continued to produce frictions even after protectionism had died. Japan's rigid banking control laws and demanding product tests were seen by businessmen in other countries as governmental "nontariff barriers"; restrictive procurement policies on the part of public corporations like the Japan Telephone and Telegraph Company were viewed similarly. Informal import cartels were also said to exist in a number of raw materials sectors. Still, Japanese also found much to complain about in the trade policies of the United States and some European countries, and it would seem that allegations on all sides of nontariff barriers would be a continuing feature of world trade as industrial markets became increasingly competitive.

Most contemporary analyses of Japan's world competitiveness in many product sectors emphasize the importance of her technological improvement programs and related high productivity. By the 1970s Japanese plants produced up to 350 motorcycles per man-year in contrast with outputs of 11 motorcycles per man-year from the U.S. Harley Davidson and 14 units from Britain's NVT group. Similarly, the time required to produce a color television set in the United States and Europe was from two to three times that needed in Japan, and Japanese factories could turn out far more cars per labor input than plants in some European countries.

Yoshi Tsurumi surveys some of the general features of Japanese R & D policies that have contributed to the currently high levels. In the early periods of development—the 1950s in some industries and the 1960s in others—the Japanese government carefully allocated foreign exchange and import licenses to technological imports deemed needed for key-sector development. The key-sector approach to technology imports plus rapid diffusion of technology among domestic firms and subsequent technological innovation in Japan meant that Japan was able to "leapfrog" in a number of industries from the position of follower to that of world leader in a relatively short period of time. Indeed, the past 30 years has witnessed a process by which Japanese industries first imported foreign technology, then contributed important technological innovations, and finally became net exporters of technology. In some areas the Japanese breakthroughs came because of government-industry joint research projects and other forms of government help. But Japanese companies themselves have spent heavily on research and development and continue to do so in their efforts to attain domestic and world market leadership.

Both cheaper labor and governmental leadership were undoubtedly major factors in Japan's competitiveness during the 1950s and even into the 1960s. Yet, the major factor in Japan's foreign trade success must be recognized to be its technological leadership, particularly process technology, which is reflected in high productivity, superior quality control levels in many product areas, and in the development of products desired in markets throughout the world.

Research and Development

Where do the technological strength and weakness of Japanese industries lie? What are their research and development (R & D) policies?

RESEARCH AND DEVELOPMENT ACTIVITIES AND TECHNOLOGY

In order to grasp what the roles of technology are in the industrialization processes of any country, we should define technology since kinds of technology have different impacts on a nation. We have found that the following three types of technology offer useful guides to policymakers.

Product-related technologies emanate from identifiable products, which are new to countries. These technologies are often the proprietary possessions of the firms and/or individuals who invented them.

Production process-related technologies stem from identifiable manufacturing processes. These technologies are also often proprietary property unique to the firms and/or individuals who invented them. Although specific products are concrete results of production process-related technologies, the company or individual inventor has the technological advantage of possessing unique manufacturing processes not held by local firms or by foreign competitors.

Institution-related technologies result from the experience from a specific technology related to products as well as to production processes of firms. This institutional skill is difficult to separate from the firm and employees performing it. The firm's way of organizing and motivating employees to produce specific products or services is but one example of such technology. One example in this category is "management skill."

Naturally, the operational demarcations among these three categories of technologies are often blurred. The successful utilization of production process-related technologies depends upon the successful manipulation of institution-related technologies in the inevitable interaction between worker and machine. And product-related technologies, of course, require specific methods to produce them. However, these specific production methods can be improved by firms and individuals other than the inventors of the product-related technologies.

R&D activities refer to the specific activities of researchers in industry, government (and military), and academia who are aiming at producing combinations of the above three categories of technological innovation. Today, when firms are involved in the rapidly changing business and political environment, and when technological frontiers are far more complex than decades ago, the concerted efforts of a company's R&D activities require well-coordinated work of various research groups representing different research areas. This is why R&D activities today are significantly different from the individual "tinkerers' activities" of the past. As a result, the financial risks of R&D activities are becoming greater and the outcome of such activities, more uncertain. The lead time required for the fruition of R&D activities is becoming longer and longer.

When the R&D activities of a company's laboratories produce either product-related technological innovations or production process-related innovations, the company's own institution-related technology—its management skill—determines the necessary lead time to commercialize these new products of their R&D efforts from the laboratory prototype to their ultimate contributions to production and sales of the company.

CHARACTERISTICS OF JAPANESE TECHNOLOGY

Industrialized nations differ in their ability to produce industrial technology. For example, the United States is noted for its many innovations and inventions of product-related technology. Japan, on the other hand, produces technological achievements dominated by production process-related technology. The United Kingdom has shown a balanced achievement of both product-related and production process-related technologies. France and West Germany have shown somewhat greater achievements in production process-related technologies.

There is nothing mysterious about these differences. The R&D activities of companies are closely related to the social and economic stimuli of different countries. For example, such economic attributes of the United States as high wages and high income have motivated many American firms to invent labor-saving products (for both industrial and consumer use) and luxury household appliances geared to high-income groups. On the other hand, Japan's efforts to catch up with the United States have motivated Japanese firms to invent such production process-related technology as mass-production systems designed to cut production costs of products without sacrificing product quality. At the same time, since Japan must import various expensive industrial raw materials, Japanese firms have focused their R&D activities on technological innovations that would save vital raw materials or on the utilization of raw materials of diverse grade without sacrificing the quality of their final products.

In Japan, since the 1950s, over two-thirds of R&D expenditures have been made by private industry. This is a marked contrast to the United States where over two-thirds of R&D expenditures are made by the government and the military. As a result, Japanese R&D activities are often typed as being particularly effective in the commercialization of general technological and scientific knowledge.

Since World War II, Japanese industries have continued to upgrade their technological capabilities. First, massive infusions of foreign (notably American) technologies took hold as firm after firm concluded technological licensing agreements with American and other foreign companies. Once they absorbed these technologies, Japanese firms went on to adapt these foreign technologies to the socioeconomic conditions of Japan. After acquiring this adaptive capability, Japanese firms moved on to the ultimate stage of producing their own truly innovative products and production processes.

A case in point is the Japanese color television industry. During the 1950s, Japanese companies absorbed the technology of black and white television sets. At that time, their technological capability was considered

10 to 15 years behind the United States. By the mid-1960s, however, Japanese firms had mastered the technology of color television sets and caught up with the product-related technology of their American competitors. From the mid-1960s to the early 1970s, Japanese television manufacturers concentrated on producing incremental innovations in the product-related technology of color televisions as well as on refining their production processes to mass-produce their color television sets with a commitment to "zero defects." Sony's Trinitron TV set epitomizes these efforts in both product- and production process-related technology. By the end of the 1960s, Japanese firms like Sony and Panasonic leapfrogged their American competitors in the field of color video cassette recorders.

Similar stories can be told about the automobile, steel, computer, and semiconductor industries in Japan. The industrial growth of Japan after World War II was made possible by the cumulative technological innovations of Japanese firms.

TABLE 4.1

Ratios of R&D Expenditures to Gross National Product in Japan, 1948–78

Year	Ratio	R&D Personnel
1948	0.3%	14,500
1953	0.5	26,633
1957	0.9	52,077
1960	1.2	82,149
1965	1.3	117,596
1968	1.5	157,612
1970	1.7	172,002
1975	2.2	192,115
1978	2.4	205,668

Note: R&D personnel include full-time researchers in the industry and government only, excluding research support personnel and researchers at colleges and universities.

Source: Compiled by the author from *Keizai Tokei Nempa*, 1950–78, Bank of Japan; *Kagaku Gigutsu Makasho*, 1970–78, Agency of Science and Technology.

The steady increase in R&D activities in Japan can be seen in Table 4.1, which summarizes the ratios of aggregate R&D expenditures to the Gross National Product for the years 1948–78. Since Japan's Gross National Product increased rapidly, compounding 8 to 12 percent per year from the end of the 1950s through the early 1970s, R&D expenditures easily doubled every five years.

DOMESTIC DIFFUSION OF TECHNOLOGICAL INNOVATIONS

In addition to the level of R&D activity, the speed with which any technological innovation spreads from one firm to the next determines the total technological level of a nation. This domestic diffusion of technological innovation is often the key to the industrial development of a nation. The new technologies that are absorbed from abroad by certain firms spread domestically through the competitive imitation process. Likewise, domestic technological innovations developed by certain firms are soon imitated by their competitors.

The government can encourage a rapid diffusion of technological innovations through such means as patent regulations, sponsorships of industrial and technological exhibitions throughout the country, and general exhortation of inventions and technological innovations.

Since the 1870s when Japan embarked on industrial growth through massive infusion of Western technologies, the domestic diffusion rate of technological innovations in Japan has been characterized as very rapid. Fierce competition among private firms and entrepreneurs underlies this fast rate of domestic diffusion of new technologies. Since Japanese firms have long been accustomed to dynamic competition at home and abroad, they are alert to new market and technological developments worldwide. New market opportunities at home and abroad perceived by innovative firms and entrepreneurs trigger their concerted R&D efforts.

RESEARCH AND DEVELOPMENT POLICIES
OF JAPANESE INDUSTRIES

The R&D policies of Japan are tied to targeted commercialization of new scientific and technological knowledge. The government also scans the world and points industries in the direction of new technological frontiers they should conquer. In order to expand these technological frontiers, government research institutes often carry out joint R&D projects for basic development projects with selected private firms when national goals demand concerted efforts to pool technological and financial resources. Such efforts to pool information and basic R&D efforts are closely linked to the specific industrial policies of the nation.

In fact, the R&D policies of Japan have been largely guided by the long-term "supply management" of the Japanese government. New bellwether industries are chosen by the government and private sectors to receive the government's preferential allotment of such scarce resources as capital, technology, and guaranteed market (sometimes government purchases act as an economic primer). This economic planning with the government only indicating the direction of Japan's industrial development has helped Japanese private industries target their own growth goals and gear their R&D efforts to these goals. The ultimate risks associated with R&D activities will have to be absorbed by private firms undertaking them.

The expansion in scope and depth of Japan's R&D activities was made possible by national educational policies that supplied increasing numbers of trained scientists and engineers. The fact that since the 1870s Japan has been emphasizing industrial development through improvements of human resources (bottom-up types of education) has enabled Japanese industries to undertake the expansive tasks of complex R&D activities.

RETRAINING OF PRODUCTION WORKERS

The fruits of these R&D efforts would be wasted unless they were promptly commercialized. This process of commercialization requires the cooperation of production workers in moving the R&D products from the laboratory onto the actual production floors and into sales activities. New products and new production processes require constant retraining of production workers, engineers, and marketing personnel. More important, an in-plant atmosphere that permits engineers to mingle and work closely with rank-and-file production workers may well be a key to the commercialization of R&D fruits. Such an atmosphere, in which close consultation and shared goals and responsibilities are encouraged among research and development, marketing, and production groups, will determine the success of the commercialization of R&D fruits (see Chapter 1 for the discussion of corporate organization in Japan). Without their commitment to product quality and the improvement of production processes, no firm can succeed in bringing R&D products to the markets at home and abroad.

As compared with American competitors, Japanese firms have always emphasized constant retraining of rank-and-file production workers and motivated them to participate in the perpetual improvement of their production processes. In fact, the cumulative training costs of Japanese rank-and-file workers may be added to total research and development expenditures of their firms if we were to devise a gross index of Japan's overall R&D activities.

Moreover, effective R&D efforts require the long-term growth commitment of the firm's management. If management is merely interested in such short-term profit performance indicators as quarterly profits and earnings per share, such strategic investments as R&D activities and continuous retraining of managers, engineers, and rank-and-file employees are likely to be deemphasized in the interest of short-term profit performance. And without long-term commitment by rank-and-file employees and engineers to the growth of their firm, their retraining costs will be wasted when they leave their firm for better opportunities elsewhere.

THE FUTURE OF JAPAN'S
RESEARCH AND DEVELOPMENT EFFORTS

From the early 1970s, it became increasingly apparent that Japanese firms were forced to emphasize their own independent and innovative R&D activities as their past licensors, notably American firms, grew reluctant to sell their new and proprietary technology except in cross-licensing agreements. Japanese firms are now showing a fair degree of success in innovative R&D efforts as reflected in the increasing exports of Japanese proprietary technology.

Japanese technology that has found eager purchasers in developing countries, most notably in Asia, is distinguishable from that purchased by industrialized nations. The recent fruits of Japanese R&D efforts in the fields of electronics, automobiles, chemical and petrochemical products and production processes have been mainly exported to the United States and Europe. New semiconductors, such as diodes, and synthetic paper are being licensed to American and European firms. And newer production processes such as operational know-how of cold strip milling by steel plants and the production expertise of steel fabrication are also sold by Japanese firms to American companies. In contrast, older technologies such as drawing wires and standard machine tools are purchased by firms located in developing countries.

In addition, the increased technological capabilities of Japanese firms have permitted many firms to move their new technologies to the United States and elsewhere through direct investments. In the case of Japanese firms opening manufacturing plants in the United States and elsewhere, they are groping their way to adapt Japanese management skill to the American environment. This international transfer of Japanese production process-related technologies also requires the transfer of the key elements of Japanese management pratices—the basis of the corporate culture needed for the successful adaptation of Japanese production processes to the United States scene.

Yoshi Tsurumi

BIBLIOGRAPHY

Tsurumi, Yoshi. *Transfer of Technology and Foreign Trade: A Case of Japan, 1950–1965*. New York: Arno Press, 1980.

Cheap Labor

A few years ago Japan's economic success at home and in export markets was attributed in part to the cheapness of labor. But recently this situation is said to have changed. Just what is the situation of Japan's labor market in comparison with that of other countries, and will Japan ever import cheap labor as Germany and other northern European countries have done?

WAGES AND LABOR COSTS IN JAPAN

The phrase "cheap labor" conjures up an image of workers receiving wages close to the subsistence level while working extra long hours. Such an image may have been somewhat correct for Japan in the years before and just after World War II but has not been a true depiction for the past two decades. Japan's economic success at home and in export markets cannot be seriously attributed to low wages and long hours. Unquestionably, Japan's level of real wages, including monetary fringe benefits, has been rising steadily during the past two decades and, translated into dollars, is now close to that of the United States and of the most industrially advanced countries of Western Europe. With the appreciation of the yen against the dollar, the rise has been especially rapid during the 1970s. According to the Japan Ministry of Labor, real hourly earnings of Japanese production workers in manufacturing enterprises with five or more employees shot up from less than one-fourth in 1970 to more than two-thirds of the American average by 1978. This advance occurred even though in monetary terms U.S. hourly wages themselves climbed about two-thirds since 1970. In the same period hourly wages in Japanese manufacturing leaped almost three times. The story is repeated to a greater or lesser degree when comparisons are made with West Germany, the United Kingdom, France, and other countries. In fact, by 1978 average hourly earnings in Japanese manufacturing actually exceeded the British figure and were about equal to the French. While some may dispute the statistics because a number of rough assumptions have to be made to undertake the computations and comparisons, the general trend is clear: Japan is no longer a low-wage country.

Nor are labor costs low on the average. Wage earnings alone do not include all the items that make up labor costs paid for in whole or part by employers. There are also fringe benefits such as pensions, retirement pay, children's allowances, unemployment and health insurance, workmen's accident compensation, training expense, meals, housing, recreation, medical facilities, and the like. Some of these are required by law; others by agreement, work rules, or custom. Fringes vary considerably country by country. For Japan, the Ministry of Labor estimates that in 1978 fringes added at least 19 percent to cash wages—a little above the extra cost for fringes estimated for the United States. As a percent of wages, the legally required payments in Japan slightly exceed those in the United States; but in both cases they are somewhat less than half of all the fringe benefits paid. Neither country comes close to matching either West Germany or France, where legally required fringes as a percent of wages reach to more than 20 and 30 percent respectively (but both Germany and France are quite low for fringes not mandated by law).

However, comparisons such as the above require careful analysis. For example, they reflect differences in demographic patterns. It is likely, for example, that Japan's labor force, which is now comparatively young, will age rapidly in the next few years. As a result, under the Japanese system of shared contributions by employers and employees, pension and retirement allowance costs in Japan should rise substantially. Housing for employees also represents comparatively large burdens on Japanese companies.

Total labor costs in Japanese enterprises with 30 or more workers each averaged $1,253 per month in 1978 (using the average exchange rate for the year). On an hourly basis per production worker in manufacturing, they stood at about two-thirds the American and West German levels, almost the same as France, and nearly 50 percent above Great Britain.

DECLINING HOURS

One reason for the rapid climb in hourly wages and labor costs in Japan is the sharp decline in the average hours worked per week, month, and year since the early 1960s without reductions in wages and benefits (most Japanese workers are paid by the month). While the Labor Standards Law (LSL), which was adopted in Japan in 1947 as one of the major labor reforms under the occupation, set (with a few exceptions) a maximum of 8 hours per day and 48 hours per week without required overtime payment, in 1960 the number of hours actually worked per week for firms employing 30 or more workers, on the average, was 46.8, with 5.1 hours of these requiring overtime payment. That was the postwar peak. Average hours of work have declined substantially since that time. The decline took place steadily until the mid-1970s, with ups and downs reflecting the course of the business cycle. By 1978, the average hours worked per week had fallen to 40.4 with 2.8 hours of paid overtime—almost as low as the average for American production workers and less than in the United Kingdom, West Germany, and France. In the largest firms (1,000 or more employees), total hours in fact averaged about 39.8. In small firms with 10 to 29 employees, however, they still were about 46 hours per week. An especially sharp decline in hours worked took place following the 1973–74 oil crisis. As a result, the 40-hour week has become prevalent for close to a majority of all Japanese workers. The five-day work week, at least once or twice a month, now applies to almost three-fourths of Japan's wage and salary earners; and it is widespread on a regular weekly basis among large-size companies.

Another indication of reduced working time in Japan is the increase in paid days off and vacation. Special days off with pay, other than the regular weekly rest day required by law and the five-day work schedule, have been growing. These, like the five-day week, are usually established by collective bargaining agreements or stipulated work rules. They now average a little over 16 days a year, a growth of almost two days since the early 1970s. They usually are granted for national holidays (of which there are 12), year-end and New Year holiday periods, May Day, company anniversary day, and/or summer time (commonly the Buddhist Solstice holiday). In addition, under the law workers are entitled to annual leave with pay. The minimum requirement is six days for workers who have been continuously employed for a year with an 80 percent attendance record. For each additional year of such continuous employment, the law requires one more day of leave with pay up to a maximum of 20. Many firms grant more than the legally required minimums. In fact, days off in firms with 30 or more employees, including annual leave, rest days, and holidays, averaged over 102 in 1977. The spread of paid days off and leaves in Japan has contributed sizably to the reduction of average work hours per week, month, and year in approaching Western levels. Further decreases are expected as the five-day week becomes more and more common. It should be noted, however, that Japanese workers tend not to take off all days to which they are entitled—usually reflecting long-standing habits of work and leisure taking in Japan.

WAGE DIFFERENTIALS IN THE JAPANESE LABOR MARKET

Averages, however, disguise relatively wide disparities in wages and working hours, although the steady rise of the average wage level and decline in hours have led to the narrowing of wage differentials among various types of workers in Japan. Differentials have been notably large in relation to age and length of service, sex, size of firm, and level of education. The continued existence of such differentials probably explains why Japan still gives the impression of remaining a low-wage country.

Some of the most prominent differentials in Japan are those based on age and length of service, more popularly known as the "seniority-based" or nenkō wages. Under the nenkō system, wages, promotions, other benefits are supposed to be rewards for continuous employment in the same firm rather than for work performance or value of a particular job. A 1977 survey of wages by the Ministry of Labor, indeed, shows that male workers in the 15–17 age group earn less than half those in the 35–39 age group and about one-third those in the 50–54 age group. Wage levels drop precipitously after age 55. This is primarily the result of mandatory retirement from a company, ending one's participation in the nenkō system even though a large proportion of older workers do not actually retire but continue to seek paid employment. While there has been a trend among companies toward extending the compulsory retirement age beyond 55, only a tiny percentage of companies have gone beyond age 60. Presumably the nenkō compensation system is an inducement for workers to remain permanently in a firm for most of their career after graduation from school—the so-called "lifetime employment" institution.

It is probably correct to observe that, relative to their productivity, under the nenkō system workers are "underpaid" in the first half of their careers and "overpaid" in the last half up to their retirement between the ages of 55 and 60. However, over this career span, productivity and wages probably equalize. Moreover, nenkō, where practiced, usually does not come in pure form. A substantial portion of a worker's wage may be directly related to the job, performance, ability, or other factors unrelated to length of service.

It should be strongly emphasized, also, that only a minority of the wage and salary earners in Japan—perhaps only about 30 percent of the total—are employed under the nenkō system. Those who are under nenkō are almost entirely males hired by large-scale private enterprises or government agencies as permanent workers from the time they are initially recruited from school. (Workers hired in their mid-career are usually placed at a lower level on the nenkō scale than their counterparts recruited from school.) Almost all temporary, part-time, and casual workers are excluded from this system. Very few women are subject to nenkō, since not only are they often hired as temporary and part-time employees but they usually withdraw from a work force at an early age because of marriage or childbirth to return to work 10 to 20 years later. In the medium and small-scale companies, there is little resembling nenkō: wage workers in these firms are paid primarily for their jobs or skills, in accordance to the labor market; and many are employed as unpaid workers in family-owned work shops.

As in the United States, wage differentials by sex are notable in Japan. Women wage earners now average less than 60 percent of male wage levels. Part of this is due to fewer hours worked than males per week, month, or year—somewhat because of the legal limitations on overtime work. But the main reason for the sex differential is that women largely perform only unskilled or semiskilled jobs (often dubbed "women's work") that have relatively low productivity. Although the law mandates equal work for equal pay regardless of sex, it is infrequent that men and women work at the same jobs. This situation indicates that relatively few females are given training to advance to the more skilled work performed by men. Most are protected, however, by a system of minimum wages under the law.

Level of education in Japan also makes a decided difference in the wages for workers the older they become, especially in the case of males. While most employees tend to be at about the same wage level in their early years whether they are university, high school, or junior high school graduates, or white- or blue-collar workers, after they reach their late twenties differentials emerge in favor of higher educational attainment and continue to grow wider until close to the mandatory retirement age. By the time employees reach their early fifties, male university graduates tend to average about 30 percent above male high school graduates and 50 percent above male junior high school graduates. Roughly speaking, this corresponds to the difference between white- and blue-collar employees. After "retirement," however, the gaps tend to close steadily.

Since the nenkō system is not a prominent feature of smaller-scale firms and since small firms tend to hire larger proportions of females and lesser proportions of workers with advanced education compared to large enterprises, it is not surprising that significant differentials by size of firm exist in Japan. Fundamentally, of course, the differentials reflect differences in labor productivity levels. In the mid-1970s, for example, wages for workers in manufacturing firms with 10 to 49 employees each averaged only about 60 percent of the wages of workers in firms with 1,000 or more employees each. The discrepancy may also be due somewhat to collective bargaining pressures, since unionization in Japan is concentrated primarily in the large-scale enterprises and is relatively infrequent in the smaller-firm sector. Size-of-firm differentials in Japan appear to be considerably greater than in the United States and Western European nations, where the average difference between the largest and smallest is usually little more than 25 percent.

ECONOMIC DUALISM

The continued existence of wage differentials is the product of the "dualism" of the Japanese economy extending back almost 100 years. One must recall that Japan, in attempting to catch up with the West, superimposed an advanced industrialized sector requiring scarce skilled labor upon an "underdeveloped" economy based on agriculture and traditional industry with surplus unskilled labor. However, this dualism has steadily dissipated, especially during the very rapid growth period from the mid-1950s to mid-1970s. As a result, the wage differentials described above have been gradually diminishing and no doubt will continue to do so in the years ahead as economic growth, even though now more modest than in the past three decades, continues. In fact, with the advance of Japan's industrial economy, labor shortages have developed, especially among the younger workers, and with the rise in educational levels, all workers have been able to command higher and higher wages.

While rising wage levels and narrowing wage differentials indicate growing labor shortages, Japan has not imported many low-wage foreign workers as has been the case in northern Europe and the United States. It is not likely that Japan will in the years ahead. (During World War II, however, Japan did employ a considerable number of Koreans as forced labor because of such shortages. Many have remained in Japan.) Aside from the difficulties that many immigrants encounter in adapting to Japanese society and culture, there are two main reasons why such a development is unlikely for the foreseeable future. On the one hand, the Japanese economy is turning increasingly to labor-saving industry at home and investing in labor-intensive industry abroad. On the other hand, Japan is still in the process of upgrading workers from low-productivity to high-productivity enterprises and occupations. While the transfer of labor out of agriculture to industry now appears about exhausted, there still remains potential for considerable improvement for women, "retired" workers, employees in small-size enterprise, seasonal workers, and unemployed, among other sources of labor supply. As long as these sources are available, importation of foreign labor remains far off.

To describe wage levels, wage costs, and wage structure is only one side of the coin. The other is purchasing power of the worker and his/her family: what wages actually buy in terms of goods and services, that is, what standard of living do they provide? This is a highly complex question, especially in making comparisons among countries. The measurement of wages may differ. The components of wages may or may not contain certain items, depending on the levels and proportion of various money and nonmoney fringe benefits. Also, the bundles of goods and services purchased by workers in one country are not likely to be the same as in another country as the result of custom, taste, saving habits, price, and availability. There is again the problem of what exchange rate to utilize, especially as they often fluctuate, as has been the case of the dollar and yen in recent years. Finally, different rates of inflation among countries may be involved in comparing changes in the cost of living.

While not dealing solely with wage income, a recent United Nations study of international comparative purchasing power uses a far more complex formula (known as international price weights) than the current exchange rates. This study found that 1978 living standards in Japan on a per capita basis not only averaged about 56 percent of the American level, but also showed only relatively modest improvement over the 1970 comparison with the United States prior to the recent rapid acceleration of the yen. The figures, however, do show that the Japanese average per capita standard of living has risen above Italy's, about equaled Britain's, and remained below that of France and West Germany. This does not mean that Japanese living standards will remain below those of the United States, for a country such as Japan has been investing one of the world's largest percentages of GNP in economic growth. In the long run such an investment rate should produce more goods and services at a faster rate in Japan than in the United States as well as most other countries. If present rates of growth and investment continue, Japan could catch up with the living standards of the United States within the next several decades, perhaps even within this century.

Solomon B. Levine

BIBLIOGRAPHY

Shirai, Taishiro, and Haruo Shimada. "Japan." In *Labor in the Twentieth Century*, edited by John T. Dunlop and Walter Galenson, pp. 241–322. New York: Academic Press, 1978.

Funahashi, Naomichi. "The Industrial Award System: Wages and Benefits." In *Workers and Employers in Japan: The Japanese Employment Relations System*, edited by Kazuo Okochi, Bernard Karsh, and Solomon B. Levine, pp. 361–98. Princeton and Tokyo: Princeton University Press and University of Tokyo Press, 1973.

Japan Institute of Labour. Japanese Industrial Relations Series: *Wages and Hours of Work*, Series 3. Tokyo, 1979; and *Labor and the Economy Illustrated*, Series 4. Tokyo, 1980.

The Contemporary Myth of Japanese Protectionism

Some of the Western media accuse Japan of being protectionist, insisting that Japan maintains import tariffs and quotas, special supports for exporters and nontrade barriers in various areas. What is current Japanese trade policy and practice, and is it reasonable to make these kinds of assertions?

BACKGROUND

Japan's postwar foreign economic policy has been motivated by extreme resource dependency and at times a governmental interventionist approach to economic policy. Heavily dependent on foreign sources of industrial raw materials, Japan has long been concerned with ensuring its overseas sources of supply. In the prewar and wartime eras, the desire to maintain access to Chinese iron and coal and Southeast Asian rubber and oil was a major factor in expansionist military policies. Since World War II, and particularly after 1952, concern for maintaining adequate exports to support necessary imports of raw materials has been a leading consideration in all of Japan's domestic and foreign economic planning. Japan has also had an interventionist approach to the relationship between government and the economy at various points throughout the period of modernization beginning in the mid-nineteenth century. While the degree of government intervention has varied, Japan's government has never hesitated to play a strong role in stimulating and channeling economic development through centralized planning and use of bureaucratic controls and incentives. These two factors—extreme resource dependency and a tendency toward strong government roles vis-a-vis economic activity—underlie heavy governmental concern for the state of Japan's foreign economic relations in recent periods.

Since the 1950s Japan has sought to pattern economic development through a series of indicative plans fairly similar to those used in France. Central to the Japanese planning effort and related industrial policy was the "key-industry" development concept. Through a variety of policies the Japanese government sought to encourage development of selected technology and capital-intensive industries that were to be both internationally competitive and form the core for domestic economic progress. In the 1950s and 1960s major stress was put on development of the steel, chemical, shipbuilding, and electric power industries, and Japan's subsequent competitive advantage in steel and shipbuilding was in part the result of industrywide "rationalization" and development plans. Later, emphasis was placed on support for the automobile, heavy machinery, nuclear power, and computer industries. The planning process and policies toward specific industries, which economists feel were more important than the plans, encouraged heavy investments in technology and plant improvements, selective mergers where excessive competition was believed injurious to industry viability, market cartels in some instances, and a variety of import controls and export supports. The greatest part of these developmental activities were carried out in the 1950s and 1960s; their foreign economic policy components were phased out by the early 1970s, and at present only residual elements of the foreign economic policies of the growth period remain.

IMPORT QUOTAS

Japan's postwar system of import controls took preliminary form in 1949 with the passage of the Foreign Exchange and Foreign Trade Control Law. This law provided for a quota licensing system, which was initially designed primarily to protect Japan's inadequate foreign exchange resources. However, the quota and licensing system was also used as a device to protect Japan's industries during the postwar period of rehabilitation and rationalization as well as during the subsequent early periods of postrehabilitation growth. By the late 1950s, continued use of import quotas and other protectionist devices was being challenged by elements within Japan's government and business community, even as other governmental groups argued for their continuance. Thus, the 1950s was the period during which quotas and other controls were used most extensively, and by 1962–63 preliminary efforts had been begun toward dismantlement of the quota system. After Japan accepted Article 11 of the General Agreement on Tariffs and Trade (GATT) international agreements in 1963, the moves to liberalize foreign trade controls were accelerated. In the period between 1962 and 1970, the number of items under quota restriction were reduced from 492 to 133, and later in the 1970s, the list was further reduced to 73 items (see Table 4.2). (Meanwhile, the number of items under residual restriction in accordance with the GATT agreement, i.e., items where quotas were to removed by commonly agreed upon GATT policy, were reduced from 466 to 31.)

At present Japan's import quota system consists of restrictions on mainly agricultural products. Some other products, such as certain medicines and drugs, explosives and military weaponry, and fissionable materials, which are deemed threatening to morals or public safety, are also restricted. Very few manufactured products remain under quota, the most notable of these being leather products and certain chemicals. By the

TABLE 4.2

Japanese Import Quota Restrictions, 1962–80

Date	Quota Restriction Items	GATT Residual Quota Items
April 1962	492	466
April 1963	229	197
April 1964	174	136
October 1965	161	122
May 1966	168	126
October 1968	164	121
October 1969	161	118
September 1970	133	90
April 1972	79	33
April 1973	83	32
November 1973	82	31
October 1974	84	30
December 1975	82	27
April 1977	80	27
April 1978	79	27
January 1980	73	27

Source: Compiled from information supplied privately by the Ministry of International Trade and Industry.

late 1970s Japan maintained import quotas at roughly the same level as those of Germany and the United Kingdom. The Japanese residual (GATT) quota system was actually less comprehensive than that of France, but more extensive than the import quota system of the United States (see Table 4.3).

Japan's overall quota system—the system unrelated to specific GATT provisions—is somewhat larger than that of the United States (the number of items restricted is also larger than the GATT list in both countries). All of the items restricted by the United States, including various agricultural products controlled by the Department of Agriculture as well as other types of materials, totals 47, in contrast with Japan's quota list of 73 items. However, the import quota system of these two nations is not strictly comparable, in that Japan restricts the import of drugs and weapons through import quotas, while the United States uses a different approach.

TABLE 4.3

Number of Commodity Items under Residual (GATT)
Import Restrictions, 1976

Country	Total Number of Items	Agricultural and Marine Products as Percent of Total
France	74	52
Germany	39	49
Japan	27	81
United Kingdom	25	76
Italy	20	60
United States	7	14

Source: Ministry of International Trade and Industry, *The Import System of Japan 1977* (Tokyo: MITI Background Information Series Number BI25, 1977).

If roughly comparable categories of items are compared Japan now maintains quotas on 68 items as compared with 47 in the United States.

Thus, in contrast with the widespread idea that Japan continues to be a protectionist nation, the import quota systems of Japan and other industrialized nations are simply not all that different in terms of numbers of restricted items. More importantly, Japan's current import quota system focuses mainly on agricultural products, similar to the case in most other industrialized countries. Indeed, the United States, which maintains import quotas on various steel products, controls imports on more industrial products than Japan.

TARIFFS AND FOREIGN CAPITAL IMPORT CONTROLS

Paralleling the liberalization of Japan's import quota system in the 1960s and early 1970s was a comparable relaxation of import tariff regulations. Between 1967 and 1972, major shifts in Japan's import tariff system compared favorably with those of other advanced industrialized nations. For example, in 1973 the Ministry of Finance estimated that Japan's average tariff on imports from abroad was 8.8 percent, a figure identical to that for the United States and only slightly higher than the 8.2 percent average for the European Common Market's member countries.

Governmental controls over foreign investment in Japan followed a similar pattern to developments in the import quota and tariff systems. A foreign investment control law was enacted in 1950, motivated in part by fear that uncontrolled foreign investment in Japan could introduce destabilizing capital flows in a nation with severe foreign exchange problems. The foreign investment control regulations were also motivated by concern that foreign companies would enter the Japanese economy and dominate domestic industries, an attitude reflecting both a traditional Japanese concern for remaining free from foreign domination as well as the specific vulnerabilities of the postwar Japanese economy.

Beginning in 1967, the Japanese government "liberalized" foreign investment in *new* business ventures in a series of five "rounds." By 1973 and thereafter, Japan met the internationally agreed upon foreign investment code of the Organization of Economic Cooperation and Development (OECD), in that there were controls on foreign capital inflow only in certain problem industries where case-by-case screening of proposed projects was believed necessary. Free establishment of 100 percent foreign-owned enterprises is consequently now possible in many industries in Japan. An exception was made for agriculture, forestry, fishery, and leather and leather products (all of which are characterized by extremely small-scale production, representation by strong political interest groups, and/or some special considerations, such as the "caste" prejudice problem associated with employment in the leather-working industry and a resulting governmental effort to protect and develop this industry). Certain security and autarchy-related industries such as aircraft, atomic power, and energy are also not completely open to foreign investors, and are controlled on a "case-by-case" basis.

Regulations regarding acquisition of stocks in existing Japanese companies are somewhat more restrictive than controls over new investment, while following some of the same general principles of regulations affecting new firms. Permanent foreign residents of Japan may freely acquire stocks of Japanese firms in most cases as long as their holdings do not exceed 10 percent of the company's total shares (after which point controls and screening procedures are set in operation). Additionally, 100 percent collective foreign ownership is possible in the case of many industries, although only 50 percent total foreign ownership is permitted in a restricted industry group that includes data processing, mining, small retail trade, and real estate. Finally, more restrictions involving a limitation of a maximum of 25 percent foreign ownership are applied to investments in petroleum, large-scale retail trade, leather and leather processing, and primary production activities in agriculture, forestry, and fisheries, as well as in some special cases in the data processing leasing and manufacturing and real estate industries.

Another common opinion outside of Japan holds that the Japanese government engages in a system of direct subsidies of foreign export industries. Generally speaking, this is simply untrue at present, nor was it ever true in a literal sense. The major export industry incentive operative in postwar Japan was a corporation tax exemption for export trade profits. This system was abandoned in 1964 consequent upon Japan's acceptance of full responsibilities under the GATT agreements. Likewise, special export-related depreciation allowances were reduced and/or terminated during the 1970s, so that the contemporary situation resembles that of the United States where various indirect supports to export industries are given through government foreign trade promotion activities and the normal commercial activities of overseas embassies. It is also sometimes alleged that the Japanese practice of commodity tax rebates in the case of exports is an example of governmental subsidies to foreign export industries. But, in reality, the commodity tax is a domestic sales tax applied to all sales within Japan's territories, and as such cannot even legally be applied outside of Japan.

Much of the restrictive foreign trade practices found in Japan in the 1950s and early 1960s were thus eliminated in the decade beginning in 1962–63, even though this fact has not been widely recognized in the American and European media and business circles. Nevertheless, there are still aspects of Japanese bureaucratic policies that result in complaints from business and farming interests in Europe and the United States (just as Japanese continue to complain about related practices in other countries and areas). Included in the activities in Japan that have been seen as either formal trade barriers or nontariff barriers are quotas on some agricultural imports, a variety of administrative practices seen as restrictive by foreign businessmen, alleged import cartels, restrictions on activities of foreign banks in Japan, and "buy Japan" government procurement practices in some areas.

AGRICULTURAL PROTECTIONISM

While import quotas have been eliminated on most manufactured goods, Japan, as we have observed, still maintains quotas on several kinds of agricultural imports. Imports of most citrus fruits are severely restricted, leather products are imported under a quota system, and there are allegedly protectionist tariffs on pork. Beef import quotas have also been one of the areas stressed in recent American government complaints (even though the United States is a net importer of beef).

Some expansion of the quota on beef was achieved in the 1978 Strauss-Ushiba agreements on U.S.-Japanese trade practices. At the same negotiations, quotas on imports of citrus fruits and products were also expanded by as much as 400 percent. However, the citrus quota limits, which represent a response to pressures from Japan's important citrus industry to limit imports to "tolerable" levels, are still seen as unduly restrictive in American eyes. In a similar vein, leather products are restricted in order to protect domestic tanners. Despite the fact that roughly 25 percent of Japan's caloric food intake is imported, and much of these imports come from the United States, the cited areas of protectionism—not unlike agricultural protectionism in many other countries—continue as a sore spot in intergovernmental trade negotiations between Japan and the United States, and also present problems in ties between Japan, Australia, and New Zealand.

NONTARIFF BARRIERS

Foreign trade interests also see various Japanese government practices as "nontariff barriers" (NTBs) at present, even though there is little evidence that the practices were meant systematically to have the effects alleged by their overseas critics. In the area of product standards, for example, Japanese administrative officials were initially loathe to accept foreign tests of products to be imported into Japan and required tests to be made in Japan, which necessitated representation by local agents and sometimes long administrative delays. While testing procedures were identical to those applied to domestic Japanese producers, foreign exporters felt disadvantaged. Eventually political pressures from abroad led both MITI and Japan's Transportation Ministry to accept overseas or special testing procedures for electric appliances and automobiles. In the case of electric appliances, Japanese product standard decisions are now clarified for foreign companies' representatives, with standards being translated into English for easy comprehension by foreign companies. The Ministry of Transportation in turn now sends inspectors overseas to certify foreign automobile models at the place of origin in some instances. Similarly, the Ministry of Health and Welfare has altered its testing procedures in certain cases where complaints were received from abroad.

Meanwhile administrative practices and traditions continue to be a target for foreign complaints in such areas as chemical imports (where MITI is said to restrict imports of diammonium phosphate by administrative guidance), automobiles (where domestic taxes based on automobile engine size and local registration procedures are attacked as NTBs), and banking (where foreign banks cannot make consumer loans and are barred from participation in domestic clearinghouse and wire transfer systems). It is also argued that MITI tacitly permits cartels in such import markets as aluminum, copper, naptha, and caustic soda.

Many of the foreign complaints about NTBs in Japan reflect a failure abroad to recognize that Japanese practices and administrative traditions are simply different from those in the respective home countries. While it cannot be denied that domestic practices have consequences for importers, domestic administrative restrictions rigorously channel and control *domestic* producers' activities within Japan (banking is a case in point) in addition to affecting foreign trading interests. Also, it should be noted that Japanese government officials point out that the roughly 80 "voluntary" quotas imposed on Japanese exports in past negotiations with the American government constitute as severe a barrier to free trade as the traditional administrative and marketing practices in Japan that foreign business interests find objectionable. Indeed, intergovernmental negotiations on business practices such as those regularly conducted between the United States and Japan *actually* reflect very similar frustrations on both sides of the Pacific regarding governmental practices in the other countries.

CONCLUSION

At present a variety of efforts are being made bilaterally and multi-laterally to resolve some of the tensions created by alleged trade barriers and remaining quota systems. For example, both the United States and Japan have created special roving foreign trade ambassadors in recent years; these officials' duties have included both representation of national industrial interests and promotion of resolution of trade problems, including both alleged NTBs and other "threatening" practices engaged in by private companies. Currently, there is a United States-Japan Trade Study Group, which is a governmental and private body that addresses itself to resolution of bilateral trade problems. There is also an inter-governmental Trade Facilitation Committee that regularly meets to address itself to alleged instances of restrictive trade practices in both member countries. Similar contacts exist between Japan and other trading partners in the EEC, Australia, and New Zealand.

Japan's foreign economic policies in the postwar era have more than anything else represented the expression of traditional practices in the economic arena. Unlike the adversary relationships existing between business and government in the United States, important elements within the Japanese business community have long accepted a corporatist relationship with the large administrative ministries like MITI, Transportation, and Finance. The major economic ministries themselves differ from their American counterparts in that they combine the policymaking and statistics-collection functions of American government departments with the regulatory powers of the American regulatory commissions and agencies. This gives the Japanese economic ministries great power, in addition to the aura of authority conveyed by a tradition of statism, and results in a capability to centrally regulate minute and detailed aspects of business activities that seem repugnant to at least American businessmen. In reality, it is possible that the combined activities of national, state, and local authorities in the United States result in similar levels of governmental intervention in business activities to those found in Japan with the exception of controls and inducements related to economic planning and industrial policy functions. But the centralized nature of governmental controls in Japan, as well as a tradition of corporatism, does manage to convey the impression that controls are numerous and pervasive in impact in the Japanese case.

Bradley Richardson

BIBLIOGRAPHY

Department of the Treasury. *Import Quotas*. 1977.

Hatakeyama, Noboru. "The Image of Japanese Trade Policy." *Mainichi Daily News*, various issues, November 1978.

Ministry of Finance. *Manual of Foreign Investment in Japan*. Tokyo, 1974.

Ministry of International Trade and Industry. *The Import System of Japan*. Tokyo, 1977.

————. *Import Notice*. Tokyo, March 1980.

U.S. Department of Commerce. *Business America*, May 1980.

U.S. Government Printing Office. *Export Stimulation Programs in the Major Industrial Countries*. Washington, D.C., 1978.

————. *Task-Force Report on United States-Japan Trade*. Washington, D.C., 1979.

5

INCOME DISTRIBUTION, PURCHASING POWER, AND THE CONSUMER MARKET

To the resident of the United States, accustomed to urban poverty, crime, and slums, Japanese urban communities afford quite a contrast. Nowhere are there major slum areas such as exist in most American cities. In fact, there seems to be little difference in the quality and size of housing between the various districts of Tokyo, with the exception of areas inhabited by the very well-to-do. Housing conditions, one of the best indicators of income distribution, suggest that income distribution is fairly egalitarian in Japan and that there are not large sectors of poor people in the population.

Albert Keidel II addresses the problem of income distribution in Japan and presents evidence that the Japanese patterns are the most egalitarian in the present industrialized world. Many factors contribute to this state of affairs. Rural poverty, for example, is not a problem in Japan as it is in so many countries. The postwar land reform created an agricultural sector of small farmers who own their own land, while subsequent farm price supports have guaranteed some degree of parity between farm and city incomes. Decentralization of industry, a major Japanese government policy since the 1960s, has meant that members of farm families can earn factory wages to supplement household incomes from farming; this is another factor contributing to a leveling of differences between rural and urban income levels. Former landowners before the reform actually lost wealth after the reform, as inflation wiped out the value of government bonds given them as compensation for their land; this was a further leveling influence in the rural sector itself.

Events have also favored the urban working class in Japan, at least in recent years. Because of high growth in the late 1960s and early 1970s, Japan, which had been a labor surplus economy earlier, actually experienced labor shortages. Because of these shortages, which were especially acute among skilled workers and artisans, and also strong pressure from Japan's unions, workers' salaries rose dramatically in the 1970s; these wage rises, especially significant among employees of large firms, also had a leveling effect on the overall pattern of income distribution in Japan.

The egalitarian nature of income distribution in Japan in a period of relative affluence has favored the development of a large, domestic consumer market for such durables as household appliances, stereos and television sets, and automobiles. Indeed, first-time purchases of consumer durables was an important market trend in the high growth years. Still, the comparative affluence of most Japanese in terms of consumer durables ownership does not mean that purchasing power in Japan is equivalent to that in all other industrial nations. Food and housing are especially expensive in Japan, and absorb resources that families could otherwise spend on other kinds of goods and services.

Nevertheless, Japan is obviously an affluent country. As Yoshi Tsurumi points out, Japanese levels of ownership of appliances and automobiles are closer to those of the United States than Great Britain. Also, the Japanese have spent a great deal on foreign travel in recent years, another indicator of their relative affluence. Interestingly, the consumer market in Japan is far less dependent on consumer credit than is the case in the United States. Although credit buying is on the increase in Japan, many people prefer bank-sponsored savings plans that enable them to make major purchases with cash, or at least permit a large cash down payment. The practice in large companies of giving bonuses that are equal at times to several months' salary has also favored cash buying of consumer durables in the years when companies could afford to give sizable bonus awards.

Income Distribution in Contemporary Japan

Many people say that Japan is a society without poverty and slums. Is this true? What is the pattern of current income distribution in Japan? In addition, what can we say about Japanese living standards in comparative terms?

It is widely observed and hence generally expected that as an economy grows to industrial maturity, its distribution of personal income will become more equal and poverty as such will become less pronounced. This aspect of modern economic growth has been so rapid in Japan, however, that by the 1970s she succeeded in all but eliminating the more visible forms of poverty, making her probably the most egalitarian of the non-Socialist economic powers.

But income equality and poverty are notoriously difficult to measure and understand, and the Japanese case is no exception. Income distribution per se has not had the same importance in worldwide economic theory and national policy as growth and industrialization. Hence, comprehensive data on poverty are relatively poor almost everywhere. In addition, many of the same measurement complications that make it difficult to compare international standards of living also make it difficult to compare international levels of poverty. Who are a nation's poor? There is no simple statistical answer.

Nevertheless, a great deal of information points to dramatic changes in levels of well-being in Japan since the 1950s, and although the fruits of Japan's postwar growth have by no means been equally shared by all, many of the sources of prewar inequality and poverty in Japan have disappeared or been greeatly reduced. As difficult as they are to apply fairly, international measures of both average welfare in Japan and its distribution indicate that although the Japanese still trail the United States absolutely in many important categories (though not all) of well-being, the equal sharing of those benefits has probably occurred faster in Japan. In addition, the vitality and high quality of Japanese urban life, when compared to the abandonment, decay, and squalor of American inner cities, has meant that the most visible forms of poverty, both for foreign visitors and for Japanese themselves, are all but eliminated.

INCOME EQUALIZERS: LAND REFORM AND RAPID INDUSTRIAL GROWTH

There are numerous historical reasons for the recent evolution of equality in Japan, reasons related to war destruction, allied occupying policies (particularly land reform and labor reform), inflation, low unemployment, relatively equal education, and a host of factors directly related to rapid growth itself.

For most countries, and in particular for countries in transition to industrial maturity, one of the single most important sources of overall income inequality is the poverty of rural farm workers, tenants, and marginal landholders. In Japan, three important forces have eliminated and perhaps even reversed this pattern. Between 1946 and the Korean War, the large prewar landlord holdings were broken up and distributed to individual cultivators by American occupying forces. It is difficult to overemphasize the central importance of this ownership reform in what was then probably Japan's single most valuable productive asset.

Second, delays in electoral reapportionment compared to the pace of urban migration have maintained uneven national representation in favor of farmers. Japanese government policy has accordingly supported extremely high grain, meat, and dairy prices, resulting in rural-urban terms of trade greatly favoring farmers.

Third, the density of Japan's population in general and the decentralized nature of much of Japanese small and intermediate manufacturing have provided greatly increased part-time nonfarm employment for farm owners and farm workers alike. Supplementary employment has become so important that a great deal of the rapid farm mechanization in Japan is not for farming more land with fewer individuals, but is rather to allow individuals to spend less time on their own lands and more time in subsidiary employment. This subsidiary income was so great by even 1970 that on the average farmers with the smallest holdings were actually earning more than larger farmers, while in 1955 their income had not been 70 percent of the latter's.

In the context of asset redistribution, it is also important to remember the equalizing impact of the rapid post-World War II inflation. Redistribution of land as well as the confiscation of concentrated industrial assets were legally compensated with long-term bonds. Without inflation the former land and industrial asset owners would have remained just as wealthy on the income from these bonds. As it turned out, the nominal face value of these bonds was fixed, and extremely rapid inflation in early postwar years all but wiped out their purchasing-power significance.

Off the farm, urban and industrial incomes themselves have become more equal, largely because of Japan's sustained high economic growth and the resulting shortage of industrial labor that appeared in the 1960s. Beginning with the industrial boom during World War I and the importation into Japan of sophisticated machine tools and other equipment, skilled workers commanded much higher wages than unskilled. Firms paid significant wage differentials to keep high-quality operators, and managers, in their permanent employ, but wages for unskilled workers were by and large regulated by income levels in rural areas. This "dual" industrial wage structure came to be seen most clearly as a striking difference between wages in large modern capital-intensive industries on the one hand, and those in the extremely large number of smaller and less mechanized firms on the other.

The "income-doubling" growth of the 1960s, however, brought with it unskilled labor shortages as well, and the wage differential began to narrow. Compensation to small-firm employees was well less than 60 percent of that in larger firms in the late 1950s, but by the early 1970s the ratio had risen to roughly 70 percent. Other wage differentials, for example those associated with different industrial sectors and subsectors, have narrowed as well, as have even the differential incomes of male and female office workers. While females had earned less than 40 percent than their male counterparts in the latter 1950s, the same percentage had risen to roughly 48 percent by the early 1970s.

It should also be remembered that Japanese unemployment has been extremely low in postwar decades (between 1.0 and 1.8 percent in the years of most rapid growth from 1960 to the 1970s oil crisis and recession, during which it still did not go above 2 percent). The combination of this information with other factors above does a great deal to explain Japan's overall pattern of increasing equality and the very great reduction, if not disappearance, of visible urban poverty (Japan is roughly 75 percent urban).

THE STATISTICAL RECORD:
INCOME DISTRIBUTION BY SIZE

There are, nevertheless, serious shortcomings in our knowledge about many aspects of Japanese income distribution, just as there are for most other nations. Most serious are the exclusion of capital gains from our measures of income and problems of consistent units for income recipients. By 1973, wages had increased by 9 times when compared to their 1952 level, but the price of urban land had increased 58 times and the Tokyo stock exchange index had risen 19 times. Thus, very large windfall capital gains were added to the incomes of the owners of those assets, a group believed to represent only a small portion of the population.

It should be noted, however, that for measuring poverty in an economy, these errors are less serious, as they usually reflect only adjustments to the upper end of the income distribution. A more troublesome shortcoming of statistical measures of inequality is the shortage of information on the incomes of small owner-operated businesses, for which business finances and individual income are difficult to separate. These and other difficulties, such as the valuation of income in kind in rural areas, plague estimates of income distribution in any country. Nevertheless, there are roughly corresponding sets of data for several industrial and industrializing countries in the early 1970s, and they confirm the international standing of Japan's recent gains in equality.

Table 5.1 provides information on income distribution "by size" for a selection of countries. The method of reporting is fairly simple. Each population is divided statistically into groups of equal size, beginning with the poorest 10 percent down to the richest 10 percent, and even the richest five percent, as shown in the left-hand column. The data then show the size

TABLE 5.1

Income Distribution by Size—International Comparisons

Richest % of Population	Percent of Total Income Received							
	Japan-1	Japan-2	U.S.-1	U.S.-2	U.K.	West Germany	East Germany	Brazil
0-10	3.4	.5	1.5	.8	2.3	2.2	4.0	.9
10-20	5.4	3.3	3.4	3.1	4.3	3.7	6.4	1.5
20-30	6.3	4.9	4.7	4.4	5.4	4.7	7.5	2.2
30-40	7.2	6.1	5.9	5.8	6.5	5.8	8.4	3.1
40-50	8.3	7.3	7.1	7.1	7.8	7.0	9.3	4.2
50-60	9.2	8.8	8.6	8.8	9.2	8.3	10.3	5.6
60-70	10.5	10.3	10.4	10.8	11.0	10.2	11.1	7.5
70-80	12.1	12.5	12.8	13.5	13.2	12.5	12.3	10.5
80-90	14.5	15.7	16.6	17.6	16.4	16.5	13.8	15.9
90-100	23.1	30.6	29.0	28.1	23.9	29.1	16.9	48.6
95-100	14.2	20.4	18.1	16.6	13.7	18.2	9.2	36.0

Note: Data years are: Japan 1971, U.S. 1971/72, U.K. 1968, West Germany 1970, East Germany 1970, Brazil. 1970.

Source: Shail Jain, *Size Distribution of Income: A Compilation of Data* (Washington, D.C.: Johns Hopkins University Press for the World Bank, 1975), relevant pages.

Used with permission.

of the share in total income received by each respective group. If income were perfectly equally distributed, each ten percent of the population would receive just 10 percent of total income, and there would be no "richer" or "poorer groups. As it is, the size of the poorest group's share is obviously the smallest (0.9 percent for Brazil's poorest 10 percent), while that of the richest group is the largest (48.6 percent for Brazil).

The most interesting comparisons are for the poorest and the richest groups. Two sets of data each are presented for the United States and Japan, to give some idea of the differences in estimation procedures and data interpretation used by researchers. One set for each country shows more egalitarian results, while the other set is less flattering. Taking the more equal estimates (Japan-1 and U.S.-1), we can.see that the Japanese distribution is considerably more even than that for the United States. The reverse is true for the second sets of estimates (Japan-2 and U.S.-2), which are similar except for adjustments that have been made in the richest and poorest categories by researchers (O. R. Wada and Simon Kuznets, respectively). These allow for estimates of data felt to be missing from the more official interpretations of the first sets. The adjustment in the lower "tail" of the Japanese series was clearly more severe than that for the United States.

Thus, although there is uncertainty about the poorest 10 percent, overall the data indicate that the distributions are about the same in both countries, or if anything, Japan's income is more equally divided. Using the first Japanese set of data for comparisons with essentially official estimates for the United Kingdom and West Germany, we also find that overall the Japanese distribution is more equal.

Comparison with East Germany, however, shows the reverse to be true. This result is consistent with other measures of income distributions in Eastern Europe: they tend to be the most equal in the industrial world, and are often taken as an international standard of the practical limits of equality. At the other extreme, Brazil is internationally notorious for its poor income distribution, and although data problems are even more severe in such a developing country, a large number of estimates have been made, and the figures given are a fair representation of Brazil's actual distribution, one of the most unequal in the world.

The above data, then, allow us to put Japan's relative poverty into international perspective. In less than 30 years she succeeded in not only breaking all economic growth records, but she has at the same time evolved a distribution of income approaching the best in the world.

VERY LITTLE URBAN SLUM HOUSING

A traveler to Japan, however, does not need sophisticated statistics to know that the Japanese, and in particular the urban Japanese, enjoy a high standard of living that seems to be shared by all. Visible signs of poverty are difficult if not impossible to see. Housing is poor, and in some cases even dilapidated, but the degree of personal care and upkeep for even such poor housing is so high that there is no feeling of it being in any way "slum quarters." It should be noted that a slum is more than poverty, crowding, and poor housing; it involves the "inferiority" of the residents in some sense, and it has about it an air of destitution and social brakdown. Such conditions are very rarely seen in Japanese cities today.

It is true that slums have existed in Japan since at least the Meiji era, when studies and reports documented their squalor in Tokyo, Osaka, Kobe, and other major Japanese cities. Nevertheless, the Japanese themselves say that this kind of poverty disappeared sometime between the 1950s and 1970s, though there is no available statistical information referring directly to urban slum areas. Specifically, "poverty line" calculations showed that by 1967 there were only 6 percent of the population actually in poverty, down from 15 percent just seven years earlier. When it is remembered that these data are for pretax and pretransfer incomes, the incidence of government expenditures such as for the national health insurance program most likely reduces the number of poor even more. Based on these data, the Japanese declared that poverty was disappearing from Japan, and given the cleanliness and order in Japanese cities, one is inclined to believe that slums have all but disappeared as well.

The quality of life in Japanese cities, especially in the latter 1970s when great improvements had been made in reducing air pollution, is just one sign of the level of welfare achieved by the Japanese as a result of their postwar success. This new level of welfare includes tangibles as well as intangibles, and a very important example of the latter is the safety of Japanese city streets, even at night, and even for women and the elderly. The extraordinarily low incidence of crime is one form of income that benefits all, and for which there is no money measure.

A EUROPEAN STANDARD OF LIVING

Attempts to measure Japan's level of welfare and compare it to other nations runs into the considerable problems posed by all such comparisons, but the results are interesting and show that although in per capita income she trails the United States, in literacy and other indicators of social success she surpasses the United States and many other nations of the world.

International comparisons of per capita income must solve the problem of the different currencies used by each country. It is not acceptable to use the market or official exchange rate between the two currencies, because that represents only equilibrium relationships for traded goods, and the bulk of income is usually spent on nontraded goods. Any traveler knows that the exchange rate can change because of some shift in international financial conditions or capital movements, while the incomes and expenditures of citizens of the respective countries have hardly changed at all. For the United States and Japan, since the goods Japan trades are relatively low priced by world price patterns, and expenditures on food and housing are high, use of the exchange rate results in an estimate for Japanese income in dollars that could buy much more food and housing in the United States than the corresponding yen could buy in Japan. Since income is only useful for what it can buy, some way of converting foreign currencies to "real" income is needed.

The most exhaustive comparison to date has used "average" or "international" relative prices, and its results give as close an estimate as is currently possible of the differences in average real incomes, as reflected in the goods and services they can actually buy. Table 5.2 gives the results for a few selected countries from 1967 to 1975, using the United States as a benchmark value of 100.0.

TABLE 5.2

**Indexes of Per Capita Real Gross Domestic Product
(in international dollars, U.S. = 100)**

Country	1967	1970	1973	1974	1975
Kenya	5.6	6.3	6.1	6.2	6.1
South Korea	n.a.*	12.1	14.6	15.9	16.9
Japan	48.3	59.2	64.0	63.2	65.1
United Kingdom	61.9	73.5	60.6	60.5	62.0
France	n.a.	73.2	76.1	78.6	79.5
West Germany	n.a.	78.2	77.4	78.9	79.2
United States	100.0	100.0	100.0	100.0	100.0

*Data not available.

Source: Irving B. Kravis et al. *International Comparisons of Real Product and Purchasing Power: United Nations International Comparison Project—Phase II* (Baltimore: Johns Hopkins University Press for the World Bank, 1978), p. 14. Used with permission.

We can see, that in terms of purchasing power, the Japanese average per-person output was worth half that for the United States in 1967, but that by 1970 it was already almost 60 percent, and in 1975 it was fully 65 percent. Several other studies have shown that Korea in the mid-1970s was close to Japan's condition at the time of the Korean War, and if that is true, the data in Table 5.2 outline Japan's impressive improvement in her standard of living in just over 20 years.

There are still reasons why the above statistics are not a complete summary of comparative national welfare. First and perhaps foremost, the Japanese, no matter how much they produce, will never be able to buy bigger houses and home gardens as a nation, because there is too little good land for the population. This is just one example of elements in the quality of life that cannot be measured with money. In a similar example, the Japanese have very few parks in their urban areas, an average of 1.2 square meters per person, while the corresponding figures for the United States, England, and West Germany are 19.2, 22.8, and 20.3, respectively.

But not all such "social indicators" leave Japan in a bad light. Japan has more college students as a share of that age group than the European Common Market countries, though she still lags far behind the United States. Per capita newspaper circulation is as high as anywhere in the world, as is life expectancy, considerably longer than in the United States. It is difficult to draw any conclusions from these and similar statistics, but they do point out that although Japan's measurable material welfare is lower than that in the United States, it compares favorably with European industrial powers, and some of her nonmeasurable benefits, such as safety from crime and violence, might tip the scale if they were weighed with a dollar sign.

To sum up, Japan's record of economic achievement has been remarkable for the degree of equality in income it has also brought. In spite of measurement hurdles, statistics show that poverty has all but disappeared, and there is little if any urban poverty in identifiable slums. Although equality itself is an important component in many people's estimate of a nation's quality of life, measures of real income and intangible benefits show that Japan has also raised her overall standard of living into the ranks of the world leaders.

Albert Keidel

BIBLIOGRAPHY

Chubachi, Masayoshi, and Koji Taira. "Poverty in Modern Japan: Perceptions and Reality." In *Japanese Industrialization and its Social Consequences*, edited by Hugh Patrick. Berkeley: University of California Press, 1976.

Consumer Spending in Japan

The development of a consumer market and credit spending have been features of twentieth-century life in some Western nations. What are the main patterns of consumer goods purchases and ownership in contemporary Japan, and to what extent are these financed by credit systems, such as charge accounts or credit cards?

Since 1968, Japan's Gross National Product has ranked a consistent third in the world after that of the United States and the Soviet Union. Japan in 1980 still ranks only third in terms of her Gross National Product, but it is expected that she will overtake the Soviet Union sometime during the 1980s. As late as 1965, Japan's Gross National Product was a mere one-tenth of that of the United States, placing her behind Great Britain and West Germany as well. By 1980, however, Japan's Gross National Product has reached a level approximately one-half that of the United States. And in terms of per capita income, but not in terms of purchasing power, Japan is approaching the U.S. level.

More interestingly, rapid economic growth and resultant growth in income in Japan have concurrently narrowed the gap between upper- and lower-income brackets to the extent that, in 1980, more than three-quarters of the Japanese population consider themselves to be members of the middle-income group. Monetary wage rates of Japanese rank-and-file production workers are now well ahead of those for their European counterparts, with the exception of the West Germans. Even if the monetary equivalents of fringe benefits and the guaranteed job security provided by lifetime employment are excluded from consideration, the wages of Japanese factory workers are estimated to be three-fourths of the comparable figures for American workers.

MOTORIZATION IN JAPAN

Nowhere has this rapid rise in household income been more dramatically apparent than in Japan's headlong rush toward private ownership of passenger cars. In the mere 15 years prior to 1980, more than 54 percent of Japanese households have come to own at least one passenger motor vehicle. One out of two persons eligible to drive (16 years of age and older) now possesses a driver's license. This situation compares favorably with that of the Netherlands and Belgium. At present, the daily life of a Japanese household resembles more closely that of an American household than that

TABLE 5.3

Household Ownership Rates for Selected Products, 1979

	Japan	United States	United Kingdom
Color TV sets	98%	72%	55%
Refrigerators	99	99	75
Washing machines	98	78	73
Piped-in tap water	93	97	99
Flush toilets	60	96	98
Telephones	41 per 100 persons	72 per 100 persons	39 per 100 persons
Daily newspapers	526 per 1,000 persons	287 per 1,000 persons	388 per 1,000 persons

Source: Economic Planning Agency, *Kakei Shohi no Doko* [Trends of Household Expenditures] (Tokyo, 1979); and other government publications.

of a British household. Table 5.3 shows recent ownership percentages of a few appliances used in daily life and reading materials.

In addition, Japanese consumers have been buying such luxury appliances as tape recorders, stereo equipment, cameras, electronic games, and calculators. They are also spending an increasing amount of both time and money on domestic and international travel as well as on both participatory and spectator sports. Fashionable clothing is eagerly sought after by young and old alike. The age of mass consumption has already come for the Japanese.

PREFERENCE FOR CASH PURCHASES

Compared with American consumers, however, Japanese have maintained their strong propensity toward the purrchase of consumer appliances with cash rather than through the use of credit or installment plans, although such large consumer items as passenger cars are sold mainly on an installment basis. Even in the case of automobile purchases, however, typical financing arrangements for Japanese buyers consist of a 25 percent cash down payment, with the balance to be paid over a 20-month period. Despite the offering by commercial banks of "auto loans," "piano loans," and other types of bank financing for purchases of durable consumer goods, a majority of Japanese consumers prefer to have financing arranged by retailers.

In comparison with the cashless economy of the United States, where personal checks or credit cards are used heavily, Japan's is still very much a cash economy. Monthly charges for utilities and telephone service are either paid in cash to door-to-door collectors or are deducted automatically from ordinary savings deposits kept by households with nearby commercial banks. The use of credit cards is spreading slowly. Yet, the majority of credit-card holders appears to limit voluntarily their use of credit cards to dining out, short-term credit purchases of small consumer items, or for brief travel.

Two idiosyncrasies of Japanese society seem to have produced a propensity toward preference for cash purchases and avoidance of excessive personal debt. First, a system has evolved in Japan since the end of World War II under which managers and rank-and-file employees are paid the equivalent of 18 months' salary each year. Twice a year, in June and at the end of December, Japanese workers receive a lump sum equivalent to three or four months' regular salary as a ''bonus'' in addition to their monthly salaries. As a result, most Japanese households have developed a habit of living on regular monthly salaries while using their twice-yearly bonuses to make large purchases of applicances or to save for planned future expenditures. Even the lowest-paid worker often receives a summer or year-end bonus large enough to enable him to make a 25 percent cash down payment on a stripped-down model of one of the popular compact cars. His remaining obligation to the automobile dealer is often arranged so as to permit larger repayments during bonus months than during the rest of the year.

A second observation is that, although this tendency has weakened gradually over time, a mental block still exists among Japanese mass consumers with regard to incurring a large amount of personal debt. This has been identified as a major reason for the slow spread of credit-card use and installment purchases by consumers in Japan. Many consumers join special savings plans having such descriptive titles as Overseas Travel Plan, or the Piano Purchase Plan, or Sewing Machine Ownership Plan, which are offered by commercial banks, household appliance manufacturers, and travel agencies. With a specific target in mind, consumers concentrate on saving money each month until they have accumulated at least enough funds to afford a cash down payment, which is usually 25 to 50 percent of the purchase price.

Incidentally, this Japanese tendency to save for a coveted item rather than go into debt for it was cleverly exploited by Janome Sewing Machine Company during pre-World War II days when it decided to dislodge Singer Sewing Machine from its dominant position in the Japanese market. While

Singer offered installment purchases, Janome "sold" a Monthly Purchase Reservation Plan, concentrating its efforts on the growing market composed of single working girls. These future housewives did not wish to bring personal debts to their new husbands and preferred Janome's plan to Singer's installment repayment plan. Even today, this traditional attitude lingers on rather strongly among female customers.

THE FUTURE OF CONSUMER BORROWING AND SPENDING

Although Japanese households still display their tendency to save even under inflationary periods and thus act to apply the brake on the runaway inflationary pressures, they are gradually acquiring the taste of consume now and pay later. For example, according to the Japanese government statistics (Prime Minister's Office, 1980), during 1979, the Japanese household had, on the average, the outstanding debt of 1.49 million yen, an 18.1 percent increase from the comparable level of 1978. On the other hand, the average household had the savings of 4.02 million yen, an 8.1 percent increase over and above the comparable level of 1978. Although the savings exceeded the outstanding debts, some observers were alarmed by the fast growth rate of the debts owed by the average household.

A further analysis of the debts of the Japanese household revealed, however, that most of these debts consisted of the mortgage loans on the house used by the same household. The second largest item of such debts was the installment repayment loans on automobiles and other household appliances. At the same time, the amounts that Japanese consumers owed to various credit cards were rapidly increasing from 1978 to 1980.

Some people predict that Japanese consumers will begin to reduce their savings and spend more. However, Japan is still very much the country where one's retirement life has to be planned privately. The firms assist their employees' savings and purchases of their own homes. The government encourages such savings by providing special income tax reliefs to such savings. Accordingly, the high saving tendency of Japanese households is most likely to remain as an integral part of the Japanese life.

The aforementioned situations in Japan make a good contrast to the Unitd States. In the United States, the personal debts that combine consumer credits and residential mortgages far outweigh the personal savings. For example, in 1979, there were about $840 billion of residential mortgage and about $310 billion of consumer credits (debts) that were still outstanding. Altogether, $1,144 billion of personal debts outstanding were translated into about $5,720 of personal debts for every living individual of the United States who is counted into the total population of the nation.

Since the average household of the United States consists of 3.5 individuals, statistically speaking, total personal debts of the United States correspond to about $20,020 per household.

On the other hand, the personal savings of the United States tend to fluctuate from year to year between about $80 billion and $67 billion depending upon the general economic conditions of the nation. Statistically speaking again, the personal savings outstanding in the United States are about $1,400 per household, less than one-tenth of the comparable figure for the average Japanese household (translated at the prevailing exchange rate of 1979–80). This difference between the two nations reflects the difference in the basic economic structure. The Japanese economy is still very much shaped by the savings-investment activities of the economy while the U.S. economy is shaped by mass consumption and the housing industry.

Yoshi Tsurumi

BIBLIOGRAPHY

Tsurumi, Yoshi. *The Japanese are Coming*. Cambridge, Mass.: Ballinger, 1976.

PART III

THE JAPANESE BUSINESS ENVIRONMENT

6

LAW IN JAPAN

A comprehensive, working legal code is necessary for the operation of any modern economy and society. Whether the legal system originated in custom or in positive legal codes is irrelevant. What matters is that rules exist that provide for orderly social behavior and commercial transactions, and that these rules be honored and enforced. These requirements are met in Japan through a blend of imported legal concepts and native social traditions.

Before the beginning of Japan's explicit modernization in the Meiji period (1868–1912), Japan's legal code consisted of Chinese public law, Japanese custom, and a commercial code based on Japanese experience. After the Meiji Restoration, Japanese officials visited Britain, France, and Germany in a search for models for a "modern" legal code. The German example was the most dominant influence, and the constitution, the civil code, and the commercial code enacted in the late nineteenth century in Japan reflected strong German influences. For example, the constitution closely resembled that of Prussia in its embodiment of a strong cabinet system and qualified civil rights.

The Japanese legal system was further developed after World War II during the American-dominated postwar occupation (1945–52). The Japanese constitution was rewritten under American influence, and the code of criminal procedure, the civil code, and the code of civil procedure were all revised in order to provide for greater guarantees for civil rights, due process, and equality between the sexes. The commercial code and other laws were either revised or rewritten in order to strengthen the position of corporate stockholders, protect the rights of labor, and promote free competition between firms, all aspects of the economic democracy advocated by occupation officials.

In addition to changes in various legal codes, the position of the Japanese judiciary was also substantially changed during the occupation period. Among other things, the American reformers provided for an autonomous judicial system and for judicial review of legislative and administrative actions such as are found in the United States. Simultaneously, the status of lawyers before the courts was enhanced through legislative action, the training of lawyers was upgraded, and rights to counsel were enshrined in the relevant codes on procedures.

Basically, the occupation authorities introduced elements of Anglo-American procedures into a system that had been dominated by the administrative law thinking of Europe; in the process they furthered the Westernization of the formal legal system of Japan. The Japanese legal codes today are remarkably eclectic in that they blend different foreign traditions, while Japanese legal concepts and social practices further influence the imported codes and their application. One of the contributions of Japanese tradition and institutions is seen in the relatively low levels of litigation. Very few disputes are taken to court in Japan, partly because of traditional cultural preferences for consensual procedures and partly because of various institutional barriers. There are very few lawyers in Japan, and court cases take a very long time for resolution. Also, various kinds of informal mediation services are provided by the government. Divorces, for example, can be obtained by an extremely simple process of filing the relevant forms and appearing before a family problems counselor; the services of an attorney are not needed.

Perhaps the prevention of crime and resolution of criminal cases exemplifies the blend of foreign legal codes, traditional practices, and modern administration that characterizes Japan's legal system. A comprehensive criminal code reflecting both indigenous and foreign influences defines criminal activity in Japan. Modern, well-organized, and well-trained police enforce the law using techniques common to all advanced countries. However, the police also work closely with ordinary citizens in a way unknown in at least the United States, and the social cohesion of Japanese community life favors both deterrence and effective investigation of crime. Local Japanese policemen are assigned to neighborhoods where they are expected to know and work with all resident households in the areas under their supervision. Simultaneously, the compactness and cohesion of these communities and neighborhoods discourage persons from engaging in crime (through fear of nonconformity), while also permitting fast identification of criminal elements and even motivating criminals to confess their guilt through strong feelings of obligation. Because of these mutually reenforcing influences, crime is remarkably low in Japan, even in urban centers that are the locations of flourishing crime in some other countries like the United States.

At the pinnacle of Japan's postwar legal system is the Constitution of 1947. The postwar Constitution is quite modern in the degree to which it guarantees civil and economic rights. The Constitution also thoroughly reworked Japan's parliamentary system, so that Japanese government now resembles the political systems of most Western European democracies. One of the most famous and internally controversial provisions of the Constitution committed Japan to abandonment of war as an instrument of foreign policy; under current interpretations Japan has only defensive military forces! Experience has shown the Japanese Constitution to be more than a documented ideal, and most of Japanese postwar political experiences suggest a very optimistic prognosis for the future success of constitutional government.

The Japanese Legal System

What are the main features of Japan's legal system? Is it basically similar to Western systems or is it somehow fundamentally different?

BACKGROUND

The Japanese legal system is a complex combination of European civil law and Anglo-American common law concepts placed against a background of unique Japanese attitudes and practices toward law. The result is a legal system that is almost entirely Western in its formal structure and operation. The result in a particular case may differ since the particular legal rules are interpreted or applied according to the social or commercial context in Japan, but this degree of difference is usually present among the various legal systems of the West as well. Given this proviso, the Japanese system as it appears on paper is quite similar to the Western systems on which it is based. One hestitates to answer the question so simply, however, because the manner and extent to which the formal machinery of the system is used in Japan is quite different from the role of formal law in most of the rest of the industrialized world. A knowledge of the formal structure of the courts or of the import of a particular article of the Civil Code, therefore, may not be as useful or important in a Japanese context as in many Western countries.

Before the Meiji Restoration of 1868 when Japan began its institutional response to the West, Japanese law was a mixture of borrowed Chinese law concepts and Japanese custom. The Chinese influence was essentially limited to public law—theories of the organization of the state and society and criminal law. The basis of society was natural law, i.e., society was seen as reflecting the natural order as derived from Confucian principles. The positive codes and rules were merely the embodiment of this natural order. Alongside this very abstract public law realm, there developed especially toward the end of the Tokugawa period (1603–1868) a detailed body of customary commercial law that was almost entirely free of Chinese influence. This law merchant grew in response to the growth of a nation-wide rice trade and the need for rules to govern complicated commercial transactions, transactions that were totally unrelated and often antithetical to the Confucian view of society that animated public law. The attitude of officialdom to commercial development in general and to commercial disputes in particular was therefore at best ambivalent, and there was no perceived need for a general commercial court system with specialized personnel applying clear, officially sanctioned rules of behavior and interpretation. Nonetheless, a discrete body of commercial customs were practiced and understood by the commercial world and enforced through a combination of government courts and private sanctions. The later introduction of Western ideas of commercial law, therefore, merely confirmed much of what had already developed indigenously within Japanese commercial society. Basic concepts such as the importance of written contracts, judicial persons, the holder-in-due-course doctrine, and the bona fide purchaser were already understood in Japan.

LEGAL INSTITUTIONS OF THE MEIJI ERA

The position of commercial law and the structure and role of the legal system underwent fundamental changes in the three decades after 1868 so that few of the Tokugawa institutions were to remain by 1900. Both in recognition of the inadequacies of the traditional system and in response to external demands for legal reform, the Meiji elite soon turned to the wholesale adoption of Western legal institutions. Scholars and members of the elite themselves were sent to Europe or the United States to study Western legal models, and foreign legal scholars were invited to Japan to serve as advisors and teachers. Schools were established to study Western law and translations of major Western codes or treatises were prepared, which often meant the invention of a new Japanese vocabulary to express legal concepts hitherto unknown in Japan.

By the end of 1885, considerable progress had been made in the drafting of new codes, the elimination of the use of torture and other aspects of the former law particularly offensive to Western mores, and the drafting of a new constitution. At this time supporters of the English and French models for the commercial and civil codes were dominant, but by the late 1890s the influence of Germany had largely displaced both, and the codes eventually promulgated in 1898 (Civil Code) and 1899 (Commercial Code) were most heavily influenced by the new German codes, then only in draft form in Germany. The German influence was even more dominant in the new Meiji Constitution of 1889 partly because the more authoritarian nature of German public law appealed to the Meiji leaders' desire for the strong executive and a revered position for the emperor.

By the turn of the century, there was in place a virtually complete Westernized legal system boasting a written constitution, which, although quite conservative, reflected Western theories of state and society, and a set of codes that were generally as "modern" as most of Europe's. The connection between the positive law and the functioning of society, however, was frequently tenuous and more often nonexistent. Although the adoption of Western law served its major purpose of helping to abolish the unequal treaties forced on Japan in the nineteenth century, Japan's leaders were not at all inclined to have the individualistic premises of German, French, or British jurisprudence penetrate beyond the surface. Nor could they have done so even if the government had wished them to. Until Japanese scholars, lawyers, and judges not only became familiar with the abstract Western gloss of the codes, but also began creatively applying these concepts in the Japanese context, the imported laws would remain nothing more than a veneer intended to satisfy and delude foreign observers. Meanwhile traditional customary law retained much of its force.

POST-WORLD WAR II CHANGES

The process of adapting the Western codes to Japanese social reality began in the first three decades of the twentieth century, but was cut short by the triumph of militarism and the consequent disintegration of the legal system during the 1930s. Before it could resume in 1945, a second wave of foeign influence and reform again transformed Japanese law with the reforms of the Allied Occupation. The mandate of the Occupation staff was to democratize Japan, and legal reforms were central in their plans. The constitution was completely reworked so that it is perhaps the most liberal major constitution in the world today, guaranteeing explicitly many of the rights only implied or not provided at all in Western documents. The basic codes were also revised to implement the new due process, right to counsel, and other procedural guarantees of defendants. The substantive Criminal Code was less affected, being revised only where its provisions conflicted with the constitution. The provision that punished an adulterous wife but not a husband, for example, fell before the equality of the sexes provision of the constitution. The Civil Code was similarly revised mainly in the area of family law to break the authority of the family patriarch, who had legally controlled family property and the marriage of the members, and to abolish legal sexual inequalities. The Code of Civil Procedure was also left mainly intact, but certain changes were made that resulted in a significant shift from the German inquisitorial model of trial procedure, which relies on an activist interventionist bench, toward the American adversary model with its emphasis on the initiative of the parties and their counsel.

The revisions of the Commercial Code, the most extensive of which dealt with company law, stand somewhat apart from the constitutionally based reforms and are best understood as part of the Occupation's attempt to democratize the Japanese economy and business structure. They attempt to strengthen the position of shareholders and clarify management obligations with the objective of promoting corporate democracy. They reinforce the provisions of the various specific statutes in the economic area and particularly the Securities Exchange Law, which was modeled after American securities laws. Other significant economic reforms include labor laws establishing minimum standards for working conditions and implementing the constitutional right of collective bargaining; the Antimonopoly Law and related statutes that attempted to break up prewar concentrations of economic power in the zaibatsu and established the Fair Trade Commission to administer and enforce various American-inspired provisions directed at the maintenance of fair and free competition; and reforms in the statutory and structure of the tax system, again based on American models.

A third area of major Occupation reforms concerns the status of the judiciary. The Meiji Constitution of 1889 had established some important aspects of judicial independence including guaranteed tenure and had fostered the development of a professional judiciary independent of the rest of the bureaucracy and imbued with high standards of personal and professional integrity. Full judicial independence, however, was not possible because the Minister of Justice had general administrative power over the judiciary including considerable power to manipulate personnel policies and to induce promising judges to leave the judiciary and enter the Ministry itself as general administrators where the pay, prestige, and opportunities for promotion were better. Even more damaging to the judiciary as a coequal branch of government was the separate system of administrative courts that had exclusive competence to review the legality of official government action. Although separate administrative and civil court systems do not necessarily preclude the development of independent judicial review by administrative judges—witness the example of the French administrative court system—the administrative courts remained very much a tool of the executive in prewar Japan and never developed the independence or professionalism of the prewar civil judiciary.

Allied reforms, especially the Constitution of 1947, radically changed the position of the judiciary. The administrative court system was abolished, and the American system of constitutional and statutory judicial review review of administrative and legislative acts was firmly established. The full independence and autonomy of the courts is guaranteed with personnel and administrative supervision (except impeachment) entirely within the power of the Supreme Court. The justices of the Supreme Court are appointed by the Cabinet, but lower judicial appointments are controlled by the Supreme Court.

These judicial reforms greatly increased the need for competent private attorneys. The right to counsel in criminal cases, the new emphasis on the attorney's role at trial, and the general elevation of the status of the judiciary meant that the private bar would have to be considerably improved before these reforms could be substantially realized. The prewar bar, although enjoying occasional moments of glory, had generally been kept in a subservient position by the Ministry of Justice, which had had considerable supervisory power over attorneys. Lawyers had been denied equal professional status with judges and public procurators (prosecutors) and occupied a considerably lower social and political position.

The Lawyers Law of 1949 was the vehicle for the fundamental improvement in the private bar. First it granted the bar autonomy. The screening of applicants and the registration and discipline of lawyers were entrusted to the profession, now organized on a nationwide basis as the Japanse Federation of Bar Associations. Second, and even more significant in the long run, the training of lawyers was merged with that of judges and procurators. All three must pass the extremely selective National Legal Examination and receive two years of government training at the Legal Training and Research Institute, an agency of the Supreme Court. If anything, the social status of lawyers is now better than that of the other jurists. Their income is considerably higher, and the recent growth of a politically active public-interest bar has given substantial credence to the Japanese bar's consistent claim to be the defender of the ideals of the Constitution of 1947 and postwar democratic reforms.

The independence of the judiciary and the bar, the political and legal guarantees of the new constitution, the elimination of separate administrative courts, the substantial revisions of the five codes, and the passage of complementary legislation have radically transformed the Japanese legal system to an extent comparable with the reforms of the Meiji period. The infusion of American concepts during the Occupation has removed the legal culture significantly from its European roots, although the civil law tradition remains dominant in the private law fields. The increase in the importance of judicial precedent, the emergence of a politically assertive and litigation-oriented bar, and the heightened interest in legal sociology and the social efficacy of law and litigation within university law faculties all reflect this new American influence. The basic direction of the postwar reforms, however, is probably better perceived not as the introduction of narrowly American ideas but as the culmination of a 100-year-long process of "Westernization" of the legal system—the triumph of the individualistic premises of nineteenth-century liberalism over the hierarchical familial Confucian statecraft of premodern Japan and the evolution of a rule of law that is as thorough, at least institutionally, as that of most liberal democracies.

SUMMARY

The evolution described above has resulted in a legal system that is basically similar to those of Western Europe and the United States. It is at times a curious mixture of civilian and common-law components, e.g., a criminal procedure heavily influenced by American constitutional principles but a substantive criminal law modeled closely on nineteenth-century German concepts. The mix does not always work smoothly, but the formal system as a whole is remarkable mainly because of its eclectic origins, not because of any fundamental departure from Western legal principles. To approach Japanese law solely from the perspective of its institutions, however, would be a serious mistake. Like every legal system the Japanese one functions within a particular social context, and to ignore that context would limit the observer to a very superficial understanding of the way law works in Japan. This is not to say that the institutions of the formal legal system—the courts, the bar, the constitution, and so forth—are merely foreign imports with no connection to Japanese society. That would be an equally mistaken conclusion. But to understand the role of law in Japan, one must understand the way the Japanese use these institutions, their view of litigation, their attitude toward crime and the police, their relationship with their neighbors and their government. These aspects of the Japanese legal system are addressed in the questions that follow.

Frank K. Upham

BIBLIOGRAPHY

Haley, John O., ed. *Current Legal Aspects of Doing Business in Japan and East Asia*. Chicago: American Bar Association, 1978.

Noda, Yosiyuki. *Introduction to Japanese Law*. Tokyo: University of Tokyo Press, 1976.

Tanaka, Hideo, ed. *The Japanese Legal System: Introductory Cases and Materials*. Tokyo: University of Tokyo Press, 1976.

Von Mehren, Arthur C., ed. *Law in Japan: The Legal Order in a Changing Society*. Cambridge, Mass.: Harvard University Press, 1963.

Litigation in Japan

I have heard that the Japanese do not use lawyers and litigation as much as Westerners, and that lawyers correspondingly play a less-crucial role in business decisions. If this is true, how do Japanese (and especially Japanese businesses) solve problems for which we use lawyers and why isn't the legal system used more?

OVERVIEW

It is certainly true that the Japanese use litigation markedly less than most Westerners, and, if anything, the gap is widening with time as the litigation rate in Japan is now less than it was in the late 1920s and early 1930s. Since the war, the annual rate of litigation has remained virtually stable at between 140 and 180 formal trials per 100,000 persons. To give this statistic some perspective, the number of trials commenced in all of Japan with 113 million inhabitants in 1970 was approximately 175,000; the number commenced in the American state of Ohio with 10.6 million was 138,643 in 1970 (not including juvenile and probate cases). Nor is the contrast limited to the United States. Some sources indicate that the Danes sue approximately four times as often as the Japanese, the British three times, and the West Germans almost twice as often.

But such statistics can be exceedingly unreliable and deceiving. Definitional problems abound and many Westerners, especially Americans, must use courts for many matters such as divorces that are rarely handled legally in Japan. The situation is perhaps more effectively presented by two studies of personal injury litigation in Japan in the 1960s. One investigated railroad accidents and discovered that of 145 accidents causing physical injury in which the given railroad was involved, not one case was brought to litigation and attorneys were involved in only two. Similarly a study of Tokyo taxicab companies showed that of a total of 2,567 accidents causing either physical injury or property damage, only two cases were filed.

THE ROLE OF CULTURE

It is commonly believed that this remarkable lack of litigation can be traced to social and cultural factors that have historically led the Japanese to prefer extrajudicial, informal means of dispute settlement. Traditional Japan, as represented by the archetype rural village, was a society that valued harmony and compromise. Stable interpersonal relationships were of the utmost importance and there was a strong expectation that open conflict would not occur. The values of such a society are antithetical to litigation, which admits formally and publicly the existence of the dispute and accentuates conflict and mistrust between the parties. Instead of relying on the participation of the parties and the leaders of their community to bring about a solution that both parties can accept with grace, the judicial process represents the application of abstract, inflexible, and impersonal standards not only to resolve the dispute but often to assign moral blame as well.

This rather romantic vision of a traditional Japan where the individual's interests were voluntarily sacrificed to the goal of social harmony is still frequently cited as the fundamental reason for Japan's low litigation rates. But the truth is certainly much more complex. Even if one assumes that traditional Japanese values were as depicted, how does one explain the apparent drop in litigiousness from the 1920s and 1930s to the postwar period? Certainly the normative hold of village Japan has been loosened, not tightened, in the last three decades. A second explanation of Japan's low litigation rates emphasizes not the strength of traditional values but the objective political and institutional factors that have historically discouraged litigation. According to this interpretation, the rulers of Japan from the Tokugawa shoguns to today's Liberal Democrats have consciously and consistently worked to limit litigation and channel social disputes into what they have perceived as less-disruptive modes of resolution.

INSTITUTIONAL BARRIERS

First, institutional obstacles are placed in the way of the potential litigant. In the contemporary context perhaps the most salient of these obstacles is the lack of lawyers. There are approximately 11,000 attorneys available to serve a population of over 113 million, or about one attorney per 10,250 people. By contrast, the per capita population of lawyers in the West ranges from a high of one lawyer for every 630 citizens in the United States, to a low of one lawyer for every 5,900 citizens in France. The scarcity of Japanese lawyers is not a matter of chance or the result of supply and demand, but a conscious government policy. To become a lawyer in Japan, one must receive two years of training in the official Legal Training and Research Institute. To enter the Institute, applicants, typically graduates of an undergraduate law faculty, must take the National Legal Examination. This examination is extremely difficult to pass. In 1975, for example, 472 out of 27,791 passed, a rate of 1.7 percent. In 1977 the rate fell to 1.6 percent. The successful applicant has on the average taken the exam five times. These figures should dispel any preconception that Japanese do not want to be lawyers. The number per capita of Japanese taking the judicial examination in 1975 was in fact slightly higher than that of Americans taking a bar examination. The difference of course is that 74 percent of the Americans passed.

The official rationale for the low passage rate is the maintenance of high-quality lawyers. Given that the 25,000–30,000 who take the exam each year are already heavily self-selected, however, this explanation seems disingenuous at best. It is hardly likely that an increase in the passage rate to 3 percent—an increase that would almost double the number of lawyers—would flood the legal profession with shysters and dolts. It seems much more likely that the consequences of a lawyer shortage are viewed with equanimity by the government. At present Japanese lawyers are kept so busy and are able to charge what to the Japanese seem as such high fees—a factor that explains the private bar's ambivalence to increasing its own numbers—that most individuals are denied access to the courts for anything but matters of the most vital importance.

Another subtle, but important byproduct of the scarcity is that lawyers are kept so busy litigating private land disputes, contract and debt actions, and personal injury cases that they have little time to pursue the political and social cases that have made litigation and lawyers so important in the West and particularly so in the United States, the country with which the Japanese are most familiar. Since lawyers in Japan have always been considered as outside the ruling elite, a status that most lawyers emphasize and enjoy, the government is anxious to keep them from playing a larger social and political role, especially through the courts.

Even if the litigant perseveres and initiates litigation, the shortage of judicial personnel—judges also must pass the National Legal Examination and attend the Institute—make the process agonizingly time consuming by any standards. It is not at all uncommon for cases that reach the Supreme Court to take 10 years for final decision. If they are politically controversial, they may well take even longer.

The government does not leave Japanese society without means to resolve its disputes, however. Just as actively as it discourages resort to litigation, the government promotes the use of less formal, less public, and less disruptive means of dispute resolution. The most common are conciliation and mediation whereby the parties are brought together and given a chance to resolve their dispute with or without the intervention of a third party. Although a common means to resolve any dispute anywhere, the Japanese are famous for preferring conciliation or mediation to litigation. One reason has undoubtedly been the government's provision of official conciliation services for a broad range of disputes from landlord tenant to pollution cases. Although compulsory before the war, submission to officially sponsored conciliation now is legally voluntary. Resort to formal litigation is available at any time, but conciliation remains the preferred mode. The reasons are clear. It saves time and money since neither lawyers nor formal adjudication is involved, and it preserves the parties' relationship. By reaching a compromise, it also reduces the risk of an all or nothing decision, a risk that is heightened by the fact that the loser usually must pay the winner's litigation expenses. The assessment of expenses and the absence of a contingent-fee system are themselves further obstacles to litigation.

THE ROLE OF LAWYERS

Whether the Japanese avoid litigation because of a cultural adversion to it or because the government has made it virtually unavailable is unanswerable. It is undoubtedly a combination of these factors. The fact remains, however, that lawyers and litigation are relatively rare and that the Japanese, including Japanese businesses, do not use legal expertise and institutions as they are frequently used in the West. The shortage of lawyers alone practically precludes their functioning as general corporate counselors in matters such as taxation, contract drafting, or business negotiations. In fact the introduction of an attorney into a domestic business conference is often considered an unfriendly act, an implied threat of litigation since businesses have traditionally used lawyers only for that purpose. Although Japanese businessmen with considerable international experience are accustomed to the role of corporate lawyers in the West and are often in constant communication with American law firms in New York or the West Coast, reliance on lawyers as corporate counselors in domestic matters remains limited. There is a growing number of specialized corporate firms in Tokyo and Osaka whose significance will continue to grow in the future, but institutional and cultural factors will probably preclude the constant dependence on lawyers common in the West.

Even domestically, however, legal expertise is needed for corporate planning in areas like tax and patents, and, although Japanese contracts are famous for being as short and flexible as possible, they do exist and have to be drafted or at least reviewed by someone with a legal background. Although a few lawyers are now being consulted on such matters in Tokyo and Osaka, businesses are much more likely to rely on various types of nonlawyer legal personnel. Two of these are patent agents and tax agents, which are licensed professions almost as difficult to enter as the bar. Regulated by the Ministry of International Trade and Industry and the Finance Ministry respectively, patent and tax agents must take examinations and demonstrate a high level of expertise in their fields. The patent agent can litigate as well as advise on patent, utility model, design, and trademark questions. The tax agent, on the other rhand, is limited to nonlitigative activities such as drafting tax returns, filing applications for review of assessments, and counseling on tax matters. Lawyers can also perform these functions, as can certified public accounts (CPAs) in the tax area, but they are less likely to do so in practice.

In addition to these specialists, most large companies (and government agencies) have their own legal staffs with employees who are usually law faculty graduates but who have not passed the judicial examination or received the official training necessary for the formal practice of law. It is they who are the major dispensers of corporate legal advice in Japan and who do much of the work handled by corporate counsel in the United States or by solicitors in Great Britain. As legal matters have grown in complexity and importance, large companies have put more emphasis on the drafting of contracts and the legal aspects of corporate planning, and the status and expertise of corporate legal departments have improved. Although clearly not possessed with the professionalism or broad competence of members of the bar, their technical knowledge of corporate law is often greater than that of many lawyers.

FOREIGN LAWYERS

For the foreign businessman doing business in Japan, there exists a third type of legal professional, the foreign lawyer practicing in Japan. Of these there are only a very few, no more than 20 and mostly American nationals, are now licensed to practice in Japan. Until 1955 Japanese language competence was not a requirement for foreign lawyers to be admitted to the bar. Thereafter, the requirements for Japanese and foreigners have been identical and, except for Korean nationals born and raised in Japan, the chance for a foreigner to practice formally in Japan is practically nil. There are, however, quite a few Westerners practicing informally in Japan and available to foreign clients. The legal status of these foreign lawyers is unclear, but several international law firms have offices in Tokyo and employ both Japanese and foreign lawyers, the latter sometimes under the guise of "law clerks." In addition there are a growing number of purely Japanese law firms made up of English-speaking lawyers who have often worked in American or European law firms and are familiar with the needs of foreign business clients.

The legal aspect of international business in Japan, however, remains a very small and relatively insignificant exception to the general rule that the Japanese do quite well without lawyers. To Americans especially, who often feel themselves beset by lawyers at every turn, it may be revealing to know that the Japanese rarely use lawyers in divorces, virtually never to buy a house or plot of land, get a loan from a bank, or file an income tax return. Even within the domestic business world with the company legal staff available, the fine points of a contract are rarely haggled over, and negotiations over a business project, although they may be prolonged, are often more a process of establishing mutual trust than working out the details of a contract that will protect each party from all foreseeable occurrences. Once that trust is established, both parties put great emphasis on maintaining the relationship over the long term. That attitude often means foregoing short-term profits that could be gained by shifting to another buyer or supplier and being willing to be flexible about the terms of a contract when the other party is under unusual pressure or short-term difficulties. Although perhaps guilty of overstatement, a leading American lawyer familiar with the Japanese business environment explained it:

> The law, which purports to sort out human relations on supposedly objective bases, goes directly contrary to the Japanese feeling that relations (even business relations) should be based upon a warm subjective relationship which can solve every practical problem by mutual compromise and accommodation, regardless of formal rights and obligations (Stevens, p. 1272)

Whether or not this is an accurate description of the reality of Japanese business relationships, and many would argue that Japanese businessmen are as interested in the "bottom line" in the long run as businessmen anywhere, it captures well the Japanese businessman's own ideal of what animates his behavior. And to a certain extent, it represents the way most

Japanese prefer to picture themselves. Whether a myth or not and whether caused by a unique heritage or official manipulation, the average Japanese eschews the entanglements of the law and perceives his society as generally more compassionate and efficient than the law-plagued, overly rational West.

Frank K. Upham

BIBLIOGRAPHY

Haley, John O. "The Myth of the Reluctant Litigant." *Journal of Japanese Studies* 359 (1978).

Kawashima, Takeyoshi. "Dispute Resolution in Contemporary Japan." In *Law in Japan: The Legal Order in a Changing Society,* edited by Arthur C. Von Mehren, p. 41. Cambridge, Mass.: Harvard University Press, 1963.

Stevens, Charles, "Japanese Law and the Japanese Legal System: Perspectives for the American Business Lawyer," 27 *Business Law* 1259 (July 1972).

Crime in Japan

> Japan is said to have a very low crime rate. Is this true, and if so, what is the role of society, the police, and courts in preventing crime in Japan? Moreover, what are the defendant's rights in Japan and is the criminal process different in Japan than in America?

A woman walking on a poorly lit street, an unsteady businessman in a deserted entertainment district, an elderly person crossing a park in the inner city—tense, fearful scenes for many Westerners. For the Japanese, however, they are commonplace and not particularly frightening. Street crime is extremely rare in Japan. In fact Japan has by far the lowest crime rate among major industrialized nations.

The figures are startling and consistently low for virtually all forms of crime. Government statistics indicate that a New Yorker was almost nine times more likely to be murdered in 1973 than a Tokyo resident. The U.S. national homicide rate is 4.5 times higher than the Japanese, the incidence of rape 5 times higher, and perhaps the most startling of all, the incidence of robbery—the taking of property by force—is a staggering 105 times higher in the United States. The comparison need not stop with the Americans; Japanese are much safer than the French, British, and Germans as well. In 1977 they suffered (and committed) 2.3 times less homicides than the

Germans, 28 times fewer robberies than the French, and one-fourth as many rapes as the British. Equally important, the Japanese are much more likely to solve crimes once they are committed. The overall clearance rate in Japan in 1973 was 58 percent versus only 28 percent in the United States.

Perhaps even more remarkable than the differences in the crime rates is the striking difference in the trend in crime. Crime seems to rise inexorably in the West, and we begin to assume that crime is a natural concomitant of contemporary life. In Japan, crime rates are falling. The total number of crimes committed in Japan was less in 1973 than in 1946, despite the increase in population. The decrease in per capita crime is even more dramatic and is not limited to comparisons with the chaotic postwar years. In the decade after 1967, serious crime generally decreased, and in the five years from 1974 to 1978 the rate for homicide, robbery, assault, forcible rape, and homicides associated with robbery all declined. By contrast, the rate of serious crime in the United States increased approximately 60 percent from 1967 to 1977.

The crime picture is not entirely rosy. If one looks closely, he will find that the illicit use of drugs has increased sharply since 1970, that in 1977 the number of juveniles placed under official "protection and guidance" was at a ten-year high, and that the gangs of the Japanese underworld continue their participation in the gambling, drugs, and protection rackets. Small as these problems are in relation to similar ones in the West, they cause concern among Japanese that Japan may be moving toward the situation in Western countries. Japanese religiously lock their doors and windows against what they seem to perceive as inevitable burglary should they forget even once. To an American, however, the depth of Japanese concern over problems like burglars or young "hot-rodders" racing around urban expressways, a problem that receives frequent and anxious attention in the media, merely confirms the difference in magnitude of the crime problem in the United States and Japan.

Statistics can be deceiving of course, and comparative crime rates are particularly susceptible to reporting and definitional discrepancies. American scholars have estimated, however, that underreporting of crime is greater in the United States than Japan. Even if there are some definitional differences, therefore, the published statistics should be accepted as evidence of a profound difference in the incidence of crime. Statistics are only part of the story of course; personal experience of foreigners in Japan more than corroborates the very real difference of living in a relatively crime-free society. As one American commentator on the Japanese police stated:

> Americans who live for a while in Japan soon begin to experience a liberating sense of freedom; they forget to be afraid. They learn to walk

through city streets by night as well as by day and not fear the sound of a following step, the sight of a lounging group of teenagers, or the query of a stranger for directions (Bayley, p. 9).

SOCIAL COHESION AND LOW CRIME RATES

But what is the significance of the Japanese success? Surely it is of interest to foreigners visiting or residing in Japan and to Westerners who are simply interested in learning about Japan, but its greatest significance must be in what the Japanese experience can tell us about our own societies. To learn from the Japanese and perhaps to apply some of those lessons to crime control in other countries, however, we must first have some idea of the reasons for Japan's success. For, if they lie in unique social or cultural factors, we must be cautious in applying them elsewhere.

The reasons for Japan's success are complex and not susceptible to precise or dogmatic articulation, but certain generalizations are possible and practical lessons can be learned. Perhaps the clearest is that some of our popular assumptions about crime need reassessment. We often assume that urbanization in an industrial society contributes to crime. Japan, however, is one of the most densely populated countries of the world with all the problems of pollution, congestion, and anonymity that one associates with large cities, except crime. In fact crime in urban areas in Japan is no higher than in rural or suburban areas. The huge high-rise apartment complexes that encircle Tokyo, Osaka, and the other major urban centers are not unusually beset by crime. Nor is crime an inevitable concomitant of low-income neighborhoods. Finally, one should note that Japan is not a noticeably more pacifistic society than the West. Television violence is common, and political violence, both in the form of terrorism and assassinations and in the more acceptable form of labor strife and political demonstrations, is probably as common in Japan as elsewhere.

But if Japan has many of the same characteristics of other modern societies, to what can we attribute the low crime rate? First let's look at those aspects of Japanese society that distinguish it from technologically similar Western societies. Although one must be careful to avoid over-simplifications and clichés, the cohesion and homogeneity of Japanese society is remarkable and surely contributes to effective law enforcement. The Koreans form the largest ethnic minority in Japan. Even when combined with the Chinese, who constitute the second largest ethnic minority, they make up less than 1 percent of the population. Even including the descendents of former feudal outcasts, the total population of socially disadvantaged and discriminated-against groups is less than 3 percent of the population. The other 97 percent of Japan's population share not only an ethnic and cultural identity but also a set of common values. Although the stereotype of Japan as conformist and group oriented ignores strains of individualism and social dissonance present throughout Japanese history, it remains true that group identification with the family, the local neighborhood, and, as is often the case in contemporary Japan, with the husband's employer is of great importance to the Japanese. This group orientation may be under considerable strain as the mobility of industrial life erodes its traditional bases in the family and rural village, but the particular nature of the Japanese company has to a certain extent provided a new focus for urban life and enabled many Japanese to retain a sense of belonging that is more difficult in the more individualistic societies of the West. The role of the firm is complemented by the cohesiveness of most Japanese neighborhoods, which are held together by a panoply of quasi-official associations and self-help groups. Again, mobility has weakened these social ties, but they still exist and function, even in the middle of Tokyo and Osaka, and are of undoubted importance to law enforcement.

THE JAPANESE POLICE AND JAPANESE SOCIETY

The Japanese police do not only profit from this social cohesion, they actively encourage it and become part of it. As a result, they are much closer to the community they serve than are, e.g., American police. There are many reasons for this. First, there is a physical proximity and accessibility. Japanese patrolmen are stationed in police boxes spread over a neighborhood rather than concentrated in central police stations. From the police box the patrolmen make frequent foot patrols during which they consciously cultivate personal relationships with neighborhood residents. These relationships are broadened and strengthened by periodic visits to each home in the district when the police office gathers certain information—family members' names and birthdays, their occupations and employers, whom to contact in emergencies—and discusses occurrences and problems in the neighborhood. Although ostensibly voluntary, practically everyone cooperates. Another means of cooperation and contact with the residents is the panoply of voluntary groups supported by the police—crime-prevention associations, traffic-safely associations, "youth assistants," and volunteer welfare caseworkers, probation officers, and human rights commissioners—all of which are in regular communication with the police.

Their closeness to the community enables to police to play a role in society that goes well beyond crime control. Like police everywhere they are called on to settle disputes and to help those in need, but unlike the American police, they do not see such activity as secondary or as interfering with their crime control function. On the contrary, they go out of their way to provide social services of various kinds from visiting the elderly, especially those living alone, to loaning wayward drunks taxi fare home. They serve as counselors for people with problems ranging from marital discord to money management or finding an apartment. Citizens know that the police will listen patiently and respectfully even if no concrete help is possible.

These efforts pay off in crime control. The community assists the police spontaneously through tips or through the more formal channels of the police-support organizations. In fact the police and the community form a partnership, and the dividing line between the citizen and formal authority is not sharply delineated. This is undoubtedly one of the reasons not only that crime control is so effective but also for the success of the Japanese police in solving crimes that are committed. The Japanese apparently understand that the primary responsibility for social control lies with the community and that members of society must not only discipline themselves but also actively help maintain order. They realize a truth that at least American police and civilians often forget—that crime control cannot be, as one observer phrased it, "a game of cowboys and Indians, with honest citizens playing the part of the trees" (Ames, p. VI-1).

Before one grants the police superhuman status, however, one should remember the vital role that the cohesion and unity of Japanese society plays in this process. Evidence for this role is the increased difficulty the police have in dealing with groups, such as the Koreans, the descendents of feudal outcasts, and leftists, that either do not share the common set of values that animate police-community relations generally or that feel persecuted or oppressed by the society or police. There are also several objective factors that make law enforcement easier. Japan is a virtually unarmed society. The use of guns by criminals is limited almost entirely to underworld gang warfare, and even there it is unusual. The relatively low youth unemployment rate in Japan for the last two decades and the small number of extremely poor Japanese must also play some role in crime control although empirical proof of the relationship is lacking.

CRIME AND THE JAPANESE COURT SYSTEM

Although perhaps the most important, the police are not the only institution involved in crime control. Without competent prosecutors and efficient courts their effectiveness would be greatly diminished, so let us now turn to the role of these other legal institutions. Both prosecutors and judges are career civil servants, selected by means of an extremely rigorous examination (less than 3 percent pass) to receive two years of official legal training. At the end of the two-year course each of the class of approximately 500 trainees chooses to become a private attorney, enter the Ministry of Justice as prosecutors, or become career judges. Judges and prosecutors, therefore, are generally extraordinarily able, at least in terms of passing written examinations, and the professionalism of court personnel, like that in most European systems, is in striking contrast to the frequently poor quality found at lower levels of the American court system.

At this juncture one might reasonably ask what has been the cost of this success. A low crime rate would be of little interest or value if achieved through the sacrifice of civil rights and personal freedom. The picture of a centrally trained and directed police force with encyclopedic knowledge of each neighborhood across the country—even to the degree of knowing the occupation of each resident in each home—is not an entirely pleasant one, particularly in a nation that has so recently experienced a militaristic dictatorship supported by a police force not completely unlike the present one.

Return to the police practices of prewar Japan, however, is impossible under the new Constitution of 1947 and the 1948 Code of Criminal Procedure. Article 38 (2) of the Constitution, for example, explicitly excludes involuntary confessions from use as evidence, no matter how reliable the confession may be. Based on this provision, the Japanese Supreme Court has ruled that a confession induced by a prosecutor's promise of leniency could not be a truly voluntary act. Negotiated confessions are of course a regular, if frequently criticized, tactic of American law enforcement officials. A Japanese defendant also has the various procedural rights familiar to Europeans and Americans: the right to consult an attorney immediately upon detention and to counsel at trial, the right to be informed of the charges against him, freedom from search or arrest without a judicially issued warrant, the right to a speedy trial before an impartial judge, the full opportunity to confront prosecution witnesses and compulsory process for his own, and the right to remain silent. In addition there are provisions specifically directed at prewar police practices, such as the constitutional provision that no person shall be convicted on the basis of his confession alone. This requirement of additional evidence is directed against the prewar tendency of the police to rely entirely on confessions, many of which were of dubious reliability.

The Japanese defendant, therefore, has most if not all of the formal protections that are available to defendants anywhere. What is fascinating, however, is that they are relatively rarely called on. Defense attorneys, for example, rarely meet their clients until after they have confessed, not because the police have actively prevented the suspect from contacting an attorney, but because the police are so adept at the psychology of interrogation that most defendants—professional criminals, political offenders, and white-collar suspects are often exceptions—soon want to confess. In interrogation the police again utilize traditional Japanese values just as they do in establishing themselves in a neighborhood. They seem to play the role of social worker or clergyman to establish an emotional dependence in the defendant, a belief that the police think he is a good person who has merely made a mistake. Once the police have developed this rapport, they can fully exploit the difficulty most Japanese have in resisting someone in a position of authority. The result is that 95 percent of those interrogated by the Japanese police confess.

None of these police techniques is unique to Japan. What makes them work so well is the manner in which the Japanese police adapt them to the specific mores of their society. That Japan's success in controlling crime is based ultimately on aspects of its social structure, however, should not be a pretext for dismissing the Japanese experience as irrelevant in the European or American contexts. Westerners would be foolish to view their success as further evidence of Japanese "inscrutability." There are lessons to learn and they go beyond police practices to raise fundamental questions about the relationship between our social structure and crime. But in applying those lessons, we must remember the importance of social context and not treat Japanese techniques as immediately applicable to Paris or New York.

Frank K. Upham

BIBLIOGRAPHY

Ames, Walter L. *Police and Community in Japan*. Berkeley: University of California Press, forthcoming.

Bayley, David H. *Forces of Order: Police Behavior in Japan and the United States*. Berkeley: University of California Press, 1976.

Ross, Ruth A., and George C. S. Benson. *Criminal Justice from East to West*, 25 *Crime and Delinquency* 76 (1979).

The Japanese Constitution

The Japanese constitution is essentially an American document. How has that origin affected its operation, and will some reversion to a more Japanese document occur some day? Relatedly, do Japanese enjoy the same civil rights and liberties that Americans do?

JAPAN'S MODEL CONSTITUTION

The Japanese Constitution of 1947 is indeed a remarkable document, and not merely because of its foreign origin. Although largely drafted by American reformers on the model of the U.S. Constitution, it goes further and makes explicit many features of contemporary democracies left implicit or absent totally from the U.S. Constitution. These include not only civil rights and liberties such as the equality of the sexes before the law, the absence of which is of course a matter of current controversy in the United States, but also broader, affirmative duties of the state to provide minimal living conditions for its citizens, which anticipate a form of social welfare state hardly contemplated by the eighteenth-century draftsmen of the American document. Of course such far-reaching ideals, particularly when imposed by a foreign conqueror, are easier proclaimed than implemented, and Japanese society inevitably falls short of the norms expressed in the constitution. One should not assume, however, that this shortfall is any greater in Japan than elsewhere or that it is rooted in a fundamental rejection of the spirit of the Constitution as foreign or "un-Japanese." As the decades have passed since its adoption, the Constitution has grown stronger, not weaker. It has been thoroughly accepted by the Japanese people despite occasional attempts to revise it along more "Japanese" lines. Courts and politicians have adapted its more starkly alien features to the actuality of Japanese society, but have not weakened the strength of the democratic principles that form its foundation and animate Japanese political and social life today.

PREWAR VERSUS POSTWAR
JAPANESE CONSTITUTIONS

It is common to contrast the present constitution with its prewar predecessor, the so-called Meiji Constitution of 1889. The latter was a basically authoritarian document heavily influenced by nineteenth-century

German constitutional theory. It provided for few civil rights or liberties and even those could be limited by Diet legislation. Perhaps more important historically, however, was the position of the emperor under the old constitution. The sovereignty of the state flowed from the emperor. The Constitution was merely a "gift" from the emperor to his subjects and was formally contingent on the imperial will. The emperor's status as the transcendent object of loyalty and the formal locus of state power actually increased during the almost 60 years of the Meiji Constitution and, combined with ambiguous provisions concerning the constitutional position of the military, eventually contributed to the tragedy of the 1930s and later to World War II itself.

All this was dramatically changed in the 1947 constitution. Sovereignty now rests with the people and the emperor is relegated to a purely formal role as the "symbol of the State and of the unity of the people." The maintenance of military forces is severely limited by article 9 and, to the extent a military establishment exists as the Self Defense Forces, it is clearly under civilian control. But it would be a mistake to exaggerate the break with the prewar Meiji Constitution or to dismiss the latter as irrelevant or destructive to the democratic development of Japan. Although basically authoritarian, it did establish a type of rule of law in that citizens' legal rights were guaranteed by an independent judiciary. Equally important, the constitution provided the framework, albeit flawed, for a strong centralized state with a professional bureaucracy, an elected legislature, and an executive at least partially responsible to that legislature. Given the feudal institutions of the Tokugawa period, these were important first steps toward democracy, and the vigor of party politics in the 1920s should demonstrate that democratic political development was not foreclosed by the Meiji Constitution.

It is certainly true, however, that the prewar constitution was not strong enough to protect Japan's nascent democracy from the militarism and ultranationalism of the 1930s. Nor was it designed to foster affirmatively a pacifistic and democratic consciousness among the Japanese people. These goals clearly required a new constitution. But on September 1, 1945, when the Occupation authorities informed the Japanese cabinet of the need for constitutional change, the resulting Japanese revisions of the Meiji Constitution were minimal and far from sufficient, maintaining even the sovereignty of the emperor. The Occupation's draftsmen then, in the remarkable period of two weeks, prepared their own version, which was given to the Japanese authorities as a "guide" to what was needed. The response of the Japanese politicians was surprise and dismay at the radical nature of the American document and at its almost total lack of connection with Japanese tradition. They had little choice, however, and in time a slightly modified draft was adopted by the Diet as an amendment to the

Meiji Constitution. The resulting document is thus foreign not only in its basic ideology, but even in its language. Even a middle-school student can tell that it is a translation that as one observer phrased it at the time, "sounds quaintly and exotically American."

Japan's postwar constitution provides for political institutions that are as democratic in potential as any in the world. The prewar governmental system in which cabinet members could not be removed by the parliament was replaced by a conventional system of prime ministerial and cabinet responsibility. The Prime Minister of Japan is elected by the National Diet's two houses and in turn appoints a cabinet, a majority of whom must be members of the parliament. The prime minister and his cabinet can also be removed by a vote of nonconfidence, or by the failure of a vote of confidence, in the parliament.

Popular elections were introduced in Japan in 1890, when the first members of the House of Representatives, the lower house of the National Diet, were elected. A typical restricted suffrage was gradually expanded, and all adult males were given the vote in 1925 while women gained the franchise in 1946. As a result of the postwar governmental reforms, some of which were built into the constitution and some of which were enacted in separate legislation, the membership of Japan's upper parliamentary house became elective after 1946; prefectural governors were also elected for the first time in the postwar era.

Because Japan's postwar national politics have generally been dominated by the Liberal Democratic Pary (or conservative coalitions before 1955), prime ministers and cabinets have been less vulnerable to recall than the constitutional arrangements would imply. Still, Japan's postwar political system has worked extremely well, and since the 1950s there has been no indication that a return to the authoritarian politics of the prewar era is possible or desired by any major political groups. Indeed, Japan's new political institutions have worked remarkably well, and after some desire to return to a Japanese style constitution in the 1950s and early 1960s, even moves for constitutional reform have dwindled in strength and plausibility.

CIVIL AND ECONOMIC RIGHTS

The heart of the new constitution's guarantees of fundamental human rights is found in the 31 articles of chapter III, entitled the Rights and Duties of the People. The expected rights and freedoms found in the American constitutions are all there: equality before the law for sex, race, creed, social status (to eliminate remnants of feudal hierarchy), and family origin; universal adult suffrage and a secret ballot; freedom of thought and conscience and of religion; freedom of assembly and speech; academic freedom; an ambiguous provision for due process; and the right to own or hold property. Other guarantees implicit in a liberal democracy but not explicitly provided in the U.S. Constitution are also present: freedom to choose and change an occupation and residence and the freedom to emigrate; the duty of the state to treat all citizens as individuals; the right to work; the right to sue the state for redress of wrongs committed by the state or a public entity; and guaranteed access to the courts. There are also provisions specifically tailored to eliminate uniquely Japanese obstacles to democracy. The prime example is the constitution's effort to redress the traditionally subservient status of women in Japanese society. The inclusion of sex in the article 14 guarantee of legal equality, for example, is reinforced by article 24's provisions guaranteeing freedom of marriage based on the mutual consent of both sexes and requiring that all legislation concerning the family and marriage, including laws governing the disposition of property, "be enacted from the standpoint of individual dignity and the essential equality of the sexes."

The above description can be characterized as the imitation, adaptation, and perfection of the American constitution and of the European liberal ideology on which it is based. That ideology can be fairly summarized as emphasizing individual freedom and rights and as viewing the state's role as providing a neutral structure within which the individual members of society can operate autonomously with minimal assistance or interference from the government. Although such a conception of society is perhaps dominant in the Japanese constitution, it is not a complete description. The constitution goes beyond pure liberal ideology to anticipate many of the concepts of the welfare state that characterize twentieth-century societies. Implicit in the ideology of the welfare state, for example, is the limitation of individual rights for the common good. Absent from the explicit language of the U.S. Constitution, American courts have implied such a limitation primarily since the New Deal of the 1930s. The Constitution of Japan, on the other hand, explicitly states that the Japanese people "shall refrain from any abuse" of their rights (the European abuse of rights doctrine), and "shall be responsible for utilizing them for the public welfare." In return, society as embodied by the state owes something more to the individual than merely leaving him alone to compete equally with his fellows. Article 25, for example, gives all people "the right to maintain the minimum standards of wholesome and cultured living" and requires the state to promote and extend "social welfare and security." Article 26 grants all Japanese a "right to receive an equal education correspondent to their ability" and guarantees free compulsory education. Other articles provide that standards for working conditions will be fixed by law, prohibit the exploitation of child labor, and guarantee workers the right to organize and bargain collectively. Although none of these provisions was new even in 1947, their inclusion as constitutional norms, rather than being established by statute, sets the Constitution of Japan apart from its American model and brings it more into accord not only with twentieth-century welfare state concepts, but also with the communitarian, less individualist traditions of Japan.

RENUNCIATION OF WAR

Perhaps the best known of the constitution's articles, however, draws upon neither Western nor Japanese traditions. That is article 9, which unilaterally renounces war and the use of force as a sovereign right of Japan. Paragraph 2 goes on to provide that "land, sea, and air forces, as well as other war potential, will never be maintained." Unique to Japan's constitution, article 9 was the expression of the Allies' determination to elminate Japan as a potential military rival for the foreseeable future (a point which the United States, now pressing Japan to assume substantial military responsibilities, would perhaps like to forget). As such it is the frequent target of conservative and right-wing politicians who claim that it demeans Japan as a sovereign state.

These cries for revision of the "peace constitution" have so far elicited only insignificant support. One would expect the opposition parties, especially those that oppose Japan's military relationship with the United States, to oppose revision, but the concern for article 9 goes much, much deeper than partisan politics. For most Japanese the defeat in 1945 was a devastating experience. Not only had Japan never suffered defeat in war before, but the military government did nothing to prepare the people for it, stressing to the bitter end the need to defend the empire and the glory of patriotic death. The defeat, when it came on the heels of Hiroshima and Nagasaki, therefore, thoroughly discredited the military and transformed Japan almost over night into one of the most pacifistic nations in the world. While the visceral reaction to war and militarism is perhaps fading as the population moves farther away from the experience of World War II, the sentiment in favor of article 9 remains strong and prospects for its explicit revision are slim.

IMPLEMENTATION

The true measure of the Constitution of Japan, however, lies not in the idealistic language of article 9 or the ringing guarantees of human rights and social justice. For that one must ask whether these norms have been implemented and how seriously they are taken by the government and its citizens. This is of course a difficult question to answer across the board. Japan is without doubt a "free" country where there exists a vigorous and free exchange of political and social ideas, but there also exist areas where the promise of the constitution has not yet been fulfilled. One such area is the guarantee of a "minimal standard of wholesome and cultured living," which has been interpreted to be of only oratorical effect without specific legislation. Similarly Japanese courts have been reluctant to interpret constitutional provisions as broadly as the language itself might indicate. Nor have the courts been eager to strike down legislation or administrative action as unconstitutional, even with the right of constitutional judicial review explicitly guaranteed by article 81 of the constitution itself. In fact it was not until the 1960s that the Supreme Court first definitively exercised its power to declare a statute unconstitutional.

Instead of boldly asserting its power of constitutional review, the court has chosen to avoid constitutional issues whenever possible. One prime example is the question of the constitutional status of the Self Defense Forces. Despite article 9, the Self Defense Forces now has one of the 10 largest military budgets in the world. The courts, perhaps wisely, have generally chosen to invoke the political question doctrine when faced with this question, although the prevailing interpretation is that the Self Defense Forces remain constitutional as long as they are capable of only "defensive" action. Similarly in social issues such as sexual equality, the courts have not played the active role that American courts did in the civil rights movements in the United States. Part of the reason is the disinclination of the Japanese to use litigation either to resolve private disputes or to achieve social or political ends. Another aspect, however, is undoubtedly the realization by the courts that many of the constitutional norms we have been discussing need time to sink roots in the society of Japan and that to push provisions such as the no war clause of article 9 or the sexual equality guarantee of article 14 to their logical ends would be premature and threaten the broad public support that the constitution now enjoys.

That is not to say, however, that the fundamental human rights of the constitution are or should be subordinate to contrary aspects of Japanese society. There is instead a continual dialectic between society and the constitution whereby the latter, both indirectly through its substantial moral force as a generally accepted statement of the ideal and directly by its implementation through judicial decisions, contributes to the continued "democratization" of Japan while simultaneously being adapted to Japan's special circumstances. As that process goes on, the Supreme Court has become more comfortable with its role and more assertive in enforcing the constitution. In a 1976 decision, for example, the court declared the Diet apportionment, which heavily favors the generally conservative rural voters over the more liberal urban voters, invalid as a violation of article 14's requirement of equality before the law. Even in this modified "one-man, one-vote" case, however, the ambivalence of the court toward its own role caused a majority of the justices to stop short of invalidating the previous Diet election. To do so would have taken the court beyond the limits of its consitutional powers in their opinion.

Even with a somewhat more active court, therefore, there is no reason to expect that Japanese constitutional law will develop along strictly American lines. There is, after all, nothing that requires that the same language in a constitution will mean the same in two very different societies. In fact, if there were, the Japanese constitution would be the "foreign" document that it is sometimes criticized as being and, undoubtably, would have been revised long ago to meet the realities and needs of Japanese society.

Frank K. Upham

BIBLIOGRAPHY

Henderson, Dan Fenno, ed. *The Constitution of Japan: Its First Twenty Years, 1947–1967.* Seattle: University of Washington Press, 1969.

Itoh, Hiroshi, and Lawrence Ward Beer. *The Constitutional Case Law of Japan: Selected Supreme Court Decisions, 1961–1970.* Seattle: University of Washington Press, 1978.

Maki, John M., ed. *Court and Constitution in Japan: Selected Supreme Court Decisions, 1948–1960.* Seattle: University of Washington Press, 1964.

7

THE POLITICAL ENVIRONMENT

Politics is obviously important to business; the political environment has at times been of even greater importance in Japan than in most other industrialized nations. Japan's rapid national development was guided in its early years by government policies, and postwar high growth has followed at least the general direction provided by indicative economic plans, even though planning by itself was not the main determinant of growth. Indeed both domestic and foreign policy have been extensively supportive of economic growth and trade expansion, although Japanese economic success has probably been due as much or more to market factors and business leadership than to governmental initiative. Finally, postwar Japan has been stable politically, which is in itself no small factor contributing to business predictability and success.

Japan has been governed for 30 years by the same political movement. Represented by different parties up until 1955, and one party during most of the ensuing period, Japan's conservative camp has managed to win a majority in the national parliament in every general election since 1946. (Splits in the conservative camp permitted Socialist participation in government in the late 1940s, the only breach in total conservative dominance in the postwar era.) Despite declining electoral support in the 1960s and 1970s, the conservative movement—represented currently by the Liberal Democratic Party—remains in power today and even rallied to win a substantial increase in its share of Diet seats in the Spring 1980 elections.

Conservative dominance in postwar Japan has meant by and large a favorable climate for business. Supports for business growth in selected areas were provided as part of the overall economic policy effort, while the general political climate was receptive to business interests. Foreign trade policy in the 1950s and early 1960s was clearly oriented toward protection of domestic industry and promotion of exports. The residue of supportive trade policies exists even today, as government after government seeks stable relations with all nations—a prerequisite for trade—and explores the potential for trade with such difficult partners as the People's Republic of China and the Soviet Union. Current energy problems have, if anything, sharpened governmental sensitivity to the links between trade and politics, and even though Japanese foreign policy does concern itself with other matters such as national security, economics is the major motivating force in Japan's contemporary foreign stance.

In two essays on Japanese politics, Bradley Richardson shows the importance under conservative hegemony of the frequent business-government identity of interests to both domestic and foreign policies. But the presence in Japan of a dynamic multiparty system with active leftist parties, as well as a growing middle-of-the-road sector, should not be forgotten. The comparatively strong and vociferous, albeit fragmented, opposition has ensured that the conservative movement has paid attention to "postindustrial" issues like pollution and quality-of-life problems even more than the Conservatives' "catchall" posture of responsibility to the whole nation might have provided for. Also, while there has been a rough identity of long-term goals between business and government in Japan, there have been many disagreements over short-term policies; the presence of these often overlooked differences between various business sectors and government, as well as pressure from a multitude of other groups, has meant that Japanese politics have been highly pluralistic much in the vein of competitive politics in other complex industrialized societies.

For political reasons as well as in response to the "objective" forces of Japan's own special vulnerability to pollution, considerable attention has been given to environmental problems since the early 1970s. As Frank Upham points out, Japan's response to pollution initially was developed in a series of famous court suits wherein injured persons sought damages for the debilitating or even fatal toxic effects of effluents from chemical and metallurgical factories. Subsequently, the pollution "logic" of Japan's crowded space became more apparent both in the already developed cities and elsewhere as factory districts expanded into former farm areas and the automobile population grew sevenfold in a decade. The ensuing governmental response to pollution provided for a fairly comprehensive system of ambient and emission standards, which have been enforced fairly successfully in the nonadversarial climate between business and government in Japan. Automobile emission standards exceeding those in the United States were imposed along with other controls, and air pollution has actually decreased as a result. The Japanese government also authored an innovative pollution compensation approach by which contributions are made by all firms in a district to a central pollution damage fund for that area. Still, environmental impact assessments are not currently required, and the present emphasis is more on controlling existing polluting activities than the prevention of development of future sources of pollution.

Japan's answer to the social problems accompanying industrialization and urbanization has been much like those of other countries. There are now sizable pension and health care systems in Japan as well as smaller-scale efforts at income maintenance, given the diminished size of unemployment during the recent high growth era and earlier rural underemployment. In addition to many similarities to other countries, the Japanese social welfare system still has distinctive provisions, as John Campbell points out. For one thing, because of extensive private participation in the form of corporate pension plans, Japan's overall social security system is very complicated and fragmented. Corporate pension plans have also been one factor in the traditionally lower public outlays on social programs in Japan in comparison with other industrialized nations. Notwithstanding past trends, public social programs have expanded in recent years due to political pressures for increased coverage. Budgetary outlays have also increased substantially both in response to program growth and due to the aging of the Japanese population. Like many other countries, Japan is actually faced today with the question of how to continue financing a comprehensive social program while costs are beginning to spiral and will continue to do so in the foreseeable future.

Political stability is an essential ingredient to economic stability and growth. By and large Japan has been stable throughout the postwar era (and even earlier barring some troubled periods). Domination by one political movement has by itself been an element of stability, even though factional conflict within conservative parties has at times suggested that instability at the top could break out at any moment. But somehow the conservative parties have held together. Moreover, while stormy sessions are not uncommon in the Japanese Diet, all of Japan's postwar political parties have been supportive of constitutional government in marked contrast with political movements in many countries. Consequently, the main threat to political stability has been in the form of mass protest movements, and more recently in extremism and terrorism in a number of locales both inside and outside of Japan.

As Richardson demonstrates, protest takes different forms: mass protest demonstrations and extremist groups are quite distinctive in style and motivation (at least at the present). Since the wane of the student violence that characterized the late 1960s and early 1970s, mass political protests have occurred in Japan mainly among the components of large institutionalized groups like labor, farmers, or consumers. These groups inevitably have a stake in Japan's current political system, however violent their protests may be on occasion. In contrast, Japan's small extremist groups are typically alienated from contemporary institutions and processes. The small size of the extremist groups, however, and, typically very effective police control, minimize the destabilizing effects of these groups. Also, there is a substantial continuum even among extremist groups, and some groups seem to pretty much adhere to the present political arrangements even while others are totally alienated from today's politics. This continuum in attitudes is reflected in variations in the degree of violence and terrorism engaged in by the groups themselves.

The most striking aspect of the political environment in Japan is the degree to which business and government maintain a relatively cooperative relationship, even in the presence of shared differences in interests at some points. Upham argues that while business-government ties in the United States might be described as adversarial, formal, and multipolar, those in Japan could best be called consensual, informal, and bipolar. There is a basic agreement on long-term national goals between the major business interests, the majoritarian Liberal Democratic Party, and the economic ministries. Business, the bureaucracy, and Liberal Democratic leaders each want stability, satisfactory economic growth, and expanded trade. While disagreements often occur on short-term issues, the long-term identity of purpose between business and government provides for a less-strained environment than would otherwise be the case. Ongoing political decision making also includes representatives of business in an informal, consensus-building process that emphasizes prior consultation to the degree that decisions themselves at times become self-enforcing. Bureaucrats and businessmen meet in advisory committees to discuss economic and industrial policies and where there are disagreements over treatment of particular firms or industries these are ultimately dealt with through consultation rather than lawsuits or formal hearings. Even if there is more conflict within these processes than has appeared to be the case to many foreign observers, the contrast in goals and style between the Japanese approach to government-business relations and that of other industrialized countries is still striking.

Political Interests and Political Parties

Government in Western industrialized countries has certain common themes: left-right ideology and political parties, multiple interest groups or lobbies, and parliaments/legislatures that legislate with lessening degrees of independence, given the complexity of modern lawmaking and the predominance of bureaucratic expertise in overall policymaking processes. What is the nature of politics and legislation in Japan? What are the main ideologies and party cleavages, what are some of the important interest groups and how do they operate, and where and how are policies made in Japan?

JAPANESE POLITICAL PARTIES

Politically speaking Japan looks more like Europe than the United States. There is currently a multiparty system in which five parties—the Liberal Democrats, Japan Socialists, Democratic Socialists, Clean Government Party, and Japan Communists—have meaningful representation in the two-house national parliament. Multipartisan competition has persisted throughout the postwar era, although the configurations of party competition were different from those at present at several points. In this same period the main axis of ideological conflict was between the conservative camp, now represented by the Liberal Democrats, and the reformist or leftist camp composed of the Japan Socialist and Japan Communist Parties and sometimes other groups.

From 1948 the conservative movement dominated the Japanese political scene at both the national and the local level for two decades. Conservative coalitions, or the post-1955 Liberal Democratic Party, were the main force in national parliamentary politics throughout the 1950s and the 1960s, and conservative politicians held major posts in local and prefectural governments throughout the nation.

However, there was a long-term decline in conservative power from a high point in the early 1950s. Until recently, this decline did not affect the operation of national politics, as the conservatives continued to have a working majority in the parliament. But after the 1976 House of Representatives election, conservative and opposition representation in both houses of the National Diet was almost equal. There were also important parallel shifts in power in local politics that brought more leftist candidates into office in many urban and even rural places. Also, political competition in the 1970s became increasingly complex as middle-of-the-road groups, especially the Clean Government Party, assumed a larger role in both national and local politics, while the Communist Party became a stronger force in the leftist camp at the expense of the Japan Socialists (see Table 7.1).

TABLE 7.1

Party Strengths in the Japanese House of Representatives 1947–80

Party	1947	1952	1960	1969	1980
Conservatives-Liberal Democrats	60%	70%	63%	59%	56%
Democratic Socialist Party	—	—	—	6	6
Clean Government Party	—	—	—	10	6
Japan Socialist Party	31	24	31	19	21
Japan Communist Party	1	0	1	3	6

Note: Minor parties are omitted. Parties are arranged vertically on a left-right spectrum. "—" means that the party did not exist.

Source: Compiled by the author from Japan Ministry of Home Affairs documents.

IDEOLOGICAL TENSIONS BETWEEN JAPANESE PARTIES

Ideological divisions between the conservative forces and the opposition leftists were especially intense in the 1950s and 1960s. The greatest intensity was felt by the leftist camp, which had a clearer ideological position and was keenly frustrated by its seemingly permanent minority position. By the middle and late 1970s ideological conflict had scaled down, and there were important trends toward moderation in the form of stronger middle parties and substantially less-combative positions on the part of the Japanese left.

The ideological positions of the long-dominant conservative movement have always been complex in that the party resembles the catchall parties of the United States, Germany, and Great Britain more than the narrower ideological parties still found in some European countries. Typical of such catchall parties and movements, there has always been considerable diversity of opinion among conservatives, especially on defense policy and relations with Communist bloc countries.

In addition to their internal diversity, the Liberal Democrats and predecessor conservative groups have not always been as conservative as their conservative classification implies. Conservatism has been visible in some wings of the movement in attachment to older constitutional forms, concern for prewar moral curricula in education, and support for the imperial institutions and some muted forms of Japanese nationalism. But the party has also advocated some welfare state programs, especially in recent years. A kind of socially responsible capitalism was urged in the 1950s and 1960s, which combined both public and private medical care and social security programs. In the 1970s the Liberal Democrats moved toward support for expanded public social welfare programs, including free medical aid for most older people. Closely affiliated with big business throughout the postwar era (although not always having identical views) the Liberal Democrats also initially favored economic growth over deference to environmental concerns and attention to consumer problems. However, a shift in political emphasis to environmental and quality-of-life issues occurred in Japan around 1970 much as it did elsewhere in the past decade, and current conservative party statements are replete with proposed solutions for pollution problems and other quality-of-life questions.

POSTWAR LEFTIST ISSUE POSITIONS

The "traditional" ideological position of Japan's leftist parties consisted of opposition to capitalism and capitalist countries coupled with preference for neutralist solutions of international tensions. Both the Japan Socialists and the Japan Communists were, in the beginning, Marxist class parties. The rhetoric of these two parties in the 1950s and the 1960s indicated a particularly virulent form of anticapitalism and antiimperialism (as was also typical of some European leftist movements and the Socialist bloc nations of the times). By the 1970s, however, adaptation to both a changing political scene and recognition of the need to make appeals to a broader constituency than the industrial working class brought moderation to both the Japan Communists' and the Japan Socialists' position. (Significantly, more adjustments were made by the Japanese Communists than by the Socialists!) Advocation of a neutral role for Japan, which includes both downplaying of the Japanese defense effort and a position of independence between the traditional Socialist and capitalist blocs, continues. But rapprochements between Japan and Peking and emergence of economic ties with all of the Communist nations in East Asia have stolen much of the force of the left's earlier pleas for warmer relations with the Socialist counties and less dependence on the United States and the West. At the same time, Japan's enormous economic power in the 1970s has meant some inevitable adjustments in the United States-Japan relationships, which served to undermine the appeal of leftists for greater independence. Domestically, the Communists and Socialists have come to talk more of transportation, pollution, and price problems than revolution and nationalization of industry, the themes of earlier years.

THE POLITICAL PROCESS

During the period of Liberal Democratic dominance of Japanese politics (1955–76) policies in different substantive issue areas were made in different "places" within the governmental system. Highly ideological issues, such as security and foreign policy alternatives were actively debated and decided by the political parties in the National Diet even if the Liberal Democrats and their bureaucratic allies usually had their own way. In contrast, many interest group issues were resolved in complex negotiations between the Liberal Democratic Party, which championed the groups, and representatives of the bureaucracy acting as guardians of the purse. In a third scenario, the major economic ministries such as International Trade and Industry, Construction, Transportation, and Finance often defined macroeconomic policies like the budget and economic plans, as well as dictating specific industry policies. Often the bureaucracy and ruling conservatives operated in tandem, but ministerial initiative was usually the most decisive element in policymaking.

Under conservative dominance, mass interest groups, such as small businessmen, farmers, and pensioners, worked through the conservative party (or parties) to present their claims on government. The resulting complex of farm price supports, farm extension programs, pension programs for veterans, payments to persons displaced after the loss of Japan's colonies, and economic support packages for small businessmen are not unlike their counterparts in other countries. Many of these programs continue today, and many of the established groups continue to work through long-standing relationships with the Liberal Democrats to lobby for such items as restrictions on imports of American and Australian beef or American citrus fruit.

Business interests have been active in national politics in diverse ways. The big business sector is often internally divided in its ideologies and attitudes toward government. Some business leaders have wanted more government support for their industrial sector in times of both development and retrenchment, while others have wanted government to maintain a hands-off posture. Some business leaders have been internationalists, while others have been protectionist. The complexities of intrabusiness outlooks have resulted in different demands being placed by different groups (and at different times) on government policymakers. The complexity and shifts in economic policymaking in postwar Japan have been linked to the nature of business attitudes as well as to other factors. Thus, Japan's shift from protectionism to freer trade provisions in the early 1960s represented an accommodation to demands from abroad as well as shifting opinions among business groups, conservative leaders, and the economic ministries. Policies on China trade and attitudes toward investments in Soviet Siberia have also reflected the complexity in business opinions as well as the diversity in other influences.

Relations between labor and politics have also been complicated. The labor union movement itself is very diversified and includes points of view ranging from ardent leftist commitment through pragmatic trade unionism. The most visible labor participants in politics have been the leftist unions of the Japan General Council of Trade Unions. These are predominantly unions of government employees in education, the nationalized railways, and postal services. The General Council of Trade Unions has long been closely linked with the Japan Socialist Party in defense of common fronts on foreign policy issues. More recently the leftist union movement and the Socialists have been united in defense of the environment and consumer interests, both of which positions reflect a common antibusiness bias. The General Council of Trade Unions is also a frequent antagonist of the government over wages in the public sector and has been championed by the Socialist Party in its demands for preservation of labor's postwar economic rights and defense of local individual autonomy and rights. The success of leftist labor has been mixed. At times, through operation of a "de facto" veto by Socialist Party obstructionism, leftist labor has been in the winning coalition that successfully resisted passage of conservative proposals in the national parliament. But on many occasions the ministries and conservative parties have overcome or ignored union and Socialist opposition. Probably leftist labor's greatest postwar accomplishment has been in its 1950s "defense" of the postwar constitution in alliance with the Japan Socialists.

In contrast with the prominence of leftist labor's political roles, political action by the "middle-of-the-road" Japanese Confederation of Labor has been much more muted. The Japanese Confederation of Labor has operated much more like a "conventional" pressure group by seeking representation of its steelworker, autoworker, and other sector membership's economic interests through an alliance with the Democratic Socialist Party and occasionally through approaches to conservative politicans. The major role of the Japanese Confederation of Labor has been its electoral support for middle-of-the-road and conservative candidates, as both its smaller size (in comparison with the General Council of Trade Unions) and its more moderate ideological approach has resulted in a lower-key role in policymaking. (Recently the relatively close ties between the General Council of Trade Unions and the Socialist Party and the Japanese Confederation of Labor and the Democratic Socialist Party have been breaking down, to be replaced by more complex and less stable electoral alliances between unions and parties.)

JAPANESE POLITICS AND THE FUTURE

At present, the Liberal Democratic Party still rules Japan and its policies dominate the Japanese political scene. Should the long-term trend of decline in conservative party strength—which actually stopped in recent elections—continue, two alternative coalition and policy outcomes are possible. The most likely outcome is that the Liberal Democrats will form a coalition with the Democratic Socialists, and possibly also with the Clean Government Party. This conservative middle-of-the-road coalition will continue current conservative policies with only fairly minor changes, such as the 1970s emphasis on postindustrial quality-of-life concerns. If the less likely event of a middle-left coalition occurs (which is currently impossible because of strong animosities between several of the plausible coalition partners), the trend toward ideological moderation on the left means that whatever departures occur from "traditional" postwar policy emphases in Japan will be only partial steps rather than the dramatic shifts that might have been expected at earlier time points. In domestic policies a less than radical shift in emphasis on social policies can be expected as the result of the sobering experiences of leftist governors and mayors who tried to revolutionize local social programs. Shifts in emphasis favoring quality-of-life issues, while present, would also be somewhat muted, given ultimate restrictions in physical and financial resources. Meanwhile, policies toward Japan's role in a complex international society, while perhaps slightly more "neutralist" than its present close ties with the United States and European Economic Community, ultimately would involve only modest departures from current preference for healthy and widespread trade contacts, some form of security arrangements and defense forces, and relations with Communist as well as with non-Communist political systems.

Bradley Richardson

BIBLIOGRAPHY

Flanagan, Scott, and Bradley Richardson. *Politics in Japan*. Boston: Little, Brown, 1981.

Ward, Robert E. *Japan's Political System*. Englewood Cliffs, N.J.: Prentice Hall, 1978.

Movements and Political Stability

Like most industrialized countries, Japan has both active leftist movements and ultraright groups. Both are highly visible on the streets of Tokyo and other cities. What is the current state of these movements, especially those which attract youths? What does this say about the feelings and frustrations of contemporary Japanese, and do those movements pose a threat to political, economic, or social stability?

CONTEMPORARY POLITICAL PROTEST IN JAPAN

One of the more striking sights in contemporary Tokyo is the small convoys of olive-drab trucks, festooned with Japanese flags, and manned by angry-looking young men in military uniforms who scream right-wing slogans and play World War II marches, which appear and disappear in prominent places. These right-wing protesters are most visible in the streets around the Soviet and Chinese embassies. But they can be found anywhere in downtown Tokyo's government district and in the major streets of the capital's financial and business areas.

What do these protests mean? Are Japanese youths turning to right-wing attitudes? After a period of enthusiasm for peace and opposition to military forces, are Japanese returning to moods such as those of the militaristic 1930s? And what of the other protest movements regularly seen in Tokyo, such as the thousands of labor union marchers who protest controls over government workers' right to strike, or the lines of women marching in protest against inflation and high consumer prices? Are these protests expressions of major elements in public opinion? Do they imply widespread antisystem feelings and, most importantly of all, are they a threat to political stability?

The roots and meaning of political protest movements are one of the more difficult phenomena of politics in any country in that elements of organization and spontaneity, traditional and modern expectations, and volatility and permanence are always interwoven in complex ways. In contemporary Japan there are essentially two kinds of protest movements. The first form of protest is highly ideological in motivation, and is found in expressions of both extreme right- and left-wing sentiments, while the second type of movement is less extreme and more stable organizationally.

EXTREME RIGHT- AND LEFT-WING MOVEMENTS

Currently there are a large number of relatively small right-wing movements, such as the Greater Japan Production Party, the National Comrades Society, the Yuzon Society, the Japan Youth Society, the People's Council, the People's League, the Greater Japan Patriotic Party, and many others. These groups appear inherently unstable in many cases, as they are ridden by factionalism and many are in an almost chronic state of reformation under shifting leadership and new names. Yet they also vociferously express a fairly unified ideological theme of strong nationalism that includes opposition to Soviet occupation of the "northern islands" (the four southernmost islands of the Kurile chain which Japan claims), support for traditional "morals" education courses such as those that fostered patriotic feelings before World War II and sometimes advocation of a more Japanese-style constitution, and strong anticommunism.

These right-wing ideological movements are paralleled by left-wing ideological groups that have some of the same organizational traits of their right-wing opponents. The most famous of the ultraleft-wing groups is, of course, the Japanese Red Army, a terrorist group responsible for violent acts within and outside of Japan on several well-publicized occasions. However, the Red Army is only one of a number of small, faction-ridden leftist movements dedicated to complete elimination of the contemporary social and political "system." In commitments to revolutionary solutions and extremism in demands and behavior, these groups are not dissimilar to the much larger groups of left-wing student protesters of the late 1960s. In a sense, they represent an extension into terrorist activities of a postwar tradition of combative student leftism and highly faction-ridden and organizationally unstable student leftist groups.

The small ideological groups of both the right and the left represent a blend of extreme individual alienation with more traditional, almost romantic ideas of total sacrifice on behalf of a cause that reflects themes of Japanese life during the feudal period. While it is said that the right-wing movements at least are supported by rich benefactors, which implies some kind of involvement in the mainstream of Japanese life, the participants in both extreme right- and left-wing movements seem far more alienated than most other Japanese, including the many hundreds of thousands of participants in other kinds of protest movements in Japan. In other words, neither the right- nor the left-wing extremists appear representative of any mainstream in Japanese opinion these days. Indeed, their behavior is mocked by other Japanese, or in the case of terrorism, lamented and condemned. Even if heroic protest may have certain links with traditional, romantic ideas about heroism on behalf of one's cause, the ideological content of these

movements has little general support. In addition, these movements'
organizational fragility in most cases makes them inherently very weak.

INSTITUTIONALIZED PROTEST MOVEMENTS

A second kind of protest movement in Japan falls much closer to the
mainstream of Japanese thinking and behavior, and reflects much more
permanent organizational forms than are found among the extremists.
During every week of the "political year" when the Japanese parliament is
in session, long lines of protesters pass along the streets of Tokyo's government quarter of Kasumigaseki in advocacy of such causes as the political
rights of labor, higher wages for public workers, farm price supports, limits
on imports of farm products, or an end to comsumer price inflation. While
these larger movements occasionally get out of hand, such as in the case of
protests against the United States-Japan Security Treaty in 1960 or the
opening of Japan's new international airport at Narita, both of which gave
the appearance of small-scale civil wars, most large-scale protest movements are very orderly. As such, they represent a little-discussed Japanese
political tradition of peaceful petition of political authority, which typically
takes the form of an orderly presentation of a political demand supported
by a display of support by an assemblage of ordinary citizens. If governmental authorities respond to the demonstration by a substantive
commitment, or in some cases if they simply indicate symbolically that
they will consider the needs of the particular group, the movement's
membership is often satisfied. Indeed, orderly protest of this kind represents a kind of ritualized participation involving petition by subjects to a
political authority who is assumed to be ultimately consensualistic and
benevolent in acceptance of the rights of a particular group. In fact it is only
when such groups gain no sense of government responsiveness or when the
government actually indicates a "high-handed" commitment to pursue
policies to which the group objects that such otherwise orderly mass
citizens' protests run to more violent (although nonterrorist) forms of
behavior. These were precisely the routes to violent protest displayed
when the government overrode a large segment of public opinion to pass
the United States-Japanese Security Treaty, permitted American nuclear-
powered naval vessels to visit Japanese ports, and built the Narita airport
against the protests of some local citizens (admittedly reinforced by near-
terrorist, antigovernment groups from other places). Similarly, in many
other cases where the government gave the appearance of irresponsibility
and arrogance, the mass protest "ritual" turned into more violent con-
frontations.

Political protest movements thus represent an important and legitimate component of traditional Japanese political culture. Throughout Japanese history local communities, or even groups of persons, such as poor peasants, within these communities have used public protest to make their political demands known. Just as in other areas of Japanese political behavior and more general social interactions, responsible actions by leadership in the form of a concession to the demand, or even simply an indication that the demand was legitimate, ended protest activities and prevented violence. In contrast, authoritarian arrogance and abandonment of the subtle rules of consensualistic participation and decisionmaking typically served to exacerbate bitterness and conflict.

PROTEST, QUALITY-OF-LIFE ISSUES, AND JAPANESE POLITICAL ATTITUDES

Mass political protest in contemporary Japan has roots in modern substance as well as in traditional political culture concepts. Despite Japan's dramatic economic "miracle" of the 1960s and 1970s, which raised per capita Gross National Product from one-seventh of that of the United States to near parity with American economic levels, there are many areas of real discontent in Japanese life. Some of these are very specific, and relate to occupational or consumer interests. Others are more general. For example, high-growth economics produced pollution problems (discussed elsewhere in this book) that were probably the most grave in the modern world. Economic success also produced a boom in family automobile ownership which, in addition to being one of the causes of pollution, also led to staggering traffic problems on Japan's already overcrowded roads and highways. Affluence likewise made it possible for many people to buy a home in the suburbs, which in turn overloaded public transportation systems and overwhelmed suburban governments' ability to provide adequate paved roads or modern sewage disposal systems. Land prices also rose so dramatically that by the mid-1970s fewer and fewer people could even continue to dream of having "my home" whatever the associated problems.

The real limitations in Japan's ability to expand the amenities of modern life where space is so restricted and accompanying development costs are so great have meant that many modern Japanese see no end to the deprivations of high pollution, crowded transportation, or overcrowded and expensive apartments and homes even in the face of Japan's "arrival" as the world's third economic power. This means that expectations of a better life congruent with collective economic success appear to never be completely capable of being met.

These frustrations have been reflected in specific movements for redress, such as relief from industrial pollution. The frustrated expectations have also affected general political attitudes. Among adults frustration has led to much higher levels of political distrust and disenchantment with government than are found in most other modern, industrial countries. They also tend to condemn their political parties, even in many cases having negative images of the very parties that they support at the polls.

Frustrations with the inherent limitations in Japan's ability to provide a quality of life commensurate with her high degree of economic success seem particularly acute among younger Japanese. There has long been a kind of stylized or "modish" alienation among Japanese university youth, which presumably reflected reactions to Japan's highly institutionalized, entrance-examination-oriented and careerist educational system as well as the influence of "pop-Marxism." Whatever the causes, Japanese university youth have been negative toward political and social authority for a long time. But this postwar style of negativism and cynicism has also apparently been enhanced recently by the more general mood of political dissatisfaction found among all Japanese. Thus, recent worldwide opinion polls conducted by the Japanese Prime Ministers Office have shown Japanese youths to be from two to five times as unhappy with their political system as youths in other major industrialized and nonindustrialized countries.

So there is in Japan a well of general dissatisfaction with politics that is especially acute among youths, as well as a variety of political claims specific to particular communities or groups. This general mood of cynicism clearly contributes to political protest in some cases. Japanese who are cynical about politics (according to their answers to polls) *and* who are also members of labor unions and other groups turn out to protest in favor of some political action or in opposition to some political policy more than politically satisfied citizens. This is true at the microcommunity level, where thousands of local groups protesting air, water, noise, and sunshine pollution or further regional industrial development were formed in the late 1960s and early 1970s. It is also true at the macrocommunity or national level where members of Japan's powerful agricultural organizations or governmental employees' labor unions protest in massive movements on the streets of Tokyo. In other words, participation in mass protest demonstrations vents citizens' general political frustrations as well as serving specific causes.

Membership in some organization, whether it be a local community or a national, mass organization, also probably controls and institutionalizes mass protest behavior as well as sustaining it. This is a kind of irony that explains why Japan can have so much popular dissatisfaction while also maintaining ultimately very high levels of political stability. All of Japan's mass organizations are at the national level closely related to political parties that subscribe to maintenance of constitutional government and support Japan's parliamentary institutions. At times these groups may advocate their own interests to the point of engaging in minor violence through stoppage of major Tokyo streets or surrounding government or political party offices (as has occurred when farmers' groups have virtually held Liberal Democratic Party senior officials hostage during emotional disputes over price subsidies). As such they express their own political demands in the most vocal of ways, and also give vent to the general political frustrations of their memberships. Yet at another level these mass organizations are supporters of the contemporary political system, and do not advocate (as have recent crowds in Iran or El Salvador) a complete overturn of Japan's political institutions. The same is true of the myriads of citizens' movements whose concerns for rectification of local injustices did not imply antisystem sentiments of a fundamental kind, even if their protest behavior sometimes verged on violence.

So, political protest in Japan today, while often massive in terms of numbers of participants and reflective of pervasive sentiments of political frustration at both the national and community levels, is generally not a threat to the stability of Japan's political institutions nor its political life. Instead, protest reflects a traditional aspect of Japan's political culture coupled with "modern" frustrations with quality-of-life or more specific political problems. Simultaneously, right- and left-wing extremism, while dramatic and disturbing in its forms and emotionalism and even temporarily disruptive of normal life, does not reflect widespread antisystem sentiments. While Japan's modern history has been complex, and there have been a few periods of acute political instability caused in part by protest movement activities, generally Japanese have been committed ultimately to stable and institutionalized political solutions more than the peoples of many other rapidly developing countries.

Bradley Richardson

BIBLIOGRAPHY

Massey, Joseph. *Youth and Politics in Japan*. Lexington, Mass.: Lexington Books, 1976.

Richardson, Bradley. "Political Cynicism and Political Protest." In *The Japanese Voter*, edited by Bradley Richardson, Scott Flanagan, and Joji Watanuki. Manuscript in preparation.

Pollution Problems and Response

Environmental pollution and related problems are found in all industrialized nations. What has been the trend in pollution problems in Japan, what has been the Japanese "solution" or response to these problems and how do pollution control systems affect the cost considerations of Japanese companies?

In a society that is perhaps romantically perceived by the West as imbued with the reverance for nature peculiar to Zen Buddhism, one might expect an environmental policy that would reflect this unique attitude toward nature. That has not been the case. Instead, Japan has suffered probably the world's worst industrial pollution with a series of pollution disasters unrivaled anywhere in the West. Recently, however, the government has taken important steps to prevent future problems and to rectify some of the damage of past indifference. The result is an environmental policy that is now in many ways more sophisticated than that of the United States, but which still lacks an effective system for protecting the natural environment.

The reasons for Japan's environmental deterioration are simple: extremely rapid and unrestrained industrialization in a country with very little living space. The growth of Japanese industry between 1955 and 1970 needs no comment here, but the physical and demographic characteristics of Japan as shown in Table 7.2 illustrate the uniquely narrow margin of error that public and private planners have in trying to balance industrial growth and the maintenance of even a minimally livable environment. To focus on the comparison to the United States, Japan has over 10 times as many automobiles and almost 25 times as much industrial output per inhabitable square kilometer.

Despite these physical limitations, there was little concern about the environment in Japan during the late 1950s and 1960s when the rate of industrial expansion reached its peak, particularly in highly polluting sectors like petrochemicals and heavy manufacturing. New petrochemical complexes and steel plants were concentrated in the center of large urban areas with no consideration of their effect on the residents' health. The resultant air pollution was actually welcomed as evidence of Japan's industrial rebirth after the devastation of World War II. The rapid increase in automobiles in the late 1960s further exacerbated the problem so that by 1970 there were few areas of the world with worse air pollution.

But it was water, not air pollution that eventually provided the dramatic incidents that shocked the nation and forced the government to

TABLE 7.2

International Comparison of Indices of Economic and Social Activity

Unit	Nominal GNP ($100 million /100 ha of habitable area, 1974)	Energy consumption (million tons/ 10 ha of habitable area, 1973)	Motor vehicle ownership (No. of vehicles /ha of habitable area, 1974)	Vegetation (ha of forests + agricultural land ha per 1000 persons)	Habitable area (ha per 1,000 persons)
Japan	356.4	30.7	2.10	271.1 ('72)	116.0 ('72)
United States	21.9	3.9	0.20	3,434.5 ('69)	3,038.4 ('69)
United Kingdom	86.9	14.4	0.71	369.5 ('73)	400.8 ('73)
France	68.6	5.7	0.43	895.9 ('72)	765.2 ('72)
West Germany	218.8	20.4	1.05	332.1 ('73)	283.4 ('73)

Source: Environment Agency, *Quality of the Environment in Japan,* 1978.

take effective action. The destruction of urban rivers and bays by organic substance pollution accompanied the deterioration of urban air quality, but it was heavy metal poisoning of rural rivers and bays that caused several incidents of unparalleled suffering and death among fishermen and farmers who ate the polluted fish and used the water to irrigate their rice paddies. The most extreme and best known of these incidents was the mercury poisoning incident at the City of Minamata in southern Kyushu. For over 15 years Chisso Corporation, at that time one of the technological leaders of Japan's chemical industry, poured untreated effluent into Minamata Bay. Mercury in the discharge entered the food chain, first accumulating in fish and shellfish, and then in the brains of the local fishermen who ate them. The result was progressive brain damage and eventually death.

The first victims of what came to be called Minamata disease appeared in the early 1950s. Robust men and women who had hitherto enjoyed good health suddenly found their hands trembling so violently that they could not strike a match. They next had difficulty thinking clearly, and it became impossible for them to operate their boats. Eventually control of all bodily functions was impaired. Victims became bedridden, at times completely incoherent, and eventually subject to wild fits of thrashing and senseless screaming. Hundreds have died and thousands face a life of unrelenting pain and varying degrees of disability. Similarly dramatic although less widespread incidents of heavy metal poisoning occurred in other areas of Japan in the mid-1960s.

Despite overwhelming evidence to the contrary, the government's response to Minamata disease was to deny that it was caused by industrial pollution and to support Chisso in its attempts to avoid responsibility. Although perhaps understandable given the low level of awareness of environmental issues at the time and the very real need for industrial growth, the problem would not go away. Instead, with the discovery of other cases of heavy metal poisoning elsewhere and the continuing deterioration of the urban environment, pollution became a major political issue in the late 1960s. With assistance from the leftist parties, pollution victims were able to utilize the mass media to put their case before the Japanese public repeatedly and effectively in a way reminiscent of the civil rights movement in the United States. The resulting political pressure eventually convinced the leaders of the Liberal Democratic Party and the government that forceful action was imperative, for the sake of their political future if not for the future of Japan itself.

Once the ruling coalition of businessmen, party leaders, and bureaucrats reached a consensus that action was necessary, movement was fast, effective, and far-reaching. A preliminary step was the passage in 1967 of the Basic Law for Environmental Pollution Control. It set the stage for stronger specific statutes to be passed in 1970, at the height of the antipollution movement. The next year saw the creation of the Environment Agency and the beginning of full-scale implementation of the major environmental statutes.

The results have generally been impressive. As shown in Figure 7.1, concentrations of carbon monoxide and sulfur dioxide have declined dramatically since 1968 and that of nitrogen oxides has leveled off. Progress in containing most forms of water pollution has been comparable. There was a steady annual decline in toxic substance pollution (cadmium, mercury, organic phosphorous, hexachrome, and so forth) from the late 1960s to the late 1970s so that by 1978 the Environment Agency was able to report noncompliance at less than 1 percent of its monitoring stations. Success in eliminating other types of water pollution, chiefly biochemical oxygen demand and chemical oxygen demand, however, has been uneven. Some rivers and coastal areas have improved significantly while others have actually deteriorated.

To achieve this remarkable progress in less than a decade, the Japanese government used the same basic tools used elsewhere—ambient and emission standards set and enforced by administrative agencies. There are, however, several aspects of the Japanese experience that deserve special note.

FIGURE 7.1

Changes in Annual Density of Major Air Pollutants

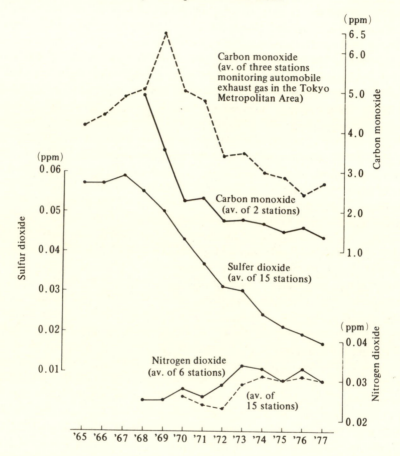

1. Carbon monoxide measurements by automobile exhaust gas monitoring stations are given in terms of calendar years.

2. Saltzman coefficient of 0.72 is used for nitrogen oxides.

Source: Japanese Environment Agency, *Quality of the Environment in Japan*, 1979 (p. 4).

First, there was a broadly and deeply held national consensus that effective steps to preserve and restore the environment were necessary. This conviction was largely shared by the business community, which meant that the bureaucracy was able to secure business's voluntary cooperation rather than being faced with the constant legal and political challenges that have delayed the implementation of American environmental policies and essentially made their formation in the United States an adversary process.

One example of this cooperation is automobile emission control. Japan virtually copied American standards in the early 1970s, both because of automobile exports and because the Japanese government was convinced that the United States would not set technologically impossible standards. The standards were greeted in both countries with immediate and fierce resistance from the automobile industry. The way the industry reaction evolved, however, is indicative of Japanese government/business relations in the environmental area and a prime reason why Japan now is meeting much stricter standards than any other nation. The American industry response was predictable: a unified lobbying effort supported by litigation challenging the Environmental Protection Agency's (EPA) standards. Eventually after acrimonious legal and political debate, which is still continuing, the EPA was forced to back down and grant extended postponement of the implementation of standards. By contrast, the Japanese automakers, although by no means pleased with the standards, did not resort to litigation. Instead they entered into a continuous process of negotiation with the government. They were successful in 1975 in convincing the Environment Agency to extend the 1976 standard for nitrogen oxides to 1978. Unlike in the United States, there was relatively little pressure to change the hydrocarbon and carbon monoxide standards, which in fact were not substantially modified. The focus then shifted to the 1978 nitrogen oxide (NOx) standards with Toyota and Nissan (Datsun) pushing for further relaxation. At this point, however, the automakers' united front broke. In January and February of 1976 four of the smaller companies, Mitsubishi, Toyo Kogyo (Mazda), Honda, and Fuji Heavy Industries (Subaru), publicly announced that they could meet the 1978 nitrogen oxide standards on schedule. Nissan soon followed. Toyota, increasingly isolated and publicly criticized as "selfishly" profiting from dirty air and human misery, eventually fell into line in 1977. Although foreign manufacturers continued to complain, Toyota's capitulation essentially ended the controversy. The result is that Japanese cars have been meeting emission standards since 1976 (1978 in the case of NOx standards) that American cars may not even meet by 1980.

Both countries started with similar standards and similar technical problems. Why has Japan been so much more successful in producing attractive, economical automobiles that meet stringent environmental standards? The answer is complex, but one factor is certainly the cooperative relationship between the industry and government. Instead of a legal attack against the standards across the board, the industry met those it could while persuading the Environment Agency to postpone the more difficult NOx standard. The large number of automobile manufacturers also played a key role since a unified position became difficult and then impossible to achieve, leaving the field open for technological competition in meeting the emission goals. The underlying reason, however may have been the widely shared conviction in Japan that air pollution had to be dealt with effectively. This consensus put pressure on both the government and the industry and convinced smaller manufacturers that advertising a "clean-air" car would be effective in cutting into Nissan and Toyota's market share.

Another aspect of Japanese environmental policy deserving mention is its innovative scheme to compensate victims of pollution. Although we often prefer to ignore it, environmental pollution is not cost free. In fact, the total cost to society of air, water, and noise pollution is enormous, ranging from dramatically increased rates of emphysema in highly polluted cities to the loss of recreational opportunities because of the elimination of wilderness and wildlife. Due to restrictive laws and enormous problems in showing causation, however, few of these costs are borne by the polluters. The Japanese have by no means attempted to internalize all these costs, but they have gone further than most other countries by forcing the polluters to bear some of the health costs caused by their activity. Although rather complicated in its implementation, the concept is simple. The Environment Agency officially certifies heavily polluted areas and pollution-induced diseases. If a resident of a designated area, Osaka or Tokyo, for example, suffers from a designated disease, he is generally eligible for compensatory cash payments from the government. The government in turn collects from stationary polluters within the certified area according to the amount of their individual emissions and from automobile owners as a weight tax on all cars.

The aim of this administrative scheme is twofold. First, it enables persons injured by environmental pollution to collect compensation without resorting to litigation. Second, it forces polluting enterprises to shoulder more of the external social cost of their operation. To the extent that the cost is eventually passed on, the ultimate consumer is paying a price that is closer to the actual cost of the product. By imposing a levy based on the amount of emissions, there is also an incentive for the polluter to continue to lower his emissions below the emission standards set by the Environment Agency. And, by taxing more heavily polluters within desig- nated polluted districts, there is an incentive to deconcentrate industry. Finally, as is true for pollution control efforts generally, the compensation levy accelerates the trend to shift the Japanese economy to cleaner industries by putting high pollution plants overseas.

FIGURE 7.2

Trends in Pollution Control Equipment Investments by Private Industry

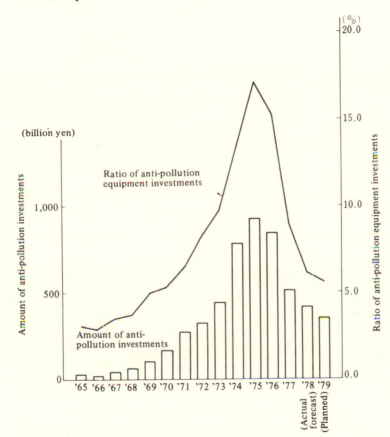

1. Pollution control investment data are from companies with Capital of ¥50 million or more for fiscal 1965–71, and companies (other than mining companies) with capital of ¥100 million from fiscal 1972.

2. Figures are on payment basis.

Source: "Trends in Pollution Control Expenditures in the Private Sector," by the Ministry of International Trade and Industry (survey of September 1978).

TABLE 7.3

**Total Expenditure of Pollution Control
as a Percentage of Total GNP (1971–75)**

Country	Total Expenditure (% of total GNP)
United States	0.8
Germany	0.8
Sweden	0.5–0.9
Italy	0.4
Japan	3.0–5.5
Netherlands	0.04

Source: Organization for Economic Cooperation and Development, Economic Implications of Pollution Control, 1974, p. 3, from Julian Gresser, Koichiro Fujikura and Akio Morishimo, *Environmental Law in Japan* (Massachusetts: MIT Press), 1980. Used with permission.

The improvement in the general environment and innovative programs like the administrative compensation of pollution victims did not come cheaply. Environment Agency officials have estimated that the automotive industry spent approximately 115 billion yen in 1971–72 alone in meeting the emission standards. Similarly, the Keidanren estimated that the 1979 levies for victim compensation would approach $300 million, with some firms liable to pay $20–30 million each. As Figure 7.2 shows, pollution control investments by private industry reached 928.6 billion yen (almost $4 billion at Y250/$1) in 1975, over 16 percent of total private investment. To put this expenditure in international perspective, Table 7.3 sets out the total environmental cost burden for the first half of the 1970s. Although these figures may overstate Japan's expenditures, they demonstrate the particularly heavy burden on Japan. Some of this difference is due to the dire state of the Japanese environment in 1970—Japan simply had a lot farther to go to reach a tolerable environment than most countries. Playing catch-up is not the whole story, however, since the physical, demographic, and economic characteristics of Japan mean that she will likely continue to spend more than the international average in the future.

To help private enterprise bear this sudden and enormous burden, the Japanese government has initiated a series of steps designed to support and encourage antipollution investment. Tax incentives, largely accelerated

TABLE 7.4

**Ratio of Subsidization Equivalence Value to
Private Pollution Control Investment**

Country	Ratio
Japan (1975)	2.6
West Germany (1975)	9.1
Netherlands (1974)	1.1
Norway (1975)	14.2
Sweden (1975)	5.3
U.S.A. (1975)	4.5

Source: Organization for Economic Cooperation and Development, Environment Policies in Japan, 1977, p. 76. Used with permission. Secretariat estimates.

depreciation for pollution control devices, were valued as equivalent to 35 billion yen in 1977. Loans below the commercial rate are an additional measure available as are antipollution public works aimed at lowering antipollution costs to the private sector. Despite these direct and indirect subsidies, however, the Organization for Economic Cooperation and Development has estimated that Japan subsidizes its antipollution efforts less than most industrialized countries, as shown in Table 7.4.

Before the reader gets the impression that Japan is an environmentalist's paradise, with businesses eager to trade profits for clean air and government imbued with the spirit of the Friends of the Earth, some words of caution are needed. First, although the Japanese environment is now tolerable, pollution has by no means been eliminated. Given the density of population in Japan's cities, the average Japanese probably suffers more from air pollution, noise, and assorted other irritants than most citizens of even some countries with statistically worse pollution. Nor is there any reason to think that the improvement in environmental conditions will continue in the 1980s. The Environment Agency 1979 year-end report on air and water quality showed no overall improvement for that year and actual deterioration in nitrogen oxide standard levels, and the national consensus supporting environmental measures has largely dissolved with the solution to the most-pressing problems and the appearance of the energy crisis.

On a more subtle level, Japan may in fact be sliding farther behind in terms of quality-of-life concerns as opposed to statistical measures of the physical environment. Perhaps because of their history as exemplified by the Minamata tragedy, the Japanese tend to view pollution as a human health problem. Although neighborhoods often mobilize effectively to protest local development projects, there is no longer a national environmental movement of any strength. As a result, once the threat to the urbanite's lungs and eyes was substantially eliminated, the push for environmental protection lessened. One reflection of that attitude is the government's approach to the preservation of nature in the abstract. Despite the dearth of wilderness and other natural recreational areas near major urban centers, government bureaucrats still seem disinclined to consider the preservation of such areas seriously in planning industrial development. Although the passage of a National Land Use Law and increasing affluence may influence that attitude in the future, Japan is practically alone in not requiring an environmental impact assessment for major government projects. The various ministries and agencies have their own standards for various projects so the situation is far from unregulated, but there is little or no check on bureaucratic decision making. As long as it is a question of short-term public health, there is no doubt that the government is concerned and effective. In terms of the long-term quality of life and the preservation of the natural environment, however, there is more reason for the environmentalist to be concerned.

Frank K. Upham

BIBLIOGRAPHY

Environment Agency. *Quality of the Environment in Japan.* Published annually in Tokyo. (This is an English version of the Environment Agency's annual report to the Diet on the state of the environment.)

Fujikura, Koichiro, Julian Gresser, and Akio Morishima. *Environmental Law in Japan.* Cambridge, Mass.: MIT Press, 1980.

Business and the Bureaucracy

The relationships between Japanese businesses and the bureaucracy are said to be very intimate. How do Japanese businesses get their voices heard within government administrative organs; do they appear before the agencies in formal hearings as in the United States, or do they use more informal means? Also how do Japanese bureaucratic organs control business behavior, if they indeed do so? In other words, if administrative policy is important, how is it implemented?

The formal legal structure of business/government relations is essentially similar in Japan and the United States. Administrative policy is formed in both countries through a mixture of formal hearings and informal consultations and implemented likewise through a system of formal and informal legal sanctions, threats, and cajolery. Within the official rules of the game, however, there are wide variations in the degree of formality involved, both within and between the two countries. As one would expect, the closer, more harmonious the relationship between the particular bureaucracy and the regulated business, the less legalistic or adversarial their dealings, whether it involves the Japanese Ministry of International Trade and Industry (MITI) or the American Department of Commerce. Because of the very different political and social attitudes toward business and economic growth in Japan, however, the informal mode of government/business interaction is much more common in Japan than the United States, a contrast that has produced the controversial phrase "Japan, Inc." to describe the cooperative relationship of big business and government in planning and regulating the Japanese economy.

Although one should be cautious of oversimplification and stereotypes, it is probably accurate to describe contemporary U.S. bureaucratic policymaking as adversarial, formal, and multipolar. It is adversarial in that the parties involved perceive their respective interests as in conflict; it is formal in that significant portions of the information-receiving and decision-making processes are conducted at public or quasi-public, hearings, by lawyers, operating in a framework of legal rules, and with the explicit and constant threat of eventual judicial review; and it is mulipolar in that diverse, frequently conflicting interests participate equally— consumer, labor, and environmental groups as well as business—with the administrative agency unable to establish a close working relationship with any one set of interests. A contrasting characterization of the Japanese process, on the other hand, would note that it was consensual, informal, and bipolar. The two interests represented in the process, big business and government, most typically MITI, have generally complementary goals and the time and latitude to develop a working relationship that enables them to search informally and largely privately for the compromise that will maximize both of their interests without worrying about fractious intervention by other interest groups.

As is implicit above, the key to the Japanese business/bureaucracy relationship is an agreement on long-term goals that in turn enables them to work out specific problems on the basis of cooperation and consensus. The question of how constant, short-term conflict is avoided remains, however, since each side's immediate interests may frequently conflict, despite an abstract agreement on the desirability of economic growth in the long run. Part of the answer lies in MITI's conscious attempt to create a consensus for any major policy decision by maintaining an ongoing interaction between the career bureaucrats and particular industries. As a general rule, this interaction leads to the ideas that serve as a foundation for MITI's industrial policy and for proposed legislation.

The factors contributing to the success of this interaction are many. One is the continuity and quality of the Japanese bureaucracy. Whether one is considering MITI's efforts to encourage mergers or cartels in a declining industry like textiles or to build up an emerging one like computers, it takes extended periods of time to develop such projects and considerable expertise and competence to implement them. Japanese bureaucrats have both. Entry into the elite of the Japanese civil service is highly prestigious and selective, and ministries such as MITI can claim the very best university graduates almost as a matter of course. And once a young man (there are virtually no women in either the top ministries or the top positions in business—perhaps another often unmentioned factor in the close personal relationships that frequently develop) enters a ministry, he will remain. The American phenomenon of the promising young bureaucrat leaving for the private sector as soon as he has acquired the experience necessary for a high level of competence is unknown in Japan. These two characteristics of continuity and competence combine to form a career bureaucracy that parallels the private bureaucracies of the companies that it regulates, thereby fostering the development of long-term relationships based on mutual trust and confidence.

The nature of the Japanese bureaucracy is certainly the foundation for consensus policymaking, but that in itself would not be enough without constant communication before any decision is made. To cite again the MITI example, one method of communication is through government committees composed of business leaders and staffed by the MITI secretariat. Committees are appointed to consider wide ranges of issues that might concern a particular industry. Industry itself aids the process of interaction by forming its own councils to facilitate exchange of information and aid in the formation of policy. Finally, each bureau of MITI is in daily communication with the businesses in its corresponding industry. Through this constant process of dialogue, MITI arrives at policies and decisions that are amenable to the industry while serving the larger goals of MITI. One example is the decision of a joint MITI and industry committee that for purposes of economy of scale no ethylene production plant would be built that had less than a 300,000-ton capacity.

Constant prior consultation and consensus building means that the decision once made is often self-enforcing. That of course is not always the case, however, since a consensus is frequently not possible and some actions are not conducive to extended prior consultation. It would be stretching the Japan, Inc. caricature well beyond its limited accuracy to picture the implementation of government economic policy as simply a process where all parties gladly cooperate even when against their own short-term interests. Conflict arises and ministries like MITI must be able to enforce their policies against unwilling firms or even against whole industries. In such instances, statutory authority for legal enforcement is usually available. MITI, for example, administers 109 separate laws that provide it with authority to establish certain institutions, control and develop industry, regulate prices and market operations, provide for quality control, regulate patents, and participate in certain aspects of environmental protection. Such broad authority is common for other ministries as well, but a description of agency authority in terms of legal enforcement power is both incomplete and misleading. Although MITI could usually rely on strictly legal means to enforce its policies, it rarely does so, preferring instead to use informal means of coercion and persuasion even when truly voluntary cooperation is impossible. Such informal means are often successful even in those not infrequent cases where agency authority to act formally is doubtful or even clearly absent.

Perhaps one or two examples will help to illustrate this process. In the mid-1960s the Japanese steel industry faced a recessionary decline in demand, and MITI responded by requesting each major manufacturer to cut back production by specific amounts. The Sumitomo Metal Mining Company, however, was dissatisfied with its production quota and refused to abide by the recession guidelines. MITI responded not with direct formal legal action that might bring into question MITI's somewhat questionable authority to set production quotas in these circumstances, but instead by reducing the foreign coal import quota for Sumitomo, an action for which it had clear statutory authority under the Foreign Exchange and Foreign Trade Law. Sumitomo did not immediately challenge MITI's action and the recession ended before the situation resulted in a formal confrontation.

Another example of MITI's preference for informal methods is Japan's response to the 1973–74 oil crisis. Because of its almost total reliance on Middle Eastern oil, Japan was exceptionally hard hit. Immediate steps were necessary and much of the legislative authority for reacting to the price rises was dispersed among the various ministries, but, as often happens, MITI quickly took steps to coordinate price and consumption control. The first step was revived import quotas on petroleum under the Foreign Exchange and Foreign Trade Law and the concurrent announcement of consumption controls on heavy industrial users of oil and power. MITI requested all large consumers of electricity and 11 major oil-consuming industries to reduce consumption by 10 percent across the board. There were no elaborate formulas for determining each firm's "fair" consumption amount; nor was a special administrative agency formed to monitor compliance and handle grievances, appeals, exceptions, and so forth. Industry complied voluntarily with these measures despite the absence of any clear statutory authority for them.

During the following months the government did agree upon legislation, the Petroleum Supply and Demand Adjustment Law, after considerable consultation between government agencies and business. Even after passage of the legislation, however, MITI continued to rely primarily upon persuasion to obtain price cuts in oil and other areas, avoiding legislative regulation in favor of voluntary compliance. As had happened in the Sumitomo case, however, the oil industry eventually reached a point where its interests were too much at odds with those of the government and they refused to cooperate on voluntary oil constraints. By the time voluntary compliance was breaking down, however, the oil crisis too was beginning to ease. Had the crisis continued, there were provisions in the legislation for sanctions if needed, but these were never used. Characteristically MITI did not respond to the oil crisis with a flurry of regulations or legislation drafted in secrecy to prevent companies from raising prices before a freeze. Throughout the crisis period the government worked closely with business, announcing each proposed measure well in advance and relying heavily upon the voluntary cooperation of business. The assumption throughout was that the industry shared MITI's concern with the general economy and could be trusted to comply voluntarily and in good faith as long as industry leaders were consulted and felt that government policy was fundamentally fair.

This partnership between government and business, if indeed partnership is the correct term, has frequently been pointed to as one of the contributors to Japan's rapid and sustained economic growth and a potentially fertile ground for American imitation. Other observers have tended to minimize the government's contribution to Japan's growth, but whatever causal role one attributes to governmental economic policy, the mutual understanding between business leaders and the bureaucracy that helps form and carry out that policy is based on several factors that may be unique to Japan and may in fact have begun to erode even there. By far the most important of these factors is a genuine national consensus on the overriding importance of economic growth. Although weakened by the rise of the consumer and environmental protection movements in the 1970s, this consensus has allowed policymakers to ignore or minimize the consideration of interests that would have conflicted with those of business and industry. As long as this political consensus holds, therefore, both business and government can assume that their long-term interests are complementary, rather than inimical, and the informal and close relationship can continue.

If the consensus breaks down, however, the whole process of administrative policymaking will be drawn into question. At present Japanese administrative law doctrines of standing, ripeness, and procedural fairness give the bureaucracy considerable leeway to exclude potentially disruptive elements from significant access to policymaking. If the social consensus for economic growth begins to erode significantly and there develops strong political pressure to open the decision-making process to participation by a wider group of interests, however, legal doctrines will be of only minimal help in maintaining the informality of the administrative process. Just as restrictive doctrines limiting legal liability for pollution damage were of little help in protecting industry from the legitimate demands of pollution victims, a shift in the political consensus would undoubtedly affect the range of interests effectively represented in ministries like MITI. The less-certain but more-interesting question is whether the shift from an essentially bipolar government/business dialogue to a multipolar one allowing consumer, environmental, or labor groups to wield real power would necessarily mean losing the consensual and informal aspects of the present system as well. Although observers used to the formalistic and lawyer-ridden American administrative system may prefer to view that as inevitable in a pluralistic democracy, it would be foolish to discount the resilience and effectiveness of informal means of dispute settlement in Japan.

Frank K. Upham

BIBLIOGRAPHY

Haley, John O., ed. *Current Legal Aspects of Doing Business in Japan and East Asia*. Chicago: American Bar Association, 1978.

Henderson, Dan Fenno. *Foreign Enterprise in Japan: Laws and Policies*. Chapel Hill: University of North Carolina Press, 1973.

Kaplan, Eugene J. *Japan: The Government-Business Relationship. A Guide for the American Businessman*. Washington, D.C.: U.S. Bureau of International Commerce, Government Printing Office, 1972.

Japanese Foreign Policy

What is Japan's contemporary foreign policy? What are the main themes regarding Japan's participation in international organizations, what are Japan's main foreign policy postures, and what are the most plausible future scenarios for Japan's foreign policy orientations?

Japan's foreign policy in the 30 odd years since World War II's end has been motivated by first, a concern for national security; second, a desire for access to vital raw materials and world export markets; and third, a wish for a legitimate and effective role as a member of the international community. Like the foreign policies of other nations, these concerns have intermingled in at times fairly complex ways. Moreover, much of Japan's foreign behavior has necessarily been reactive to the policies of other nations and the general international climate.

During the 1950s, Japan's most vital concerns were reacquisition of legitimate status as a member of the international community and provision for security in a bipolarized world whose conflicts increasingly threatened the stability of northeast Asia. Japan regained autonomy in the management of its foreign affairs with the signature in 1952 of a peace treaty with most of the powers who had been her opponents in World War II. Once independence was regained, Japanese leaders systematically sought to reestablish diplomatic relationships with the nations of the world and to gain membership in important international organizations.

Early efforts for Japan's entrance into the United Nations Organization were frustrated by a Soviet veto. However, Japan did gain entrance into the International Monetary Fund and the World Bank in 1952, and the General Agreement on Tariffs and Trade in 1953. In 1956, Japan was finally admitted to the United Nations and in 1958 she became a nonpermanent member of the Security Council. Membership in the Organization for Economic Cooperation and Development came roughly a decade later in 1963. Each of these events, and particularly entry into the United Nations Organization, marked a step toward legitimate international status that was widely supported inside Japan. The Japanese public did not suffer from strong feelings of collective guilt over the events of World War II, since it was generally felt that those events had been out of the control of the general population. Still, reacquisition of legitimate international status was broadly welcomed by the Japanese media and public.

Japan's postwar political alignment with the anti-Communist bloc of nations was assured even before completion of the peace treaty arrangements in 1951–52. The postwar military occupation of Japan, while multinational in form, was dominated by the United States with assistance from Britain, Canada, New Zealand, and Australia. Early occupation policies favored punitive dismantlement of Japan's industrial capacity and discouragement of Japan's maintenance of any kind of military forces. This orientation was soon reversed in reaction to cold war events outside of Japan and fear of the emerging domestic Communist movement by both conservative Japanese leaders and the American occupation authorities. After the outbreak of war in Korea in 1950, a National Police Reserve of 75,000 men was established to serve as a brake on the threat to internal security from the emerging Japanese Communist movement. The police reserve was a precursor of a defensive military force. Negotiations with the United States toward a bilateral security relationship also took place in this period of extreme tension in Northeast Asia and real anxiety within Japan about Soviet intentions in the Far East.

SECURITY AND DEFENSE

The United States-Japan Mutual Security Treaty, signed in 1951, became the keystone of Japan's security policy throughout the postwar era. Under the 1951 treaty the United States gained bases in Japan and was responsible for Japan's external defense and partially responsible for new internal security. While the American motivation for the treaty came from its anti-Communist containment policy, as well as feelings of strong interest in Asia dating back to the late nineteenth century, the security treaty was welcomed by Japan's governing elite as a reasonable approach to the perceived threat of advancing communism. Even though questioned by some elements within the conservative movement and strongly opposed by Japan's leftist parties, the mutual security treaty was strongly defended by Japan's political leadership of the time as the best solution to the problems of Japan's defense.

In the late 1950s the United States-Japan Security Treaty was modified after Japan's requests for greater control over the deployment of American forces based in Japan. Restrictions were added to the new treaty that specified the duration of the treaty and forbade use of American forces to quell domestic disturbances in Japan. Parliamentary ratification of the revised United States-Japan Mutual Security Treaty in 1960 became the most controversial political issue of the postwar era. However, in the face of stiff opposition the ruling Liberal Democratic Party strongly supported the bilateral relationship and continues to do so today even in the face of growing support for the idea that Japan should have more responsibility for its own defense. At present, the United States-Japan Mutual Security Treaty continues in force with the tacit agreement of both contract parties.

Japan's commitment to maintain a limited defensive military establishment dates from the early 1950s and has been continued up until the present. In 1953 a National Safety Corps with a total personnel complement of 110,000 men was decided upon; this was followed in 1954 by establishment of the tri-service Self Defense Forces; the Self Defense Forces continue to exist today as Japan's organized military arm. Opponents of Japan's maintenance of any form of military forces strongly fought establishment of the defensive arm in the 1950s (citing among other arguments the antiwar clause in Japan's postwar constitution, originally written at the suggestion of the occupation authorities). Yet the Self Defense Forces have been maintained until this day and have gradually gained acceptance among both the populace as a whole and the opposition parties. By 1980 even the Japan Socialist Party, which had opposed the Self Defense Forces since its inception, indicated that maintenance of the defense forces is warranted.

The Self Defense Forces, while a central component of Japan's postwar security policy, have not actually become a large military arm. Currently, the authorized strength of the Self Defense Forces remains slightly under 300,000 men, while the sea component maintains 72 fighting and patrol ships and the air arm has 520 aircraft. All of these figures are substantially smaller than the relevant statistics for the Republic of China (Taiwan), South Korea, and North Korea, all of which have much smaller populations and economies than Japan. The Japanese military component is also dwarfed by the Far Eastern military forces of the Soviet Union, some of which are deployed within minutes by air and hours by sea from Japan's northernmost island of Hokkaido. Comparisons of Japan's defense forces with the military establishment of the People's Republic of China indicates a similar disparity of commitment even when the large Chinese population is taken into consideration. Putting matters slightly differently, Japan's current military effort is seventeenth in rank in numbers of persons bearing arms among the nations of the world, even though Japan is the world's third largest economy.

Japan's defense policy since the 1950s has repeatedly emphasized qualitative improvement in the Self Defense Forces over increases in size. In each of Japan's major defense plans, replacement of older equipment by up-to-date aircraft, vessels, electronic equipment, and firepower have been the key concerns. This emphasis on quality of defensive armament led Chinese observers to point out in the 1960s that Japanese firepower was several times that of the World War II era, a time when Japan had vastly larger military forces. These statements clearly indicate the nature of Japan's postwar military posture, i.e., one of quality over quantity.

Statistics on Japan's budgetary expenditures on defense, meanwhile, clearly indicate the limited nature of the Japanese military commitment when compared with that of the Soviet Union, the United States, members of the NATO and Warsaw pacts, South Korea, and Taiwan. Annual defense budget outlays of 1 percent or less of Gross National Product have been among the lowest in the world among advanced, industrial powers as well as being substantially lower than the proportionate defense figures for some developing countries. (However, in absolute terms the outlays have been larger than those of many other countries simply because of Japan's enormous Gross National Product. For this reason, while Japan's relative commitment is very small, its absolute outlays are ninth in the world at present, and current modest increases in the defense budget will not alter this rank.) Japanese commentators have noted that defense budgets have usually been lower than annual expenditures by the public on the Japanese equivalent of pinball. Whatever meaning such statements have, they do serve to underline the limited defensive nature of current Japanese military commitments.

JAPANESE-U.S.TIES

Japan's entire foreign policy from the early 1950s until the present has been closely, albeit complexly, linked with American foreign relations and policies. From the time of the Korean War through at least the late 1960s the leadership of both countries in most cases manifested common anti-Communist sentiments. Ideological outlooks were not completely identical. Nor was there universal agreement on policies toward the Asian Communist powers among all political elites in both countries. Still, the grounds for a close security relationship and a common anti-Communist posture existed.

Closely related to the mutuality of American and Japanese outlooks on communism and security in the cold war era were shared economic interests. America became Japan's major trading partner after World War II, replacing China's role in the prewar period, as U.S.-Japan trade came to account for up to one-third of both imports into Japan and exports from that country. The basic economic relationship and interdependence clearly helped cement close ties between the governments of these two countries, even while also providing the basis for frictions on many occasions.

It was these frictions over trade and economics, as well as differences in opinion and timing on China policy after the early 1960s, which have at times made Japanese-American relations appear to be on the brink of severe ruptures. On the Japanese side, American resistance to free exports of Japanese textiles, television sets, and steel led to periods of sharp tensions between the two countries. Japanese leaders also chafed under American restrictions on their trade with China under the CHINCOM and COCOM lists of restricted products for trade with Communist nations at some points, and were frustrated by the sudden reversal of U.S.-China policy in 1971–72 without consultation with Japan. Other decisions by American leaders, such as the unilateral floating of the dollar, import surcharges, and temporary embargoes on soybean exports from the United States had similarly negative repercussions in Japan. On the American side, governmental leaders and business interests were convinced that Japanese firms were guilty of "dumping" steel, television sets, and other products in the American market, while maintaining various kinds of barriers to free entry of American products into Japan (discussed elsewhere in this book).

Differences of opinion also emerged over Japanese-American security relationships at times. In the 1950s these differences focused on such issues as the virtual extraterritoriality of American forces and bases in Japan, and other aspects of the initially one-sided security treaty relationship. Later, Japan's desire for reversion of the Ryukyu Islands (including Okinawa) to Japanese control became a subject for lengthy negotiations between the two countries. During much of this period, some Japanese leaders and political observers were critical of what was termed Japan's overdependence on the United States, while American opinion on Japan was often less than well-informed, and consequently both insensitive and out of date. However, by the 1970s, relationships were on the whole less one-sided, even if many differences of opinion still existed.

Some of the "structural" problems surrounding U.S.-Japan trade frictions have been echoed at several points in Japan's relationships with the European Economic Community nations. Indeed, it is not unreasonable to expect that fairly deep divisions of interest will exist between the advanced economies of the world during the 1980s, as competition increases in areas of declining differential advantage. Readjustments in trading patterns between Japan and other countries will doubtless occur in response to long-term problems of "structural" competition, greater Japanese direct investment in productive capacity abroad, and the increased costs of energy and possibly other raw materials resources.

RELATIONS WITH THE USSR AND CHINA

Japan's relationships with her Communist and non-Communist neighbors in Asia have also dominated her foreign policy concerns at many points. After an initial period of very cool relations, Soviet-Japanese contacts thawed somewhat after a 1956 agreement that reestablished diplomatic ties between the two countries. Nevertheless, relations between Japan and the USSR have been repeatedly strained by differences over fishing rights in the Northwest Pacific and the intransigence of Soviet claims to sovereignty over several islands in the Kuriles Chain adjacent to Japan's northernmost island of Hokkaido. Because of these frictions over Soviet territorial claims, no peace treaty has been signed between Japan and the USSR even though full relationships were in fact established by the 1956 normalization agreement. While the issue of territorial claims continues to erupt sporadically during exchanges of visits by leading Japanese and Soviet politicians, economic ties between the two countries have developed somewhat. The Soviet side sees obvious economic advantage in Japanese involvement in the development of eastern Siberia. Japanese response to various Soviet proposals has not always been as extensive as the USSR would prefer, but a substantial economic relationship wherein Japanese industrial products are exchanged for Siberian raw materials has developed.

During the 1950s and 1960s relations between Japan and the People's Republic of China were affected by many factors. Pressures from the United States kept Japanese companies from exporting many materials to China after China's involvement in the Korean War. The pro-Taiwan, anti-Mainland sentiments of such Japanese leaders as Prime Minister Yoshida (1948–54) were in themselves also major barriers to both economic and political relations. Led largely by Osaka business interests and some "deviant" Liberal Democrats, various cultural and trade mission contacts between Japan and the People's Republic of China were nevertheless begun in the early 1950s and increased in frequency as the decade progressed. Subsequently, during Premier Ikeda's term (1960–64) even closer economic ties were developed with the People's Republic of China, and Japan began the export of whole plant packages to China under various deferred payments plans. Still, continuing strong pro-Taiwan feelings and some deference to American interests kept Japan from having effective political ties with the Mainland until after the surprise shift of U.S.-China policy during the Nixon era.

Once the United States took the initiative, and Japan was freed from the restrictions of American residual cold war policies, Japanese elements of political and business opinion in 1971–72 openly favored closer ties with the People's Republic. Although pro-Taiwan elements in the Liberal Democratic Party and elsewhere in the nation's economic elite continued to resist rapprochement with Peking, Premier Tanaka negotiated a "normalization" agreement with the Mainland government in Autumn of 1972 that provided for dramatically improved political relations and expanded trade between the two countries. Six years later, Prime Minister Fukuda presided over signature of a peace agreement with Peking. During this period, China became once again a supplier of raw materials to Japan, while Japan shipped heavy industrial goods to the Mainland. Trade between the two countries did increase substantially because of closer political ties and

China's reorientation toward non-Communist sources of supply. At the same time, China's limited ability to pay and the related difficulty of discovering financing arrangements acceptable to the Japanese government and Japanese banking concerns kept trade from growing to amounts projected by some optimists. Meanwhile, Japan's economic ties with Taiwan were maintained despite some initial strong friction after the 1972 Peking-Tokyo rapprochement, and continued to parallel in importance the growing volume of trade between Japan and the People's Republic.

ECONOMICS AND FOREIGN POLICY

Japan's dependence on imported raw materials (and its related need to export to both advanced industrial countries and to the developing countries of Asia and other areas of the world) is the dominant underlying factor in Japan's contemporary foreign policy. Whether the issue at stake be relations with the dramatically developing economies of Taiwan and South Korea (with whom relations were normalized in 1965), the developing countries in Southeast Asia, South Asia, Latin America, or Africa, the Socialist bloc nations, or the advanced industrialized nations, Japan's need for stable sources of supply and dependable, free export markets dominates political concerns at many points. Given her 99 percent dependence on foreign oil, and heavy needs for other raw material imports, Japan is unable to make foreign policy decisions independent from her economic interests. Consequently, whatever relationships emerge between the developing countries of the "south" and the industrialized nations of the north in the future, and whatever ties develop between the Socialist bloc economies, the industrialized nations, and Japan, economics will play a large role in generating both policy differences between Japan and other countries and the solutions Japan's policymakers will take to ameliorate these problems. In contrast with nations like the Soviet Union and the People's Republic of China, where geopolitics will affect policymaking for the foreseeable future, economics is the "bottom line" in Japanese foreign policymaking. Similarly, ideological interests, such as have dominated American policy at so many points since World War II, will not be the major factor in Japanese policy in the foreseeable future. Economics will generally be the driving force in Japan's future foreign policy (including at times the economics of domestic interests such as Japan's farm bloc). Security concerns, however, could become dominant should future world environments dictate a feeling of vulnerability in Japan such as has occurred vis-a-vis the USSR at some times in the postwar era. Indeed, the 1980 Afghanistan crisis performed exactly this function for some Japanese leaders.

Bradley Richardson

BIBLIOGRAPHY

Langdon, F. C. *Japan's Foreign Policy*. Vancouver: University of British Columbia Press, 1973.

Scalapino, Robert A., ed. *The Foreign Policy of Modern Japan*. Berkeley: The University of California Press, 1977.

Japan's Social Welfare System

Japanese firms are known as being especially attentive to the needs of their permanent workers. Does this mean that Japan doesn't need a social welfare system like that of Western Europe or the United States? And what about assistance to older people, since Japanese families reputedly take care of their own aged and infirm?

The social security system in Japan today is broadly similar to that of other industrialized nations, with some distinctive features that are a product of its historical development and its social setting. Also as elsewhere, political leaders have recently become concerned with the rising costs of social security, particularly in the context of the "aging society"; Japan is currently undergoing an unprecedentedly rapid rise in the number of older people, who require financial support and a disproportionate share of medical care. Japanese responses to these problems may provide helpful lessons to policymakers in America and elsewhere.

The three major components of social security will be discussed: health insurance, pensions, and employment programs. In all we may observe a fragmentation of programs caused by differential treatment of various social groups; a preference for relying on the family, community, and particularly the firm rather than direct government-to-individual benefits; and increasing pressure from the aging society.

HEALTH INSURANCE

Health insurance was the first major social welfare initiative by the Japanese government. The first program, begun in the 1920s, was aimed at keeping the labor force needed for industrialization healthy. In 1937, as Japan prepared for war, coverage was extended to the general population, particularly the farmers, who were the main source of army recruits. The contemporary system was essentially completed in 1958, and since then all Japanese have been covered by some compulsory health insurance scheme, though their costs and benefits vary considerably.

The least-generous system is National Health Insurance, which mainly covers farmers, the self-employed, and the retired or others without jobs. Participants make a monthly payment to their local government office and have 70 percent of necessary medical, dental, and hospital expenses covered. The government-managed Employees' Health Insurance program covers most employees, whose contributions are matched by their employers; it pays all medical costs (minus a small deductible) for the insured, but just 70 percent for his or her dependents. Wage replacement for the time the employee is out sick is also provided. Nearly all larger firms (those with at least 1,000 employees) have opted to form Health Insurance Societies within the Employees' Health Insurance system, with some governmental financial support. Usually the firm will bear a higher and the employee a lower proportion of costs in these societies, and benefits are ample, often including various special services as well as full coverage for dependents. The Mutual Aid Associations set up for various categories of public or quasi-public employees also provide relatively high benefits.

This fragmentation of health insurance produces both administrative difficulties and considerable inequities of coverage, which are hardly randomly distributed. The best benefits and lowest costs are for government employees and those who work for the largest companies; employees of smaller firms get good benefits at somewhat higher cost; the self-employed or those without jobs receive less and pay more. This pattern serves to reinforce the attachment of elite workers to their organizations. However, it is worth noting that the American system, while private except for the poor and aged, results in a similar pattern of high benefits and relatively low cost for those in large organizations, with less service at more cost for many others.

The Japanese health care delivery system, as distinct from the insurance system that pays for it, resembles the United States more than, for example, England's National Health Service. Most Japanese doctors are in private practice on a fee-for-service basis. Doctors dispense their own prescription drugs (mostly covered by insurance) and often operate small hospitals; naturally, hospital stays and consumption of medicine tend to be quite high in Japan.

Financing medical care has been a deficit operation for the Japanese government for many years, and costs have increased with the aging of the population. In the early 1970s, as part of an overall expansion of benefits for the elderly, the government began offering free health care (by supplementing insurance coverage) for all over 70 who could meet a rather relaxed income test. Many localities, including Tokyo, supplement this program by, for example, lowering the age limit to 65. This subsidy itself is expensive and it encourages greater use of medical services by the elderly, thereby straining the National Health Insurance system. In any case, greater numbers of old people inevitably cost money because their health costs per capita are about three times average. Hence a number of alternatives for restricting or reorganizing health care for the elderly are currently under discussion within the government.

Health insurance was Japan's first step toward the welfare state, and it remains its strongest component in international comparison. The system has some shortcomings, and certainly is expensive, but it is one factor (along with improved nutrition and public health) in maintaining a healthy population—Japan today has nearly the longest life expectancy in the world.

PENSIONS

The sequence of development of pension insurance in Japan was similar to that of health insurance, though it occurred later, and has resulted in a very fragmented system. As in other nations, the first group to be covered with old age or disability pensions was government employees. A system to cover private-sector employees was established in 1941, partly as a means for accumulating large financial reserves for investment in war production. This system fell victim to the postwar inflation and had to be completely overhauled in 1954; it is called the Kōsei Nenkin in Japanese, sometimes translated as the Welfare Pension but better referred to as the Employees' Pension system. Employees of all but the tiniest firms are enrolled, currently about 25 million workers. The worker and employer each contribute about 5 percent of wages, and the government contributes to benefits and pays administrative costs from general revenues. Benefits are figured on a complex formula that includes a flat rate amount, an amount proportionate to average earnings, and a dependent's allowance, and they are indexed to inflation. After big hikes in the early 1970s, Employees' Pension benefits became roughly comparable to those of the U.S. social security system, in money amounts and relative to the average wage level. In 1979, the "model" pension for a married beneficiary with good wages and 28 years' participation (a relatively small proportion of the elderly) was about $650 per month. The average benefit payment was about $400 a month, going to some 2 million beneficiaries, of which about 90 percent receive old age or survivors pensions, the remainder disability. (For a comparison of pension benefits with other advanced nations see Figure 7.3).

FIGURE 7.3

Pension Benefits in Five Countries

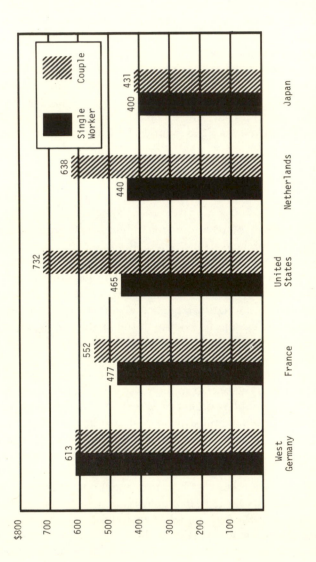

Note: Monthly benefits in 1979 for a male worker who earned $15,000 in 1978, his year of retirement. Calculated in American dollars at exchange rates of January 1979. Benefits are those for the major public system covering employees in each country, which is the Employees' Pension System for Japan.
Source: Calculated from data prepared by the Comparative Studies Staff, United States Social Security Administration, as reported in the *Washington Post*, July 26, 1980.

As with health insurance, some employees get better treatment. Public and quasi-public employees participate in Mutual Aid Associations that generally offer higher benefits, although several of these associations are now running into financial difficulties. Most of Japan's largest firms have established Employee Pension Funds, in which the employer's contribution and the employee's benefits are generally much higher than in the more general system. These are jointly run by management and the union. Since the government also contributes, this "contracting-out" plan may be seen as a mixed public-private system. Many firms provide completely private pension plans, or the traditional Japanese lump-sum retirement bonus (the model amount in 1978 was about $80,000 for college graduates), either instead of or along with a pension fund. At the other end of the scale, farmers, housewives, the self-employed, and others belong to the National Pension system, established in 1959. Here participants pay their contribution (about $15 a month in 1980) to the local government office. Benefits are determined by length of participation and run somewhat under half the amount of the Employees' Pension, it being assumed that both husband and wife are eligible.

Until about a decade ago, Japanese pensions were meager, and many older people or those with disabilities had to rely on their families for support. Even today nearly three-quarters of those over 65 continue to live with their children, although a much higher proportion of their income now comes from public sources. Still, because a long period of participation is required before becoming eligible for full benefits, the proportion of the elderly receiving adequate support is still relatively small. To provide some help, the government offers an Old Age Welfare Pension, which is non-contributory, to low-income people over age 70; in 1980 this amounted to about $100 a month.

The pension system faces many of the same difficulties as health insurance. One is the disparity between a true "pension elite" of employees of the government and large firms and those with little and no coverage, although this situation will improve as the pension schemes mature. Fragmentation causes many administrative problems and permits some double coverage: for example, wives of Employee Pension participants can enroll in the National Pension plan and ultimately receive what many see as an inequitably large, heavily subsidized benefit. The thorniest problems are financial, caused by the aging of the population. It is estimated that the number of old-age pension beneficiaries will rise from about 11 million in 1980 to almost 19 million in 2010, while the working-age population actually declines by 4 million. The financial structure of the Japanese pension plans is somewhat closer to a "funded" pattern than the basically "pay-as-you-go" American social security system, and enormous reserves have been accumulated, but before too long contributions from workers will have to be raised sharply or else expenditures somehow reduced. In 1979, it was proposed that the pensionable age for men under the Employees' Pension be raised from 60 (among the lowest in the world) to 65, the same as the National Pension. While political pressures killed this initiative, some such move is likely for the future.

EMPLOYMENT POLICY

A type of unemployment insurance dates back to 1936 in Japan, but the modern system was created in 1947 and then substantially reformed in 1974. The policy prior to that year can be called "ameliorative": insurance for those temporarily out of work, and special public employment programs for the more "hard-core" unemployed. These programs were designed to cope with the high unemployment of the immediate postwar years. When economic growth brought a shift from a labor-surplus to a labor-short economy, policy shifted toward an "affirmative" focus on stable employment, symbolized by the 1974 name change from "unemployment" to "employment" insurance.

The basic insurance scheme pays a monthly benefit of $240 to $745 (1979 figures), amounting to 60 to 80 percent of prior wages, for a period of 90 days (recipients under 30) to 300 days (those over 55 or facing some other special difficulty). Various additional allowances to encourage job retraining are also provided, as are extra payments for moving or other expenses after a new job is found. The plan in financed by equal contributions by worker and employer totaling 1 percent of wages (higher in some industries with fluctuating employment). Seasonal employees, including farmers who seek jobs for only part of the year, and day laborers are covered by separate systems.

Since the oil shock of 1973, Japan has been troubled by both cyclical and structural unemployment. A notably Japanese policy response has been to provide support for workers idled because of an economic slowdown through their employers, rather than waiting until the worker has been laid off and then giving benefits directly. From the point of view of the firm, this program allows maintenance of a trained work force through a temporary recession; from a social point of view, as with the health and pension plans described above, it serves to strengthen the bonds between worker and company. Somewhat similarly, companies in sectors that face long-term economic declines are offered subsidies for retraining their workers in new skills, and for aiding their transfers to other companies.

Another aspect of the new "affirmative" employment policy is a series of measures to stimulate employment of older workers. The combination of demographic change and Japanese employment practices—entry-level hiring, early retirement—has produced large numbers of middle-aged or older workers (ages 45–65) who have difficulty in finding jobs, particularly since 1973. The Ministry of Labor has had some success through various legal and financial devices in inducing firms to raise their fixed retirement age from the customary age 55 or thereabouts to age 60. It has also established a quota for older workers, and offers subsidies to companies who hire those over age 60. Although the problem is far from solved, Japanese programs in this area may offer some interesting suggestions to Americans, who only recently are beginning to grasp the need for some positive policy toward older workers.

CONCLUSIONS

These three areas are the most important components of Japanese social welfare policy, in terms of both expenditures and their impact on people's lives. Of course, most of the other welfare programs found in other advanced nations have their counterparts in Japan, though generally at lower levels than at least in such welfare states as Sweden. Differences in social customs account for some of what might seem deficiencies of programs. For example, the fact that so many older people live with their children reduces the need for old-age homes, and indeed the existing supply (about 80,000 beds) is adequate, although demand continues to rise for nursing homes (about 70,000 beds). The fact that larger firms provide a variety of welfare benefits for their employees presumably also reduces the need for public services, though at the expense of those not so well situated. Factors related to Japan's ethnic homogeneity and relatively flat income distribution may explain the rather low numbers receiving public assistance (under 1.2 percent of households), though it should be noted that the benefits are reasonably generous. However, even after allowing for all these factors, it is clear that throughout the postwar period Japan has pursued "cheap government," part of a policy of restraining consumption to maximize funds for investment. Holding back on social security expenditures was an important element in keeping Japanese government costs at astonishingly low levels for an industrialized country. As late as 1966, according to the standard International Labor Organization definition, Japanese were devoting only 4.4 percent of national income to social insurance contributions, compared with 19.2 percent for France, 14.2 percent for West Germany, and 7.0 percent for the United States.

However, because of the aging of the population, urbanization, and other social change, and simply increased expectations among the people, this situation has changed markedly. Although up-to-date figures are not yet available, the social welfare expenditure to national income ratio is now probably about 13 percent, comparable to the U.S. 1977 figure of 13.7 percent. Moreover, even without any new policy initiatives, the maturation of the pension systems alone will ensure that this figure will keep rising for the foreseeable future. Everybody worries about how this bill will be paid. Many conservatives are still more concerned that heavy taxes plus high benefits will induce the so-called "English disease," with a diminution of work ethic, and that the traditional Japanese reliance on family, community, and coroporate group will be lost. Hence, recently there has been much discussion of a "Japanese-style" welfare system, with restraints on expenditures and attempts to encourage, for example, older people to continue living with their children. Extra income-tax deductions, government loans for building additional rooms on houses, and special training for family members to take care of a bedridden parent are among the devices adopted to this purpose. One may doubt if these efforts are likely to reverse the trend toward a welfare state, but they are certainly worthy of attention as Japanese responses to a set of problems that trouble every advanced society.

John Creighton Campbell

BIBLIOGRAPHY

Japan Institute of Labor. Japanese Industrial Relations Series: see especially *Employment and Employment Policy*. Tokyo, 1979; and *Social Security*. Tokyo, 1980.

Leichter, Howard M. *A Comparative Approach to Policy Analysis: Health Care Policy in Four Nations*. Cambridge, England: Cambridge University Press, 1979, pp. 237–70.

Ministry of Health and Welfare. *Social Welfare Services in Japan*. Japan, annual.

Ministry of Health and Welfare, Social Insurance Agency. *Outline of Social Insurance in Japan*. Japan, annual.

8

SOCIOHISTORIC TRENDS

Business is conducted in Japan like other countries in an environment that reflects the broad historical patterns of the past. The Japanese value system reflects among other things the impact of centuries of religious and philosophical experience, and the assumptions and attitudes of contemporary Japanese businessmen are molded by past dogmas and beliefs as well as by current goals and orientation. Cultural values and the substance of Japanese experience have also reflected attitudes toward the role of the military and the importance given to military ventures relative to other kinds of activity (e.g., economic or political) at different points in time. James Bartholomew discusses the broad patterns of Japanese religious experience and the often misunderstood attitudes toward militarism in Japan in this chapter.

Contemporary Japanese religious practice is a set of contradictions. Comparatively few Japanese are active religious practitioners and attend religious services, but many Japanese are married or buried according to religious rites. A similar contradiction exists in regard to religious beliefs: fewer Japanese say they believe in God relative to the larger proportions of the population who report they have prayed to a supernatural being some time in their lives.

These seemingly contradictory patterns reflect a contemporary trend toward secularization in Japanese religious life, accompanied by residual attention to religious practices, which are the product of complex historical forces. Through a process of adaptation various foreign religions and philosophies—Buddhism, Catholicism, and Confucianism—were imported into Japanese belief systems over the past centuries. Buddhism came first and was followed in impact by Confucianism; Catholicism itself arrived during the seventeenth century. In each case the foreign belief systems were imported under political tutelage, only to be abandoned by political leaders at later dates (despite whatever broader effects on religious ideas and practices lingered). Each imported belief system at one or another time also made some adjustments to the native Shinto concepts, although Shintoism in itself was not always the most dynamic of religious forces. The resulting admixtures of primarily Buddhist, Shinto, and Confucian moral codes and religious beliefs and practices are reflected in contemporary Japanese life. Japanese are married in Shinto rites, or occasionally in Christian ceremonies; funerals and memorial services are conducted in Buddhist temples; and Confucian ideas are reflected in contemporary social codes. Because of the decline of institutional Buddhism, and the discrediting of state Shinto during World War II, Japanese do not practice religion. Even though Christianity and some new syncretic religions have enjoyed popularity since World War II, most Japanese follow a more or less rationalistic and secular path—even though the parallel European philosophical movements had little *direct* impact on popular Japanese thinking.

The effects of earlier religious movements on contemporary values are as complex as were the events that accompanied the arrival of the various foreign religions and beliefs in Japan. From Confucian thought comes an emphasis on communal values and harmony that reinforces Japanese rural social traditions. Confucian ideas also support the Japanese tendency toward hierarchical ranking in social relationships (which itself contrasts with the broad tendencies toward relative egalitarianism between social classes and groups!). Confucian and Buddhist ideas also support the Japanese individual emphasis on self-improvement, while a fatalistic adaptation to unpredictable events derives from mainly Buddhist tenets. Finally, Shinto, a totemistic religion, has left behind a symbolization of both the local and national community in its deification of local places and its support for the traditional imperial mythology.

Like many traditional religious beliefs, military values are largely discredited or neglected in contemporary Japan. Military budgets are low and defensive military forces are supported by public opinion somewhat reluctantly as a more or less necessary evil. The present deemphasis on military solutions and values contrasts markedly with Japan's twentieth-century experience, and contradicts some earlier historical trends. There have been essentially four periods in Japan's known history: a prehistorical era in which different regional tribes were the major social and political force, a period of semicentralized imperial rule when Chinese bureaucratic institutions were imitated, a long era of military feudalism, and modern constitutional rule. Military values and the military arm did not receive major emphasis in the first two of these periods. Subsequently, during the long feudal period, the samurai military class was dominant and several civil wars occurred. Still, the class basis of military involvement was fairly narrow, and military values and activities did not generally include large segments of the population—the existence of samurai-led peasant armies in no way resembled modern political mobilization.

Militarism as a glorification of military ventures and enthusiasm for military careers was actually a phenomenon of the modern era in Japan. The long samurai emphasis on heroic military leadership was of course a historical reference point for military romanticists and leaders who sought to legitimize military concepts employing past traditions. Yet, the broad inculcation of support for nationalistic goals and military solutions itself came only after the adoption of national development goals. Also, while military values and military forces were glorified at the time of the Sino-Japanese (1895) and Russo-Japanese (1905) Wars they actually reached a crescendo mainly in the 1930s and during World War II. At present militarism is pretty well discredited in Japan. Even though some intellectuals and politicians feel Japan should have more control over its own military security, the popular mood is not very supportive of greater military involvement at this time.

Militarism in Japan's Tradition

Most people these days would not call Japan a militaristic nation. Yet some people in Western countries still have such an image of Japan. Historically, was Japan always militaristic, or was this the case only at times? What is the nature of Japan's contemporary defense policy and public opinion on defense matters in Japan? And what is the near future likely to be for Japan's defense options?

Japan today cannot be called militaristic in any sense whatever. In 1945 the country was defeated by the United States in the Pacific War—as the Japanese call it, and since then has, if anything, been strongly inclined toward pacifism. Military budgets have remained below 1 percent of Gross National Product in the postwar period. The armed forces are wholly under civilian control. And nonaligned, militarily insignificant Switzerland is often mentioned in public opinion polls as the country most admired by the Japanese people. However, the persistence of a militaristic image is quite understandable in the light of modern Japanese history. From 1931 to 1945 Japan's foreign relations and in large measure its domestic affairs were dominated by the Army and Navy. Ultranationalism ran rampant, and military values thoroughly infiltrated the social mainstream via the conscription and compulsory education systems. But even these observations are somewhat misleading. Prior to about A.D. 900 a thoroughly civilianized elite dominated Japanese affairs. Possession of the symbols of sovereign power, i.e., the Throne, has never depended on military power. And even in the era of samurai preeminence, there were major obstacles to the militarization of society as a whole.

AN ERA OF CIVILIAN DOMINATION

Japan in the period of its late prehistory—roughly A.D. 200 to 500—was a loose-knit, tribalistic society of powerful warrior clans and a very weak center. Land was farmed and defended by tribal groups in common. The Emperor was little more than a first among equals. Religion and government were synonymous. Shinto religious ideals held the warrior up to acclaim, but there was no separate military establishment and the country was militarily weaker than its continental neighbors. However, the forcible expulson of the Japanese from their south Korean foothold in 562 set the stage for a major transformation. Cultural Sinification and political centralization took place during the next several decades in an effort to strengthen both the country and its monarchical institutions. Reforming elements established a permanent national capital. Land holding by tribal groups gave way to farming by nuclear family units. Bureaucratic institutions were established and the tax system to sustain them. And a military establishment energed that was based on peasant conscription.

For a time the reforms appeared to work well. Nara, the imperial capital, grew to a city of 200,000 with elegant palaces, temples, and various public buildings. The number of Buddhist monasteries grew tenfold in the seventh and eighth centuries. Frontiers were expanded northward, and the amount of cultivated land grew apace. But the bases of change were slowly being laid. The central government lacked ideological justification for the kind of centralized authority it wished to exercise. It granted tax concessions to monasteries and other powerful groups as a means of encouraging expansion. The peasants vigorously resisted conscription. And frontier elements thumbed their noses at the bureaucrats in Nara and (after 794) in Kyoto. Moreover, the structural imperatives that dictated strong bureaucratic institutions in China were lacking in Japan. Japan was an island country with no external enemies and practically none at home. And its climate was beneficent enough to assure an adequate food supply without centrally controlled irrigation.

EMERGENCE OF THE SAMURAI MILITARY ELITE

Out of these conditions emerged a new military elite. From a legal standpoint, the samurai were the disinherited offspring of ninth-century emperors. The founding fathers of the Chinese-style state system had correctly foreseen the financial and political problems that an unrestricted bequeathing of imperial family status and prerogatives to imperial descendents would engender and in 702 took legal steps to counteract their effects. The reformers provided that all descendents of emperors, excepting only the main line, would incur disinheritance after six generations. They would no longer be entitled to state subsidies. They would have to assume surnames. (Part of the Japanese imperial family's mystique is precisely the *lack* of a surname, a practice sharply at variance with the monarchical traditions of other countries.) And they would be obliged to work and thus fend for themselves. By virtue of their training, public office was the most suitable occupation for imperial castoffs and most government positions were outside the capital. This circumstance, together with the workings of the 702 law, produced a growing movement of former aristocrats to the provinces in the latter part of the ninth century; and the combination of imperial lineage and the rustification caused by frontier life in due course produced the samurai as a Japanese social type.

Samurai military provincials dominated Japanese political life for the next thousand years. Through the rest of the Heian period, they lived in uneasy symbiosis with the aristocrats of the capital, but in 1185 the Minamoto family coalition defeated its Taira rivals and thereafter created a new structure of government, the military shogunate. From the 1190s to 1334 the shogunate was based at Kamakura in east central Japan. But in 1336 a successor, the Ashikaga, seized power and removed the shogunate to Kyoto. From the 1330s to the 1570s Kyoto was thus the sole nerve center of elite politics in Japan, but many vital decisions were actually made at the local level where successions of military barons (*daimyō*) and their samurai followers held sway, sometimes plundering their neighbors, at other times developing the national wealth and providing security but invariably preventing creation of effective centralized authority. The Ashikaga regime essentially disappeared—unlamented—in 1573 and a new shogunate administration emerged only in 1600.

Adapting and subtly altering an ancient Chinese blueprint of social organization, the Tokugawa shogunate classified people into one of four groups—military, farmers, artisans, and merchants—with the military class on top. They and their families became a hereditary-ruling elite. They alone could bear arms and only samurai (high-ranking ones, actually) could hold office. All other groups were subordinated to the military and paid them formal deference. At the same time, other changes were imposed that significantly restricted samurai. Under Tokugawa law, they were denied control of the land by being forced to reside in the shadow of their *daimyō*'s castle. And their freedom of economic movement was restricted as a matter of shogunate policy. Samurai under feudal law were paid rice stipends by their *daimyō* (or in some cases, the shogun) and were generally forbidden to compete economically with members of other classes. Moreover, many were impoverished by an economically burdensome set of travel and service restrictions (the system of Alternate Attendance) imposed on them by the shogunate as a means of political control.

As the samurai grew weaker, their system of values became stronger in Japanese society as a whole. Neo-Confucianism was adopted as the official Tokugawa ideology because of its stress on the importance of loyalty between individuals. All Japanese were admonished to follow the requirements of filial piety, respect for spouses and older siblings, and above all, to be loyal to their lord or other superior. Samurai families also lived by the code of *bushidō*. Fully articulated by the end of the seventeenth century, bushidō—the "Way of the Warrior"—told them to practice bravery, self-control, benevolence, and loyalty—and most especially to value personal honor over human life itself. Bushidō was limited to samurai in its direct application, but their elite status gave it wider circulation. Socially ambitious people emulated the samurai, and as literacy and education spread, more and more Japanese became acquainted with the code of the warrior families. Whether these conditions justify a militarist label for Tokugawa society, however, is quite another matter. Samurai were supposed to be segregated from the general population. Most Japanese were not formally educated. They could not bear arms or marry into samurai families. And the combination of national seclusion (1639–1853) and restrictions on the daimyō class called the Alternate Attendance System (1642–1862) made domestic or foreign wars virtually next to impossible.

MEIJI PERIOD DEVELOPMENTS, 1868–1912

The Meiji government (1868–1912) moved to abolish samurai privileges even as their ethos was actively diffused to the general population. Swords and topknots (the distinctive samurai hairdress) disappeared with the Restoration of 1868. Rice stipends were abolished in 1876. The daimyō were pensioned off. A compensatory plan to employ beleaguered warriors in an invasion of Korea was quashed in 1873, and a full-scale rebellion of samurai against the Meiji government was suppressed in 1877. But some features of the warrior tradition survived the Restoration intact. The leaders of the new armed services, created in 1872, saw themselves, like the samurai, as the natural leaders of society. They refused to subordinate themselves to full civilian control. War and Navy ministers, responsible to the Cabinet for administering the armed services, were subordinate to the Service Chiefs of Staff by virtue of their status on the active duty roster. And the Service Chiefs of Staff had rights of direct access to the occupant of the Throne himself.

Latent militaristic attitudes were also encouraged in the general population. For most this occurred in the public school system, but for some Japanese there were other vehicles as well. The heart of the schools' moral education effort was the so-called *shūshin* course. Mostly it taught pupils such traditional virtues as filial piety, respect for teachers and obedience to parents, but other features constituted a major cult of the Throne. Everyone was taught the Shinto mythological view of the Emperor's divine origin and the divine creation of Japan. A photograph of the Emperor was placed above every school blackboard. Teacher and pupils together read the Imperial Rescript on Education (issued in 1890) every morning. And imperial photographs had at all cost to be safely removed from the wooden buildings in the event of a school fire. Further indoctrination was provided by nationalist societies and the Imperial Military Reserve Association. This organization, founded in 1906, was supposed to create "citizen soldiers" capable of moving from civilian to military life rapidly in the event of a national emergency. The Association taught traditional samurai ideals and magnified its impact by recruiting local elites. By 1912 it had about 10,000 local chapters and a membership of over a million.

THE INTERWAR PERIOD, 1919–31

Japan's power and influence grew rapidly in the years after World War I. The country was recognized as one of the Big Three (with Great Britain and the United States) at the Versailles Conference. In 1921–22 it was a leading participant in the Washington Naval Conference. Throughout the 1920s it took a leading role in the League of Nations and in 1930 attended the London Conference on Naval Arms Limitations. This record of achievement by the rules of Western diplomacy was nevertheless marred by several ugly incidents. The city of San Francisco in 1907 had ejected Japanese-American children from its public schools just a year after accepting earthquake-relief assistance from Japan. Diplomatic partners like Great Britain and the United States declined to support Japan's "Racial Equality Clause" addendum to the League of Nations Charter. And in 1924 the U.S. Congress enacted an immigration law that prevented Japanese nationals from gaining American citizenship. These events undercut a short-term trend against militarism. After World War I Japan abandoned an earlier attempt to make a satellite out of China. Military objections to an inferior naval status vis-a-vis the United States and Great Britain were overridden by the government in 1922 and 1930. And military budgets were systematically and regularly cut back in the decade of the 1920s.

Nationalist obscurantism, political uncertainties in China, and domestic economic pressures combined with opposition to military budget cutting in the unauthorized takeover of Manchuria by the Japanese field army in 1931. The Army officers who planned it hated the favoritism toward big business and exploitation of farmers effectively endorsed by antimilitarist politicians and planned their daring coup as a means of changing domestic opinion. Civilian Cabinet officials, though hostile, were forced to accept the maneuver by a tide of popular jingoism. Within two years Japan had launched a campaign for rearmament, renounced the naval arms limitation treaty and departed from the League of Nations. Early in 1937 a war began with China and Western antagonisms hardened. In 1941 the Japanese attacked American forces at Pearl Harbor when diplomatic negotiations proved abortive. However, American military and industrial might brought an end to open resistance in due course, and six and a half years of occupation and major reforms followed.

JAPANESE SOCIETY AND
MILITARY AFFAIRS SINCE 1945

Defeat marked the turning point in the fortunes of Japanese militarism. The country was forced by defeat to abandon all overseas territories and colonies. Foreign military forces occupied the home islands for the first time in recorded history. The entire military apparatus was destroyed and a clause forbidding the use or mobilization of offensive military capabilities (the famous Article 9) was inserted at American insistence into the Constitution of 1947. However, present-day opinions on defense-related matters are not simply a product of American views and initiatives. World War II was a catastrophic disaster for Japan causing 3,000,000 deaths, mass destruction of cities, transportation facilities, and industrial plant, and man's first experience with the use of atomic weapons. These experiences encouraged many Japanese to think the military had let down or even betrayed the country and led in no small measure to the present climate and policies.

Defense proved a divisive issue in the years that followed the war. Few Japanese supported the idea of a large military establishment and fewer still creation of a nuclear weapons arsenal, which many thought the Constitution precluded in any event. But no clear consensus existed for many years beyond these fundamental points. For the past 30 years, conservatives have almost unanimously supported the United States-Japan Security Treaty that came into existence in 1951 (see Chapter 7 for further details); but opposition parties (until recently) ran the gamut of opinion from unarmed neutrality (the Socialist opinion) to an alliance with the Soviet Union (favored by the Communists). American control of Okinawa, the transshipment of nuclear weapons through Japan, and relations between the U.S. bases and the Japanese public were all major issues in the 1950s and 1960s, but most of these have faded in the past few years or so. Okinawa was returned to Japan in 1970. Nuclear weapons are no longer shipped through the country, and Japanese control over American military personnel and facilities has slowly and inexorably expanded. Moreover, a 1978 poll found that two-thirds of all Japanese now consider the United States-Japan Security Treaty to be "helpful" or "somewhat helpful" to the peace and security of the country.

Japan's own military establishment, the Self Defense Force, has also become more popular in the last few years. In 1975, 79 percent of respondents to a poll conducted by the Prime Minister's Office said they considered the Self Defense Forces "necessary" while 8 percent called it "unnecessary"; but by 1978 "necessary" responses had risen to 86 percent while "unnecessary" opinion-holders had declined to 5 percent. Moreover, increasingly favorable opinions correlate with greater financial support. In 1965 Japan spent less than $840 million on defense, but by 1975 spending had risen to $3.7 billion, and in 1979 to $5.8 billion. (However, these figures employ the former fixed exchange rate of 360 yen to the dollar and therefore understate the 1975 and 1979 appropriations.) Even so, spending remains below one percent of Gross National Product and substantially below the proportional outlays of other industrial powers. In 1978, for example, Japanese defense spending exceeded that of Italy by 34 percent, but was only half that of France and just a quarter that of China.

Significant changes in defense policy seem unlikely for the short-term future at least. Even the Communist Party no longer favors a Soviet alliance. All public opinion polls show the Soviet Union as the country *least* favorably regarded by the Japanese, and many refer to the USSR informally as a *kurai kuni* (sinister place). Rearmament on any significant scale raises significant constitutional issues and the prospect of unacceptably high costs. In 1978, for example, nuclear armed Britain and France spent 5 percent and 3.6 percent of Gross National Product respectively on national defense and many experts think Japan would also have to spend 5 percent of Gross National Product on the military to have a protective posture of equal credibility. This figure repesents a fivefold increase in spending and might still fall short of the protection presently guaranteed by the American "nuclear umbrella." Finally there remains the issue of the "nuclear allergy" itself. Annual anti-A bomb rallies at Hiroshima commemorating the 1945 nuclear attack still attract hundreds of thousands of people, and even a staunch defense advocate like Yasuhiro Nakasone, former Defense Agency Chief, recommends *against* nuclear weapons for fear they might disrupt the hard-won consensus in support of the Self Defense Force.

But none of this forecloses the nuclear option forever. Japan has been understandably eager to acquire a permanent United Nations Security Council seat for some time and is keenly aware that all of the present permanent members are possessors of nuclear weapons. Moreover, India has had nuclear weapons since 1974 and some Japanese have questioned U.S. guarantees since the fall of Vietnam in the Spring of 1975. It is often pointed out that technical problems of nuclear development pose no obstacle to Japan, and some find its long delay in ratifying the Nuclear Non-Proliferation Treaty in the 1970s significant. Whether Japan chooses the nuclear option at some future time will depend on the nature of its relations with the United States, China, the USSR, possibly the United Nations, *and* its need to assure delivery of foreign energy supplies. In neither case can the future be predicted with assurance.

James Bartholomew

BIBLIOGRAPHY

Sorenson, Jay B. *Japanese Policy and Nuclear Arms*. New York: American-Asian Educational Exchange, 1975.

Weinstein, Martin E. *Japan's Postwar Defense Policy, 1947–1968*. New York and London: Columbia University Press, 1971.

Religion in Japan

What is the state of religious belief in Japan today, and what has it been like in the past? What are the main religious traditions, and, overall, are Japanese people very "religious" in the sense of going to church regularly? Are there other manifestations of religious commitment?

The contemporary state of religious belief and practice in Japan is apt to strike the Western observer as both complex and contradictory. Only 24 percent admit to having prayed, including 48 percent of those who say they consider religion irrelevant or unnecessary. More and more Japanese, by some indicators, are being married according to various religious rites, yet traditional religious affiliations and commitments are greatest among those whose weddings were not conducted at a shrine, temple, or church at all. A mere 1 percent of all Japanese appear on the membership rosters of the various Christian churches, yet public opinion surveys invariably reveal a self-professed Christian following of something like 3 percent of the total population. Such contradictions can, in some degree, be found elsewhere; but the total religious situation of Japan today defies easy comparison with that of any contemporary nation or society.

One must look to the Japanese setting to account for the contradictions. Many countries have a legacy of religious totemism—identification of kinship groups with animals or other natural objects—but the Japanese Shinto tradition lasted longer and enjoyed greater support than comparable movements elsewhere. Other societies—Germany, Russia, China, Poland—suffered terrible devastation in World War II; but in none did physical devastation produce a backlash against traditional religious ideals or institutions akin to that of Japan. Philosophical rationalism has greatly affected opinion about religion in most countries with technologically sophisticated economies, but in none outside Scandinavia has the impact on both the intellectual community *and* the general public been greater. Similarly, Japan—along with Russia—is unique in the degree to which its various political regimes systematically and successfully manipulated or abused religious sentiments and institutions to achieve purely political aims.

PROMINENCE OF SYNCRETISM

Syncretism—the tendency to combine opposing principles in a single system—is a particularly prominent feature of the Japanese religious scene. In fact, Japan is, and is likely to remain, the only industrialized country whose religious traditions are so thoroughly, almost dogmatically, syncretistic. Shinto is the oldest element of Japan's syncretic religious system and the one to which all other religions historically had to adapt. Despite the religion's antiquity, the term Shinto ("Way of the *kami*") was itself not coined until the seventh century A.D. and only then because Buddhism's arrival in the sixth century had made it necessary to distinguish between the two traditions. Confucianism arrived about the same time as Buddhism but had very little impact before the seventeenth century. Catholicism reached

Japan in the middle of the sixteenth century, but was largely extirpated in the seventeenth after a century of evangelization. These religions came from very different societies (India, China, and Europe respectively) and brought very different philosophies, moral traditions, and views of man to Japan. Nevertheless, the Japanese have long tried to produce from all of them, if not a complete amalgam, at least a placid contunuum of religious ideals and practices based on a de facto, or in the Tokugawa period (1600–1867) de jure, segregation of religious concerns and labor. Buddhism took responsibility for religious philosophy, Confucianism for ethics, and Shinto for theology. Protestantism, which arrived from the United States in the mid-nineteenth century, proved more resistant to syncretistic pressures than the other religions, but even it has not escaped them completely.

Juxtaposition of such divergent traditions has produced a religiosity that is characteristically Japanese. It is one that tends to reject absolute moral principles while everywhere investing aesthetic activities and living patterns with a sense of the Absolute. This feature is best explained in reference to the concept of *michi* or "way" (*tao* in Chinese), a term frequently associated with Zen Buddhism but owing equally as much to Shinto. The physicist Yukawa Hideki, a Nobel Laureate, describes adherence to a way as a "thorough-going passiveness [in which one] submits to the irrationalities omnipresent.in the universe by regarding them as inevitable." Religion expert Joseph J. Spae regards adherence to a way as an attempt to achieve "direct contact" with reality through the mysticism or heightened experience of the moment. This concept of way proved extraordinarily fruitful in the high cultural realm where the Japanese have developed a way of archery, a way of judo, a way of making and serving tea, and numerous other ways. By following any one of them, the devotee attains more than a purely technical proficiency; he expects rather to attain harmony, peace, integration with nature, and possibly enlightenment itself. Noting the prominence of this conception and its derivative institutional forms in Japanese religion, the well-known historian of Japan, Sir George Sansom, once remarked that the Japanese have tended to make religion into an art form, and art forms into a religion.

CONCENTRATION ON LIFE IN THIS WORLD

As may readily be apparent, Japanese religiosity distrusts intellectualism and emphasizes instead the immediate experience of the life situation. Shinto in particular disdains all truths derived exclusively from reason, and Buddhism, which initially presented a highly intellectual image of religion to the Japanese, through contact with Shinto, was wont to change its image and, in some degree, its message. After the eighth century, its emphasis on the saving power of various bodhisattvas tended to replace an earlier stress on attaining enlightenment by philosophical means. Buddhist intellectual activites did not disappear but were thereafter on the defensive. Such a prominent feature of medieval Japanese religion did the cult of mysticism and direct experience become that the great Buddhist philosopher and teacher Shinran (1173–1262) openly labeled his own voluminous writings on religion as "unreal, provisional and expedient."

Japanese religion typically emphasizes the visible world and affirms the nature of man as it is. Although Shinto has always disavowed human actions that harm society or threaten the cosmic order, its general conception of sin is shallow and its hope for man's future unlimited. A man can become a *kami* (spirits, deities, any source of power) and a kami can become a man. Buddhism and Christianity later took a more skeptical view. The former defined the world as a place of suffering due to the limitless cravings of men, while Christianity stressed the reality of Original Sin and the unique saving power of Christ. Both teachings have been influential, but most Japanese have never been entirely persuaded. In fact, it has historically been the two "foreign" religions that came to terms with Shinto, rather than the other way around. From the ninth century, Buddhist temples were frequently built in places held sacred by Shinto, and the Shinto kami were termed local manifestations of the more universalistic bodhisattvas—candidates for deliverance who postpone their own salvation to help other struggling souls through the cycle of birth, life, death, and rebirth. Catholicism held to its original beliefs but also gave ground to Shinto. In the 1930s, Pope Pius XI, after receiving assurances from Japanese officials that Shinto was not really a religion in the Western sense, authorized participation by Japanese Catholics in Shinto rites. And in some Catholic homes even now, one can find a small Shinto altar and a small Catholic altar existing side by side.

SUPERIORITY OF GOVERNMENT TO RELIGION

Negotiations between Tokyo and the Vatican in the 1930s point up the subordination of religion to government that has long influenced Japanese religious belief and practice. Successive Japanese governments, to a greater degree than elsewhere, have used religious ideals and institutions to buttress political claims, and religious establishments have generally accepted a subordinate function or role. Prior to extensive contacts with China in the sixth century A.D., the Japanese language had only a single term—*matsurigoto*—to describe "government" and "religion," and Buddhism's initial dependence on the Imperial Court for patronage discouraged any resistance to political authority. However, such quiescence and scruples began disappearing in the tenth century due to the government's weakness and Buddhism's institutional strength. Some monastic and temple communities organized armed bands of clerics for protection, and the same armed bands could sometimes force their way on a reluctant but superstitious Court, and occasionally on local territorial magnates as well. Ultimately, though, political intimidation failed, in part because Buddhism was never able to justify a significant political role on the basis of its own philosophical traditions. In 1571 Lord Oda Nobunaga, first of the three great Japanese unifiers, managed to destroy the leading Buddhist monastery and all the monks in it. After the establishment of the Tokugawa family's military government (shogunate) in the early seventeenth century, Buddhism was once again reduced to a status of almost total dependence on government.

Between 1600 and 1867, the political fortunes of Buddhism were intricately entwined with those of Catholicism and Confucianism. Successive Tokugawa rulers feared Catholicism as a force lying partly outside their control. To prevent its resurgence they forced all Japanese to register at the nearest Buddhist temple and there perform an annual desecration ritual as proof of their personal nonadherence. Buddhist priests were obliged to oversee the ritual and, on pain of death, to report all open or surreptitious lapses into Catholic practice by members of their community.

Confucianism in the same period became the government's official ideology because of its message of conservatism and sociopolitical stability. Confucianism saw the universe—nature and society alike—in purely moral terms. It held that irregular movements in the heavens presaged disaster on earth attributable in ultimate terms to the ruler's lack of virtue. Ritual observances might diminish the effects of such forces, but only virtuous conduct at all levels of society could be truly lasting or effective. Japanese, like the Chinese and Koreans before them, were thus admonished to uphold the sanctity of the Five Human Relationships (father-son, husband-wife, ruler-subject, older brother-younger brother, friend-friend), with that of ruler and subject taking precedence over all the rest. Propagation of Confucian beliefs and values had several important results. It strongly reinforced the communal orientation of traditional religiosity. It actively promoted skepticism about the moral and religious efficacy of any savior figure. And it helped institutionalize a separation of moral consciousness from formally organized religion.

COMMUNAL RELIGION

Strengthening of communalism is perhaps the most readily apparent result. Japanese have always been a communally conscious people. Shinto considered all humans the descendants of various kami and the Japanese islands themselves the creation of spiritual progenitors. Religion was traditionally more a feature of whole communities than of discrete individuals, and even today most rural Japanese hesitate to adopt a religious commitment to which they think neighbors and friends might object. Confucianism not only reinforced· but legitimated, rationalized, and even sanctified such beliefs. Humans were seen as linked to each other and to the spirit world as well. However, Confucianism's agnostic propensities about spirits created two significant bifurcations, one of which developed between morality and religion.

The first bifurcation developed out of the rationalizing of Confucianism's concept of Heaven. Heaven had long been an object of religious veneration, but it eventually became rationalized and impersonal. This divested the tradition of a transcendent spirituality and left it instead a highly systematized moralism. When there thus developed a division of authority in the Tokugawa period, it was natural for Confucianism to take control of social relations, statecraft, and public morality, leaving the more intimate or interior aspects of human awareness to Shinto and Buddhism. This particular arrangement was, in fact, actively promoted by the Tokugawa government and has continued to influence opinion about moral and religious matters. "Even today," Spae reports, "the popular mind simply refuses to assimilate religion with the structures and strictures of a [systematic] moral code."

The other bifurcation separated Japanese with advanced education from those with little or none at all. The educated in the context of Tokugawa Japan meant the hereditary ruling elite (samurai), their wives, and family dependents—about 7 percent of the total population. But the actual diffusion of education was greater than this figure alone would suggest. Because of the belief that Confucian studies could raise society's moral tone and enhance its governability, the Tokugawa shogunate was favorably disposed to a wide diffusion of "learning." There could be no fear that education would increase competition for jobs when socioeconomic status depended on family lineage alone. Moreover, samurai could be kept off the streets and out of trouble if their minds could be turned to study. (Most were legally unemployed and subsisted on doles from immediate military superiors.) These factors, combined with the prolonged peace and slowly rising income that Tokugawa conditions produced, led by 1868 to the attainment of an unprecedently high degree of literacy for a preindustrial society—40 percent of all adults. This condition in the modern period allowed, therefore, a more rapid diffusion of rationalistic ideals and beliefs about religion than would probably have occurred otherwise.

Late nineteenth-century conditions constituted a watershed in the formation of the Japanese religious consciousness today. Buddhism experienced attrition from identification with the former military government and Confucianism came formally to be viewed as the relic of a discredited past. Needing, nonetheless, to mobilize popular opinion behind a program of "modernization," Japanese government leaders chose promotion of Shinto as the most convenient device for the purpose. All Japanese were taught the Shinto myth of the country's and people's creation by the kami and were admonished to view the Emperor as the Sun Goddess Amaterasu's descendent. The Emperor's role as mediator between men and the kami was stressed. Shinto was given an official status. Public monies were disbursed to maintain shrines and train Shinto priests. And Shinto rituals became de rigeur in celebrating public events. The well-known result was the inculcation, not only of a powerful civic consciousness, but of an almost fanatical degree of loyalty to the country in general and, in the difficult interwar period, to its military and political leaders in particular.

THE POSTWAR SITUATION

Military defeat in 1945, however, had a dramatic and powerful effect, causing many people to rethink their basic beliefs and values. Shinto was disestablished by the Allied Occupation. Mythological teachings were removed from the school curriculum. The Emperor repudiated his "divine" ancestry. Numerous Shinto shrines were abandoned or destroyed. The Catholic Church and the Protestant Churches experienced a surge of adult conversions. And a number of "New Religions" became very active and popular.

These New Religions run the gamut of intellectual possibilities but often mix elements of Shinto with aspects of Buddhism and Christianity. Tenrikyō, Ōmoto-kyō, and Risshōkōseikai fit this pattern and are all considered New Religions even though their origins go back to the mid-nineteenth century. However, the best known and most successful is the Sōka Gakkai (Society for the Creation of Values) or Nichiren Shōshū movement. Sōka Gakkai was only founded in 1930, but its ancestry actually derives from the philosophy of the influential Buddhist teacher Nichiren, who lived in the thirteenth century. Unlike other New Religions, Sōka Gakkai does not mix ideas from different religious sources but stresses the exclusive importance of cultivating and displaying in a corrupt world the "Buddha nature" that is thought to be immanent in all sentient beings. Sōka Gakkai is highly organized, rather militant, and has attracted a large following. The exact number of adherents is a matter of dispute, but 7 million may be a reasonable estimate.

While the postwar religious situation of Japan is difficult to characterize, some basic features stand out. One is the rather low level of institutional affiliation. In 1978, only 34 percent of Japanese polled by the Institute of Statistical Mathematics reported having a personal faith; likewise, the Oriens Institute for Religious Research estimates active "church" membership at about 30.3 million persons. Christianity by this measure shows up surprisingly well since a third of those claiming belief (about 3 million in most polls) are actually listed on church membership rosters. Buddhist membership is put at 23 million, perhaps a quarter of the nominal adherents, while active Shinto membership is thought to have dropped to about 2.8 million. This is a tiny fraction of those who formerly associated themselves with this creed, and some authorities think active affiliation may have dropped to a mere 1.5 percent of the total population!

Another significant feature of religion in Japan today is the stratification of faith by educational level. Thirty-six percent of primary-school graduates report belief in God, but only 20 percent of high-school graduates do; and among university graduates, belief drops to 14 percent. This pattern of commitment is partly attributable to the spread of philosophical rationalism but one should take the indigenous Confucian legacy into account in drawing causal inferences. At the same time, statistics of this kind can be somewhat misleading. For example, an average belief in God of 24 percent may seem low compared to the 77 percent figure reported for Great Britain or the 98 percent figure reported for the United States. But these figures in Japan refer specifically to belief in the *Christian* God and not to Shinto kami where positive belief commitments range around 49 percent of respondents in recent polls. Considering the historicially uneven progress of Japanese Christianity, this finding might well be seen as a harbinger of greater religious commitment in the future.

Syncretism is still a powerful force in the contemporary religious life of Japan. The older pattern of the Shinto—though increasingly Christian—wedding and the Buddhist funeral is quite common. One still finds the Buddhist altar and the Shinto *kamidana* ("god-shelf") in many homes and commercial establishments. Christian Japanese will carefully observe Shinto rituals when visiting a major shrine. And interreligious worship services like those involving Ōmoto kyō and the Anglicans are, if anything, more common than ever. Japanese today would in many cases thus agree wih a comment made 20 years ago by then Prime Minister Hayato Ikeda: "I am not an atheist. Every night I pray to God, to the *kami* and to all the buddhas!"

James Bartholomew

BIBLIOGRAPHY

Earhart, H. Byron. *Japanese Religion: Unity and Diversity*. Encino and Belmont, Calif.: Dickenson, 1974.

Spae, Joseph J. *Japanese Religiosity*. Tokyo: Oriens Institute for Religious Research, 1971.

9

SOCIETY AND CULTURE

When American and European businessmen enter into negotiations with a Japanese firm, their counterparts are the products of a particular cultural and social experience. Typically, their Japanese counterparts will have been educated in the Japanese school system; they will also express the general cultural values received in their youth, which typify the attitudes of all Japanese toward social situations and roles. The counterparts' leisure habits will be those of Japanese in their own social class, and the traditional components of their attitudes will be both reinforced and challenged by the messages contained in the Japanese communications media.

Japan's educational system is a mixture of institutions and practices reflecting different educational goals at different points in modern Japanese experience. As Leslie Bedford reports, the primary and secondary school systems and the old national university system grew out of a self-conscious effort in the late nineteenth century to establish institutions that would train both leaders and masses for tasks in the modern world. Established and maintained under strong centralized guidance from the Ministry of Education, Japan's public schools offer a standardized high-quality curriculum that has produced one of the world's highest rates of literacy, even in the face of the extremely difficult task of learning the Japanese writing system. The cluster of elite national universities established during the nineteenth century meanwhile shows a strong resemblance to European institutions in the emphasis on theory over practice in the faculties of law, history, and the social sciences, which are the training ground for Japan's business and governmental elites. Grafted onto the public system is a less coherent array of private universities and schools of varying prestige, quality, and age. Some schools like Keio, Waseda, and Doshisha rank with the prestigious national universities as the desired places from which to graduate for career-oriented young Japanese to whom a degree from a top-ranked school is virtually a key to lifetime success. But others are of lower rank and quality, having developed in quite a few cases in response to the university education "boom" consequent on recent high economic growth and widespread household affluence.

Like educational systems in other countries, Japan's school system has problems and critics. Because the universities act as a conduit for persons desirous of jobs in Japan's top companies and ministries, the long-established university examination system has become an important barrier that career-oriented students must surpass, sometimes at considerable cost in time and health. The examination system is widely criticized within Japan, all the more as its extension to lower educational levels results in inordinate pressures being placed on students at the kindergarten, primary, and secondary school levels to succeed in the highly competitive tests. Indeed, the emphasis placed on examinations, the presence of "escalator" systems in which students who succeed in entering prestigious preschool systems are virtually guaranteed access to prestigious universities and jobs, and the seemingly common phenomenon of the ambitious "education mother" all highlight the emphasis placed on career-oriented schooling in the Japanese system.

Another point in question is the elitist nature of the system. Although more and more Japanese are going to school, and Japan ranks near the top in the ratios of young people who enter college, education is not an entirely democratic process in Japan. In theory anyone can get into Japanese universities, and the national universities are particularly meritocratic in their admissions policies. Still most Japanese college students are from middle-class origin. In addition to this antiegalitarian bias in recruitment, Japan's school system reflects the societywide tendency to rank institutions on the basis of prestige: most Japanese are well aware that there is a cluster of three or four highly prestigious institutions at the very top from which come over 90 percent of Japan's top political elite and 70–80 percent of its economic leaders. Correspondingly ambitious young men aspire to enter these schools. The ensuing concentration of recruitment parallels only that of France among large industrial nations in its exclusiveness.

Actually the elitist recruitment track has been partially bypassed by many of Japan's more progressive new companies in such fields as electronics, cameras, and automobiles. University (and faculty) ranking, and recruitment to elite corporations from elite educational institutions, while probably still the dominant mode of business recruitment in Japan, has become somewhat outmoded among firms in the most dynamic sectors of the Japanese business world.

Some Japanese also criticize the quality of the higher educational system. This form of criticism is found among both educational specialists and business leaders, and the latter have long wanted to have more money spent at the university level. Business wants more basic research and more training of scientists and engineers who are suitable for employment and leadership in Japanese industry and research organizations and oriented toward development of ever higher levels of sophisticated technology.

Japanese spend their leisure time in a variety of activities that truly represent the merging of native tradition with cosmopolitan experience that characterizes many aspects of contemporary Japanese society. Traditional theater like Noh and Kabuki are popular, but so are movies and Western drama. Similarly, concertgoers prefer rock as much as Japanese popular music, and enthusiasm for baseball and golf probably surpasses that for any individual Japanese sport except perhaps sumo wrestling.

The same admixture of native and foreign substance can be seen in the highly developed communications media, discussed here by Maureen Donovan. Foreign and Japanese themes can be found in programming on radio and television, and in the substance of newspapers and books. But even more important is the advanced state of publishing and the other media in Japan. Japan publishes more books and newspapers per capita than almost any other country, and surpasses even the United States in each of these fields. Diffusion rates for television and radio sets are also high, reflecting both the spread of affluence and the highly developed nature of the electronics industry in Japan. If development of the media and publications industries is a valid measure of modernization as most people claim, Japan ranks among the top two or three most-developed nations on earth.

James Bartholomew's essay on Japanese values brings together themes that have been reported at other points throughout this book. Japanese are more collectivist than anything else in their orientations to all aspects of life. They value group decisions and group activities whether these be in the local community or the modern corporation, even in spite of often intensely individualistic competition within these collectivist milieux. Japanese are also frugal to a degree not found in some other industrial nations, and this frugality is presumably a core societal value in addition to reflecting the effects of certain other noncultural influences. Cooperative work attitudes and collectivist social pressures also encourage an attitude of diligence on the behalf of workers and employees in Japan. For example, most workers do not use all of their regularly allotted vacation time, and prefer to stay on the job. Like most values, economic motivations and institutional pressures also may help explain such practices. But diligence still ranks high on the preferred characteristics of being Japanese which the Japanese ascribe to themselves, and we can safely infer that diligence is indeed a core value in Japanese culture.

The status of women in Japan today represents a complex confrontation between legal codes and social reality. As Susan Pharr reports, the Japanese constitution and postwar legal reforms guarantee equal status for women in the work place and in the home. Other social trends, such as greater affluence and education, and the growth of the cities, have also favored greater equality for women today. Women are better educated than the case just a few years ago, and affluence and appliances have made home life easier while activities outside the home are more accessible. Yet customs and informal social practices keep women in a largely inferior status in the work force, despite some perhaps remarkable progress in comparison with prewar conditions. Women make much less than men and have lower positions in business and government, in part because of their shorter stay in the seniority-oriented work place, but also because of the force of tradition. And Japanese businessmen spend perhaps a remarkably small amount of their time around home and do not generally contribute much to home tasks. Moreover, while women have the right to initiate divorce proceeedings and do so in greater numbers, the traditional practice of arranged marriages lingers among persons in the middle class and in rural districts and small towns.

Japan's Educational System

Educational institutions play an important role in any nation's society and business. What is the overall organization of the Japanese educational system and what are the patterns of university attendance? Is the system elitist or democratic (and in what specific ways)? Finally, what is the degree of emphasis placed by Japanese on access to higher education and what is the internationally known "escalator" system?

The foreign visitor to Japan, especially during the Spring and Autumn tourist seasons, inevitably encounters groups of uniformed Japanese schoolchildren, usually numbering in the hundreds, visiting one of the many national shrines. These ubiquitous field trips or the frequent articles in the English-language press about the notorious school examination system are the Westerners' introduction to education in Japan. Stories detailing how many children have killed themselves over test scores, how many adolescents are sitting for the year's round of college entrance exams, how much parents must sacrifice to pay for private universities create a sensational and distorted view of a system that is, in fact, one of the world's most effective in producing a highly literate and disciplined adult society. Since the late nineteenth century Japan has pioneered in educating its young and today ranks with the West in numbers of both high school and university graduates.

THE DEVELOPMENT OF JAPAN'S EDUCATIONAL SYSTEM

Major developments in the Japanese educational system have occurred at three distinct periods—the Meiji era, the period of the American Occupation, and during the recent era of phenomenal growth.

From the 1880s on the educuational system was structured to meet the needs of the state—for a literate if loyal citizenry and for an elite corps of university-trained professionals capable of directing Japan's modernization. Universal basic education was instituted in 1872 and extended to six years in 1907. In 1877 Tokyo University, later Imperial University, became the first and most famous of a handful of state-supported universities and higher schools. A number of private institutions were also established but never achieved the prestige of the public universities.

Following World War I the system developed into the European-style, multiple-track structure that existed until 1945: after the initial six years of primary education youngsters either left school or were channeled into one of several tracks including higher elementary schools; a variety of middle and high schools; vocational schools and five different types of institutions of higher education. The selection process became increasingly rigorous at each succeeding level; only 2 percent of the population entered a university.

The present system originated in the postwar period when the Occupation instituted an American-style system of single-track, coeducational schools of which nine years were compulsory. Higher education was also simplified and integrated into four-year universities and two- or three-year junior colleges. The Ministry of Education's powers were sharply curtailed and every aspect of education democratized.

Japan's rapid economic growth in the next decades created both the demand for a technically literate work force and the financial resources to build new schools. Newly affluent families could afford more schooling for their children. By 1960, 55 percent of these "baby-boom" youngsters were in high school; by 1975 the ratio had climbed to 96 percent. University enrollments also soared and today 38 percent of Japanese adolescents go on to college, compared to 43 percent in the United States and 17 percent in West Germany (1975).

Japanese education today reflects these several historical influences. It is both stubbornly elitist in the extent to which prewar rankings of universities dominate higher education and yet profoundly egalitarian in that all children have equal access to excellent basic education. The effects of the postwar expansion of the system, if anything, have been to reinforce these two conflicting tendencies.

A recognition of this and other major differences between the compulsory primary-middle school system and that of higher education (with high schools falling somewhere in between) is a first step in unraveling the complexities of Japanese education. The examination system, which permeates every level of schooling, unifies the system as a whole and also merits separate treatment.

BASIC EDUCATION

Although education is compulsory only for grades one through nine, the majority of Japanese children also attend preschool (64 percent) and high school. Classes throughout are large by American standards and teaching methods conservative. Elementary and middle-school students attend neighborhood schools that begin in April with Winter, Spring, and Summer breaks. The school week includes Saturday morning classes and altogether Japanese youngsters are in school about 60 more days each year than American children are. The Courses of Study for each grade, determined by the Ministry of Education and modified by local school personnel, have been made increasingly more rigorous over the years.

The academic performance of Japanese children on this compulsory level has been uniformly impressive. Their scores on international math and science tests are always the best or close to it; and achievements in music and art are equally striking. These results seem especially significant considering the difficulties of mastering written Japanese, which reputably takes Japanese schoolchildren three years longer than Americans must devote to English.

The reasons for these successes include the high national standards in curriculum; the diligence of teachers who are expected to devote long hours, including vacations, to their students; the strong support of parents through active PTAs; and overall, the impact of an essentially homogeneous society that believes academic achievement is the key to adult success.

This last point expresses one of the more salient characteristics of Japanese society, which has traditionally valued achievement, including eduational achievement. Today when a diploma, preferably from one of the most prestigious universities, is considered essential to obtaining a good job and a secure future, parents are willing to devote a great deal of their time and money to their children's schooling. In fact, education is viewed as a family responsibility as caricatured by the well-known "kyōiku mama" or "education mom" who obsessively makes her child's school success the main focus of her life.

The important role of the school in socializing Japanese children also contributes to the character, including the achievements, of basic education. The foreign visitor to a Japanese school can easily identify the methods used to encourage in even the very youngest that combination of self-discipline and self-gratification through group achievement that characterizes Japanese society. It is worth observing in the schools to see fourth graders learning group responsibility by serving lunch to their classmates or enthusiastic teams of six-year-olds, dressed identically, competing in the annual Sports Days. Such things as the popular after-school clubs, the school uniforms and songs, and the cherished overnight trips contribute to a positive school experience and offset the daily routine of mastering an increasingly difficult course of study.

Finally, because the Japanese system is highly centralized, government has the primary responsibility for determining basic educational policies and practices. Although the Ministry of Education's authority was curtailed during the Occupation, the trend since the 1950s has been a reassertion of central authority; the government is involved in literally every aspect of schooling. It screens textbooks, subsidizes teachers' salaries, advises local school boards, conducts in-service training sessions for teachers, and, with its vast financial resources, is responsible for about half of all educational expenditures in the country.

Many of the Ministry's policies—ranging from the introduction of a compulsory "morals" course for grades one through nine to the adoption of a national Teachers' Efficiency Rating Plan—have been bitterly opposed by leftist groups, particularly the Japan Teachers' Union, the nation's second largest union. In general, however, the system of basic education has retained its democratic character. The central government's expenditures on basic education, which may be the highest in the world, guarantee that every child in Japan has access to the same excellent schooling, regardless of regional economic differences. Certainly in regard to educational equality as well as academic performance, Japan's system is a great success.

EXAMINATION FEVER

In spite of its obvious successes, there are criticisms of the basic educational system. They generally center on the all-important examination system, called "shiken jigoku" or "examination hell" in Japanese. Japanese children usually sit for their first school entrance exam in the ninth grade. The test results determine placement in a hierarchy of higher secondary schools ranging from the most elite academic high schools to vocational and technical institutions. While few in number on the compulsory level, private schools account for one-quarter of the nation's higher secondary schools. They too are rigidly ranked with the best enjoying national reputations for preparing students for entrance to the most elite universities and the worst serving as diploma mills for youngsters who have failed to enter a respectable public schools.

The second and more important entrance examination—for university placement—occurs in one's eighteenth year. These tests are both arduous and extremely competitive. While, in fact, there is a place in some institution for nearly every applicant (1.3 applicants for every place in 1975), most students apply to three or four universities or separate departments, and competition for the average to good schools ranges from four applicants per opening to twelve to one. In the case of medical schools, there may be twenty-five or more applicants for each place. The numbers are swollen by the many students, who having failed once, continue year after year to sit for the exams. These people are called *rōnin*, a feudal term meaning masterless samurai, and they make up as much as one-third of each year's applicants. These days the number of *chūgaku rōnin* (students who sit for multiple high school placement tests) is growing as well.

As competition for university placement has increased, it has influenced not just the secondary but the elementary and even preschool student as well. Many people believe that examination fever has distorted the entire educational process by encouraging teachers to overemphasize test-taking skills, including rote memorization, rather than developing children's imagination and critical faculties. They fear that current plans to extend the compulsory system downward into the preschools will mean the end of Japan's traditional devotion to progressive, child-centered early education.

Often critical of the system yet eager that their own children do well, parents have turned more and more to special preparatory and remedial classes to supplement regular schoolwork. Afterschool centers or juku are very popular, especially in urban areas; for example, one Tokyo sixth grade reported 80 percent of its students attending juku. While children may see *juku* as a place to socialize with friends, their parents rely on them, tutors, and other methods to bolster their offsprings' future test scores.

This kind of pressure can be intense. Recently the rate for childhood suicides, which had been declining, went up again. There were 512 deaths in the first half of 1979, an increase of 15 percent in one year, which authorities attribute to school pressures. Any Japanese parent whose work takes him abroad must consider the negative effects on his child's academic performance of taking him out of the system even for a short time. Concerns about the low self-esteem of children who do not make the grade, or about the long hours youngsters devote to homework rather than hobbies or friendships also reflect this national preoccupation with the examination system.

In order to avoid "examination hell," some parents try to enroll their children in one of the few private schools attached to universities. Called "escalator schools," these institutions require only one entrance test. After that the student can proceed straight up through college unharrassed by examinations.

The intensely debated issue of examinations has been difficult to resolve. While most observers are highly critical, others claim that the competition not only develops character but is essential to maintaining Japan's high educational achievements. Above all, in the public mind, the examinations are viewed as brutal but objective determinants of individual merit. Everyone takes the same tests and generally they alone, independent of family wealth or background, determine school placement. Therefore the theory is that quality education—equated with entrance to a respected university—is open to anyone with enough ambition and diligence to get through the system.

This theory—called the "rags-to-Tōdai myth" by one scholar—is challenged by the realities of Japan's present system of higher education.

HIGHER EDUCATION

As indicated earlier, there is a well-established ranking order among Japanese universities. At the top are the National universities headed by Tokyo, Kyoto, Hitotsubashi, and Tokyo University of Technology followed by other former Imperial Universities and a handful of private schools (Keiō, Waseda, Dōshisha). Beneath them are the "public" universities administered by the prefectures and municipalities, followed by technical colleges and junior colleges, which are almost exclusively for women. The historic reasons for the continuing dominance of the few national universities go back to the Meiji government's decision to concentrate its limited financial resources in a few institutions. These schools, headed by Tokyo University, have always enjoyed considerable government support. Except for the few traditionally prestigious universities, private schools have had to settle for a vastly inferior status.

From the beginning the hierarchy among schools has been reinforced by the employment practices of both the public and private sectors. While the gross elitism of the prewar days is gone—when, for example, Tokyo graduates were not only preferred but paid more—recent statistics confirm what every Japanese parent assumes: the bulk of the nation's top civil servants and company executives are graduates of a handful of select schools. In other words, where you go to college is more important than what you do there.

As the national demand for higher education grew in the 1950s and 1960s, it was met not by a substantial increase in government funding but by a proliferation of private institutions. By 1972, for example, there were 290 private schools as compared to 75 national and 33 public universities. Tuition remained low at public schools, but it and other fees soared at the private institutions. The rising costs were instituted without a corresponding improvement in faculty or facilities, and the resultant drop in academic quality helped set off the student rebellions of the late 1960s. Since then government support to private schools has increased significantly but still has not—and cannot—keep up with inflation and the public's demand for higher education. In 1977 tuition at the national universities was 146,000 yen but averaged 494,000 yen or 3.4 times more at private schools.

Of course, the difference in tuition alone makes the public universities that much more appealing, which increases the already tight competition for entrance and reinforces school rankings in the public's mind.

Therefore, two factors make one question the basic assumption of the inherent equality of Japanese higher education. Because the majority of university places are in private schools, a disproportionate number of students must either be able to afford school fees or forego higher education. As the competition for the inexpensive and generally better public schools increases and anxious families turn more and more to expensive preparatory programs, the pressures on the nonaffluent become greater. In fact, recent statistics indicate that the entering students at Tokyo University are drawn increasingly from the upper strata of society.

The gross disparity between the public and private schools is one major problem, but there are others as well. It has been remarked that "Enthusiasm for education in Japan focuses on the end of the line." In many respects college entrance not graduation *is* the end of the line. Japanese college students rarely flunk out so the four years become little more than a credentialing process for youngsters whose futures have already been determined by their scores on the college entrance examinations.

Japanese businesses criticize higher education for failing to give their students sufficient practical knowledge; they and others maintain that the curriculum is too "abstract." As a result firms rely on their own training programs to educate each year's new recruits.

Finally, other criticisms would include charges that the curriculum is too specialized, teaching undervalued, funds inequitably distributed among the various departments, and interuniversity exchange too limited. Japanese higher education has had nothing if not its share of critics.

There have been several government efforts at reform. Starting in 1979 students sat for a national achievement test designed to select out those applicants qualified to take the individual university/departmental exams. This change is aimed at minimizing competition. Ministry of Education officials are also urging universities to consider student records, aptitude, and interviews in the selection process.

Another type of reform has been the creation of totally new institutions; for example, the University of the Air will start enrolling students in 1982 on a first-come, first-serve basis. Using telecommunications, correspondence, and regional counseling centers, it will educate adults as well as recent high school graduates around the country.

There are some indications that the situation may change; for example, there has been a recent increase in the numbers of youngsters choosing a vocational over a university education. But major restructuring seems unlikely. The ranking order and the examination system that feeds it are well-entrenched and seemingly, if grudgingly, supported by the public. Parents are reluctant to jeopardize their child's future by supporting major reforms; established schools are loath to relinquish their privileged positions and employment recruitment patterns remain unaltered; and most fundamentally, the system reinforces those character traits and social values traditionally admired by the Japanese.

The fact is that the present system has served modern Japan well. While it has sanctioned a narrow, even barren concept of education and may eventually undermine the nation's claim to equality of social opportunity, the Japanese system of education continues to produce generations of disciplined, ambitious and highly literate adults. Change is unlikely as long as enough Japanese can rely on achievement in education as the sure route to their vision of the good life.

Leslie Bedford

BIBLIOGRAPHY

Anderson, Ronald S. *Education in Japan: A Century of Modern Development.* Washington, D.C.: U.S. Government Printing Office, 1975.

Cummings, William K., Ikuo Amano, Kazuyuki Kitamura, eds. *Changes in the Japanese University: A Comparative Perspective*. New York: Praeger, 1979.

Passin, Herbert. *Society and Education in Japan*. New York: Teachers College Press and East Asia Institute, Columbia University, 1965.

Cultural Values in Japan

Most societies operate on the basis of some central values presumably learned early in life. For example, it is said that Japanese are group and community oriented, and sometimes it is also said that they place great emphasis on patron-client relations. Are these observations true? Japanese attitudes of diligence toward work and frugality are also commented on in the West. In reality, what kinds of examples can be given to support the thesis that Japanese are both diligent and frugal? Also, what is the case among younger people in comparison with their elders?

Group life or groupism is to Japanese what individualism is to Americans—the core value of society that substantially defines other values. One has only to watch elderly tourists following the flag of a travel agency around a public monument or a gaggle of farmers discussing irrigation at a village council to appreciate its importance for the world's second-ranking capitalist society. Groups are the basic structural unit of Japan to a degree that Americans can scarcely appreciate. If office mates decide to go bowling on a Saturday night, individuals will not be playing baseball. The work inspector may criticize one worker's production schedule, but group interest or pressure on the slackard will be his real impetus to reform. Graduate students in a seminar may privately reprimand the peer group member who dissents too vigorously from the views of the senior professor. But the relaxing effect of alcohol permits any group member indulging to let off steam to another without fear of retribution from the victim.

Americans prize their independence, but Japanese value dependence or, what is now the preferred term, social interdependence. This pattern of interdepence is termed *amae* by the psychiatrist L. Takeo Doi. It refers to an individual's desire to presume on the good will or emotional support of another and is inculcated early in life. When Japanese children misbehave, they are not spanked or disciplined in a physical manner but are instead told that social rejection will follow if the offending behavior persists. Parents place considerable emphasis on the ability of their children to accommodate to the needs and feelings of others and criticize selfishness and extreme assertion as a menace to social harmony. Of course, Japanese children do not achieve the ideal of perfect socialization any more than American children do, but the stress on cooperation is real and its results are readily apparent. Children study three to five hours after supper without being forcibly compelled to do so. Their school uniforms conceal individual differences of wealth or personal taste. And the ideal of cooperative living becomes one that persists for life.

IMAGES OF GROUP LIFE

When foreigners think of Japanese group life, they are apt to envision factory workers singing their company song or a corporate executive and his clients enjoying themselves at a geisha party. One also envisions the village headman dealing with politicians for the votes of his coresidents, white-collar workers bowing at the railroad station to the departing company president, or an eager graduate student serving green tea to his professor in the seminar room. But none of these images, while true, fully reflects what has become a very complex and multidimensioned reality. For one thing, generations of intellectuals and journalists have affected public thinking on the matter by attacking group-centered relations as an inappropriate vestige of feudalism. The widespread and explicit employment of *oyabun-kobun* (patron-client) terminology in the underworld has further sullied the reputation of groupism. Moreover, some observers predict a decline in both the symbolism and the substance of patron-client relations as a result of increasing affluence. At the same time, group structures in Japan have been remarkably adaptable, containing for example, elements of objectivity or universalism that outsiders may not readily detect. Take the case of the man who achieves a corporate presidency or a university chair by marrying the boss's daughter. Establishment of a marital tie may be essential to achievement of the status, but accession to the top is scarcely dependent on marriage. One must first qualify to marry the daughter of an eminent man by demonstrating a capacity for managing affairs or contributing significantly to knowledge as in the Medical Faculty of Tokyo University where sons-in-law of professors were selected before World War II from among the top three performers in the comprehensive M.D. examinations. As this case demonstrates, personalistic ties follow universalistic demonstrations of personal merit, not the other way around.

Japanese have become group-minded for reasons of past experience, culture, and a variety of structural or institutional constraints. Mountainous topography with its many small valleys and hidden residential pockets may have predisposed the people toward tightly knit community life in ancient times, while the demands of terraced agriculture and irrigation have been a continuing incentive to cooperation among groups. The Shinto religion, which postulates an identification of specific families with various local spirits, ties people to each other through an elaborate pantheon of deities with the Japanese emperor as their supreme earthly manifestation. A strong imperial government based on Shinto and Chinese conceptions arose in the eighth century, but its faltering in the ninth and tenth centuries encouraged challenges by scattered samurai forces and the Buddhist church. However, the church's own loose structure and inability to justify the wielding of secular power led to defeat in the sixteenth century and the entire country after 1600 was governed by the Tokugawa family's military regime or its subject daimyo. Under the Tokugawa a highly structured network of sociopolitical and economic institutions came into being. The Buddhist church became an instrument of the state security apparatus. Peasants were bound to the land. Samurai were bound to their lords. And the daimyo themselves were obliged to live part time in the shogun's capital and follow other onerous requirements to prove their loyalty to the shogun and the system over which he presided.

While the Tokugawa regime disappeared in 1868, social control by corporate groups persisted and possibly even grew stronger in the decades that followed its demise. Government propaganda in the schools before 1945 sought to convince Japanese of their biological relatedness. Militaristic discipline and loyalty to the corporate state were inculcated in local elites after 1906 by the Imperial Military Reserve Association. Commonalities of language, ethnicity, and formalized behavior patterns further underscored a potent awareness of group identity and loyalty, and various publicists attacked Western doctrines of individualism and praised the familistic character of the modern Japanese state. After 1945 there was a sharp reversal of tone in much of the media, but harsh economic realities of the early postwar years brought a resurgence of oyabun-kobun ties and of economic and social cooperation that unparalleled affluence has not, thus far, contrived to efface.

Some authorities argue that cooperation between government and the business community constitutes the strongest force behind group life in Japan in the present day. The tax structure, to begin with, favors the private sector—business investment in particular. Whereas the European Economic Community countries throughout the 1970s were generally extracting about 38 percent of all personal income for taxes and the United States about 28 percent, Japan was only extracting about 22 percent—the lighest burden in the entire industrialized world. This small tax bite has ineviably meant low levels of public expenditure in the social insurance sector (education, welfare, housing). In the 1970s Great Britain spent about

14.6 percent of its tax revenues in this area, the United States about 8.3 percent, but Japan only about 7.4 percent. And because government in Japan has not adequately provided for these needs, individuals have often had to depend on the welfare activities of large corporations. Corporate housing, for example, is not unknown in the United States and Europe but in Japan nearly 7 percent of all housing is owned by large corporations. Similarly, many Japanese companies provide stores selling household goods to employees at less than the market price, while their educational credits and insurance payments to employees may also elicit dependence.

THE NATURE OF JAPANESE FRUGALITY

Frugality is certainly a prominent feature of contemporary Japanese society. In the Tokugawa period, social mores, even of the rich, were strongly affected by the socially dominant samurai ethic of personal austerity, while the harsh demands of nineteenth-century industrialization made gratification postponement both virtuous and necessary. In much of the modern period, productivity has risen at a faster pace than wages. Spending on social-infrastructure needs has been abnormally low, while Japanese savings rates among individuals have been the envy of the entire industrialized world. In the critical postwar period of 1954–62, Japan's industrial productivity increased at an annual rate of between 6 and 10.5 percent, while wages grew at a pace of only 2 to 9 percent. In 1973, spending figures on social needs from all sources as a percentage of Gross National Product show Japan at a mere 6.7 percent level, compared to 8.1 percent in the United States, 15 percent in Great Britain, 17.3 percent in Sweden, 19.7 percent in France, and 21.8 percent in West Germany. Similarly, Great Britain's personal savings rate in the 1960s averaged about 5 percent, that of the United States about 7 percent, and France some 10 percent, while that of Japan was exactly double that of France!

These data are not, however, proof of intrinsic self-indulgence among Westerners or intrinsic frugality among Japanese. What they show instead is that personal savings rates have been high in Japan and wage rates (until recently) low due to certain structural constraints of the Japanese industrialization process. For many decades (though not at present) the Japanese economy suffered serious shortages of capital mostly due to a lack of foreign trade in the Tokugawa period. This legacy contributed significantly to low wages and to a pattern of work discipline that was severe by American standards. A lower rate of investment in the social insurance sector was one result and high rates of personal saving were another: individuals necessarily provided for their own wants and need when other resources were absent. In the post-World War II period, "frugality" has been encouraged by two other features in the system of household economy. Consumer-installment credit systems were underdeveloped, and a significant percentage of salaries were paid out seasonally in large, lump-sum bonuses. Families thus had to purchase larger items with cash while living day to day at a level of consumption that their total income belied.

DILIGENCE AND ITS USES

Diligence in the work place has been one of the means by which Japanese workers changed their life-style from one of austerity to one of affluence. In 1953, some 55 percent of respondents in a national survey conducted by the Institute of Statistical Mathematics chose "diligent" as the most representative national trait. In 1973, some 66 percent thought that diligent was the term that best characterized the Japanese. Many surveys show that employees in industry often choose to work when they could be paid simply by staying at home. And a 1973 study of work attitudes among young adults in ten countries conducted by the Prime Minister's Office shows that these attitudes are shared by the younger generation. The study reported that more than a third of Japanese youth (34.5 percent) said they worked as a means of self-fulfillment, whereas the percentages of respondents choosing this explanation for working in other countries ranged downward from 30.3 percent in the United States to 15.3 percent in West Germany and only 13.8 percent in Great Britain. Only Brazil, where 42.4 percent of those questioned said that they worked for self-fulfillment, ranked higher than Japan.

Nor is evidence of diligence confined only to personal attitude surveys. Japanese objectively work longer hours and they take fewer vacations than industrial workers in other countries. In 1973 West German and American industrial workers were each averaging 38.3 hours on the job per week, while Japanese workers in manufacturing were averaging 42. American industrial workers took an average of 130 days for vacation in 1970 and their German counterparts 120 days, while Japanese workers took just 70. A 1970 study showed that only 20 percent of industrial workers took all of their paid leave available to them, while 40 percent utilized only half of their paid leave or less. Moreover, the fact that wages have often gone up at a slower pace than productivity is itself prima facie evidence for the existence of a work ethic emphasizing diligence in the work place and generalized commitment to the goals of industrial employers.

Such widely held commitments to work are scarcely fortuitous as past experience, culture, and certain institutional constraints have created and helped to maintain them. Like many prominent features of Japanese life, the work ethic represents an ideologizing of samurai values and attitudes in which loyalty, austerity, and discipline were considered beneficial to the soul as well as the body. Some of this ethic resulted from the transformation of necessity into virtue during the Tokugawa period, but the continuing harsh economic conditions (including shortages of capital and various natural resources) of the early industrialization period gave these attitudes meaning for modern Japanese as well. Unlike the United States of the 1870–1920 era, Japan's population retained a constancy of ethnic composition and a rising curve of technical skills that the American labor force often lacked because of continuing immigration and labor turnover. Methods of labor recruitment were more refined in Japan. There was less reliance on sheer chance or merely personal aspirations. Ideological traditions were helpful. Work was viewed as a desirable end in itself, not simply as a means to personal betterment. Responsibility for the welfare of individual families was assigned to the family head's activities, and organizations like the *Kyōchōkai* (Harmony Society) stressed cooperation between capital and labor and familial paternalism in the early decades of the critical twentieth century.

Work commitments have been maintained in more recent decades by a variety of institutional arrangements. Union boundaries have frequently coincided with those of specific business organizations. Significant numbers of employees have been given permanent employee status. Most employees are trained by the firm that employs them to a greater extent than is commonly done elsewhere. Jobs are defined loosely and in a manner designed to build company loyalty. And payment is most generally based on age and length of service to the firm. However, changes are in process that may alter this pattern of diligence in the work place. Unprecedented affluence has increased the temptation to slack off. A 1974 survey showed 40 percent of industrial employees now preferring more leisure time to greater income as compared to 30 percent for the reverse. And the government, responding to foreign criticism of the Japanese as mere "economic animals," has begun pushing to make the five-day work week mandatory and expand the number of holidays.

Moreover, the attitudes of younger workers are clearly changing despite generalized commitments to diligence. Younger people are less apt than their elders to choose diligent as the definitive national trait. They are less inclined to describe work as the "central concern in life." They are more apt to take the vacation time that legitimately belongs to them. And they invariably give more relaxed answers to life attitude questions in the National Character Survey than older Japanese do. A frequent response among younger workers would be something like, "Don't think about money or fame; just live a life that suits your own tastes." Respondents emphasizing sacrifice, purity, or service are nearly always from the older generation.

WILL JAPANESE VALUES CHANGE?

Are fundamental value changes in store for the next generation of Japanese? Some observers believe so. John W. Bennett and Robert E. Cole, among others, have argued that greater affluence and the loosening of cultural restraints will yield greater personal freedom, less attention to group demands, or a diminution of diligence and frugality in the future. Their argument is not necessarily that such results are an inevitable outcome of industrialization but rather that behaviors may change merely from the demonstration effect of modern communications. One cannot say with certainty at this point whether Japanese society will indeed manifest greater individualism or a more relaxed life-style by, say, the end of the twentieth century, but the evidence does admit of certain observations. First of all, Japanese society already allows greater personal freedom and individualism than it did before World War II. Confucian moral instruction is gone from the schools. Children need no longer obtain parental approval to marry. And defiance of community opinion does not lead inevitably to ostracism in the countryside. Second, however, one cannot ignore the extraordinary staying power of Japanese group structures and societal discipline. Crime rates, as previously noted (see Chapter 6), are still far lower than in Western countries. Patronage, whether labeled oyabun-kobun or not, is still a valuable aid to the job seeker. Students taking part in political demonstrations still follow their leaders to a degree that impresses outsiders—moving as a whistle directs them, for example. Children are still very sensitive to the expectations of significant adults around them. And child-rearing practices continue to stress cooperation with others or greater conformity to societal expectations than is true in the United States. All of this may make Japanese values unusual—but it scarcely makes the Japanese less "modern."

James Bartholomew

BIBLIOGRAPHY

Bennett, John William. "Japanese Economic Growth: Background for Social Change." In *Aspects of Social Change in Modern Japan,* edited by R. P. Dore, pp. 411–53. Princeton: Princeton University Press, 1967.

Cole, Robert E. *Work, Mobility and Participation: A Comparative Study of American and Japanese Industry*. Berkeley and Los Angeles: University of California Press, 1979.

Doi, Takeo, *The Anatomy of Dependence*. Translated by John Bester. Tokyo, New York, and San Francisco: Kodansha International, 1973.

Leisure and Entertainment

What are the general patterns of use of leisure time in Japan? For example, Westerners in Japan often watch Kabuki or Noh and try to see Japanese festivals. Do the Japanese themselves follow these more traditional forms of entertainment? Do they participate much in traditional festivals? To what degree are they oriented toward more modern or imported forms of entertainment? What are the most popular recreational forms?

Japanese today probably enjoy the widest range of leisure activities of any people in the world. Millions enjoy traditional games like Mah-Jongg, go, and shogi—though only the first is widely known to Americans. Indigenous martial arts like judo, karate, and kendo are not only flourishing but enjoy large followings in the United States and Europe. Noh and Kabuki dramas have their devotees, and everyone attends and actively participates in a large number of traditional festivals. But a listing like this only just scratches the surface. Baseball has been played by the Japanese for over a hundred years. Swimming, hiking, and skiing are enormously popular. Millions patronize boat, cycle, and horse races. And only one country in the world (the United States) has more golfers than Japan. Moreover, one must also at least mention such leisure activities as music (the Japanese like all kinds), movies (only three countries make more), reading (Japanese rival the Russians in the amount of material consumed), and television (where ownership of sets and viewership are scarcely exceeded anywhere).

This diversity of pastimes is intimately linked to the nature of the culture itself. Except for the two-century era of national seclusion (1639–1853), no nation anywhere has more actively appreciated intercultural exchange, yet (until recently) enjoyed such a modest amount of it. Cultural borrowing of recreational forms from China, Korea, or the Ryukyu Islands was common—karate came from the Ryukyus—but the location of Japan at the extreme edge of Eurasia's land mass made it last in the world to receive new cultural influences. Social commentator Shunsuke Tsurumi, noting this fact, thinks isolation has made his countrymen a "nation of faddists" and various kinds of evidence would bear out the point. One thinks of the baseball boom that followed Babe Ruth's Japan tour with the American League All Stars in 1934 or the popularity of bowling in the late 1960s and early 1970s. The former proved lasting as professional leagues were founded and player recruitment mechanisms systematized. But the latter shows a different pattern that is often rather common. Beginning about 1968, it appeared that bowling was destined to become the nation's number one sport. Alleys sprang up in every sizable town and everyone flocked to learn the new pastime. By 1972 paid admissions reached $455 million and investment in bowling equipment exceeded $2.9 billion. But then the situation was turned upside down. In 1973, paid admissions dropped to $407 million and new investment to $300 million, while in 1974 attendance figures only reached $136 million and new investment about $100 million!

BASEBALL AND GOLF

Baseball, unlike bowling, exemplifies the popularity of Western sports in Japan. The game was introduced early—in 1873 by some accounts—and it rapidly gained popularity among high school and college students. A much-celebrated series of victories over a team of Americans living in Yokohama stimulated national pride in 1896. Baseball exchanges between Japanese and American college teams followed. Major tours of Japan by the Chicago White Sox and New York Giants stimulated additional interest in the World War I era. Other tours followed in the 1920s, and by 1936 the Japanese had organized their first professional league. Two leagues of six teams each, the Central and the Pacific, have been in place since 1950 and game attendance per capita rivals that of the United States. With about 230 million residents, the United States generally shows a professional baseball attendance of 28 to 30 million, while Japan with 115 million people, registers an attendance of about 12 to 14 million annually.

Nor is baseball unique in its degree of popularity. Swimming is about equally popular in the two countries, similarly horse racing and golf. In the early 1970s the United States had about 5,000 public swimming pools and Japan about 2,800. Horse racing attracted 70 million fans in the United States and about 33 million in Japan, while *Golf Digest* reported the United States as having 11 million golfers in 1975 and Japan about 4.5 million. Golf's popularity is particularly striking because of the obstacles posed to it by the physical and financial environment. Space is very limited— California is larger than Japan—and land's price is very high. Nevertheless, the Japanese have somehow found room for over 1,000 golf courses (compared to 12,000 in the United States) and about 700 driving ranges. Moreover, the country has about a thousand professionals and regularly enters players in major foreign tournaments. The extent of golf's popularity in Japan is perhaps best indicated by the fact that about 1 Japanese in every 26 plays it, compared to only 1 of every 76 residents of Great Britain where the modern game was invented.

MUSIC

Music is another interest that cannot go unmentioned. Before World War II traditional ballads, often melancholy in tone or written in a minor key, were most popular, together with some Western-style popular music, including some jazz. Now tastes and musical offerings are both more diverse. There are few notable foreign ensembles or performers of jazz, rock, bluegrass, country and western, or classical music who have not been at least invited to Japan. Where recordings are concerned, a rule of thumb is that if it sells in Los Angeles, it will sell in Tokyo, too. The Beatles attracted as large and enthusiastic a crowd in Tokyo on their 1965 Japan tour as they ever did in London, and the New York and Vienna Philharmonic Orchestras have as many Japanese as American, Austrian, or German fans. In fact, Western classical music seems to be the most surprising success story of all. Before the war, it was not popular in Japan. There were few professional ensembles, only a handful of minor concert halls, and very few fans. But all that has changed in the past quarter century. Tokyo alone supports five full-time professional orchestras, at least one of world class (the NHK Orchestra), and there are estimated to be some 25,000 classical music recitals, concerts, and performances in the city every year. Only New York and London support as many and neither of them has five professional orchestras. It is perhaps a measure of classical music's success in Japan that Osaka is still the only city outside Germany to have hosted the Bayreuth Opera founded by Wagner in the 1870s. This occurred at its 1970 International Music Festival at which the $100 admission price for the opera did nothing to discourage attendance.

TELEVISION AND PINBALL

Not all Japanese play or watch baseball, golf, or bowling, let alone attend symphony concerts, of course; but everyone watches television. One survey shows viewership averaging more than 3½ hours a day per person, and males in their twenties are the only age group in the adult population for whom television viewing fails to constitute at least *half* of all free-time activity. Japanese television offers much the same fare as its counterpart in the United States, but there are certain differences. Historical dramas, often serialized, are a staple in Japan. There is more detailed and comprehensive news reporting and more programs of experts discussing political and economic events. Symphony concerts and opera performances are broadcast with greater frequency. Some of the differences are attributable to the presence of the Nippon Hoso Kyokai network, a quasi-public institution comparable to Great Britain's BBC. It presents no advertising and viewers pay a monthly fee for watching programs. (For further details on Japanese television, see Chapter 9.)

Pachinko, a variety of pinball, is another form of mass recreation that visitors to Japan cannot fail to notice. There are more than 10,000 pachinko parlors in the country (about 1,000 in Tokyo) with nearly 2 million machines. The customer stands in front of the machine ceaselessly flipping a lever that ejects small metal balls into and around a glass case. If enough balls drop into the holes with sufficient frequency, the player wins cigarettes, fresh fruit, candy, or other small prizes. Playing pachinko seems well adapted to the hectic pace of modern Japanese life because it helps to clear out one's head. In fact, the pace or rhythm of play is so relentless and hypnotic that some critics have likened it to Zen meditation!

SUMO WRESTLING

By no means all recreations of modern origin or Western derivation. Like many countries, Japan has an indigenous style of wrestling called sumo and few sports rival its degree of popular support. There are two heavy-weight contenders (each averaging about 300 pounds) in a sumo match and each tries to force the other off his feet or out of the circular ring. The contest is seldom of great duration but is preceded by extensive preliminaries of a quasi-religious nature. Sumo is a very popular participant's sport. Matches are often held in public schools and universities and there are about 680 professionals attached to various stables. But spectator appeal is mostly responsible for its popularity today. Tournaments have been held regularly since the early seventeenth century and matches are televised to every corner of the country. Wrestlers are, of course, mainly Japanese; but an occasional Korean has taken part. One major champion of the 1960s was partly of Russian background, and another favorite of the period was a native of Hawaii.

NOH AND KABUKI DRAMA

Noh and Kabuki contrast with sumo as traditional entertainments that have lost popularity. Both are products of an archaic society and tend toward depictions that audiences find remote. Some of this results from government policies of the past and some from the nature of the art forms themselves. Noh is far and away the more conservative and the more prominent victim of changes in popular taste. Its actual origins in eighth-century society were utterly lower class, but in the fourteenth century it became a highly stylized, aristocratic form and after 1600 attendance at plays and participation in the drama were exclusively reserved for members of the upper class. Moreover, Noh would be ill-adapted to mass appreciation in almost any era. Characters wear masks. There are scarcely any props. The language is incomprehensible to most Japanese. The pace of the drama seems slow and tedious to many, and practitioners themselves have resisted any updating. At the same time, Noh is highly unlikely to expire. It has managed in the modern era to attract favorable attention from intellectuals and from Western visitors to Japan as diverse as George Bernard Shaw, Ulysses S. Grant, and Ezra Pound. The *utai* or Noh chanting technique has become a distinctive interest on its own (nearly every college or university campus has a student club devoted to utai); and the national government actively supports the remaining Noh theaters and troupes with subsidies, festivals and special programs and promotions.

Kabuki has done better and will probably continue doing so. Tokyo has only a half dozen theaters where Kabuki can be seen, but performances are frequent (most days of the week, compared to once or twice for Noh) and the audiences are large. This, in fact, is similar to conditions in the past. Kabuki developed in the early seventeenth century as a lower class entertainment and reached its zenith about 1700. The costumes are brilliant, the language down to earth (for that era), the pace is lively, and the content sure to appeal. Kabuki is the original Japanese soap opera form. A typical play involves a conflict between *giri* (duty) and *ninjo* (human feelings) in which the protagonists resolve the dilemma by committing *shinjū* (lovers' suicide). In Tokugawa times people took food and saké (rice wine) to the theater and stayed all day; and even modern audiences get very involved with the action. Kabuki can regularly be seen on television. It has incorporated some new techniques and has given as much inspiration to other theatrical forms as it has borrowed from them. Kabuki is at least as popular in Japan today as Shakespeare's plays are in the United States, and nothing about this is very likely to change.

FESTIVALS

Attitudes toward, and participation in festivals are in no way similar to the role of Noh or Kabuki. Such traditional festivals as *O-Shogatsu* (New Year's), *O-Bon* (Buddhist All Souls Eve), *Tanabata* (Festival of the Stars), and *Gion* are enormously popular. They have always been popular, and it is likely they always will be. Practically all festivals manifest a religious inspiration but aside from that commonality, their functions differ widely. The Gion Festival, associated with the Yasaka (Shinto) Shrine in Kyoto, began as a ninth-century antidote to an outbreak of plague. Residents of the city parade about every day for a week in July with elaborately carved and decorated *yamaboko* (portable shrines) and beat huge gongs to frighten evil spirits thought responsible for the disease. It is unlikely that many participants nowadays consider these actions medically effective; they rather consider the festival a summer celebration. Yamaboko, in fact, are somewhat akin to floats in Pasadena's Tournament of Roses Parade, except that the structures are designed to be permanent and are carried by human bearers.

Tanabata is a popular festival based on an ancient Chinese legend. Ancient belief said people could gain success in agriculture and weaving by appealing to star deities ensconced in the Milky Way. One was Altair, patron of farming, and the other was Vega, patroness of weaving. Supplication was accomplished by household displays and offerings of food. Young women hoping for wifely success place tables holding five threaded needles in their gardens while members of their families set out offerings of peaches, cakes, pears, and melons in hope of impressing the heavenly patrons. In modern times, Tanabata has also featured colorful displays of paper streamers and cranes, symbols of peace, while cities like Sendai hold parades and colorful exhibitions.

O-Bon expresses traditional beliefs in the importance of family and ancestors. Unlike most major festivals, it is exclusively linked to Buddhist teachings about existence after death while symbolizing a Confucian respect for the permanence of family lines. Because the faithful expect to communicate with the spirits of the dead, O-Bon is often compared to the Christian All Souls Eve. But the range of contemporary observances of the former is greater than that of the latter. Japanese typically make a major commitment to O-Bon religious observances. City people travel to homes in the country from which they have long since migrated. Graves are visited and cleaned. Family altars have offerings of food placed in front of them. And serious efforts are made to contact the deceased. A typical family will light a bonfire in front of the home to attract departed members while certain family members guide the spirits to the home with lanterns and torches. People converse in the home as though ancestors were actually present and departing spirits are later led away in the same way they arrived. Departure ceremonies are the most striking observance of all. If the home is near water, candles or lanterns will be placed on tiny boats that are thought to carry the spirits via the waterways to the abode of the dead, while groups of sympathetic neighbors dance by homes of families who have suffered recent bereavements in an effort to cheer them up.

O-Shogatsu is as cheerful as O-Bon is sometimes melancholy. It is the major holiday or festival of the Japanese and continues for three full days. The emphasis is on anticipation, renewal, hopes for the future, and the strengthening of personal ties. Like O-Bon, New Year's requires traveling as people strive to spend time with family and friends. Greeting cards are sent like Christmas cards in the United States. People decorate their homes with pine boughs, bamboo stalks, ropes with hanging paper strips cut in zigzag patterns, oranges, and paper lobsters symbolizing long life and freedom from evil spirits. Inside the home, families prepare many special foods and eat elaborate meals preceded by ceremonial drawing of the first water of the year and followed by a visit to the local Shinto shrine. Many people call on absent family members or friends on New Year's and certain games like battledore and shuttlecock or the card game *hyakunin-isshū* are played.

The continuing popularity of festivals points up the reality of distinctive cultural patterns in the Japanese recreational scene. Not *all* Western sports are popular. Soccer has a very modest following and football almost none. (However, efforts were being made with mixed success to promote football via exhibition games and TV broadcasts in the late 1970s.) Patronage of innumerable bars, cabarets, and nightspots has some particular features and even baseball is not played exactly as Americans would expect. The Japanese have their own ideas about training. They are more group-oriented than Americans. And there is greater formal politeness among them. These characteristics all carry over into leisure activities and pusuits. For example, Japanese place great emphasis on achieving expertise in a *particular* sport. Four-hour pregame warm-ups are common among baseball players, and the kind of multidimensional athletic interests common among American professionals are absent among Japanese. One does not find Japanese athletes making reputations in two or three major sports at once, even in their preprofessional days. And even Japanese amateurs tend to choose a favorite sport and work almost exclusively at it. One also notes in sports like sumo or baseball a formal politeness that is more than ritualistic. Wrestlers bow to each other and help each other up; while in baseball, brushback pitches and blocking the bases to a base runner are forbidden.

Still, homogenization of recreational styles may be occurring across the two cultural boundaries. White-collar workers in Japan still socialize more together without spouses after work than American counterparts do. But Japanese couples go out more together than formerly and certain drinking establishments in the cities cater to women more than men or even to both equally. It is too soon to say whether cultural diffusion via television or unparalleled affluence and wealth will alter centuries-old habits fundamentally, but the possibility is there and the Japanese may be fulfilling it.

James Bartholomew

BIBLIOGRAPHY

Haga, Hideo, and Gordon Warner. *Japanese Festivals*. Osaka: Hoikusha, 1968.

Japan National Tourist Organization. *The New Official Guide: Japan*. Tokyo: Japan Travel Bureau, 1966

Miyake, Shutaro. *Kabuki Drama*. Tokyo: Japan Travel Bureau, 1948.

Nogami, Toyoichiro. *Japanese Noh Plays*. Tokyo: Bureau of Tourist Industries, Japanese Government Railways, 1935.

Obojski, Robert. *The Rise of Japanese Baseball Power*. Radnor, Pa.: Chilton, 1975.

Roden, Donald. "Baseball and the Quest for National Dignity in Meiji Japan." *American Historical Review* 85(June 1980):511–34.

The Media in Japan

What is the current development of written and electronic communications media in Japan? Do Japanese follow the media as much or more than Westerners, and who do they like to read and watch?

One of the impressive features of contemporary Japanese society is the proliferation of mass communications media. Although its role as a produer of hardware—television, radios, computers, cameras, and so forth—is better known in the West, Japan is also one of a handful of world leaders in the production and consumption of information and entertainment. Throughout the twentieth century sustained growth has been reached in virtually all sectors of the media industry, so that some believe that a saturation point may have been achieved. In a country where nearly every man, woman, and child already reads books, magazines, and newspapers regularly and where television viewership is at an average of more than three hours per person per day, media executives are starting to wonder how much longer the industry in its present form can continue to grow. As a result they are looking to new areas and are experimenting with the latest technology in order to maintain their leadership.

Respect for learning, a heritage from the Confucian tradition, has contributed to what seems to be a national passion for knowledge. Experts in various fields are frequently asked to comment on recent developments in the media. Professors at major universities write articles and books for the general public that sell respectably and occasionally even become best-sellers. In 1965 a 26-volume *History of Japan* written by leading scholars became the number one best-seller in the country. Educational television is popular, including such regular features as courses in foreign languages. When a course on computer programming was carried on TV, more than a million copies of the textbook accompanying the course were sold.

BOOKS AND MAGAZINES

The high level of literacy in Japan, which is very close to 100 percent, makes much of this success possible. Already by the mid-nineteenth century an estimated 40 percent of Japanese could read, and the numbers grew rapidly after the introduction of compulstory education during the Meiji period (1868–1912).

Books, magazines, and newspapers became mass oriented early in the twentieth century. Even before World War I the market had begun to expand and during the interwar period Japan became one of the world's leading publishers. The high point in the early development was reached right before World War II broke out: 31,996 books were published in 1936 while the largest number of magazines—13,268—was reached in the following year.

The growth in literacy had created the mass market and enterprising publishers had moved to capture it. Noma Seiji, a former secondary school teacher who founded the publishing house Kodansha in 1909, was the most successful. He created a number of popular magazines, including one which had 1.4 million subscribers by 1926, and in the 1930s his firm produced almost two-thirds of all magazines read in Japan. Kodansha continues to be a giant in the industry. In 1978 it issued 1,500 books, far more than any other publisher, as well as 4 weekly, 14 monthly, and 3

TABLE 9.1

Magazines Published in 1978 by Subject

Kind of Magazine	Number Published
General interest	328
Politics, current events, history, sociology, law, education, religion	584
Economics, finance, statistics, commerce	284
Literature, language, philosophy	260
Science, medicine, engineering, agriculture	882
Art, music, theater, dance, entertainment	221
Sports	104
Women's magazines, homemaking, cooking	130
Children's magazines	140
Other	109
Total	3,042

Source: Based on data in *Shuppan nenkan* [Publishers Almanac], 1979 edition (Tokyo: Shuppan News Sha), pp. 61–62.

TABLE 9.2

Total Number of Journals Published in 1978 by Type of Publisher

Type of Publisher	Journals Published
Publishers	4,206
Schools	3,938
Government	2,260
Groups	3,190
Societies	2,297
Companies (public relations)	1,726
Total	18,317

Source: Based on data from *Nihon zasshi/soran*, 1979. [*Directory of Japanese Magazines*] (Tokyo: Shuppan News Sha), 1979 edition.

FIGURE 9.1

Estimated Number of Books and Magazines Published

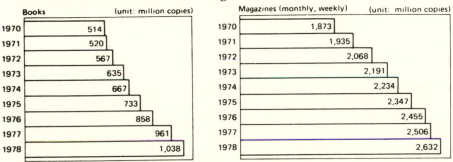

Source: Shuppan nenkan [Publishers Almanac] (Tokyo: Shuppan News Sha), 1971–79 editions.

quarterly magazines. In the same year Kodansha ranked 185th in profits in a listing of all Japanese companies regardless of industry.

Many Japanese publishers, like Kodansha, issue both magazines and books. Although over 18,000 journals are currently published by various organizations in Japan, 3,042 are issued by publishers for the general market. For publishers, proceeds from magazine sales have normally been greater than those from book sales: in 1973, for example, books sales from all publishers brought in $1.1 billion while magazine sales and subscriptions exceeded $1.7 billion. Novels and books are carried in serialized form in magazines and newspapers frequently, a feature which owes much to the joint activities of the publishers. Although in the West this practice is normally associated with the era of Dickens, in Japan it is still considered to be a major factor in attracting sales and subscriptions.

The combination of activities has made it possible for Japanese publishers to develop sophisticated distribution networks. There are about 27,000 retail outlets for magazines and books in Japan, including 15,000 true bookstores, approximately the same number as in the United States. However, in Japan, which is roughly the same size as the state of California, this means that except in the smallest and most remote villages no one is ever far from a local bookstore. Distribution of books and magazines to these stores is done by large wholesalers who are able to provide fast and efficient service. Once a book or magazine issue is published it is available for sale in the major cities on the very next day. Deliveries to more distant areas never take more than 3 to 5 days. Because most Japanese purchase books and magazines at local bookstores, book clubs have never become

popular. Publishers have tried to keep the prices low—there is a psychological ceiling of 1,000 yen for popular titles—and bookstores keep the
shelves stocked with the latest titles, making the system more convenient
than American book clubs. These bookstores do a brisk business: in 1977
the average household spent 45,938 yen ($200) on reading and audiovisual
materials.

The Japanese developed the habit of buying books in the 1920s. By
contrast, this was the period when the concept of the public library was
taking hold in the United States. While public libraries exist in Japan, most
do not get the public or financial support they obtain in the United States
and their purchases account for only about 2 or 3 percent of books sold.
Multivolume sets containing the great works of Japanese and world literature, art, history, and other subjects are very popular, as are encyclopedias
of all sorts. Many Japanese readers purchase them to form the foundation
of their own home libraries. For example, *The Complete Collection of
Modern Japanese Literature* in 63 volumes, which began publication in
1926, recorded a total of 600,000 subscribers by the time it was completed.
More recently, the multivolume *Biographical History of Japanese Women*
reached number six on the national best-seller list for 1977.

While some of the trends in book buying are different in Japan, in many
respects Japanese readers are remarkably similar to American readers.
Books on how to make money, lose weight, enjoy sex, and read fortunes
are the staples. Television adaptations become popular overnight.
Japanese have a strong interest in their own culture and its history and in
how Japan is viewed by other countries and are interested in current
developments around the world. General fiction, historical novels, science
fiction, detective stories, and romances are all popular genres. Translations
account for about 10 percent of all books published and American best-
sellers are frequently high on the Japanese lists: Richard Bach's *Jonathan
Livingston Seagull* was number one in 1974 and Alex Hailey's *Roots* was
number two in 1977.

Small-circulation magazines and books, issued by groups, societies,
and special interest organizations, are part of a phenomenon that is called
"mini-communications" in Japan. They carry everything from literary
works, local history, and autobiographical essays to in-depth reports on the
pressing social problems of Japan. The proliferation of such publications
drew attention in the early 1970s, and more recently there has been
speculaton that their lovely formats, the enthusiasm of their editors and
writers, and their personalized, grass-roots character may influence some
of the more staid and impersonal mass-oriented magazines. These publications show that the Japanese are not merely mass consumers of the media
but are interested in making their own contributions as well.

FIGURE 9.2

Number of New Book Titles by Category

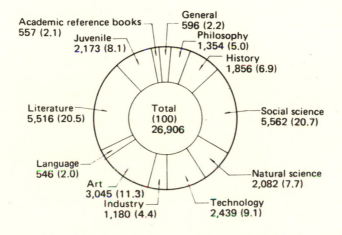

Note: Data as of 1978. Figures in parentheses indicate percentages.
Source: Shuppan nenkan [Publishers Almanac] (Tokyo: Shuppan News Sha), 1979 edition.

Although the influence of books and magazines in Japan remains high, television has clearly become the dominant medium and there is concern that the younger generation may not prove to be the avid readers that their parents and grandparents were. In 1978 a survey of college students revealed that 46.6 percent spend less than 30 minutes per day reading and many do not read at all. Among those who do read, comic books and similar materials are the most popular items. In the same year a newspaper survey of 3,000 people over the age of 20 showed that 43 percent had not read anything in the past month. These surveys mark an abrupt change; as recently as five years before, nonreaders amounted to 5 percent or less in most polls. In a country where reading has been an ingrained habit the findings are shocking, but it is still too early to estimate their long-range meaning and effect.

TABLE 9.3

Leading Newspapers of the World, 1978

Country	Newspaper	Circulation (1,000 copies)	
Japan	*Yomiuri Shimbun*	Morning	8,145
	Asahi Shimbun	Morning	7,322
	Mainichi Shimbun	Morning	4,460
U.S.	*New York Daily News*	Morning	1,825
	The New York Times	Morning	822
	The Washington Post	Morning	559
Great Britain	*Daily Mirror*	Morning	3,778
	Daily Express	Morning	2,467
	Daily Mail	Morning	1,933
	The Times	Morning	294
France	*France-Soir*	Evening	511
	Le Monde	Evening	429
	Le Figaro	Morning	327
West Germany	*Bild Zeitung*	Morning	5,853
	Frankfurter Allgemeine	Morning	356
Italy	*Corriere della Sera*	Morning	571
USSR	*Pravda*	Morning	10,600
	Izvestia	Morning	8,500

Note: Japanese newspapers also publish evening editions, while other countries' newspapers publish only morning or evening editions. *Izvestia*'s Moscow edition is an evening paper.

Sources: Editor & Publisher 1979 Yearbook (New York: Editor & Publisher); For Japan: *Nihon Shimbun nenkan* [Japan Newspaper Yearbook] (Tokyo: Nihon Shimbun Kyōkai), 1979 edition.

NEWSPAPERS

Japanese newspapers are probably the most impressive indicator of how avidly Japanese consume media products. Japan's two leading daily newspapers, *Yomiuri* and *Asahi*, have the highest circulation in the non-Communist world, while *Mainichi*, which ranks third in Japan, is fourth after Germany's *Bild Zeitung*. In total newspaper circulation Japan is third in the world after the USSR and the United States, although its population is half or less. The statistics reveal that many Japanese households subscribe to two or more newspapers.

TABLE 9.4

Circulation of Daily General-Interest Newspapers

Country	Year	Number	Circulation Total (thousands)	Circulation Per 1,000 population
Japan	1974	180	57,820	526
USSR	1975	691	100,928	397
U.S.	1975	1,812	61,222	287
Great Britain	1975	111	21,700	388
West Germany	1975	334	19,298	312
France	1975	98	11,341	214
Italy	1975	78	6,296	113
Canada	1975	121	4,872	—
Sweden	1975	135	4,678	572

Note: For the purposes of this table a "general-interest newspaper" is defined as a periodical publication devoted primarily to recording general news; it is considered to be "daily" if it appears at least four times a week.

Source: Statistical Yearbook, United Nations Educational, Scientific and Cultural Organization, 1977.

Although literacy rates and the desire for knowledge are important factors lying behind these high subscription rates, the fact that the major newspapers are national papers rather than local papers is probably the major reason for their success. Local and regional newspapers were more popular in the early twentieth century, but by the 1930s a pattern of centralization had been established. The high quality and efficient distribution of the national papers effectively halted the growth of many local papers and although local papers are still issued, their importance has been eclipsed by the national papers.

Daily newspapers are published in a 24-page format imposed by the railways to make transport possible. Each prefecture has a headquarters where local editors and reporters insert one page of news for publication in that prefecture only. Home delivery accounts for 95 percent of all newspapers sold, but the system is becoming increasingly difficult to maintain and alternatives are being sought.

The size limitation has enormous impact on the newspapers. First of all, it has restricted the amount of advertising which they carry. Thus, the Japanese newspapers have a very different appearance from the typical American newspaper. They are also spared from the pressure that influential advertisers put on a newspaper's editorial stance. Since the papers have to rely heavily on revenues from circulation to run their operations, they are very sensitive to the opinion of the general readership, therefore, even though they are pressed for space the newspapers carry a full range of features, including columns for personal advice, sports pages, one or more comic strips, letters, serialized books, and columns from news commentators. Furthermore, readers demand a very high quality of news coverage and are sensitive to the differences among the leading newspapers. In order to attract readers the newspapers have sometimes engaged in "circulation wars" by carefully timing the release of news "scoops." Although universally deplored, this practice is probably inevitable given the importance of circulation revenues.

Newspaper publishers strive for "objectivity" in reporting the news, however, the interpretation of this principle has often led to controversy. Throughout most of the postwar period newspapers have taken an opposition stand against the ruling Liberal Democratic Party. In the mid-1970s, as the Liberal Democratic Party and the opposition parties came closer together and with the resolution of some of the major points of contention, such as establishment of relations with China and withdrawal of American forces from Okinawa, the tables turned. Newspapers were even accused of collusion with government officials. For example, they were upbraided for not having reported the facts about Prime Minister Tanaka's financial dealings until after the story broke in a magazine. More recently, the influence of Watergate reporting has made the investigative style more popular. For example, the 1978 Newspaper Publishers' Association Award went to Yoshida Shin'ichi, a 28-year-old newly hired reporter for *Asahi* in Fukushima Prefecture. He published a 200-installment report on the local page of the paper exposing political corruption that ultimately led to the governor's arrest.

In addition to the national dailies, there are local papers and special interest papers, including those dealing with economics and sports, as well as several English-language papers.

TELEVISION

Although Japanese read prolifically they also find time to watch a great deal of television. One recent survey showed that viewership is at an average of 3 hours and 40 minutes per day. Television programming is similar to that in the United States in many ways. News and weather, quiz shows, soap operas, movies, sports, special reports, and situation comedies are all carried regularly. Other features are more similar to those found on England's BBC, including the large variety of educational and cultural offerings.

The major network, Nippon Hōsō Kyōkai (NHK) or Japan Broadcasting Corporation, is run much the same way that the BBC is. It is a public corporation charged with conducting its broadcasting "for the public welfare and in such a mannner that its broadcasts may be received all over Japan." A Board of Governors appointed by the Prime Minister with the consent of the Diet oversees its operations. Income is derived from monthly subscription fees paid by viewers under contract with NHK; there is no commercial advertising. Nippon Hōsō Kyōkai runs two networks, one general and one educational, and it has strict guidelines governing the percentages of news, educational or cultural programming, and entertainment that can be carried on both of these channels. Japan also has about 90 private, commercial, television broadcasters. These enterprises, which draw their revenues from advertising, carry a higher percentage of entertainment than NHK does but they also have news and some educational or cultural programs. Some of them have ties to the major newspapers.

Television in Japan offers some surprises. There is a great amount of violence, even on children's cartoon shows. It has been said that there are 44 violent deaths on Japanese television every day, many more than are shown on American TV. Yet Japan is a peaceful society with one of the lowest crime rates in the world. One reason why the violence on television has not had a negative influence on the society may be the fact that in Japan the face of the victim suffering in pain is frequently shown, while this rarely occurs on American television.

Quiz games on Japanese TV are popular and sometimes very elaborate. One show recently flew contestants to the United States, taking them from city to city and eliminating one contestant at each stop. Some popular shows depict the life of typical "salaried men," or white-collar, middle-class workers. NHK broadcasts annual historical dramas also, running them once a week for a year. They dramatize popular periods of Japanese history and are shot on location at historic sites. These dramas are extraordinarily popular and viewers take enough interest to provide feedback to NHK as the drama develops over the year.

Cable television has spread throughout Japan. It began as a means of improving reception in rural areas, but now separate programs are also carried. Many hotels use the cable system to provide English-language broadcasts for foreign visitors. Experimental projects exploring the possibilities of further development in many areas, especially interactive TV, are in progress. Tama Coaxial Cable Information System is one of the most ambitious of these projects. At Tama New Town in the Northwestern section of Tokyo this "wired city" has been established providing retransmission of VHF TV, transmission of independent, locally produced programs, TV requests, still-picture requests, newspaper and community information, and other features. The Higashi-Ikoma Optical Visual Information System, near Osaka, is a similar system featuring simultaneous two-way communication on TV screens in each home. Its developers are exploring the ways that such advanced systems can be used to foster the development of a cohesive local community.

Japanese social analysts believe that the country has reached a stage that they call the "Information Society," in which information is given as much or even greater value than material objects. They see the permeation of urban life-styles throughout the country as one of the most distinctive features of this stage. The emergence of this Information Society has drawn protests from those concerned about the abuses of the media. Controversies over the right of access to the media, the role of the government in controlling the media, the nature of media responsibility, and the influence of the media on youth have stirred in recent years, much as these same issues have attracted the attention of Americans.

Maureen Donovan

BIBLIOGRAPHY

Edelstein, Alex S., John E. Bowes, and Sheldon M. Harsel. *Information Societies: Comparing the Japanese and American Experiences.* Seattle: Intternational Communication Center, 1978.

Lottman, Herbert R. "Publishing in Japan." *Publishers Weekly* 214, no. 16 (1978): 49–95.

The Status of Women

What is the status of Japanese women today in the labor market, in the family and society, and in politics, and how has their status changed in comparison with the situation in the past?

The status of contemporary Japanese women has undergone profound change since World War II. The legal basis for women's gains over the past

35 years was laid down during the period of the Allied Occupation (1945–52) with the introduction of a series of reforms aimed at guaranteeing women's equality in the family, the work place, and in politics. Since the war, a variety of forces operating in postwar Japan, from rising economic prosperity to the spread of mass higher education, have created a climate of greater opportunity for women. At the same time, however, many customs, attitudes, and informal practices in the employment sector, education, politics, and in family life continue to reflect to a degree the values of prewar Japan in which women, both in the laws and in custom, were assigned a status that was inferior to men's. For the average Japanese woman today, it is sometimes difficult to mesh legal norms with social reality.

The overall pattern of change affecting Japanese women, then, is one in which women have made significant gains in virtually all areas of social, political, and economic life, but in which numerous issues and problems remain. In general, the barriers to further improvements in the status of Japanese women are to be found in customs and attitudes rather than in the laws, and the challenge to women is to take full advantage of the legal guarantees available to them.

The Constitution of 1947 introduced during the occupation period laid the groundwork for improvements in the situation of women by including an explicit guarantee of women's equality. In Article 14, it forbade "discrimination in political, economic or social relations because of race, creed, sex, social status or family origin." In Article 24, it took the same principle of equality into family life by guaranteeing the "equal rights of husband and wife," and by providing that "with regard to choice of spouse, property, inheritance, choice of domicile, divorce, and other matters pertaining to marriage and the family, laws shall be enacted from the standpoint of individual dignity and the essential equality of the sexes." These and other constitutional guarantees, along with more specific provisions introduced during the occupation period in the revised Civil Code and in other basic laws, established a legal framework for improving women's status that was progressive both then and now in comparison to the legal framework for women's rights to be found in a number of the other advanced industrial societies.

The legal reforms were seen by the occupying forces and by many women's groups in Japan as necessary to correct the situation in force prior to 1945 in which women, both in the family and outside it, had been fundamentally unequal to men under the law. They had been denied the right to vote and to run for political office; their education beyond elementary school had been carried out in a separate "girl's track" that normally did not include the possibility of advancing to the university level and that provided a curriculum explicitly designed to produce "good wives and wise mothers''; and family law had consistently favored the husband in matters relating to marriage, divorce, inheritance, property rights for married women, and other areas. Over the period from 1945 to 1952, all this changed. In 1945, Japanese women gained full political rights. The multitrack educational system was replaced in 1947 with a new single-track system that standardized the curriculum and offered women equal educational opportunity and equal access to higher education. In the postwar reform of the Civil Code, husbands and wives were placed on legal parity in the marriage relationship. Women gained the right to negotiate contracts without their husband's consent and were given equal recourse to divorce under the law. The Labor Standard Law enacted in 1947 carried provisions that led to major improvements in the situation of women workers. Although some of the measures, modeled on women's labor laws then in effect in the United States, fall in the area of protective legislation, and are the target of reform efforts on the part of a number of women's groups today in Japan, there is no question that in the early postwar period the labor reforms provided a much-needed basis for rectifying abuses of the past. How these various legal reforms of the occupation period affect the situation of women in Japan can be seen as we turn to consider the status of Japanese women today in the work force, in the family and society, and in politics.

JAPANESE WOMEN IN THE WORK FORCE

In 1979 women made up 39 percent of the Japanese labor force. Half of the female population of 15 years of age and over were in the work force. In the early 1970s, the labor force participation rate of women decreased slightly, but since 1976 the rate has shown an increase. Two factors have had a major effect on the overall work force participation rate of women in recent years. The first is a striking increase in the number of older women who entered or reentered the labor force. In 1979, 62.4 percent of women between the ages of 40 and 54 were working. The second, countervailing trend is the decrease in the number of younger women in the work force as more and more women seek a higher education and thus delay their entry into the labor market. It was this latter factor that is thought to be responsible for the slight decrease in women's overall work force participation rate in the early 1970s.

The increase in the number of older women workers reflects some very significant changes in the roles and attitudes of women. Traditionally, wage jobs in Japan were held by younger, single women who worked for several years and then quit their jobs to become full-time housewives. This pattern, which is still many people's stereotype of the situation in Japan, has undergone profound change. The average age of women workers had increased to 34.1 years by 1978, not far below 37.2 years for men. Whereas in 1962, 55 percent of women workers were single (consonant with the traditional pattern just described) and only 33 percent were married, the figures are reversed today. In 1979, only 33 percent were single, whereas 57 percent were married. Increasingly, the dominant pattern of women's employment in Japan, as in the other advanced industrial societies, is one in which young women enter the work force after their education is concluded, continue work after marriage until they have their first child, and then return to the labor force after their children are in school.

This change has meant that the average length of service of women workers has been increasing. In 1978, it was 6.1 years (as compared, for example, to 5.8 as recently as 1975). However, women's average length of service, due to interruptions for child rearing and to other factors, is still well below that for men, which was 11.1 years in 1978. The somewhat younger age of women workers relative to men and their shorter term of service tend to limit their chances for promotion and operate, along with other factors, to keep the level of women's wages low. The average women's wage was reported in 1980 to be only 55 percent of the average for men, and the gap appears to have widened over the past few years.

Like women workers in most countries today, Japanese women workers still predominantly hold jobs that require low levels of skill. In 1979, 32 percent of all women workers did clerical work, 13 percent were service workers, and 23 percent were factory operatives; thus 69 percent of all employed women held jobs in those three categories. In the same year, women constituted only 5.1 percent of managers and officials, 2.5 percent of lawyers and judges, 5.1 percent of scientists, and only 9.6 percent of physicians. These figures reflect major gains that women have made in the professions and managerial work in the postwar period in comparison with the situation before the war. Virtually all jobs in such fields as law, architecture, accountancy, and government service were then held by men. However, women's entry into the professions has been slow in the postwar period, despite legal guarantees designed to ensure equal employment opportunity, and the gains in the 1970s have been far less than many other countries. For example, the percentage of women physicians in Japan remained unchanged over the period from 1960 to 1975. Similarly, a United Nations report issued in 1974 indicated that of 54 nations studied, Japan ranked next to the bottom, behind only Pakistan, in the percentage of women in nonclerical positions in the national administrations of their countries.

In the Japanese labor force, women workers are found in three broad categories: salaried employees (who have been the focus of the discussion up until now), the self-employed, and unpaid family workers, most of the latter of whom are in farming or forestry. The overall trend is one in which the percentage of women who are salaried employees has been increasing, while the percentage of family workers has been declining. Two patterns not discussed so far stand out in any overall characterization of women's work force participation in Japan. One is the large number of women who are engaged in part-time work for wages. In 1979, almost 2.5 million women were engaged in part-time work (defined as working fewer than 35 hours per week) and well over 1 million others did industrial piecework in their homes. These types of employment represent important avenues into the labor market for large numbers of married women, who are looking for ways to combine income-generating activities with household responsibilities. Another pattern, strikingly different from the situation in most other advanced industrial countries, is that of the central role played by women in agriculture. Women made up 51 percent of the agricultural labor force in 1979 and in many cases had sole responsibility for managing the farm enterprise. The role of women in Japanese agriculture has been increasing as a result of a number of forces at work in the countryside. Japanese land holdings typically are too small to support families comfortably, so increasingly, male heads of the family and younger family members seek greater economic opportunity by working for wages in nearby factories or firms. When this happens, typically the wife stays behind to manage the farm. Since many types of farming in Japan, including rice growing, are labor intensive despite a high level of mechanization, the result of these changes is a heavy work load and long working hours for the farm woman.

JAPANESE WOMEN IN SOCIETY AND THE FAMILY

Multiple forces operate to affect the lives, roles, and status of women in the family and society. The democratizing reforms introduced during the occupation period upgraded women's legal status within the family, as already noted, and laid the basis for further change. The economic prosperity that Japan has enjoyed, especially since the late 1960s, has also had profound impact on the situation of women in the family. Studies show, for example, that when Japanese families have only enough resources to send one child on to higher education, typically they will educate a son over a daughter, regardless of the relative ability of the two. But when family resources are adequate, as has increasingly been the case over the past two decades, they will provide higher education for children of both sexes. The increased prosperity of the average Japanese family has made it possible for them to purchase household conveniences that improve the quality of life for housewives and to engage in leisure activities as a family. A recent survey indicates that the amount of time housewives have for social, cultural, and recreational activities has doubled in compaarison with the prewar period. Urbanization is another significant force operating indirectly to improve the status of women. In the prewar period, women's position of inferiority within the family was based on the low status of the wife in relation to other family members in an extended family arrangement that was very common before the war. The wife was subject to the authority of her mother-in-law, who ran the household. Japanese fiction is filled with accounts of the suffering experienced by young wives under this system. As urban migration has continued in Japan, however, the nuclear family has become the norm. Japan today is over 70 percent urban. The average size of household decreased from 4.0 in 1965 to 3.6 by 1970. Within the nuclear family the young wife has far greater authority and independence than in the extended family, and the marriage relationship itself is characterized by greater closeness between husband and wife. Finally, demographic and other social factors have supported improvements in the lives of women. Average childbirth expectancy had dropped from over 5 in the prewar period to 2 by 1979. Birth control measures, including legal and inexpensive abortions, are readily available in Japan, freeing women from unwanted pregnancies and making it possible for couples to engage in family planning.

One important area of change in women's status in Japan relating to family life is in the mate selection process. Traditionally, Japan has had an arranged marriage system that was the normal route to marriage in the prewar period, particularly among upper-class and middle-class families. Today arranged marriages continue to predominate in villages and small towns, but in urban areas well over a majority of young people—over 60 percent of couples in large cities—meet and marry on their own. The arranged marriage system has itself undergone profound change in recent years. Whereas in the past, young people were frequently pressured by their elders into marriage with persons they had barely met, today couples who say that their marriage was arranged may mean little more than that they were initially introduced to one another by their parents or by a go-between. Defenders of the arranged marriage system point out that it operates much like computer dating in the United States except that the persons arranging the introduction know the principals better than any computer can.

The divorce rate in Japan has undergone major fluctuations over the past 100 years. In the Meiji period (1868–1912) when Japan was industrializing and social change was occurring rapidly, the divorce rate reached a point far higher than it is today. But the high rate was an indicator of the low status of women, for virtually all divorces were initiated by husbands on grounds that reflected their superior status in the family, such as the wife's inability to get along with his parents. In the postwar period the number of divorces initiated by the wife has increased, and on such nontraditional grounds as the husband's unchastity. These changes are as significant, if not more so, than changes in the rate itself. The divorce rate of 1.17 cases per 1,000 population in 1979 was low in comparison with that in many advanced industrial countries, but it reflects a steady increase in the 1970s. Numerous factors operate to keep down the divorce rate, one of which is economic. Japanese law makes no provision for alimony. Public assistance is available for divorced women, but the amounts of aid are extremely small, and divorcees in Japan typically face extreme hardship as well as social criticism in a society that places a high value on family harmony.

The position of women within the family has improved dramatically in the postwar period. The nature of marriage itself in the 1980s still has continuities with the past, however. Japanese husbands continue to play very little part in home life compared to husbands in many Western countries. A Ministry of Labor survey in 1977 found that the average Japanese husband spent only 6 minutes a day on housework. Men, especially white-collar workers, typically stay long hours at work, and may spend much of their leisure time with male coworkers. Within the family, however, the wife has considerable autonomy in a wide range of areas from child discipline to handling the family budget.

Increased educational opportunity for women has had major impact on women's status in the family and society. Women's advancement in education has been increasing rapidly at all levels throughout the postwar period. Since 1969, the percentage of females entering senior high school has exceeded that for males. Today 95 percent of all girls enter senior high school, as compared to 93 percent for boys. Meanwhile, the percentage of women in higher education has increased 32-fold since 1950. In 1979, 33.1 percent of all women of college age entered higher education, as compared to 5 percent in 1955. The rate for women is well below the male rate of 41.1 percent, however. Despite these advances, there are many differences in the patterns of education of women and men. In senior high school, males tend to take the general education course if they plan to go to the university, or the vocational course if they plan to work immediately after high school. Females, in contrast, are more apt to take the general education course whether or not they plan to go to college. The great majority of young women thus leave high school without specialized skills that might lead to better-paying technical jobs. In higher education, women are more likely to attend junior colleges, where they make up 89 percent of the enrollment, than four-year institutions, where they make up only 22 percent of the students. Once in college, women disproportionately gravitate to a few majors, notably literature, followed by teacher training. The percentage of women in preprofessional areas of concentration such as law, politics, engineering, or economics continues to be relatively small, although the figures are increasing.

JAPANESE WOMEN AND POLITICS

On April 10, 1946, Japanese women voted and ran for public office for the first time, ushering in a new era of equal political participation for women. In the first postwar national election, there was a gap of 11.5 percent between the voting rates of women and men. Thereafter, however, the gap began to close, and since 1968 the voting rate for women consistently has exceeded that for men. In the October 1979 lower house election, for example, the rate for women was 68.6 percent, as compared to 67.4 percent for men.

Despite these changes in the area of mass political participation, women continue to be underrepresented when it comes to holding office. In the first postwar election in 1946, 39 women gained seats in the House of Representatives, but women's showing in subsequent elections has been far more modest. Since 1947 typically they have held between 7 and 12 seats in the lower house, and between 12 and 19 seats in the upper house, the House of Councillors, thus comprising under 3 percent of the total membership in the two houses. Women's level of representation is still lower at the prefectural level, where they make up only 1.1 percent of the total membership in prefectural assemblies, and at the village level, where they hold only .5 percent of the seats in village assemblies.

As indicated earlier, the number of women in the national bureaucracy is extremely low in Japan in comparison with the situation in many countries. Only two women have served in the cabinet, both of them for short-term appointments.

Outside the public sphere, Japanese women have an extensive organizational life, and some of the groups have roots that go back to the prewar period. In the 1920s, Japan had an active suffragist movement. Though it was not successful in its own day in gaining the vote for women, a number of its leaders have been active in politics and in the leadership ranks of women's organizations in the postwar period. Organizations and clubs such as the Women's Democratic Club, the League of Women Voters, the Association of University Women, and the Women's Christian Temperance Association are all very active. Through a network of regional clubs, over 6.5 million women are affiliated with a National Council of the Federation of Regional Women's Clubs and almost 3 million women are similarly linked to the National Council of Women's Organizations of Agricultural Cooperatives. In addition, there are a number of groups for women in the various professions, such as the Women Lawyers' Association. One of the most active and influential of women's organizations is the Housewives' Association, which has been concerned with a broad range of problems, from inflation to political corruption to truth-in-packaging issues.

Many women's organizations have been concerned with issues relating to the problems of women. The Women's and Young Workers' Bureau in the Ministry of Labor, which was created in 1947 under pressure from occupation officials to oversee the implementation of the occupation's reforms in the area of women's rights, has played an extremely active role in promoting improvements in the status of women. During International Women's Year in 1975, an Advisory Council on Women's Affairs was created in the Prime Minister's Office. The group has been instrumental in drawing up a National Plan of Action in the area of women's rights for the period ahead. The plan calls for greater participation of women in policy decision making, the attainment of equal rights of women in employment, greater recognition of the work done by housewives, and a variety of other improvements in the status of women by 1985.

Susan Pharr

BIBLIOGRAPHY

Cook, Alice H., and Hiroko Hayashi. *Working Women in Japan: Discrimination, Resistance, and Reform.* Ithaca, N.Y.: Cornell University Press, 1980.

Lebra, Joyce, Joy Paulson, and Elizabeth Powers. *Women in Changing Japan.* Boulder, Colo.: Westview Press, 1976.

Ministry of Labor, Women's and Young Workers' Bureau. *The Status of Women in Japan.* Tokyo, 1980.

————. *Women Workers in Japan.* Tokyo, 1980.

Pharr, Susan J. "Japan: Historical and Contemporary Perspectives." In *Women: Role and Status in Eight Countries,* edited by Janet Giele and Audrey C. Smock. New York: John Wiley, 1977.

Szalai, Alexander. *The Situation of Women in the United Nations,* report no. 18. New York: United Nations Institute for Training and Research, 1973.

U.S. Department of Labor and Japan Ministry of Labor. *The Role and Status of Women Workers in the United States and Japan.* Washington, D.C.: U.S. Government Printing Office, 1976 (A joint United States-Japan study.)

PART IV

TRADING WITH JAPAN

10

ENTERING THE JAPANESE MARKET

There are many myths regarding the difficulties of entering the Japanese market that impede serious consideration of trade with Japan by many firms. There are also realities of the Japanese marketplace that must be understood in order to trade effectively. Japanese tastes and preferences may differ from those abroad and distribution practices are markedly different from those in the United States in that multiple layers of middlemen are involved in highly institutionalized marketing channels linking producers and retailers. Because of these and other differences, as well as frequently an indifference to the possibilities of export trade, many American producers have ignored the potentials of the Japanese marketplace. In this chapter, Yoshi Tsurumi illustrates some of this potential as well as indicating areas where customs differ and some adjustment by foreign businessmen is necessary.

Japan is certainly an affluent society and one where foreign goods can compete effectively. Foreign fashion designs and automobiles are valued by well-to-do Japanese, while foreign whiskies and some other consumer items have a wider market. Consumer luxuries thus do well in Japan despite the frequently phenomenal price markups resulting from import monopolies and multiple markups in complex distribution channels. Except for the political restrictions imposed on some agricultural products, the future for imported consumer luxury goods in Japan is good.

Still, luxury imports are only a drop in the bucket in the vast Japanese home consumer market. Foreign goods could be competitive in the mass consumer market as various successes with such products as Hershey's chocolates and California avocados demonstrate. Even American automobiles could do much better. However, the low import levels of American automobiles in Japan indicate some of the considerations that lead to high price markups which impede greater success in the Japanese market. Like other consumer markets, only perhaps more so, most Japanese consumers have specific needs and tastes, e.g., for small cars; they are also accustomed to good maintenance and repair service from domestic manufacturers that importers of foreign products may not provide (witness the poor service records that eliminated some European automakers from the American market in the 1950s and 1960s). Homologization costs may also be a problem, unless products are designed specifically for the Japanese market, presumably on the assumption of high-volume sales. These typical problems in competitive export merchandising are augmented by some Japanese practices, such as high dealer margins, which provide additional barriers to effective market entry. A foreign firm desiring to enter Japanese consumer or industrial goods markets must consequently know the Japanese setting well and plan both production and marketing strategies carefully in order to achieve success.

Small firms in the United States and elsewhere have typically not been export oriented. Yet experience shows that in cases like medical instruments, apparel, and kitchen utensils, small firms can successfully penetrate the Japanese market. What is required is commitment and access to the necessary managerial skills and funding. One way to meet these needs is through trading companies, such as those in Japan. Formation of such companies has in fact been discussed in the U.S. Congress. Short of the existence of such companies, there are some other viable strategies available: firms can enter into agency representation agreements, or distribution agreements; it is not necessary to have a direct sales or production subsidiary to enter the Japanese marketplace. Among the various options, joint ventures have proven themselves as one of the most effective ways to approach the Japanese market.

What is required more than anything else is know-how. This know-how can be acquired: generic know-how, financial advice, and information about distribution channels can be obtained from agents, market consultants, the government, and those banks that have international divisions. Specific financing help can be obtained, along with export insurance and customs clearing assistance, from government agencies. Tsurumi suggests specific private and public sources for each kind of information or service.

Once generic information and advice is acquired, specific evaluations of product life-cycle timing and potential success must be carried out as Japanese, American, and European producers become more competitive in each other's markets. Tsurumi feels that awareness of the need to trade will come in the 1980s and that even small firms will become by necessity more export oriented. Once the myths of Japanese nontrade barriers are recognized for the cultural differences that they are in so many cases, and once firms make a definite commitment to export to Japan, a satisfactory entry strategy can be devised in many instances even by small firms.

Realities of the Japanese Consumer Imports Market

> Both foreigners in Japan and Japanese note that some imported consumer goods like meat cost five or six times in Japan what they would in the producing countries. Why is this the case? What will the future be?

At airport duty-free shops in Hawaii, Los Angeles, and elsewhere, Japanese tourists can frequently be seen busily buying expensive items such as brandy, scotch, bourbon, cigarettes, Gucci bags, and other luxuries. They purchase these things mainly as souvenirs for friends, relatives, and bosses back home in Japan, and are well aware that these well-known luxuries cost at least twice as much in Japan. But more importantly, they realize that the recipient in Japan will greatly appreciate the prestigious image of these items.

Nor do Japanese tourists limit their souvenir buying to the popular luxuries mentioned above. Nowadays, American beefsteak, honeydew melons, Sunkist oranges, grapefruits, Canadian herring and salmon roe, and certain prized varieties of seaweed have joined the list of popular souvenirs purchased by Japanese tourists. Again, the Japanese love these delicacies, but their prices in Japan are normally twice as high as those found at duty-free shops overseas. With such a strong demand for these products in Japan, why can't they be imported to Japan in quantity at reasonable prices?

FORMIDABLE BEEF AND ORANGE LOBBIES IN JAPAN

As the United States-Japan trade relationship took on a confrontational outlook during 1978 and 1979, California citrus growers argued that Japan should import California oranges more freely, and American and Australian cattle breeders demanded that Japan totally liberalize its imports of beef and other agricultural products. These beef and orange wars were very much reminiscent of the chicken war that was waged earlier across the Atlantic from the end of the 1950s throughout the 1960s. Even today, the same California citrus growers who demand that Japan import more oranges are dead set against the importation of Japanese and Chinese raw tangerines. These American citrus growers echo the protectionist sentiments of Japanese farmers in that they do not want foreign products to swamp their domestic markets, thereby lowering the prices of their own products. This feeling is shared widely by American beef cattle breeders and dairy farmers who want to keep out Australian and New Zealand beef, mutton, and dairy products, although these same groups demand that Japan allow the free trade of agricultural products into Japan.

The political power of Japanese farmers over the ruling party is much stronger than the comparable clout of their American counterparts. Since seats in the Japanese Diet, the center of political power, are apportioned on the basis of the national census taken in 1947 when the bombed-out cities were denuded of their population, rural areas possess much greater proportional representation in the Diet than the urban or industrial areas, even though these urban areas regained their population during the 1950s and 1960s. The ruling Liberal Democratic Party has been kept in power by the faithful support of rural voters. This is why the Japanese government appears unreasonably timid and stubborn in its refusal to liberalize imports of various agricultural goods.

Like the American government, the Japanese government subsidizes farmers. One financial source of these farmers' subsidies has been the import duties that are levied on products deemed as threats to Japanese farmers. Accordingly, subsidies to beef cattle breeders in Japan are paid for by the high duties charged on imported beef. Before beef imports were permitted, an outright ban on imports kept domestic prices very high. This protectionist umbrella of price supports has turned beef trade into a lucrative business in Japan. Several layers of wholesalers and distributors intervene in the distribution of beef and other agricultural products in Japan, each tacking on their own handling commissions to the price of beef and other products.

This system of pyramid pricing is further compounded by the economic inefficiencies of small retailers and butcher shops. In Japan, small corner grocery stores and butcher shops are still very much a way of life. In order to earn enough revenues with their small volume of sales, these small stores charge high markups. The justification for these high markups is the delivery and other customer services these stores provide "free of charge" to their customers. For example, at a typical Japanese butcher shop, Japanese housewives make daily purchases of extremely small portions of meat, portions as small as one-tenth of a pound of "deboned" and "well-sliced" meat. Japanese diets and recipes permit four to five family members to share two-fifths of a pound of beef cooked together with vegetables. At present, over 50 percent of the Japanese protein intake comes from sea produce, although the consumption of pork, chicken broilers, and beef is definitely on the rise.

HIGH PRICES FOR CONSUMER LUXURIES

Foreign luxury goods are considered by Japanese consumers to be high-status prestigious imports (*hakurai*). There is a sizable pocket of wealthy consumers who are willing to pay high prestige premiums (monopoly profits to importers) for luxury imports. Consequently, both foreign and Japanese importers (and foreign exporters) of varying foreign consumer items charge high markups to cater to this pocket of wealthy consumers. In this market, very few Japanese products provide any meaningful competition. Both Japanese and foreign dealers in imported consumer items consciously follow a market strategy of "high markups and small volume."

In the past, the Japanese government charged high luxury taxes on luxury imports. However, these taxes were easily passed along to wealthy Japanese consumers. The resultant high prices of these imports not only created an image for them as being prestigious and expensive but also excluded the Japanese mass consumers from this luxury market.

Beginning in 1979 and continuing in 1980, the United States-Japan trade dispute over automobiles has intensified. Ailing Ford and Chrysler blame the decline of their sales in the United States on rising imports, although American consumers left large gas-guzzling models on their own volition. This was because neither Ford nor Chrysler had high-quality and fuel-efficient cars that Americans demanded.

In order to drive home the argument that Japan discriminates against American cars, American automobile firms made much of the celebrated incident of $6,000 American cars being sold in Japan for $12,000. American automobile firms and the United Auto Workers made much of the fact that Japanese exports of cars to the United States exceeded 1 million units per year although Japanese imports of American cars were about 40,000 units per year. They implied that this high sticker price for American automobiles was the result of Japanese government discriminatory taxes and other unfair nontariff trade barriers. They alleged that nontariff trade barriers of Japan kept American exports of automobiles at around 40,000 units per year.

Intrigued by this allegation, in 1979 the United States government (the Comptroller General) sent American investigators to Japan to find out whether or not the high sticker price on American automobiles was caused by Japanese government discriminatory practices against foreign cars. Table 10.1 summarizes the import tariff rates on passenger cars in Japan,

TABLE 10.1

Import Tariff on Passenger Cars
(ad valorem on CIF price)

Year	Japan		United States All Models	EEC All Models
	Small Cars	Others		
1967	40.0%	28.0%	6.5%	22.0%
1968	36.0	28.0	5.5	11.0
1969	36.0	17.5	5.0	11.0
1970	20.0	17.5	4.5	11.0
1971	10.0	10.0	4.0	11.0
1972	6.4	6.4	3.0	11.0
1978	0.0	0.0	3.0	11.0
1980	0.0	0.0	3.0	11.0

Source: Import Tariff Schedules, Ministry of Finance, Tokyo, 1967–80.

the United States, and the European Economic Community (EEC) from 1967 to 1980. The American investigation team discovered that the high sticker price on American cars could not be attributed to the import tariff in Japan.

Once inside Japan, the American investigators learned that the higher dealer margin is the single most important factor causing the high sticker price of imported American cars. The Japanese commodity tax, which is akin to the local sales tax of the United States, ranged from 15 to 20 percent depending on the engine size. The commodity tax was the second most important factor contributing to the high sticker price of the imported cars although these same commodity taxes were levied on Japanese cars made and sold in Japan. The third most important factor that produced the high sticker price on imported cars was the homologation costs that were incurred by the importers in order to make necessary adjustments of the imported models. These adjustments were necessary before the imported models could satisfy Japanese safety regulations to which all Japanese cars made in Japan are also subjected. All told, Table 10.2 summarizes the factors that often contributed to a doubling of the imported price.

This shows that even a total abolishment of the commodity tax could only reduce the sticker price of imported cars by 10 percent. The remaining factors are in the hands of American exporters and Japanese importers. As

TABLE 10.2

Factors Contributing to Doubled Import Prices

Factor	VWs and other West German Car Models	American Car Models
Retail Price	100%	100%
CIF price	64	43
Commodity tax	10	9
Dealer costs & homologation	26	48

Source: "U.S.-Japan Trade," General Accounting Office, Washington, D.C., September 1979, p. 46.

compared with American automobile firms, West German firms have shown better efforts to reduce the dealers and homologation costs. Otherwise, it is difficult to break the vicious circle of small sales volume and high dealer margins that in turn produces small sales volumes.

PROBLEMS IN MERCHANDISING
CONSUMER IMPORTS ON A MASS SCALE

Of all the product lines offered by the Ford Motor Company, Lincoln Continentals carry the highest prestige premium in Japan. Its competitors—Cadillac, Mercedes-Benz, and Rolls Royce—also carry very high prestige premiums. There are now enough wealthy consumers in Japan to acount for purchases of about 40,000 units of foreign automobiles each year and American automobiles have garnered a major share of this market segment.

However, in all of the other market segments, foreign products must compete head-on with Japanese products that have been designed, manufactured, and marketed to suit the idiosyncratic user habits of Japanese consumers. Japanese consumers expect their car doors to close tightly without having to be slammed shut. Since they drive on the left-hand side of the street, they want steering wheels to be placed on the right-hand side of the front seat. And Japanese customers are impatient with the slow and unreliable service provided by the marketers of foreign imports. Unlike in luxury product markets in which no meaningful Japanese substitutes exist, there are literally more than a dozen Japanese products in these markets vying with foreign imports for the patronage of Japanese consumers. Any foreign exporter of mass consumer appliances and products would have to revise thoroughly both its marketing strategies and product design to suit the Japanese market.

For instance, it should cost no more than $100 per car to install the steering wheel on the right-hand side of the front seat if this is done while the vehicle is still on the assembly line. If the volume of exports increases, the marginal cost of such a minor adjustment on the production line would be negligible. Japanese automobile exporters perform this type of adjustment routinely on their overseas models. The same reinstallation of the steering wheel, if done after its landing in Japan, can easily cost over $700 per car. Other incremental adjustments also add up to significant price differentials between Japanese and American competitor models, although Japanese import duties on cars are much lower than those levied by the U.S. government.

OUTLOOK FOR THE FUTURE

The beef and orange wars are being resolved between the United States and Japan. The final solutions to these politically sensitive issues will have to come in the form of multilateral free-trade agreements among the key nations of the Pacific Basin community. While the United States should increase its exports of high-grade (hotel grade) beef to Japan, Australia and New Zealand should be able to export mass-market grade beef to both Japan and the United States. If California citrus growers can export their oranges and grapefruits to Japan, then Japan and other Asian nations should also be permitted to export their raw tangerines to the United States. The products complement each other in terms of the timing of their peak seasons and the taste.

Unlike the problems with Japanese import barriers on agricultural products, those with the remaining barriers on ordinary household appliances and consumer products are not legal or political in nature. These barriers can only be resolved through thoughtful application of American exporters' own marketing strategies and product policies. They are able to choose whether they wish to remain only in the luxury market or whether they will confront Japanese competitors head on in the growing mass markets.

Recent studies by the American Chamber of Commerce in Japan, in Tokyo, an organization for American businesses in Japan, underscored this very same point. The studies concluded that even a total elimination of nontariff and tariff trade barriers—which are already miniscule—would not serve to increase American exports of a variety of manufactured goods ranging from industrial equipment to household items. They recommend that American firms become export-minded and that they invest time, money, and managerial attention to tackling the Japanese markets for their long-range gains rather than for short-term profits.

AGGRESSIVE MARKETING OF AMERICAN AGRICULTURAL PRODUCTS IN JAPAN

There are a number of success stories of marketing American agricultural products and consumer products and confectionaries in Japan. The recent success of "boatique America" by which the Sakura Maru floating Expo of the United States visited many Japanese ports and promoted American products indicates that the Japanese mass would love to buy American food items and consumer products. What American exporters have to do is a careful penetration of the Japanese market.

Because of the commitment of the California Marketing Board of Avocado Growers, Avocado was effectively advertised throughout the Japanese metropolitan markets. This mass advertising campaign created a growing primary demand among Japanese consumers for California avocados, which had no Japanese competition or supplement. American grapefruits are now standard items at Japanese fruit and greengrocer stores. Hershey's chocolate bars are hit items in Japan.

With a rapid spread of mass merchandising retail chain stores and convenience stores in Japan, many brands of American household appliances and notions and kitchenwares are imported in an increasing quantity to Japan. American apparel and fashion clothing are also imported to Japan in an increasing quantity. Some Japanese ready-made garment producers even opened their factories and purchase shops in New York and export clothing made in the United States to Japan. There is no reason why more and more American exporters of foods and other consumer items cannot duplicate such export success stories. Their successes will require simply careful merchandising, effective pricing for mass markets, and effective advertisement and distribution policies—those commonsense marketing approaches to any growing mass market in the world.

Yoshi Tsurumi

BIBLIOGRAPHY

Nagashima, Akira. "A Comparison of Japanese and United States Attitudes Toward Foreign Products." *Journal of Marketing*, January 1970.

Exports to Japan by Small Firms

Large companies presumably have an edge in trading with Japan because they can afford the know-how to understand the Japanese market and have the right contacts to get their goods through government restrictions. If this is true, does the small producer or trader have a chance in the Japanese market?

LACK OF EXPORT ORIENTATION BY AMERICAN FIRMS

American firms, both large and small, tend to lack the commitment to exporting held by their Japanese counterparts. In general, the position of export manager is not thought to be as important within many American firms. Even when firms have such a department, personnel turnover is often too frequent for the firm to maintain any lasting business relationships with contacts in foreign markets.

I have asked one hypothetical question to separate groups of Japanese and American executives. This question is: "Suppose your supply situation tightened up and you had to choose between servicing domestic or overseas customers. Which ones would you favor?" Roughly eight out of ten American managers replied that they would naturally favor their American customers. On the other hand, about eight out of ten Japanese managers declared that they would, of course, give preference to foreign customers.

This lack of export orientation permeates American industry from large multinational concerns down to smaller-sized regional manufacturers. Even ostensibly export-oriented firms such as the U.S. "Big Three" automobile manufacturers grudgingly provided only miniscule sales promotion support to their Japanese import agents who participated in the 1979 Auto Show in Japan. Rarely do American manufacturers revise their products to meet special market conditions that exist in Japan.

During the 1980s, American firms of all sizes will need to reorient themselves toward export drives. The nations of the Pacific Basin, in particular, have already become America's leading trading partners. By the end of the 1980s, the combined Gross National Products of Japan and other Pacific Basin countries will exceed that of the United States. In order to capitalize on this trend, American firms will find it necessary to alter their traditional, parochial emphasis on dealing with the Atlantic community.

EXPORTS BY SMALL-SIZED FIRMS

No myth seems more harmful to the future of the U.S. position in the world than the prevailing notion that export and import investment is only for large firms of the Fortune 500 variety. It is true that nearly three-fourths of American exports of manufactured goods are carried out by the large manufacturers. This has led to the misconception that one must be big and powerful in order to be able to export.

This myth, in turn, has created a "mental block" among many small- to medium-sized firms in the United States that has led them to believe export business is from the outset risky and unprofitable. These firms maintain that such routine exporting procedures as transportation, customs clearance, and, above all, the collection of foreign accounts receivable are insurmountable barriers. And this belief perpetuates the mental block on the part of smaller firms with regard to export activities.

In the case of any export market in general, and with regard to Japan in particular, successful exporting requires the exporter, at minimum, to establish a permanent, on-site presence that will enable them to monitor market developments and provide customer service. As we point out elsewhere, the American Chamber of Commerce in Japan recently reconfirmed this obvious point. The Chamber set out to identify the so-called nontariff barriers in Japan that were popularly believed to be hindering American exports to that country. They looked into such generic nontariff barriers as customs clearance procedures, harassment by Japanese government bureaucracy, and the arbitrary evaluations by Japanese customs officials of the landed values of American goods. They concluded, however, that most of these celebrated nontariff barriers had been eliminated for some time and that a total elimination of the remaining routine government procedures would not increase American exports to Japan. Their recommendation was that American firms should strengthen their permanent bases for customer service and market intelligence activities in Japan. Without such a commitment on the part of the management of American firms, they cannot possibly compete with European and Japanese competitors in Japan.

Besides, there are already many success stories of small- to medium-sized American and European companies that export increasing quantities of their products to Japan. When individual exporters are too weak financially and managerially to mount extensive on-site market development, they can pool their resources to generate Japanese consumers' primary demand for their products. In this fashion, German wine, Danish dairy products, California's avocados and citrus fruits have made successful inroads into Japan.

Japanese mass retail chains such as department stores and mass merchandisers routinely import kitchen utensils, bedding, furniture, apparel, and other household items from the United States. In the fields of precision medical instruments, a number of American firms in Orange County, California, have expanded their total sales by exporting their products to Japan.

In order to encourage small- to medium-sized American firms to export their products to Japan, in 1978 Japan sent the Buying Mission to many regional cities of the United States. This mission included the buyers from leading department stores who were ready to deal on the site. This buying mission of Japan was subsequently reciprocated by the American selling mission to Japan that included many representatives of regional chambers of commerce of the United States. Small- to medium-sized firms should take advantage of this kind of opportunity to erase their mental block about engaging in foreign trade.

EXPORT BASES IN JAPAN

Depending on the managerial and financial resources a firm can commit to cultivating and maintaining a share of the Japanese market, a firm may choose from a number of formats and possible scales of operation in setting up their permanent export bases in Japan, ranging from a straightforward import agency agreement with Japanese importers, or even with retail chains and department stores, to the establishment of their own sales subsidiaries, or even manufacturing subsidiaries.

The cost to the foreign firm of developing the know-how for understanding the Japanese market is not great. All that is necessary is to hire one export manager who would invest his time and money in studying the Japanese society and markets. Unlike ten years earlier, there are now available numerous useful, credible guidebooks and other literature in English dealing with Japanese society and markets. Once American firms make their own commitment to examining the Japanese market, there are already a number of credible consultants in Japan who could advise American firms on how best to enter the Japanese market.

AMERICAN SŌGŌSHŌSHA

As has been implied above, however, successful exports to Japan require a sizable sum of money as an initial investment as well as close managerial attention. Even when smaller firms can afford the initial financing costs involved in gaining an understanding of the Japanese market, they may not be able to find managers of appropriately high caliber who can service the Japanese market on their own or exercise effective control over Japanese import agents. Exporting to Japan on an incremental basis could also be on too small a scale to merit any initial investment of funds or managerial attention.

Sōgōshōsha of Japan, Korea, Brazil, and Singapore have thus far resolved similar problems with export barriers faced by their small- to medium-sized manufacturing firms. And Japanese sōgōshōsha and specialty trading firms can help small American exporters to enter Japan.

Canada and the United States are now debating whether or not to create their own sōgōshōsha with the support of the government. A bill has been introduced into the U.S. Congress that would permit the growth of American sōgōshōsha free from undue legal harassment by antitrust litigation, banking regulations, and other industrial regulations. To assist small- to medium-sized American manufacturing firms in exporting their products to Japan, American sōgōshōsha are economically viable ventures.

American sōgōshōsha could then expand their business operations to include the People's Republic of China and other parts of Asia. There are many pockets of business opportunities scattered atomistically throughout the Pacific Basin region. These could be pieced together by American sōgōshōsha for the benefit of their American manufacturer clients.

INTERNATIONAL TRADE FOR SMALL-SIZED FIRMS

We already challenged the myth that you have to be large and powerful to succeed in international trade. In the years ahead during the 1980s, few firms, large or small, can merely hope to survive by envisaging the future as a mere extension of the familiar past. Incremental extrapolation from past practices will court fatal disaster when the world thrusts us into discontinuous shocks into the political and economic fabrics of the world. Take the case of the automobile industry, for instance. If there is still an automobile firm that continues to think of itself as the producer and marketer of the gasoline-powered internal combustion engine, its days will soon be numbered. With the price of gasoline soaring to $5 or even $10 per gallon by 2000, not only the fuel efficiency of the car but more importantly the power (energy) source itself will have to change. People may shift their preference from the privacy of a private passenger car to the economy of a mass transit system.

At any rate, no firm small or large can remain immune to any change that will occur in any corner of the world. Small-sized American firms have for too long made themselves believe that they are there to serve only the regional market of the United States. During the 1980s, if the firm wishes to continue serving the familiar regional market of its own home country, it will have to think multinational. This is because the firm will face increasing foreign competition in its own home territory. At minimum, the firm needs to stay alert for competitive behavior of foreign firms most likely to try to edge out American firms in the United States.

Active involvement of the firm in international export and import provide the following two additional competitive edges. First, the firm can easily stay alert for any changes of market trends and important technology that will occur in any part of the world but will affect the United States profoundly. Exposure to foreign markets provides the exporting firm with diverse market and technological stimuli that prevent the management of the firm from falling behind the time. Second, export-import improves the firm's growth potential because export increases sales and profits and because import increases the supply capabilities of the firm. By importing products that you are not fit to produce, you can tap production design capabilities and production capabilities of foreign firms. By so doing, you can broaden your product lines to your customers in the United States.

The rising income of over 110 million people makes Japan a large market at which you can aim your exports. Japanese consumers' tastes have been Americanized enough to make most American products marketable in Japan. With the rising wages of the Japanese workers, Japanese manufacturing firms are increasingly inclined to adopt many labor-saving devices in which their American counterparts also take a strong interest. These similarities of both consumer and industrial markets between Japan and the United States should help American firms evaluate the export potential of their products to Japan.

This approach can also be reversed. Japan is a good place from which American small- to medium-sized firms can obtain marketable products and technologies for the United States. This import strategy can complement the product lines of American firms and should be an advantage to small- and medium-sized firms that often lack technological and financial abilities to develop new products on their own or to broaden their lines of products by themselves.

ENTRY STRATEGY

No firm is given the birthright to succeed in any market, much less in a foreign market. If there exist barriers to entry, they have to be overcome mainly by export-minded firms' abilities to cope with them.

In Japan, if foreign firms wish to enter the mass market, they must be prepared to meet fierce competition from Japanese firms long entrenched in

Japan. Accordingly, the entry strategy needs to be worked out carefully. Above all, the format of entry and the timing of the entry are the two key factors of success.

At one extreme end of spectrum of the entry format, sales (import) agency agreements with Japanese firms permit American firms to export their products to Japan without much commitment of fund and managerial attention. At the other extreme end, American firms can establish their own fully owned sales subsidiary in Japan that controls the important marketing activities in Japan.

When American firms need manufacturing and other requisite skill to back up their sales activities in Japan, and when these requisite skills cannot be readily transported from the United States or are not readily available in Japan from ordinary sources, many American firms purposely choose the joint-venture manufacturing and sales agreements with Japanese partners. Joint ventures permit American firms not only to share business risks with Japanese firms but to shorten the time required for obtaining necessary business contacts and resources for competing with Japanese competitors.

MYTHS OF NONTARIFF TRADE BARRIERS

American public opinion still lingers about the infamous nontariff trade barriers of Japan. Cumbersome custom-clearance procedures, prohibitive tariff valuations, and strict government regulations about product specifications and performances are often called nontariff trade barriers in addition to outright import quotas. The recent conclusion of Tokyo Round Multilateral Trade Negotiations has already reduced Japan's nontariff trade barriers.

In March 1980, the American automobile industry stated 11 points of Japan's nontariff trade barriers that the industry claimed have inhibited American exports of cars to Japan. Upon checking the list of the grievances submitted by the American automobile industry, six of them were found to have been eliminated completely a long time ago. Two of them were eliminated recently (but long before March 1980). The remaining three complaints turned out to be American auto firms' demands to ease Japan's standards of automobile safety and emission controls, which all the Japanese and European automobile firms in Japan are observing. One executive of a Japanese firm that is doing business with an American automobile firm was quoted by the *Nihon Keizai Shimbun,* a leading journal, as saying, "American executives do not understand why large American cars cannot be sold in Japan. If they produce cars that meet safety and emission standards of Japan, we would not have to worry about remaking their cars at tremendous costs to us . . . ."

Political arguments over the nontariff trade barriers of Japan have been emotionally amplified among American business circles. American business firms that have not been monitoring the Japanese market do not realize that most nontariff trade barriers have practically disappeared for some time. However, some people call the Japanese domestic retailer-wholesaler mazes a nontariff trade barrier that is designed to keep out foreign businesses. The cumbersome distribution channels of Japan are not the product of antiforeigner conspiracy but the remnant of the old Japanese society and mercantile practice. But this is not difficult to master. There are many American firms, small and large, that have successfully penetrated the Japanese markets by utilizing the traditional distribution channels of Japan.

JAPANESE DISTRIBUTION SYSTEMS

American firms are often baffled by Japanese distribution systems. To them the myriads of Japanese distribution systems appear inefficient, archaic, and mysterious. A more important misunderstanding concerns the implicit rules, codes of conduct, and customs that govern manufacturers, wholesalers, and retailers that are thought mistakenly to be discriminatory against foreign firms.

American managers who are familiar with the present distribution systems in the United States no doubt find Japanese distribution systems archaic and irrational. American managers would find that their predecessors from the pre-World War II era and earlier had to cope with many of the distribution systems still found in Japan today. Given the socioeconomic attributes of the Japanese economy in which social obligations between buyers and sellers are often more important than the economic transactions involved, the many distribution channels that often confuse foreigners are indeed very easy to understand.

MULTILAYERS OF DISTRIBUTION SYSTEMS

For about a decade, the number of wholesalers and retailers has not changed much. There are about 250,000 wholesalers and about 1,500,000 retailers for a Japanese population of about 110 million. There are about twice as many wholesalers and retailers in Japan as there are in the United States, which has double the population in a geographical area vastly larger than Japan. More importantly, over 60 percent of the wholesalers have less than nine employees while over 70 percent of the retailers have less than four employees. Each retailer and wholesaler covers small pockets of their markets. Usually, for such mass consumption items as drugs, processed foods, cosmetics, confectioneries, and other sundries, there are five layers of wholesalers and agents between manufacturers and retailers.

Historically, such Japanese socioeconomic attributes as the lack of mass markets, underdeveloped transportation systems, widely scattered markets, and the financially weak retailers and wholesalers have produced many layers of wholesalers and retailers. Japanese households' time-honored habits of making daily purchases in small portions have produced friendly neighborhood shops that are expected to deliver whenever and whatever their customers demand. Since they are too financially weak to build up their own inventories, these scattered retailers have become dependent on many wholesalers who not only store merchandise but also extend working capital financing to their retailer-clients. Their common use of promissory notes with 120 to 210 days of maturity reflects the economic and social interdependency that has evolved between whole-salers and retailers. Ultimately, manufacturers who attempt to manage these groups of distributors end up by absorbing the financial risks that are associated with long collection periods for accounts receivable and with the long inventory turnover.

Manufacturers often send their sales representatives to their key wholesalers and even to retailers at least once a week if not every other day. In the United States, comparable manufacturers might make similar calls once a month at most. Manufacturers and their wholesale agents must be ready to deliver necessary merchandises to their ultimate retailers at the moment of notice. In return, retailers and wholesale agents would steer their businesses to the manufacturers who can fulfill the social and economic needs of small-sized retailers and wholesalers.

MANUFACTURERS' MANAGEMENT OF
DISTRIBUTION CHANNELS

Like their American counterparts, Japanese manufacturers prefer to develop their own exclusive networks of dealers and sales representatives. Japanese manufacturers use such economic incentives as dealer margins, volume discounts, cash rebates, wholesaler and retailer supports, and prompt delivery services. These economic incentives must be combined with the technique of cultivating personal loyalty and close relationships with key wholesalers and retailers. This is needed because the exclusive distribution arrangements between manufacturers and their wholesalers and dealers are socially regarded as the binding relationships of mutual loyalty and obligation. These obligations carry implied and even strong cash value because these exclusive relationships also function as insurance against sudden economic displacement. Small-sized retailers often borrow money from their wholesalers who in turn obtain necessary funds, not from their banks, but from their manufacturer-suppliers.

The group solidarity of the exclusive chains of manufacturers-wholesalers-retailers is maintained also by manufacturers' readiness to service such social needs of their retailers and wholesalers as the training of their employees, their recreational needs (invitations to hot springs, and so forth), and the attending to family matters (e.g., assistance to the family member's funeral). Otherwise, no amount of legal contracts among them would be worth much.

This is why many foreign firms have found it difficult to penetrate Japanese distribution systems. They are pitted against Japanese competitors who have invested time and money to cultivate their own exclusive distribution channels. These manufacturers are extremely hostile to any competitors, whether they be Japanese or foreign, who try to cut into their exclusive domain.

CAN FOREIGN FIRMS CRACK JAPANESE DISTRIBUTION SYSTEMS?

Many new Japanese manufacturers have successfully established and managed their own distribution channels. Of course, they are not overwhelmed by the implicit codes of conduct that govern the distribution channels. They learn to manipulate them. Foreign firms would, then, have to employ Japanese managers who are familiar with the ins and outs of the Japanese distribution channels and permit them to invest both time and funds in building up their own distribution channels.

Of late, the rapid popularity of mass merchandising and mass discount retail chains in Japan has permitted foreign suppliers of diverse consumer goods to enter the Japanese market. Such large retail chains as Daiei, Ito Yokado, and Seiyu are the driving forces behind the distribution revolution that will intensify in the future. Now is the time for foreign firms to start studying the distribution channels of Japan.

Yoshi Tsurumi

BIBLIOGRAPHY

Yoshino, Michael Y. *Marketing in Japan*. New York: Praeger, 1975.

Export Assistance for Foreign Firms

> What kinds of services are provided for firms wanting to enter the Japanese market? How does a firm find out about market trends, government regulations, financing and distribution contacts?

Foreign firms wishing to export their products to Japan have access to an abundance of export assistance. This assistance is available in such abundance, in fact, that their selection, not their availability, could pose problems for foreign firms. Export assistance is available from both Japanese and American governments at nominal or no charge to firms requesting it. In addition, both foreign and Japanese firms can provide export assistance to prospective exporters in a variety of ways.

EXPORT ASSISTANCE: GENERIC KNOW-HOW

Either free of charge or for a nominal fee, one can obtain such generic informational assistance as guides to Japanese government regulations, banking practices, distribution channels, and even a list (directory) of Japanese and foreign firms in Japan. These aids are available from three principal sources.

First, the Japanese government periodically publishes in English and in other foreign languages useful brochures and studies that explain the government's import regulations, general economic conditions in Japan, and marketing practices on the basis of product groups and others. The Japan External Trade Organization (JETRO) is one publisher and distributor of such information. Recently, this organization is also publishing in English several quite useful guidebooks for foreign businesses that are interested in entering the People's Republic of China. The Japan External Trade Organization offices in the United States are located in such major cities as New York, Los Angeles, Chicago, and several other cities. You can easily locate the Japan External Trade Organization offices by contacting the Japanese consular offices nearest you.

Second, the Bank of Tokyo and other Japanese banks publish in English several general guidebooks on export-import financing, foreign exchange transactions, and customs clearance procedures. These materials are promotional in nature, but provide general but useful information at no charge to their prospective clients. If you wish to obtain a listing of Japanese firms classified by their main line of business and location, you can purchase the directories of Japanese and foreign firms operating in

Japan. Nomura Securities and other leading investment bankers publish in English a digest of financial analyses of Japanese firms listed on the Tokyo Stock Exchange.

Third, the U.S. government provides many forms of export assistance to American firms. The U.S. Departments of State and Commerce are the two key cabinet agencies that provide, at a nominal fee, many informational and financial assistances on exporting for American firms. The Overseas Private Insurance Corporation (OPIC), which is affiliated with the U.S. Department of Commerce, even subsidizes overseas study tours for American business managers. In addition, the U.S. Department of Commerce maintains a permanent exhibition room and offices in Tokyo. American businesses can utilize this space to show their products and contact prospective customers in Japan. American businesses can subscribe to periodical market survey information published by both the State and Commerce departments. All that is required is to contact the office of these governmental departments nearest your place of business.

Some American state governments have established permanent offices in Tokyo in an effort to promote the export to Japan of products produced in their states. By contacting your own state office, you would be able to find out whether your state has such an office in Tokyo. Even if it does not have such an office, the commercial attache at the American Embassy in Tokyo may be contacted for assistance. The services of this office to American businesses looking for informational assistance have been improved, and could help an American firm that is interested in the Japanese market.

EXPORT ASSISTANCE: PROPRIETARY KNOW-HOW

After you have familiarized yourself with the general marketing conditions in Japan, and have contacted prospective Japanese importers, your task is to conclude business negotiations successfully (see Chapter 11). Such negotiations often will require a more detailed search of prospective Japanese business partners (importers) and a survey in greater detail of the Japanese market. This proprietary information will have to be purchased.

There are a number of credible marketing and management consulting firms in Japan. They include several leading American and European firms. When you have decided what specific information on Japan you wish to obtain, you can easily contact three or four of these consulting firms and ask them to submit bids to you for their services. You would then select one of them that suits your budget and needs.

EXPORT FINANCING ASSISTANCE

Both Japanese and American banks can provide all necessary services in export financing, including the opening of letters of credit and working capital financing. Additionally, leading American commercial banks can provide international factoring services by which the banks purchase, without recourse to exporters, foreign accounts receivable held by exporters. In this manner, American exporters can minimize the financial risk associated with collection problems in the export sales on credit and fluctuations in foreign exchange rates.

The Export-Import Bank of the United States provides financing for exports of industrial equipment from the United States. One does not have to be a Fortune 500 firm to qualify for this Export-Import Bank financing. If you are concerned about collection risks for intermediate to long-term, deferred-payment exports, you can take out collection insurance from the Foreign Credit Insurance Corporation (FCIC) of the United States. This is a syndicated consortium of 25 leading insurance firms in the United States, and is backed up by the Export-Import Bank.

Also, if you are concerned about the cumbersome requirements for bonding of your demonstration merchandise at the Japanese Customs Office, you can take out in advance the CARNET arrangement (reads "Kar-nay," the certificate of pre-bond posting), with the International Chamber of Commerce in New York. The CARNET signatory nations include Japan, and the arrangement will permit you to deposit a customs bond with the International Chamber of Commerce of your own country, thereby avoiding the cumbersome procedure of having to post a customs bond at each port of entry when you visit foreign countries.

MARKET INTELLIGENCE WORK

Contrary to what is generally believed, there are many useful market information services that you can obtain either at no cost or at a nominal fee. Japanese and American banks provide various types of export financing assistance. International transportation and customs clearance services are provided by Japanese and American air cargo lines, shipping firms, and freight forwarders. Still, many American firms remain unresponsive to growing market opportunities in Japan.

As discussed elsewhere, virtually the only remaining roadblock to successful American exports to Japan is the lack of commitment of American firms to carrying out export drives. To be able to take advantage of various informational and financial services available from outside sources, prospective American exporters will have to employ at least one export manager whose primary objective is to study the Japanese market and draw up a strategy for monitoring developments in the Japanese market.

To give your export manager the kind of backing he will need, you will need to ensure that the top leadership of your firm, including the chief executive officer, take a strong, personal interest in exporting to Japan. It is also of vital importance that this commitment on the part of management be communicated clearly to all employees and managers throughout your firm.

RELEVANT THEORY OF INTERNATIONAL TRADE

In order to monitor the Japanese (foreign) market, you need a coherent and relevant theoretical paradigm with which you can observe dynamic flows of international trade. In international trade of manufactured goods, the relevant theoretical paradigm is the Product Life Cycle Theory of International Trade and Investment. In fact, many Japanese firms have developed instinctive grasp of the business policy implications of this theory and applied it successfully to their exports.

New products developed to meet the needs of one market, say, the United States, spread to other nations, just as the new product of an innovatve firm subsequently spreads to imitating competitors within the same nation-market. How soon imitators, both at home and abroad, can copy the innovator depends mainly on their technological and financial competence.

In the domestic market where new products are developed, the products go though the life cycle from introductory phase (infancy) to growth and then to final maturity. As the market demand characteristics of the product change from new innovation to mature and standard products, sellers of the products cannot count on their non-price competitive edges such as brand appeal, novelty of the products, and quality edge over competitors'. As a product matures in the market, purchasers are becoming increasingly conscious of the price of the product available at convenient shopping places. By this time, the manufacturing technology of the product is spreading throughout the world. As American purchasers of the products become conscious of their price and easy availability, suppliers with low cost production and with mass supplying capabilities will eventually dominate the market. In fact, as a product becomes standard in a given market, the mass merchandising abilities of its manufacturer becomes a crucial competitive factor. And the location of production facilities can now be separated geographically from the markets.

If an American manufacturer begins to lose its American market position to European and Japanese and other foreign producers, the viable defensive responses are essentially threefold. It can either upgrade major product lines to more innovative products and sell sales skills and customer services. Or it can overhaul its production facilities in the United States to obtain an economy of scale of production. Or it can purchase standard products from lower-cost suppliers abroad and market them through its own distribution channels in the United States.

Nowadays, many Japaneese firms have become so thoroughly familiar with the American market and have developed so extensively their own marketing contacts that they often introduce new products first in the U.S. market and then ride the international flows of product cycle to Japan and then to the rest of the world. Besides, as the income level of Japan and the United States closes its gap, the Japanese market has taken on many economic and social attributes that have hitherto been considered unique to the United States: namely high income and mass consumption, and preference for labor-saving devices and convenience. This means that American firms will have to monitor the Japanese market very carefully during the 1980s for potential export opportunities as well as for potential competitors from Japan.

Yoshi Tsurumi

BIBLIOGRAPHY

Tsurumi, Yoshi. *Multinational Management*. Cambridge, Mass.: Ballinger, 1977.

11

SOCIAL RELATIONS AND JAPANESE BUSINESS PRACTICES

The foreign businessman entering into negotiations with Japanese counterparts is entering into another culture, just as the Japanese counterparts themselves are experiencing contact with practices different from their own. Assumptions about proper interpersonal behavior are different, and the whole process of business contacts is predicated upon a different value system. This does not mean that European or American businessmen cannot get along with Japanese. But knowing how Japanese behave, what they believe, and what their expectations are can help a great deal in smoothing interpersonal contacts and business discussions.

As Yoshi Tsurumi points out, friendships in Japan are usually lifelong ties. They are not a casual matter. Nor are they the product of a meeting that lasts only a few minutes such as those after which many Americans immediately proceed into a first-name basis "fictive friendship" with their counterparts in business. Friendships for Japanese more often than not begin with shared experiences during youth. These ties of an almost brotherly nature go on through life and are renewed through sustained contact and socialization at various points in time. To be a friend in Japan involves a commitment to support each other when there are problems and stress on the job or in home life. The bond is deep and ideally is selfless. Because of the deeper and more permanent nature of friendship in Japan— which is not totally unlike that in Europe, despite the obvious differences in culture—foreigners in Japan or meeting Japanese should not assume that acquaintanceships will develop with the same speed they do in one's native culture. Still friendships can and do form between Japanese and foreigners where both partners are understanding and not explotive in their approach and where the foreigner recognizes the slower time dimension involved in Japanese social ties.

Negotiating with Japanese counterparts involves some of the sensitivities appropriate to making friends Japanese style. Japanese business negotiations are ideally conducted on the basis of long-standing relationships of mutual trust. They are not legalistic and formalistic. They involve understanding of both semantic subtleties, wherein real motivations may be concealed behind overt behavior and talk that could imply other substance. They also involve adjustment to the time-consuming Japanese process of talking things over slowly until full mutual understanding of all parties' motivations and assumptions emerges. These and other aspects of business negotiations with Japanese counterparts are discussed by Tsurumi in terms of a series of "dos" and "don'ts" to be avoided in such relationships.

Negotiation with businessmen in Japan inevitably involves after-hours social contact where Japanese practices may be somewhat different than those in the foreigner's home country. Japanese usually do not bring their wives to social events involving other businessmen, and the foreigner in Japan who brings his spouse to evening parties with Japanese counterparts may face some embarrassing situations. Drunkenness and flirting with bar hostesses is condoned among some Japanese businessmen to a degree probably not typically accepted in Europe or the United States (perhaps American convention behavior is the best point for comparison)! There are also certain protocols in Japan that must be kept in mind for relationships to go smoothly: tipping is much less common in Japan than in the United States and Europe, and is done only where extraordinary services are rendered or a long-term relationship exists, such as at a restaurant or bar normally frequented by the Japanese host. Japanese are also great gift givers in most social relationships, including those between businessmen, and reciprocal gift giving demonstrates extra thoughtfulness on the part of both partners and often helps provide the warmth and trust necessary to effective relationships in Japan.

Negotiations with Japanese Firms

Some Western businessmen say it is very hard to negotiate with Japanese. There are many subtle things which Westerners don't understand. Just what are some of the major "rules" of negotiations Japanese style and some of the areas of misunderstanding of these matters between Japanese and Westerners?

There is nothing mysterious about negotiating with Japanese businessmen. All of the rules you would normally apply in negotiations with your fellow American businessmen would be equally applicable in doing business in Japan. However, I have been investigating for some time the causes of the dismal failures of some business negotiations between Japanese and foreign (American) businessmen and have found that those failures stemmed overwhelmingly from eight principal points of miscommunication between Japanese and foreign negotiators. But the end result is the same: negotiations were not concluded successfully.

CAUSE #1:
SLICING THE PIE BEFORE IT IS BAKED

The uneasiness of foreigners regarding the hidden intentions of their Japanese counterparts is heartily reciprocated by the Japanese themselves. These hidden suspicions make for a predisposition by both parties from the outset to become preoccupied with safeguarding their respective control over the dividing up and resultant shares of the ecoonomic pie that both sides are supposedly meeting to bake together but has not yet been produced. Once this sort of adversary relationship enters into the negotiations, little hope remains for reaching a successful conclusion. Even when a fragile agreement is reached formally, it may be doomed to failure if it lacks the mutual trust between the two parties that is vital for an amicable implementation of the agreement.

The remedy for this is simple. Foreign negotiators can easily maintain the initiative in the negotiations while at the same time enhancing their personal trust with their Japanese counterparts by first concentrating on working together with the Japanese to arrive at a clear-cut understanding of what they can achieve only by working together and not on their own. The rest falls into place as both parties grow more aware of each other's contribution to their joint deal.

CAUSE #2:
SELLING THE DEAL, AND NOT THE SELLER

No American would enter into an agreement with a fellow American who seemed to be untrustworthy. This rule of human relations needs to be expanded by an order of ten when negotiating with the Japanese. The Japanese must be convinced that you are trustworthy, just as you have the right to expect the Japanese to prove themselves to you.

Unlike in the United States, where legalistic and contractual bondings are prevalent in business relationships, personal trust between negotiators is one major guarantee in Japan that business agreements will be honored by each firm. Accordingly, Japanese negotiators instinctively attempt to assess whether their foreign counterparts are well respected by peers and superiors within their firm and whether their foreign counterparts are individually trustworthy to do business with.

Haste on the part of a foreigner to sell a specific deal before selling himself is often interpreted by the Japanese as the sign of a small person with whom dealing would be too risky. To avoid this unfortunate stereotyping by the Japanese, foreigners should at least take the following two precautions. First, they should obtain a very good introduction to the executives of their targeted Japanese firms, preferably by Japanese or foreign executives who have successfully done business with the targeted firm in the past. Japanese banks and trading companies can often provide such introductions. Second, before they explain the specific business deal they have in mind, they should first take time to introduce themselves, their educational and vocational background, their family heritage (perhaps even including who their grandfathers were), and their position and functions within their firm. The tone of this personal "sales pitch" could be likened to that which is often employed at social gatherings in the United States in getting to know an interesting stranger of the opposite sex on a personal basis.

The Japanese attitude toward the business negotiation is very personal in that the negotiation is merely one process to test their counterparts' trustworthiness. On the other hand, the American attitude toward the negotiation tends to be very legalistic in that the negotiation process is a legal sparring to make as many points as possible with their opponents. Thus, Americans often assume that nothing is binding until the final signing of the detailed legal documents. Any agreements that are reached in the process of negotiations are assumed to be subject to subsequent changes as the new phases of the negotiation unfold new circumstances.

This is why Japanese negotiators often see American counterparts try to change promises and agreements reached the day before. To most Japanese who are not familiar with the American legalistic attitude toward the business negotiation, this sudden reversal of American positions unfortunately signals the untrustworthiness of American negotiators. The only way to avoid such unfortunate misunderstandings would be to set the negotiation rule from the outset that permits both parties to change any interim promises and agreements until the final agreement. Please do not assume that the other side would understand your position and rule.

CAUSE #3:
IGNORING THE HIDDEN ECONOMICS OF
JAPANESE BUSINESS RELATIONSHIPS

When American managers attempt to sell their products or services, they are prone to speak to their prospective customers only in narrow economic terms of such product- or service-specific variables as price, delivery, quality, or sales promotion. This narrow view of things will suffice in simple over-the-counter deals. But in negotiating with Japanese businesses, they should be more sensitive to such hidden but nevertheless vital economic factors as whether the deal in question will require Japanese businessmen to alter their business relationships with other Japanese firms.

What to an uninitiated foreigner might seem a simple supplier-client relationship often masks important considerations such as an outside supplier's cumulative favors to its client through its hiring of surplus or retired employees of the client firm. As a result, a narrow economic advantage such as price or quality differences between your product and that of a Japanese competitor may have to be extremely distinctive to motivate your prospective Japanese clients to forego the hidden benefits associated with their existing relationships with other Japanese firms.

CAUSE #4:
LETTING LAWYERS IN ON YOUR NEGOTIATIONS

Of course, some lawyers are superb practicing business executives. But with the exception of a case in which a foreign businessman who happens to be a lawyer is acting as a bona fide business executive, lawyers should be kept out of business negotiations in Japan. You can consult with them privately to check on the legal parameters of your business deals. But the presence of a lawyer in the negotiations will convey the unfortunate message that you do not trust your Japanese counterpart and that you are not sure of yourself as a negotiator.

In Japan, lawyers become involved only in those serious civil or criminal disputes that are beyond normal resolution by reasonable-minded adults. The feeling an ordinary Japanese might have in consulting a lawyer is akin to the sense of guilt and shame he might feel in consulting a dermatologist for treatment of certain unmentionable social diseases.

Besides, lawyers are trained to anticipate and defuse potential problems that their clients might encounter. Accordingly, their advice could be likely to steer you into the kind of adversary bargaining we have already identified as Cause #1 for the frequent failures of American negotiations in Japan.

CAUSE #5:
LACK OF SEMANTIC SENSITIVITY

Unfortunately, there are still too few American business executives who possess even a rudimentary knowledge of the Japanese language, not to mention a crucially important sensitivity to the Japanese mode of interpersonal relationships and communication. American firms desiring to establish lasting business relations with Japan would benefit considerably from the development of a cadre of their own managers and specialists who are well versed in the Japanese language and culture. Until this happens, however, American business managers or government officials who negotiate with Japanese firms or government ministries should stay alert for three typical areas of miscommunication between Japanese and American negotiators.

First, the implied meaning of the Japanese phrase which is translated as "in principle" (*gensoku to shite*) is the opposite of the English meaning. If your Japanese negotiators agree to a certain point "in principle" that is tantamount to their declaring that they will abide by it 90 percent of the time (the remaining 10 percent being subject to acts of God). I have seen situations in which American negotiators nearly blew an entire deal merely because of their mental block against the Japanese use of the phrase 'in principle." Second, the same holds true for the Japanese interpretation of "gentleman's agreement." In a society in which one's trustworthiness (gentlemanliness) carries high social and economic value, a gentleman's agreement—especially one which is witnessed by a respected third party—is, again, almost unbreakable. Third, Japanese have a tendency to say "*hai, hai*" (yes, yes), or the equivalent of "I understand," or even "I agree," while they are listening to you. These phrases merely mean that they are listening to you and that they understand your positions. Semantic miscommunication is often compounded by an innate Japanese propensity to avoid saying "no" directly. Instead of saying "no," they prefer to say "I will consider it." This makes it difficult for you as a negotiator to distinguish between their actual, serious intention to consider your proposal and a polite, but firm refusal. At a time like this you might rely on a trustworthy third party to find out for you. The judicious use of a third party is a basic skill you will need to master. Often, the individuals who gave you a good introduction to your prospective Japanese clients are able to act as a third party for you.

CAUSE #6:
INSISTING ON DETAILED DISCUSSIONS
WITH HIGH-LEVEL EXECUTIVES

In Japanese firms, the degree to which de facto authority to formulate strategic decisions is delegated to middle-echelon executives is usually far greater than in American firms. High-level executives in Japanese firms are often present at negotiations only to arbitrate various decisions recommended by their middle-level management personnel, and often do not carry overly impressive formal job titles. Many American negotiators overlook this factor and insist upon negotiating on details with their "formal" Japanese counterparts, to the latter's inordinate sense of discomfort.

CAUSE #7:
RUSHING THE NEGOTIATIONS

With the exception of instances in which a sense of urgency is already shared by your Japanese counterparts, there is no use in rushing through the negotiation process. Americans often complain that it takes an eternity for the Japanese to make up their minds on something. In turn, Japanese often complain that it takes Americans forever to implement decisions once they have been mutually agreed upon. It is standard Japanese business practice not to finalize a decision unless its implementation is also ensured and prepared for in advance. This is why your Japanese counterparts often need time to contact key bases within their firm and prepare their colleagues to help implement the deal emerging between you and them.

At the same time, you need to educate your Japanese negotiating counterparts so that they will fully understand that decision making is often separated from implementation in American firms. To avoid any distrust that may arise through mutual ignorance of respective corporate cultures, you should budget ample time for concluding negotiations with Japanese firms. You cannot hope to wrap it all up in just a few days. As your negotiation makes positive progress, it would be advisable to work out a timetable with your Japanese counterparts for implementation of the deal. In this way you would also ascertain what will need to be done to prepare your colleagues back home so that they can help you implement the new business decisions.

CAUSE #8:
ASSUMING LASTING STABILITY
OF THE AGREEMENT

Even in a marriage, it cannot simply be assumed that the relationship between husband and wife will always be peaceful, loving, or, least of all, everlasting. Neither can one take another for granted. If a marriage is to be long-lasting and mutually gratifying, one must work at it and be on guard to resolve any difficulties as they arise.

It is therefore rather strange for Japanese and foreign negotiators to enter into a business agreement without working out in advance the procedures and criteria by which their mutual relationship will be reviewed on a periodic basis. Some liken joint-venture agreements to marriage. Actually, they are more akin to contractual cohabitation. The needs of the parties change over time. According to my research findings on questions of stability in joint ventures, I have to conclude that there are inherent instabilities in any joint venture, let alone one between Japanese and foreign business partners.

In order to ensure the stability of your business agreements with Japanese partners, you would be well advised to agree on procedures and criteria for periodic review of the arrangement once the initial agreements for your business deals are concluded. With the establishment of formal procedures for such reviews, you can also handle your own corporate politics that might at least imply an evaluation of your predecessors who were involved in the initial agreements pertaining to the business deals.

The eight above-mentioned causes are quite commonsensical and straightforward. And yet, one American negotiator after another ignores them. This is often because they program themselves mentally for failure by convincing themselves that there are certain "mysterious" tricks to negotiating with the Japanese. They forget to act sensibly, thus sowing the seeds of their own eventual failure.

Yoshi Tsurumi

BIBLIOGRAPHY

Tsurumi, Yoshi. *Multinational Management*. Cambridge, Mass.: Ballinger, 1977.

Dos and Don'ts of Japanese Etiquette

Any country has its "dos" and "don'ts" of social etiquette. If a foreigner wants to observe Japanese customs in his relations with Japanese business counterparts what are some of the things he should keep in mind as far as everyday etiquette is concerned?

Since 1868, Japan has transformed herself from an agrarian and feudalistic society to a leading industrial and democratic country. This transformation has been brought about by Japan's successful assimilation and adaptations of legal, political, educational, economic, cultural and social institutions and mores that Japan transplanted selectively from England, Germany, France, and the United States. Japanese businesses of the post-World War II period have carefully studied American business practices, in particular, and adapted them to the Japanese scene so thoroughly that American business managers today find their Japanese counterparts following much of the same business and social etiquette that Americans follow.

In order to impress Japanese businessmen, therefore, foreigners only have to behave the same way as they would behave in dealing with well-educated and cultured American, British, and European businessmen. The social values that are still strongly held among Japanese businessmen, young and old, are the time-honored Japanese versions of values such as "frugality," "diligence," and "social respectability," and these are much akin to similar values in the Judeo-Christian tradition. In fact, one can make a strong case that Japan's assimilation of many Western forms of legal, economic, and other institutions and mores was facilitated by Japan's sharing similar social values as her Western mentors.

Of course, the Japanese are not without their own subtle idiosyncrasies, idiosyncrasies that occasionally baffle and embarrass foreigners dealing with their Japanese business counterparts in informal social settings. The following pointers might be useful to foreigners doing business in Japan.

POINT #1:
STAG OUTING

Although much American socializing is done in male-and-female paired couples, the Japanese definitely practice "stag only" or "business-relations only" rules for social activities. Japanese and foreign female professionals are included in "stag" outings or dinners but they are also expected to come without their dates, as equally individualistic and independent professionals should.

This tends to create problems for foreign businessmen who bring their wives with them on their business trips to Japan. As more and more Japanese become aware of the "pairing culture" of western society, they often gladly extend dinner and other social invitations to the wives of foreign businessmen. But the Japanese hosts will come stag almost invariably. If the social occasions are likely to digress or expand into informal business shop talk, foreigners would be well advised to go without their spouses or dates. Also, after-hours socializing in Japan often extends well into the night, in seemingly endless hoppings from one dining and wining spot to another.

Your Japanese hosts are simply displaying the typical behavior of the all-male "night tribe" (*gozensama*), a "tribe" composed of businessmen who return home only in the wee small hours of the morning. Their wives often sit up late waiting for the return of their past-midnight husbands. In Japan, the notion that business is very much a male domain is still unchallenged. Foreigners who insist on getting together socially with their "Mr. and Mrs. Japanese counterparts" are often politely evaded.

POINT #2:
DINING OUT

Unlike American homes, Japanese homes are usually exclusively for family members, relatives, and close friends. Accordingly, Japanese businessmen would rather invite their foreign counterparts out to restaurants and clubs for social entertainment. In addition, very few Japanese businessmen feel that their homes are worthy to show to important foreign visitors. They are being honest when they humbly apologize for not inviting you to their homes, even though their excuses usually sound rather lame.

Knowing that Americans particularly appreciate being invited to private homes, some Japanese take pride in bringing their foreign guests home. However, foreign guests are likely to discover the host's wife spending almost the entire time either in the kitchen or in serving foods and drinks to the guests and host alike. There is no use appealing to the host and his wife that both of them should join the party for this is often the way things are done in Japan.

POINT #3:
GIFT EXCHANGE

Japanese hosts often shower foreigners with many personal gifts. Chances are that foreigners will be presented with gifts specifically meant for their spouses back home. Many Westerners feel put on the spot by this Japanese generosity and wonder if they are obligated to reciprocate. Furthermore, often gifts turn out to be awkward. They may be too big to fit into an already packed suitcase or the special color and style of a gift for a businessman's wife might not be the sort that appeals to American women.

Well, you do not need to feel embarrassed about such gifts. Your Japanese hosts reap sufficient psychological rewards when they see their important foreign guests genuinely appreciate the gifts. All you have to do is send your Japanese hosts sincere notes of thanks once you return home. As your personal acquaintance with your Japanese hosts grows, and as you have a chance to visit them again in Japan, you might pick up, at the airport duty-free shop, a bottle of whiskey or a carton of cigarettes as your personal gift to them. If your Japanese hosts happen to come and visit you in your home country, that might be a good time to reciprocate their generosity, not necessarily by expensive gifts but by entertaining them the same way you would entertain your own good friends.

POINT #4:
NO TIPPING

Japan is one of the few countries where tipping has not yet contaminated the masses. Neither Japanese nor foreigners are expected to leave tips for any service personnel including taxi driver, doormen, hotel bellboys, waiters, hairdressers, and others. Your Japanese hosts prefer to retain their practice of no tipping. Foreigners' cooperation would be appreciated.

Likewise, foreigners cannot hope to grease their ways around through heavy tipping or suggestions of personal kickbacks to their Japanese business counterparts. Nor can they hope to wiggle their way out of traffic violations or other infractions by paying off policemen. Recently one American businessman was arrested and jailed in Tokyo when he attempted to bribe a traffic policeman into forgetting the small traffic violation committed by the foreigner's cab driver. The bewildered foreigner bemoaned, "Back home, that's the way we fix traffic tickets."

POINT #5:
DIETARY PROBLEMS

For whatever reasons, religious or otherwise, you might have strict dietary habits that forbid many ingredients of Japanese foods. Even if you do not follow strict observances, you might be repelled by the very mention of such esoteric food items as raw shrimps, boiled octopus tentacles, cuttle fish filet, barbecued eels, and other delicacies.

Unfortunately, many Japanese are rather insensitive to some foreigners' strict observance of certain dietary habits; however, once you tell your hosts, they are very cooperative. It is no problem for them to exclude a number of ingredients from your dishes. If you do not like the shrimps that usually come with "tempura" (deep-fried), you can have them replaced by additional vegetables or other seafood ingredients.

If you do not have any strict reasons for avoiding certain dietary ingredients but you still feel timid about trying out something you do not know, all you have to say is that you do not wish to be told the biological or botanical names of "typical Japanese ingredients" until you have had your chance to form your own opinions about them. Many foreigners have already turned themselves into avid fans of such esoteric Japanese delicacies as puffer (blowfish) and eel skin merely because they did not find out what they were eating prior to their actual tryouts.

POINT #6:
BAR HOSTESSES AND PUBLIC DRUNKENNESS

You will often be taken to night clubs and bars where stag customers are entertained by bar hostesses. Japanese call these ladies "butterflies of the night" (*yoru no chō*). They are not prostitutes, however. They may well be Japanese adaptations of traditional geisha hostesses to modern situations where Japanese-style rooms and entertainment are replaced by somewhat vulgar Western-style settings, music, and dance. Nowadays, there are many foreign butterflies of the night in Japan from Europe, other parts of Asia, the United States, and Latin American and Africa working side by side with the Japanese butterflies.

Japanese are often unable to comprehend why some foreigners feel uncomfortable in such settings because the Japanese hosts do not consider their "professional and light flirting" with butterflies of the night as immoral or as psychological cheating on their wives or fiancees. Foreign wives are often taken to night clubs and bars along with their husbands although Japanese hosts invariably come stag. Under these circumstances, a foreigner's discomfort is sometimes doubled because his wife feels quite out of place. The best solution is to have a quick drink and enjoy a floor show or two, and then to tell your Japanese hosts that you would like to return to your hotel to nurse your lingering jet lag. Just mark time and enjoy yourself as much as you can. Under no circumstances should you try to pass moral judgement on your Japanese hosts who might suddenly display dazzling talents for disco dancing with one butterfly after another.

The Japanese are expected to be tolerant of such settings as well as with the frequent end results of such settings, namely, public drunkenness. You may have heard that the Japanese have developed special settings for every type of behavior. Most of the time in their daily lives, they are expected to observe a strict code of conduct, containing their anger, frustration, and even their joy. However, bars, night clubs, or street drinking stands are places where it is socially permitted to display the feelings that they worked hard to contain during the daytime.

In fact, drunkenness is a socially acceptable excuse for the Japanese to say and do things that they could not say or do while they are sober. When they have a burning complaint about their boss, many Japanese set up a drinking outing with their boss and then, under the safe pretense of being drunk, become very frank and open with him. Even if this sometimes leads to a fist fight, any act that is committed while drunk is expected to be forgiven.

You might see a number of Japanese drunks late at night at train stations and inside subways. Do not think that they are bums, however. In the daytime, they may well be your respectable counterparts. Again, without passing moral judgement on them, simply accept them.

Yoshi Tsurumi

BIBLIOGRAPHY

Vogel, Ezra. *Japan's New Middle Class*. Berkeley: University of California Press, 1967.

Friendships with Japanese Counterparts

Many Westerners dealing with Japanese companies say they never get to know their Japanese counterparts. Others say they get along very well, and make friends among the Japanese businessmen they have met. What are the bases for friendship between Japanese and Americans, and what kinds of customs might be involved in social relations between Japanese businessmen and their Western counterparts that Westerners might not understand?

FRIENDSHIPS AMONG JAPANESE MEN

Elsewhere in this book we have already discussed the social mores for Americans dealing with their Japanese counterparts in Japan. If Americans wish to further develop their business relationships with Japanese into friendships, they must first find out how friendships develop among Japanese men.

Major daily newspapers such as *Nihon Keizai, Asahi, Yomiuri,* and *Mainichi* often carry sidebars written by leading business executives and professionals about their friends. Any survey of these columns would reveal that their lasting friendships with their peers were invariably developed during their college days when they were in their late teens and early twenties. Occasionally, you may hear someone talking with his close friends about the time they spent together in the now defunct Imperial Army and Navy of Japan. Rarely do close friends include those outside their peer group in the same age category. It is even more unusual for Japanese men to have close friends among their business contacts. Few contacts acquired after their college years develop into lasting friendships. These relationships remain at least those of close acquaintances, and are never quite the same as relationships that come under the concept of friendship.

These observations should point out two dominant characteristics common among Japanese men. First, a strong notion of social hierarchy and an age consciousness often prevents men of different age groups and of different social and educational backgrounds from becoming very good friends. Second, business friendships develop for pragmatic reasons and from a consciousness of mutual utility rather than from genuine interest. Accordingly, it would take many years of reciprocal business favors before business could acquire the mutual admiration and loyalty akin to true friendship.

The Japanese distinguish between "friends" (*tomodachi*) and "bosom friends" (*shinyu*). The former is almost the same as a close acquaintance while the latter refers to a true and deep bondage of friendship between two individuals. This is mainly because the notion of shinyu requires the two individuals to enter into a lifelong psychological contract of selfless mutual support (unlimited sense of obligation) for each other's welfare. This commitment is ultimate and is broken only at tremendous psychological and social cost to the individuals involved.

Japanese society is still very much interwoven with cumulative interlockings of diverse personal obligations. Unlike some other Western or Islamic country where a strong, political ideology or religious belief binds its population, the social stability and cohesiveness of Japan rests upon the deep-seated notion that the ancestors of the Japanese were all blood relatives to one another. This tribal mythology has survived well into post-industrial society.

People's sharing of this notion produces two opposite but equally strong reactions when they meet fellow strangers who are Japanese. At one level, the Japanese involved feel close to one another and believe that they have to be good to one another, since their ancestors might have been related. Even if they are not part of the same family, their relatives or good friends might be. When two or three Japanese men meet they immediately begin to probe each other's background, where they were born, which schools they attended, how old they are, and whether they have mutual friends or acquaintances. The Japanese rationalize this behavior by the popular saying that "even touching the sleeves of passers-by happens because they were related in the 'herebefore' [in the world prior to the present life]."

At another level, however, the Japanese prefer to avoid adding new friendships to their crowded mental ledger of complicated personal relationships. The Japanese fear that their sudden and untimely discovery that new individuals may be remote relatives or friends of their friends might complicate their ability to meet their many interpersonal obligations. Accordingly, they often tend to be very cool and sometimes rude to strangers unless they are properly introduced by respectable mutual acquaintances. The young man who pushes you aside in the elevator may suddenly become your devoted "friend" as soon as he discovers you are a close acquaintance of his friend or boss. This should not surprise you. This young man is not a hypocrite. But before he learned your connection to his life, you were a total stranger to him. Since he had no great desire to incur another interpersonal obligation, he felt most comfortable keeping you at a distance.

SHARED EXPERIENCE AS A BASIS FOR FRIENDSHIP

Japanese close personal relationships develop mainly from shared experience, rather than from common values or religious beliefs. If this shared experience is not directly related to the "give-and-take" common to ordinary business contacts, it is likely to provide the basis for close friendship. It is no surprise, therefore, that Japanese men often find their close friends only among their school-day acquaintances. School days are the time when they not only study together and help one another but can also vividly relate such shared experiences to the social and academic context.

Japanese describe this common experience as "eating out of the same rice cooker" (*onaji kama no meshiu o tabeta*). This basis of sharing experience is not racial but circumstantial. Furthermore, in order to maintain friendships based on shared experiences, small groups of individuals who are bound by their shared experience strive hard to rejuvenate regularly their past shared experience. It is not an accident, therefore, that Japanese men often form small social groupings consisting of close friends from their school days. They regularly meet to reminisce about the good old days. If a man fails to participate in such social gatherings for too long, the other members would feel that he no longer belonged. This practice of "out of sight, out of mind" often develops into a kind of social ostracism by the rest of the group.

THE BASIS FOR FRIENDSHIP
BETWEEN JAPANESE AND AMERICANS

It is not any easier for Americans to turn the utility-focused relationships of American business contacts into true friendships than it is for them to cultivate true friendships with Japanese business contacts. If you wish to have more than just business relationships with your Japanese counterparts, however, you have to practice the following two steps.

First, just as you would do with your fellow Americans, you first have to prove yourself to be an unselfishly motivated, interesting, and sincere individual seeking genuine human relationships away from business contacts. It will naturally take you more time to develop this kind of personal relationship with your Japanese counterparts. The English language difficulties of your Japanese acquaintances might limit how soon and how deeply you can convey your true personal feelings. Over a period of time, however, you will begin to develop true empathy with your Japanese counterparts.

Second, since the Japanese value highly as preludes to true friendship shared experience away from workday life, you should participate in all kinds of after-hour sharing. Strange as it may sound, bathing together in Japanese communal hot baths is one common way to create such an encounter. The Japanese have the sayings that both noble lords and their servants take a bath naked. This Japanese notion of egalitarianism has well survived into the postindustrial society. You should not be embarrassed about this since this is no more strange or queer than some Westerners' habit of sharing a hot steam bath or sauna bath.

Besides, it is almost a cult for the Japanese to take a hot bath either alone or in a group. It goes well beyond the simple notion of washing and sanitizing their body. This is why some Japanese suggest their family guests take a bath. Foreigners' instinctive reaction in silence is often, "Do I smell?" The Japanese hosts have prepared a hot bath and offered their honored guests the coveted privilege of taking it first.

If it is not convenient to take a hot bath together, you have to help your Japanese hosts and acquaintances to break down such artificial barriers as differences in hierarchical ranks and ages between you and your Japanese acquaintances. Chances are that you might be perceived by your Japanese hosts as important and noble individuals well above such human frailty as getting drunk together or doing harmless but silly things together. This might happen when your Japanese acquaintances suddenly break into even bawdy popular songs at singing bars during social outings together. They are watching you whether you are open-minded enough to endure calmly or even enjoy such silly acts. If you join them in hamming the tune, you accomplished the same effect as taking a hot bath naked together. You have just shared the experience of breaking down social and hierarchical distance between you and your Japanese counterparts.

Of course, you do not have to overdo sharing the silly acts or the cult of taking a hot bath. The important thing is that you would help your Japanese acquaintances to prepare repeatedly the circumstances of sharing the social and work experience on a person-to-person basis. Your shared experience of working long hours together and trying to understand each other's problems would naturally prepare both of you to develop mutual trust. When this happens, you are one step closer to developing lasting friendship with your Japanese counterparts.

Unlike the relationships between two Japanese male individuals, the age difference between American and Japanese acquaintances should not pose a serious psychological barrier to the development of mutual friendship. The strong age consciousness of the Japanese men is less likely to be carried into their relationships with foreigners who live outside the strong social codes of conduct of the Japanese society.

STEREOTYPES AS POSITIVE IMAGE BUILDERS

The Japanese have developed both negative and positive stereotypes about Americans just as Americans have developed both negative and positive stereotypes about the Japanese. You can simply break negative stereotypes by presenting convincing counterexamples. Accordingly, by demonstrating your genuine interest in the Japanese way of life and culture, you can easily break one strong negative stereotype that the Japanese have developed about Americans. Americans are usually assumed to be insensitive to the feelings of other people, to foreign cultures in general, and to Japanese culture in particular.

Unfortunately, however, some Japanese have developed another stereotype about Americans. They say that some Americans are trying to out-Japanese the Japanese by displaying too uncritical a fascination with such aspects of traditional Japanese culture as Kabuki (traditional theater), tea ceremony, shrine (shintoism), and temple (Buddhism). If you want to be accepted favorably as an individual, you should exploit these extreme Japanese stereotypes about Americans. This can be easily done if you demonstrate your keen interest in the Japanese culture. But you should not overdo this by asking your Japanese hosts to explain in detail anything about Kabuki, tea ceremony, flower arrangement, shinto shrine, or Buddhist temples. Few Japanese possess sufficient analytical knowledge of the traditional culture and religion of Japan to be able to intelligently describe them even in Japanese, much less in English to Americans. You can easily read up on these subjects for yourself and convey your interest in Japanese culture casually to your Japanese hosts.

There are a number of positive stereotypes that the Japanese hold about Americans. Americans are assumed to be friendly, carefree, and informal. These stereotypes permit you to take the initiative in breaking the ice with your Japanese counterparts. Rather than waiting for your Japanese hosts to invite you out drinking or on outings, you can take it upon yourself to offer drinks at your hotel and to strike up conversations about subjects other than business.

Many Japanese still hold such social values as diligence and frugality. These values are not alien to hard-working Americans. You can demonstrate your diligence by working with your Japanese counterparts from early morning till late in the evening, and even over the weekend. Once you establish your image as hard working and serious, you will find it easier to earn the respect of your Japanese counterparts. This feeling of respect is a necessary ingredient for lasting personal relationships with your Japanese acquaintances.

MUTUAL TEACHING AS A BASIS FOR FRIENDSHIP

There is one lasting friendship that often transcends age difference between two Japanese men. It is one that is based upon a mutual teaching relationship. The young learn from the old and the old also learn from the young.

Japanese and American businessmen have a lot to learn from one another. All those theories about human resources management, for instance, that are considered revolutionary in American management literature have long and successfully been practiced by many Japanese firms. Accordingly, American managers should make the most of their encounters with their Japanese business counterparts in order to pick up some firsthand knowledge about how and why Japanese managers accept human resources development and the resulting job stability as the source of their firms' growth. In this way, American managers cannot only broaden their own management philosophy but also help their Japanese counterparts develop a psychological commitment to the personal well-being of their American "disciples."

At the same time, many Japanese are anxious to learn how their American counterparts evaluate their bosses, peers, and subordinates and how the long-term growth goals of American firms are reconciled with their short-term emphasis on quarterly bottom-line profits. The Japanese are eager to learn about the political, economic, and social fabric of the United States. They are prone to develop immediate respect and warm feelings toward their American "teachers." This give-and-take intellectual relationship provides the quickest road to the lasting friendship between American and Japanese businessmen.

Yoshi Tsurumi

BIBLIOGRAPHY

Doi, Takeo. *The Anatomy of Dependence*. Tokyo: Kodansha International, 1973.

PART V

JAPAN'S MODERN EXPERIENCE

12

THE IMPACT OF MODERNIZATION ON JAPAN

The Western businessman engaging in trade with Japan is dealing with a nation that is unique in contemporary world history. No other non-Western nation has yet achieved the rank of a major economic world power. And no major nations other than Germany and Italy have become major economic powers so quickly as has Japan. Both the success and the speed of success are important to understand the mixture of cultural and social forces that is modern Japan. Contemporary Japan developed from a premodern background in which education and certain organizational and artisans' skills were highly developed. These conditions favored early takeoff and rapid growth once the commitment to modernize was made. So tradition in the Japanese case fostered rather than impeded modernization. At the same time, modernization has come so fast that many residues of older traditions remain. Indeed, the strength of tradition is so great in Japan that many aspects of tradition remain complexly mixed with behaviors and attitudes that are "modern." Disentangling these forces of tradition and modernity becomes an inevitable, frustrating, and often exciting task for virtually every scholar who deals with Japanese experience, just as every business person dealing with Japan will find elements of both tradition and modernity represented in his daily contacts and experiences. James Bartholomew deals with these intricate and complicated trends in this chapter, summarizing many of the themes of this book.

325

Modernization Versus Westernization in Japan

Many people say Japan has become Westernized or even Americanized. Looking back over time, just what has happened in Japan's process of industrialization and modernization? Has Japan become identical in style and culture with Western nations, or has it followed its own course of modernization? Putting this differently, just what aspects of Japanese life are modernized but still Japanese, and what aspects of Japanese life could be called Westernized?

In an age of high technology, rapid transportation, and seemingly instant telecommunications, it is easy to suppose that at least the entire industrialized world—and increasingly the developing world as well—is rapidly attaining a degree of standardization in values, tastes, and living style that is both inevitable and all-pervasive. One sees everywhere the same fascination with automobiles, the same clothing styles, the same spectrum of popular music, or the same frenetic addiction to fast foods, soccer, skiing, or basketball. Frisbees are the rage in Beijing (Peking). Filipinos go wild over Donna Sommer. Soviet teenagers are all wearing Levi's. And the Japanese love Kentucky Fried Chicken. From experiential evidence of phenomena like this, one might well suppose the whole world is destined to become Westernized or even akin to the United States as industrial growth and technological change proceed. In fact, Marion J. Levy, Jr., comments: "For all of their important differences, all relatively modernized societies are . . . becoming more and more alike." And Alex Inkeles agrees: "It could very well be that we will, in the future, come to have a fairly uniform world culture, in which not only nations but groups within nations will have lost their distinctive subcultures."

Certainly material culture and tastes suggest that Japan is a far-advanced case of terminal Westernization. The country has a 98 percent diffusion rate for television sets. Eighty-nine percent of all Japanese families own refrigerators. Fifty-four percent of all households own automobiles. Intercity transportation in Japan is a model of sophisticated engineering. And baseball in summer is the Japanese "national pastime." Moreover, intimate and extensive contacts with Europe and the United States, especially since 1945, have promoted changes in the country's life-style that are unimaginable from a nineteenth-century, or even a pre-World War II perspective. Chairs often replace cushions on *tatami* as the preferred mode of sitting. Japanese designers are major contributors to haute couture. Bluegrass music enjoys a large following in Tokyo. And weddings in Christian churches are increasingly popular, despite the minority status of Christianity as a Japanese religion.

Material culture and popular tastes at the same time are only one area of modernization and a misleading one at that. As social scientists use the term, "modernization" refers equally or more to changes in people's values and institutions as a concomitant or *result* of industrialization and the diffusion of high technology. Different writers stress different changes, but most use the word to specify such changes as an expansion of educational opportunities, greater mobility in one's choice of employment or residence, greater freedom in economic and political relations, greater equality in society, and a narrowing in the range or "volume" of authority in interpersonal relations. According thus to modernization theorists, such changes appear unexceptionably in all societies that industrialize.

In some areas, like education, Japan's record will impress Americans as clear-cut and utterly predictable. Japanese have far better prospects to acquire education than they did a century ago, and the growth of colleges and universities since World War II has increased their chances further. After the war, the United States Education Mission to Japan, in concert with Japanese authorities, actively promoted expansion of higher education. Simultaneously, greater social freedom was encouraged in the classroom setting and vestiges of nationalistic obscurantism were eliminated from the curriculum. The results were a more "open" atmosphere along with greater access to schooling. A farmer's son today can have access to universities that were once the preserve of the sons of corporation presidents. Scholarships and loan funds are available, and affluence has produced a broadly middle-class society. And tuition at leading government universities is a bargain by any measure. Moreover, the quality of education is generally regarded as high. Worldwide tests in mathematics achievement sponsored by UNESCO show Japanese school children at the top level of performance. Their exposure to Western literature and history is sometimes as great as in Europe or the United States. And the wide diffusion of high literacy levels in the general population (virtually 100 percent, compared to about 96 percent in the United States), and narrow disparity in per pupil school expenditures among Japanese school districts suggest a greater diffusion of "modernity" than commonly exists in the United States. It is worth noting, too, that many aspects of Japan's present education system are based on prewar trends and thus cannot be considered a result of postwar "Americanization." Compulsory education for six years was mandated in the 1870s, and coeducation in elementary schools was instituted at that time. And virtually all children of school age were attending primary schools by the beginning of the twentieth century.

Patterns of occupational mobility and economic freedom generally seem a mixture of modernity and tradition with the former appearing predominant. Japanese in all walks of life are objectively freer to choose their occupations than they were a century ago. Feudal restrictions on employment were abolished after the Meiji Restoration (1868), and expanded educational opportunities in the subsequent period have made theoretical freedoms reality. Economic status, moreover, is much less dependent on inherited wealth, family status, or lineage than it used to be and income differentials among occupational sectors are significantly narrower. Workers can and have moved freely from one production sector to another (primarily from agriculture to industry), and population movements in the postwar period from certain regions to others have been sudden and large in scale.

Nevertheless, two prominent features of the Japanese employment scene stand out to Americans and incline many to consider it traditionalistic or even antimodern. Many industrial workers, even when they possess highly sought-after skills, do not generally move from one firm to another but rather make their careers with a single employer. And remuneration is more dependent on the employee's years with the firm than on "objective" assessment of his "merit."

Permanent employment is certainly a traditionalistic practice as regards the motives of labor. Many authorities see labor's desire for permanent employment as a function of the traditional paternalism that was historically supposed to typify relations between *oyabun* (patrons) and *kobun* (clients) in the feudal social order. Others would stress the influence of an expressive culture and a pattern of child rearing in which individuals seem to acquire a particular "need to belong." However, these explanations, while pertinent, ignore structural features in the Japanese economy to which permanent employment may well represent a highly rational solution. Much of the labor force—prior to the last two decades—felt particular insecurities due to a formerly huge reservoir of underemployed (i.e., farm) labor. And management itself came ironically to favor permanent employment as a way to guarantee a stable and amenable work force.

Awareness of particular features of permanent employment and its precise historical origin is more than a little essential to a balanced view of the matter. Not all workers receive permanent employment guarantees. Typically such guarantees go to workers with higher educational backgrounds. Moreover, the system developed in the first instance only because particular historical circumstances created uniquely difficult problems for industry. Under the rule of the Tokugawa shogunate (1600–1867), there were severe restrictions imposed on intercourse with other countries. Japanese could not travel abroad and foreign contacts were limited. The result was to create a large technological gap between Japan and the Western world. Beginning in the 1850s the old regime made a concerted effort to transcend the problem, but the resulting knowledge shortfall continued to bedevil the country for the remainder of the nineteenth century. World War I made the situation even more difficult because of the opportunities it offered to industry. As a result of such military exigencies as the Allied blockade of Germany, Japanese industry was positioned to exploit a slack in production. But the unusual mobility of labor posed a serious and continuing problem. Management thus solved the problem by offering permanent employment guarantees to labor as an enticement to stay with the firm. And the results were sufficiently attractive that the pattern has continued to the present. Between 1914 and 1919, industrial production in firms utilizing permanent employment doubled; and since 1950 employers have found greater employee cooperation with the introduction of new machinery in firms that utilize permanent employment than in those that do not.

Wage payment schemes employed by Japanese firms reflect the assumptions underlying the permanent employment system. They clearly embody the traditional principle of status differences in which *kōhai* (juniors) are subordinated to *sempai* (seniors). But wage payments are pegged, not to age but the number of years with the firm. Thus, it is difficult to perceive this system as inherently irrational on its face, if experience on the job has any economic value. (Many American firms have historically felt that it does!) Moreover, wage payments are further affected by an employee's educational background. Where technical or executive-track positions are concerned, large Japanese firms usually recruit employees from a few prestigious universities. This practice, in the Japanese cultural context, helps strengthen employee solidarity with the firm—a result that has not been without beneficial effects on productivity. Moreover, the admission standards that prestigious universities maintain assure that most every graduate has attained a minimal level of competence.

Recruitment to jobs is such a strategic feature of the Japanese, or any other, socioeconomic system that additional comment seems warranted. Experts on modernization emphasize that technology-intensive societies must by definition use only objective ("universalistic") criteria in selection of employees. Yet it is very often implied that Japanese society does otherwise. The economic status of one's family may not matter but personal connections may have some effect. Candidates with proper introductions reportedly have preference over those without, and those who have followed "standard procedures" (e.g., attending a prestigious high school followed by Tokyo or Keio University) do better than those who have not. These practices can and do penalize some people with particular talents. A perhaps amazing example of irrational recruitment is the barring of the children of Japanese executives who stay abroad too long and thus lack the personal contacts to land a job in the Foreign Ministry or with a trading company, even though their knowledge of foreign languages and culture may be superior to that of other age-mates. But recruitment of personnel from prestige schools may bar many other competent persons as well.

However, compensatory mechanisms may be operating to mitigate some possibly unfavorable effects of the prestige school-oriented recruitment system. Tokyo University's Medical School in the earlier part of this century serves as an example. It was said at the time that one virtually needed to have a relative on the faculty to secure a professorial appointment—and the evidence suggests this was partially true. In 1920, there were 51 men on the faculty who had already achieved the rank of full professor at Tokyo or would eventually do so. Of this number, 24 had a relative in the medical profession; and 13 of these were professors in, or were closely connected to, the Tokyo Medical School. However, all but one of these relatives was a father-in-law rather than a blood relative! And most significantly the father-in-law had accepted the younger man as son-in-law and heir only after the latter had proven himself by graduating first, second, or third in his medical class! If such practices exist in occupations other than medicine—as casual observation suggests—we have to suppose that a formally "particularistic" recruitment process often *does* conform to our "modern" emphasis on "merit."

In at least one major respect, Japanese society does seem to have changed in the direction predicted by the theorists of modernization. There *is* greater equality than before, of both a formal and a substantive kind. Trade union congresses of the 1920s made the destruction of workers' attitudes of submissiveness toward management one of their major objectives. Certain Tokyo University professors are known to have fined graduate students using *keigo* (respect language) to excess in the 1930s. Ostentatious gift giving to superiors is increasingly frowned on, even though it persists to a marked degree in some places, and certain deference forms are less and less commonly seen. The Tokyo cab driver may still nod deferentially to the policeman who scolds him for speeding, but he will not go down on the knees like his rickshawman predecessors. Similarly, leftist student demonstrators today may even refer to the Emperor as *Ten-chan* (roughly, "Emperor-baby"), while prewar activists most often avoided criticism of the Throne altogether.

If socialization in the family has accounted for a traditional emphasis on status differences among people, greater social equality may be resulting from changes in its fundamental structure. Fewer Japanese than ever before live together in an extended family arrangement. The average urban household contains only the married couple and an average of fewer than two children (although almost two-thirds of persons over age 65 also live with one of their sons or daughters). Even more striking is the rejection of extended family living as a normative ideal, such as was implied in a 1967 murder case involving a suburban Tokyo family. In this particular instance, a young housewife strongly objected to her 80-year-old mother-in-law's tendency to urinate in the front yard, as rural Japanese of an earlier generation were sometimes accustomed to do. Failing to dissuade the old woman from the practice on the grounds of middle-class neighborly disapproval, the daughter-in-law poisoned her mother-in-law and was subsequently put on trial. The remarkable feature of the case was not the guilty verdict but the extraordinary number of letters to newspapers that said the old woman got exactly what was coming to her! (Of course, other letter writers roundly deplored the demise of the traditional filial piety that the crime so blatantly revealed.)

Yet it would be wrong to think the declining size or changing economic functions of the family imply a dramatic weakening of all collectivistic tendencies in Japan as such. Company employees still voluntarily work many unpaid hours overtime when major assignments are due. Workers sacrifice weekend outings when production deadlines are imminent. And government officials interrupt vacation plans when economic or political affairs go awry. Such occurrences are not unknown in the United States, but the extent of their frequency may be. *Chūō Kōron,* a leading monthly, reported in July 1978 the case of a Ministry of International Trade and Industry official's wife who died alone of pneumonia because the budget-making process had unavoidably distracted her husband. The magazine suggested this incident was not entirely rare and quoted the Vice Minister as saying the lady had died a "tragic death on the battlefield as the wife of a government bureaucrat."

Self-sacrificing tendencies of the kind displayed in this case are the product not only of traditional ethical systems (e.g., Confucianism) but of a particular modality of life. Until the early 1950s, most Japanese lived as they had for centuries, in rural villages, often rather isolated and self-contained. It was a common practice for decisions in such communities to reflect a broad and general consensus; in fact, extreme dissidents and malcontents were generally punished by *mura-hachibu* (ostracism). Neighbors and relatives would refuse even to recognize the existence of the offending individual or family, let alone share burdens with or assist them in any material sense. Rural Japan was the kind of society in which no one dared to be different or in any way to defy one's neighbors. Such village solidarity has been legendary, even in the post-World War II period. In 1948, a certain village near Kyoto converted en masse from Buddhism to Catholicism; but until the entire community decided, not a single individual would agree to be baptized. And even today, many rural areas will cast unanimous election ballots for favored candidates in local elections.

The degree of conformity or group consensus displayed by Japanese in many settings reveals a gulf between Japan and the West that industrialization has not effaced nor cultural diffusion destroyed. Japanese *are* far wealthier than before. They are more mobile, more egalitarian minded, and are certainly more open to outside cultural influences. What stands out so clearly from the litany of changes is the relative strength of collectivism. Clearly this results from deeply rooted tradition; but more to the point are the forces and structures that explain it. There is first of all the legacy of religion. American Protestantism is the very epitome of individualism in the realm of the sacred; Japanese Shinto historically placed emphasis on the nation as a family. Moreover, religion in the Western world has often challenged the state; religion in Japan with equal frequency has been wholly co-opted by it. Then there is the legacy of sociopolitical structure. Feudalism in the West was mostly a vestige by the early seventeenth century, whereas Japanese feudalism was still reality in the middle of the nineteenth century. (I omit consideration of some important structural changes that occurred in Japanese feudalism earlier.)

Finally there is the matter of economic growth. Contrary to what is sometimes assumed, the industrial transformation experienced by Japan in the late nineteenth century was neither very rapid nor in some ways all that sweeping. The industrial economy as a whole grew at a rate of about 2 percent a year—solid growth to be sure, but hardly comparable to the performance of the post-World War II era. Moreover, population growth between 1868 and 1945 was so large that industrialization merely utilized the talents of the rural population excess; only after 1950 did the economy grow rapidly enough to reduce the rural population in absolute numerical terms. The values and institutions of rural Japan thus continued to be influential until very recent times, and not even the removal of people to the city necessarily negated traditional patterns. In fact, what happened in many cases was a "communalizing" of industrial life, rather than an individualization of the countryside! No one can say on the basis of historical evidence that full-fledged Westernization of Japan is inconceivable or impossible. But the forces arraigned against it are powerful and they are very deeply rooted in history. Moreover, who is to say a declining United States will not choose increasingly to emulate an economically resurgent Japan?

James Bartholomew

BIBLIOGRAPHY

Bennett, John W. "Japanese Economic Growth: Background for Social Change." In *Aspects of Social Change in Modern Japan,* edited by R. P. Dore, pp. 411–53. Princeton: Princeton University Press, 1967.

Dore, R. P. "Introduction." In *Aspects of Social Change in Modern Japan,* edited by R. P. Dore, pp. 3–24. Princeton: Princeton University Press, 1967.

ABOUT THE CONTRIBUTORS

JAMES BARTHOLOMEW is an Associate Professor of History at Ohio State University and author of articles on Japanese science and medicine.

LESLIE BEDFORD is coordinator of the Ohio State University's East Asian outreach program and has authored essays on education and values in Japan.

JOHN CREIGHTON CAMPBELL is an Associate Professor of Political Science at the University of Michigan and author of *Contemporary Japanese Budget Politics*.

ROBERT E. COLE is Professor of Sociology at the University of Michigan and Director of the Center for Japanese Studies. He is author of *Japanese Blue Collar* and *Work, Mobility and Participation*.

MAUREEN DONOVAN is Japanese Cataloger and Instructor at the Ohio State University Libraries.

ALBERT KEIDEL II is Assistant Professor of Economics at Ohio State University and has written on Japanese, Korean, and Chinese economic development.

SOLOMON B. LEVINE is Professor of Economics and Business at the University of Wisconsin and is author of *Industrial Relations in Postwar Japan* and co-author of *Workers and Employers in Japan* and *Human Resources in Japanese Industrial Development*.

SUSAN PHARR is Associate Professor of Political Science at the University of Wisconsin–Madison and author of *Political Women in Japan*.

BRADLEY M. RICHARDSON is Professor of Political Science and recently was Director of the East Asian Studies Program at Ohio State University. He is author of *The Political Culture of Japan* and coauthor of *Politics in Japan* and *The Japanese Voter*.

YOSHI TSURUMI is Professor of International Business and Marketing at Baruch College, the City University of New York and was recently the Founding Director of the UCLA Pacific Basin Economic Study Center. He is author of *The Japanese Are Coming, Multinational Management, Japanese Business, Sogoshosha,* and *Technology Transfer and International Trade*.

FRANK K. UPHAM is Assistant Professor of Law at Ohio State University and author of articles on pollution and civil rights in Japan.